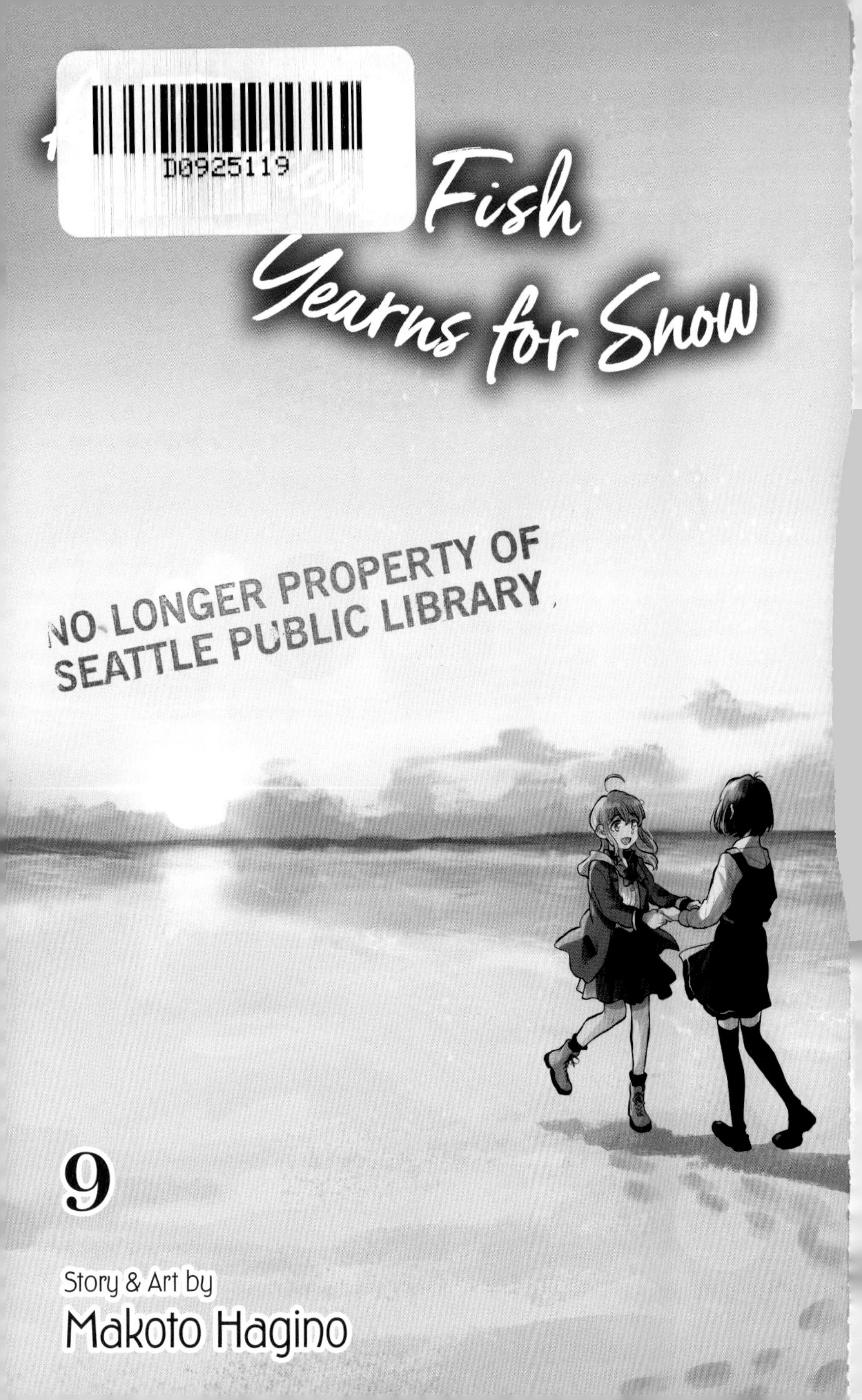
Fish
Yearns for Snow
9
Story & Art by
Makoto Hagino

The Story So Far

Konatsu transfers to Nanahama High School from the city and meets Koyuki, the only member of the Aquarium Club. The two girls naturally take a liking to each other because they're both lonely, so Konatsu ends up joining the club. A special bond forms between the two girls as they awkwardly care for each other. Summer passes, and the day of Koyuki's graduation approaches...

Characters

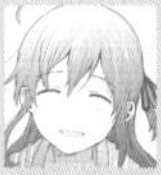

Konatsu Amano

A second-year student who transferred to Nanahama High School as a first-year. She had trouble adapting to her new surroundings until she met Koyuki and joined the Aquarium Club.

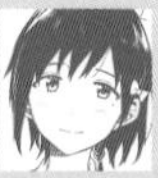

Koyuki Honami

A third-year student and president of the Aquarium Club. Everyone puts her on a pedestal, but she has gradually been breaking out of her shell.

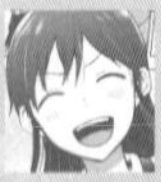

Kaede Hirose

Konatsu's classmate. Due to her perky personality, she has many friends. She's close friends with both Konatsu and Koyuki.

AUG – ~ 2022

A Tropical Fish Yearns for Snow

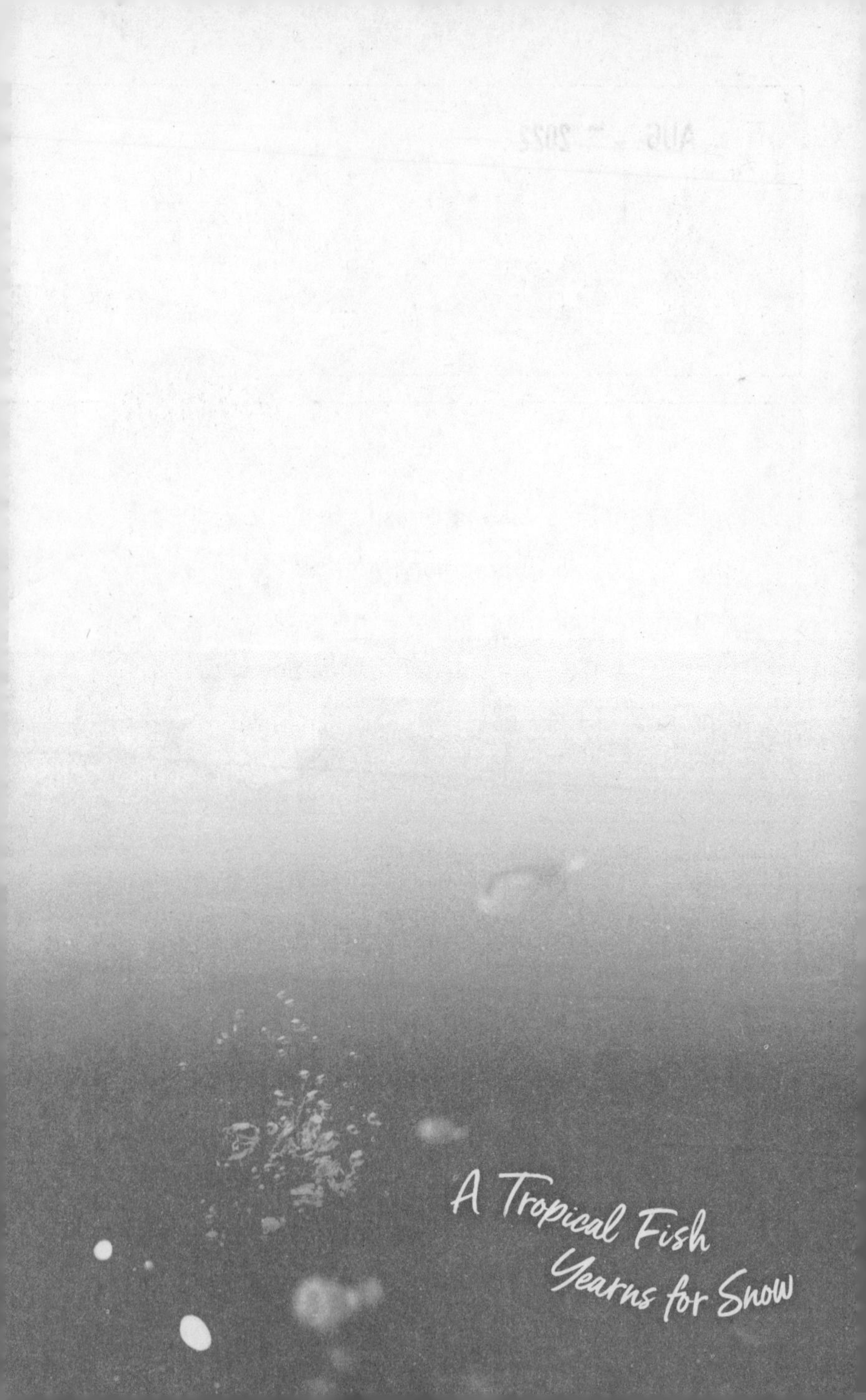
A Tropical Fish
Yearns for Snow

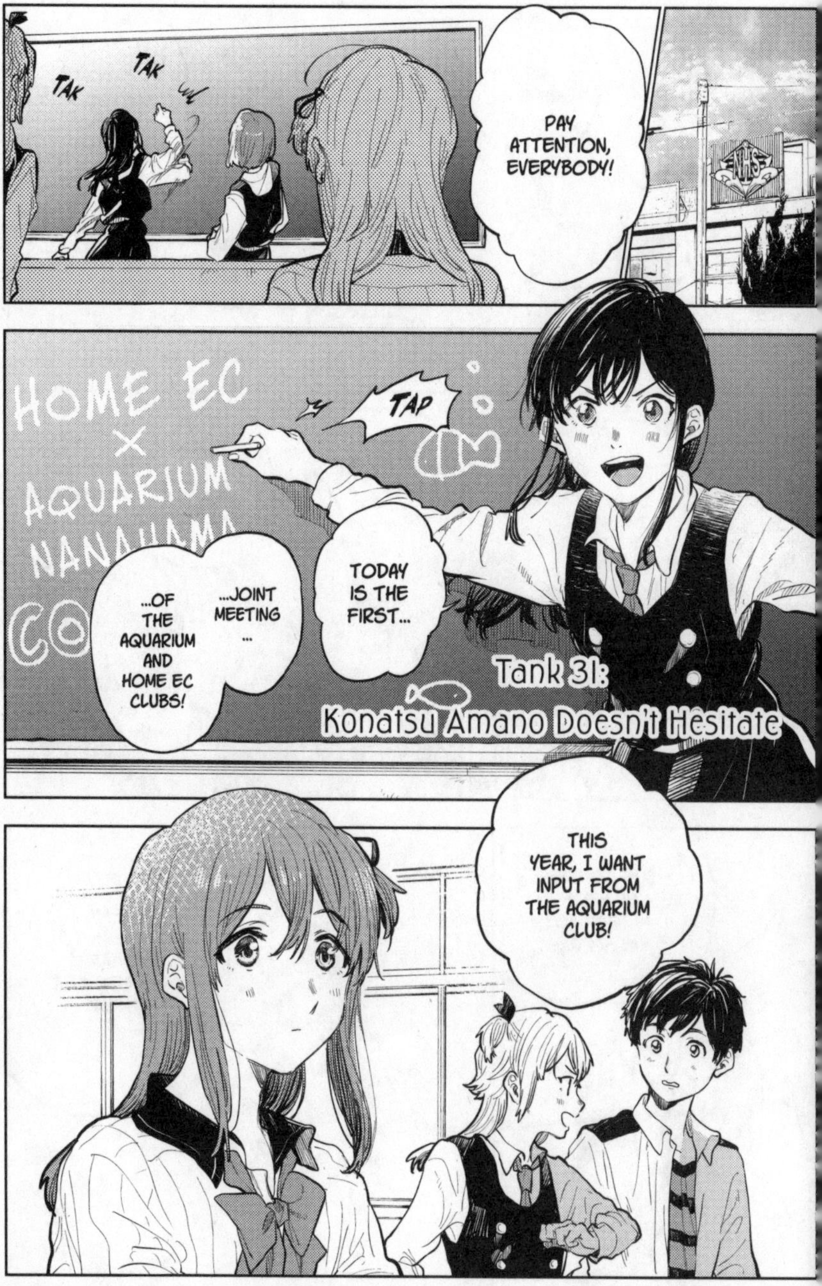
PAY ATTENTION, EVERYBODY!
TAK
TAK
TAP
HOME EC
×
AQUARIUM
TODAY IS THE FIRST...
...JOINT MEETING...
...OF THE AQUARIUM AND HOME EC CLUBS!
Tank 31: Konatsu Amano Doesn't Hesitate
THIS YEAR, I WANT INPUT FROM THE AQUARIUM CLUB!

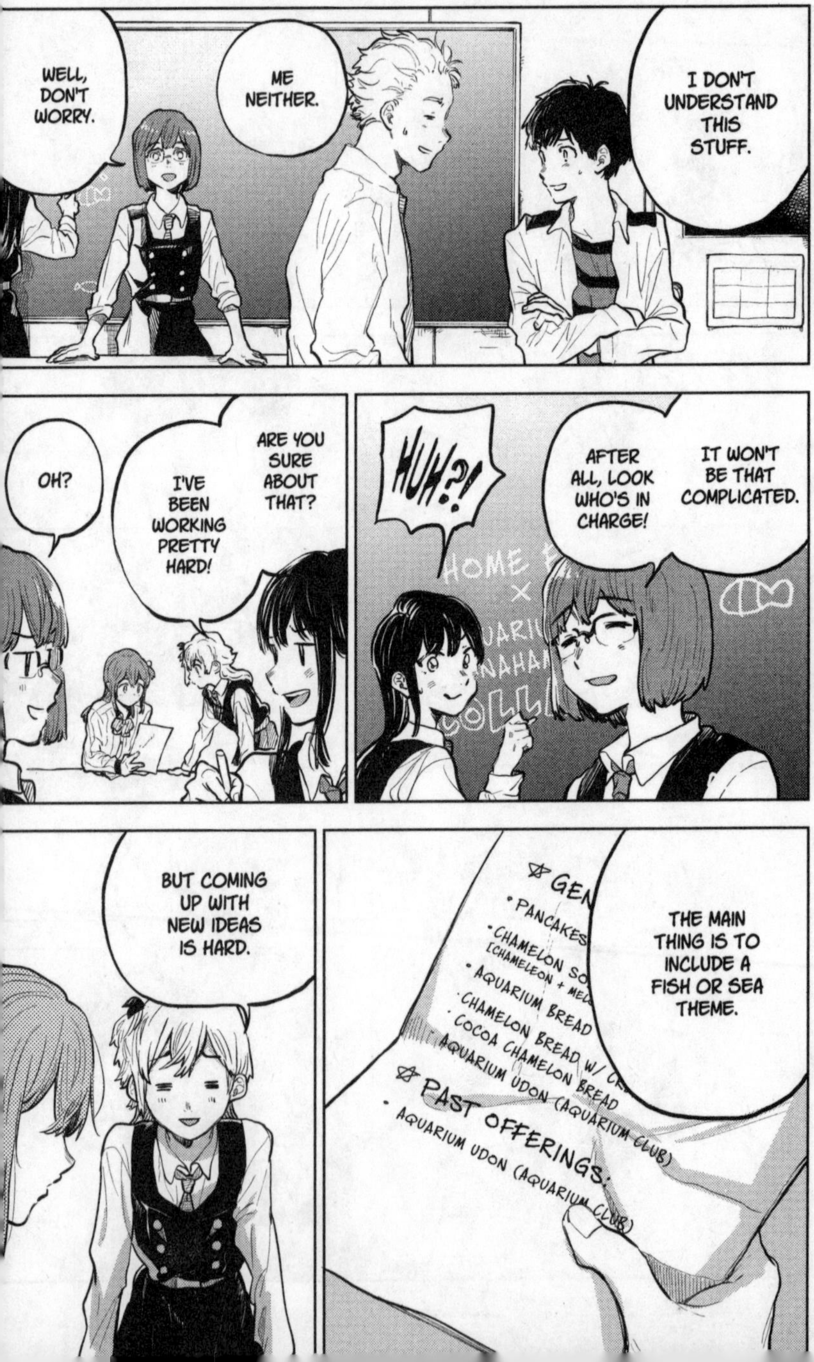
I DON'T UNDERSTAND THIS STUFF.
ME NEITHER.
WELL, DON'T WORRY.
IT WON'T BE THAT COMPLICATED.
AFTER ALL, LOOK WHO'S IN CHARGE!
HUH?!
ARE YOU SURE ABOUT THAT?
I'VE BEEN WORKING PRETTY HARD!
OH?
THE MAIN THING IS TO INCLUDE A FISH OR SEA THEME.
• AQUARIUM BREAD
• COCOA CHAMELON BREAD
• AQUARIUM UDON (AQUARIUM CLUB)
PAST OFFERINGS:
• AQUARIUM UDON (AQUARIUM CLUB)
BUT COMING UP WITH NEW IDEAS IS HARD.

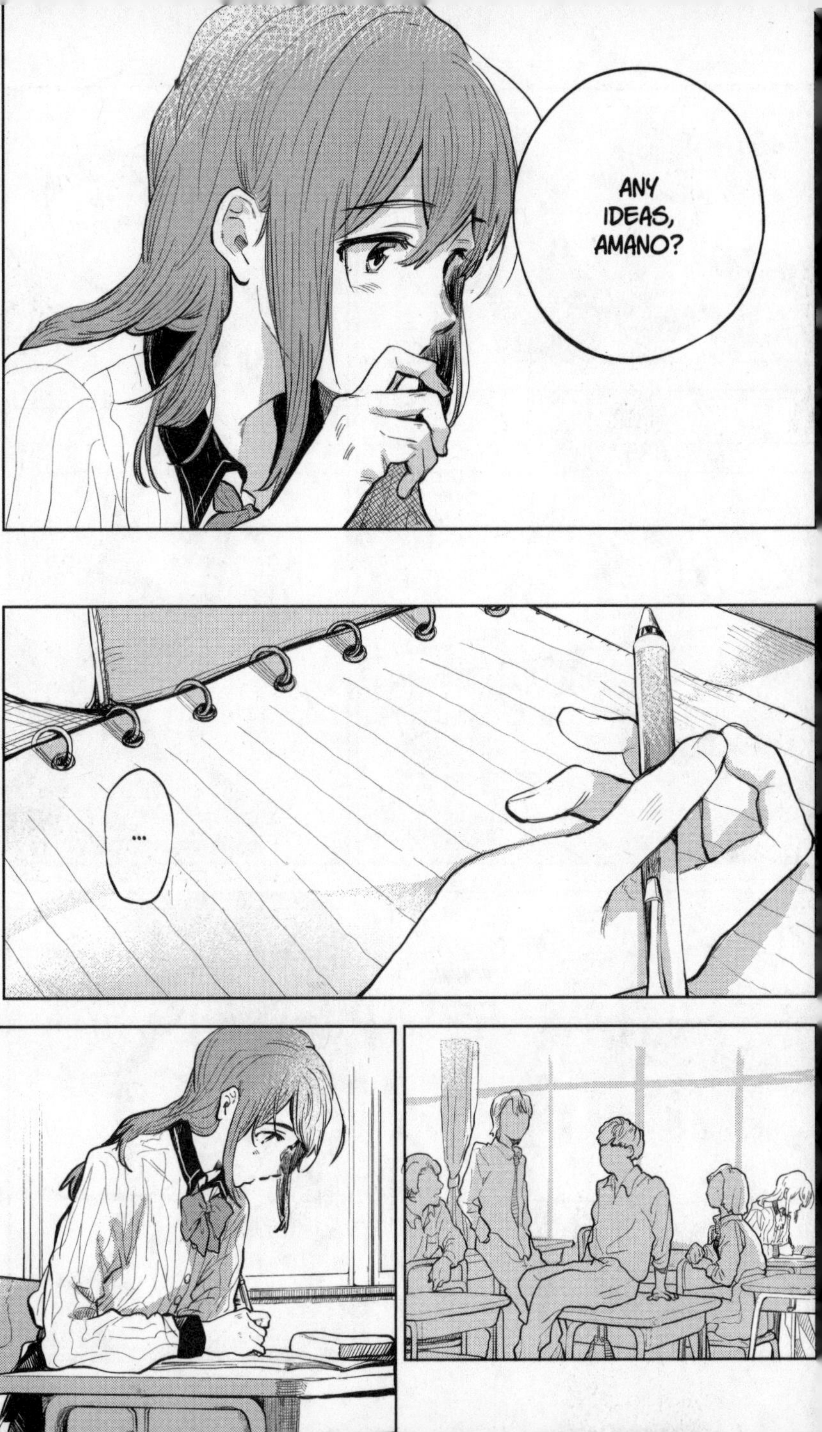
ANY IDEAS, AMANO?
...

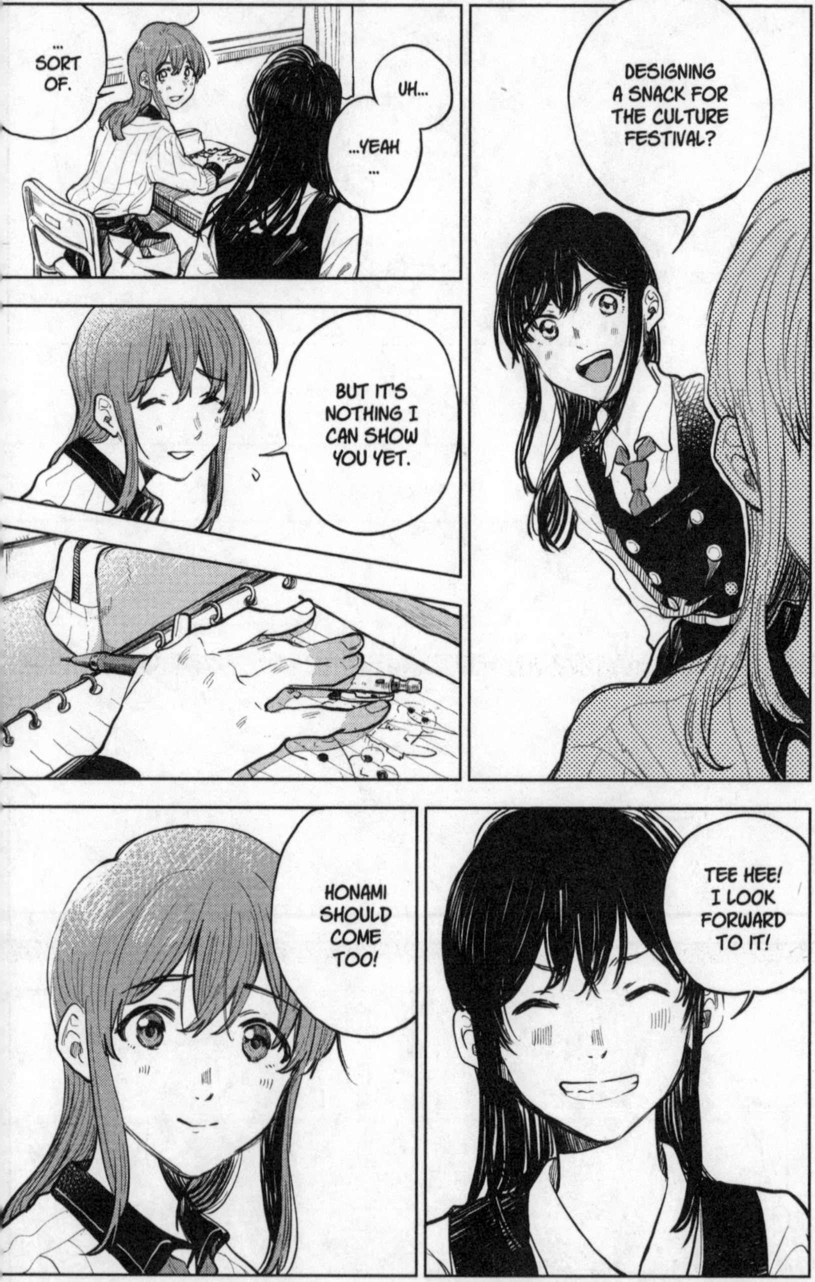
DESIGNING A SNACK FOR THE CULTURE FESTIVAL?
UH...
...YEAH ...
... SORT OF.
BUT IT'S NOTHING I CAN SHOW YOU YET.
TEE HEE! I LOOK FORWARD TO IT!
HONAMI SHOULD COME TOO!

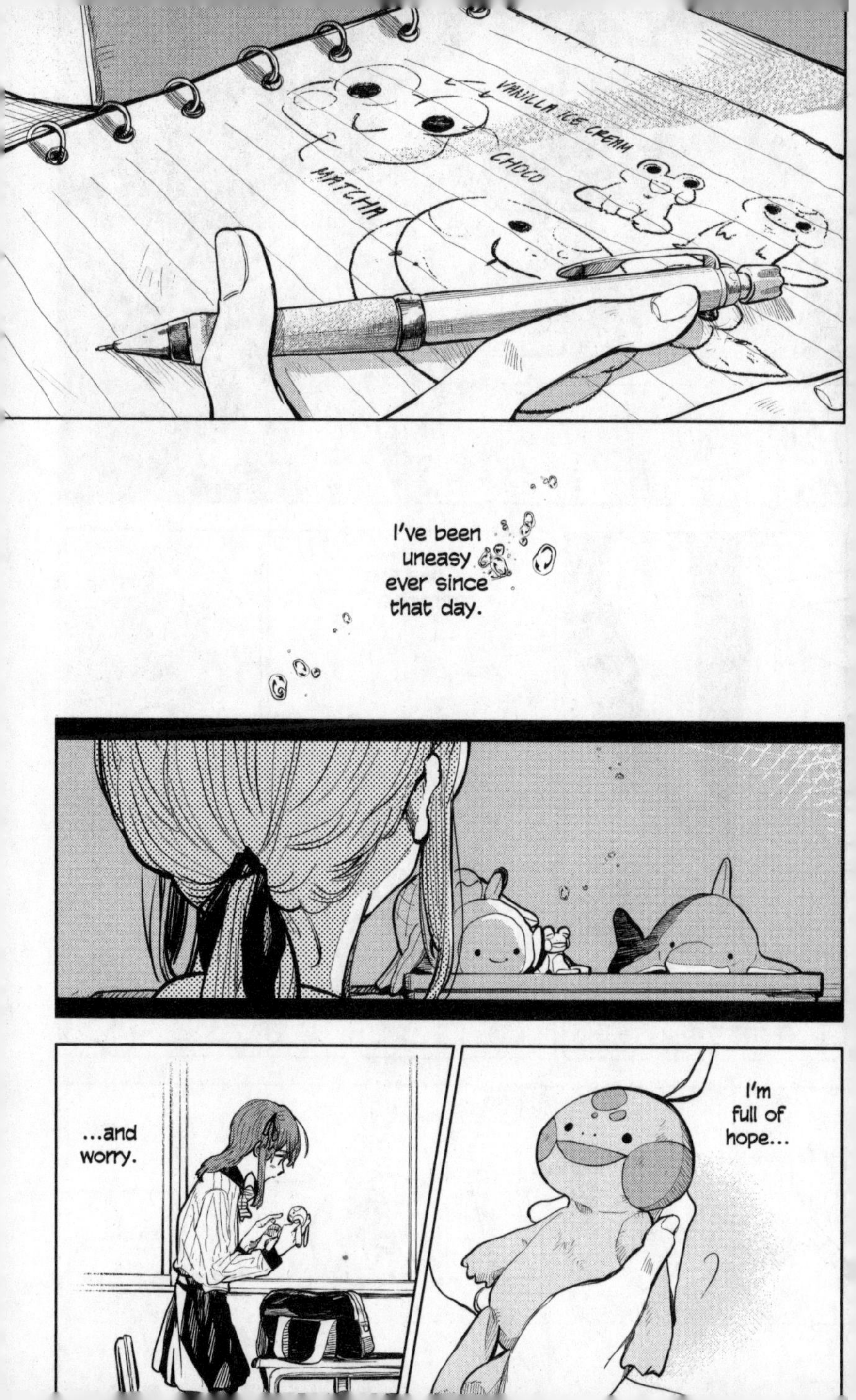
VANILLA ICE CREAM
CHOCO
MATCHA
I've been uneasy ever since that day.
I'm full of hope...
...and worry.

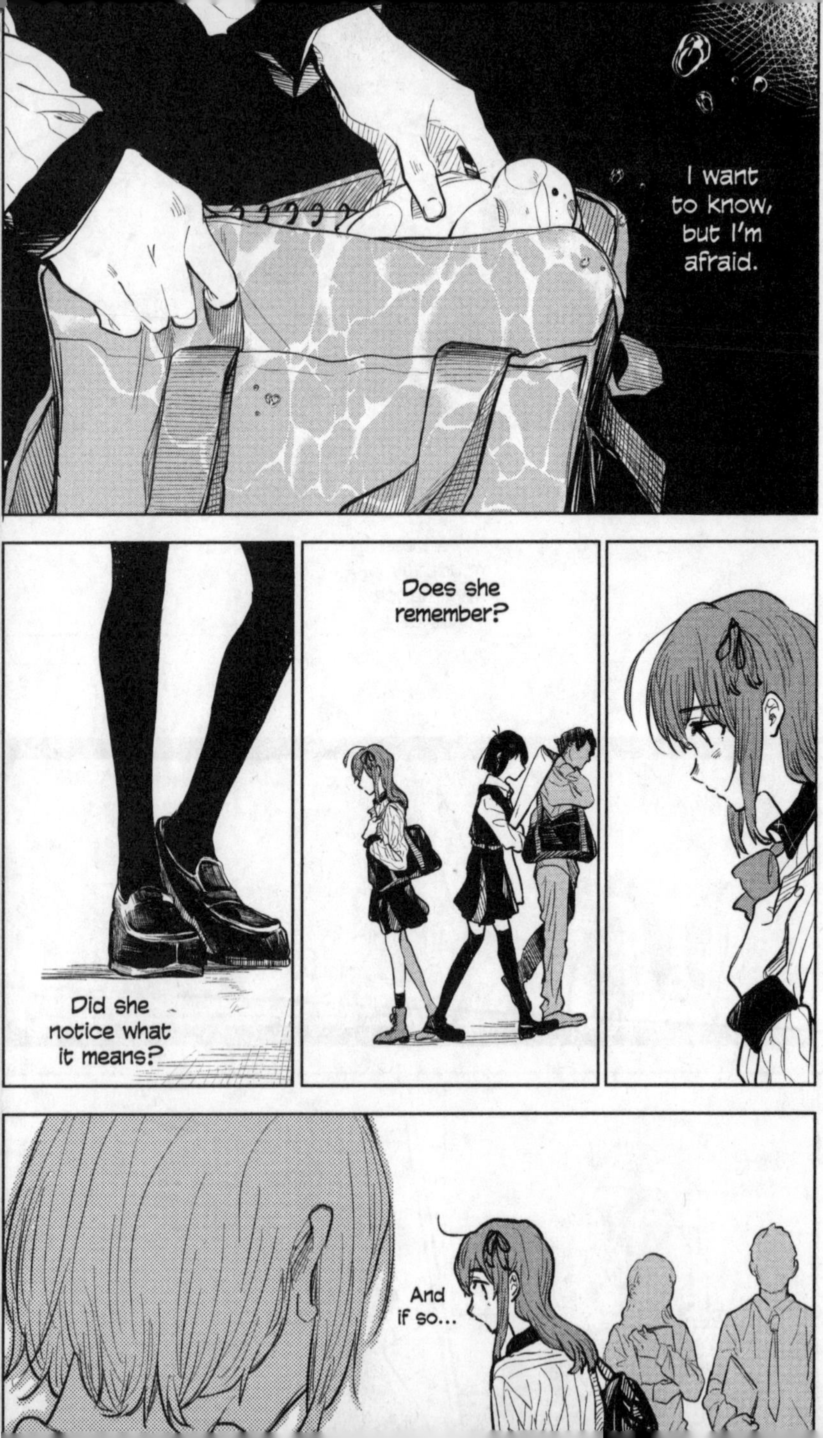
I want to know, but I'm afraid.
Does she remember?
Did she notice what it means?
And if so...

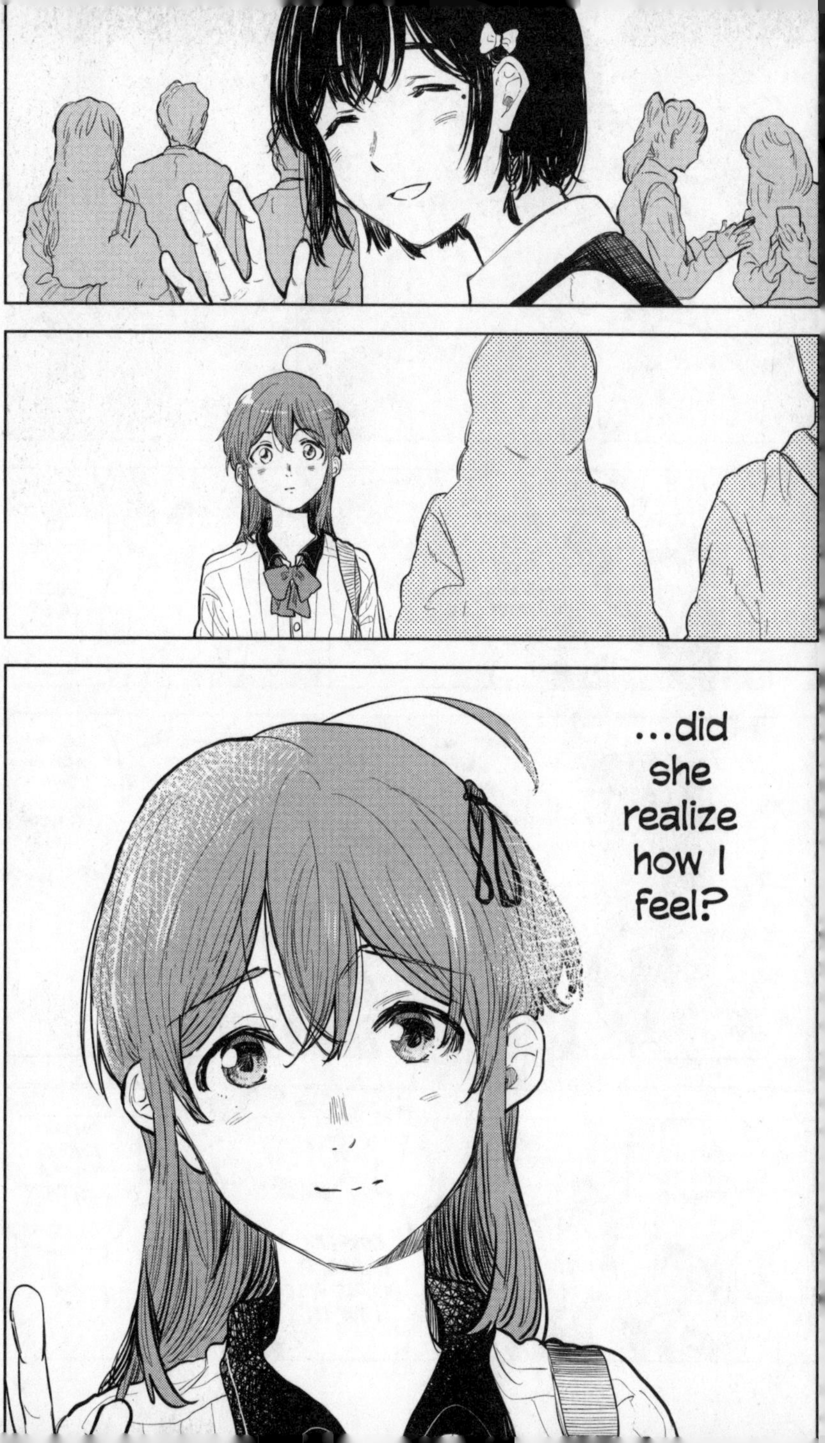
...did she realize how I feel?

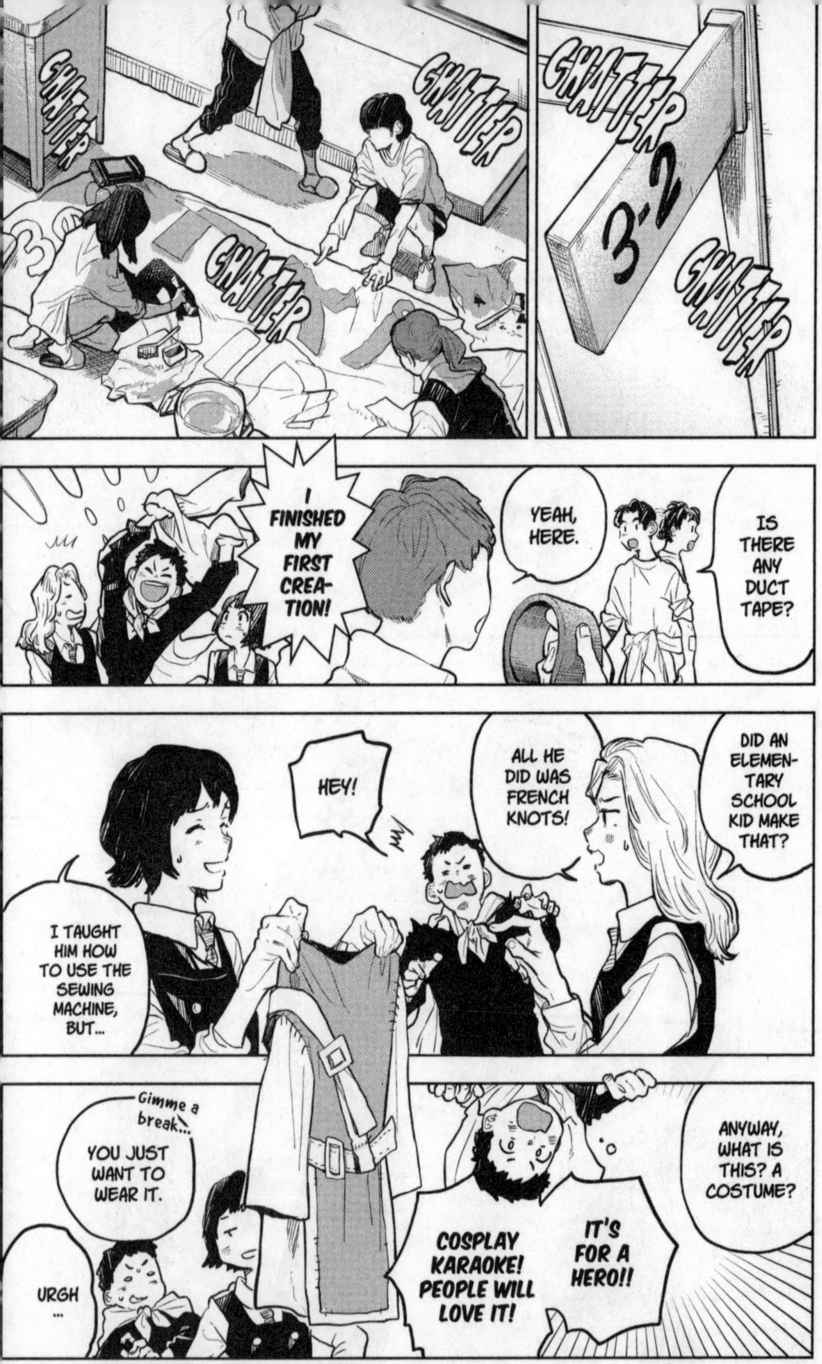
CHATTER
3-2
CHATTER
CHATTER
CHATTER
CHATTER
IS THERE ANY DUCT TAPE?
YEAH, HERE.
I FINISHED MY FIRST CREATION!
DID AN ELEMENTARY SCHOOL KID MAKE THAT?
ALL HE DID WAS FRENCH KNOTS!
HEY!
I TAUGHT HIM HOW TO USE THE SEWING MACHINE, BUT...
ANYWAY, WHAT IS THIS? A COSTUME?
IT'S FOR A HERO!!
COSPLAY KARAOKE! PEOPLE WILL LOVE IT!
YOU JUST WANT TO WEAR IT.
Gimme a break...
URGH...

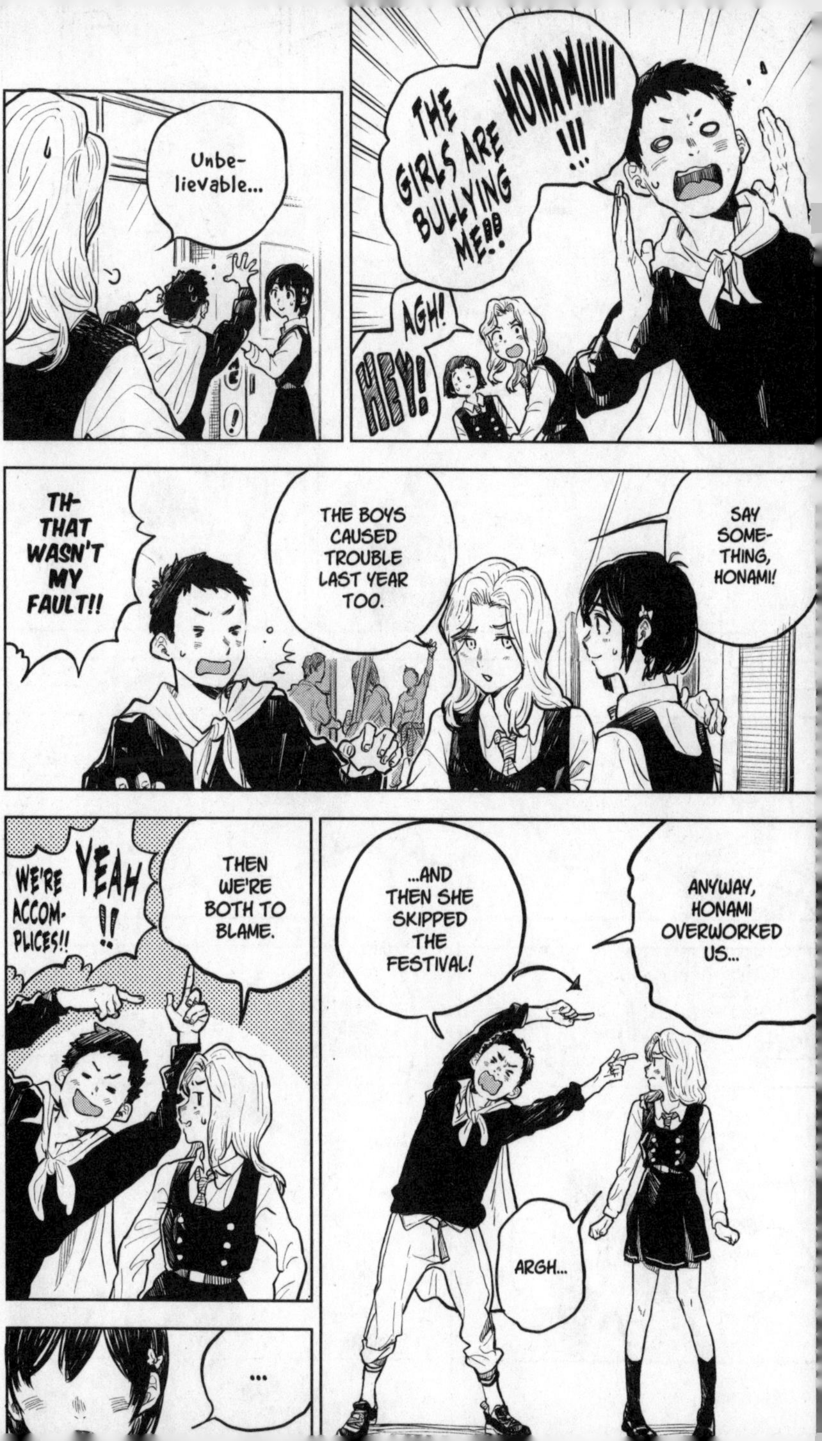
THE GIRLS ARE BULLYING ME!! HONAMI!!!!!! !!!
AGH!
HEY!
Unbe-lievable...
SAY SOME-THING, HONAMI!
THE BOYS CAUSED TROUBLE LAST YEAR TOO.
TH-THAT WASN'T MY FAULT!!
ANYWAY, HONAMI OVERWORKED US...
...AND THEN SHE SKIPPED THE FESTIVAL!
ARGH...
THEN WE'RE BOTH TO BLAME.
YEAH!!
WE'RE ACCOM-PLICES!!
...

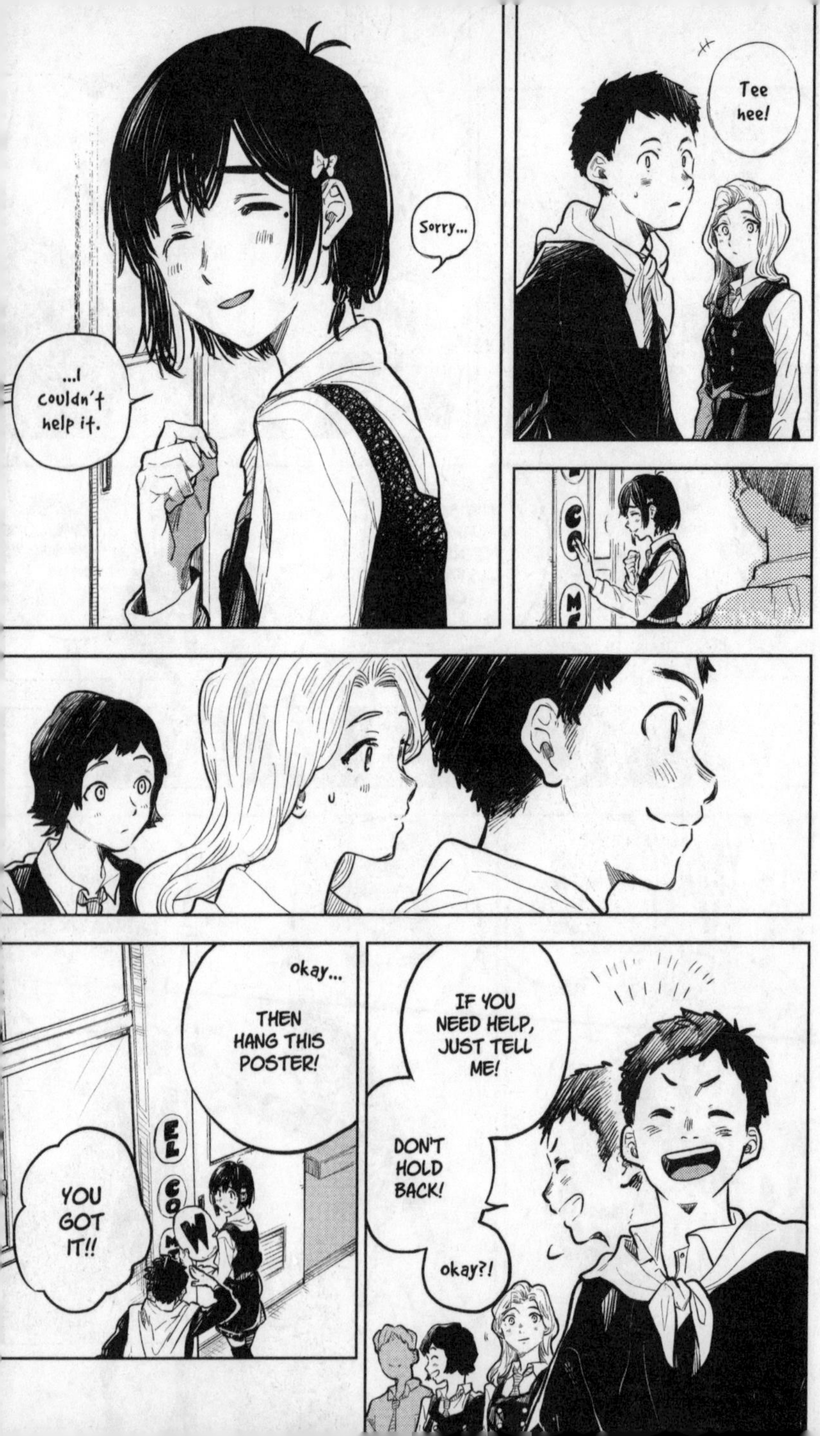
Tee hee!
Sorry...
...I couldn't help it.
IF YOU NEED HELP, JUST TELL ME!
DON'T HOLD BACK!
okay?!
okay...
THEN HANG THIS POSTER!
YOU GOT IT!!

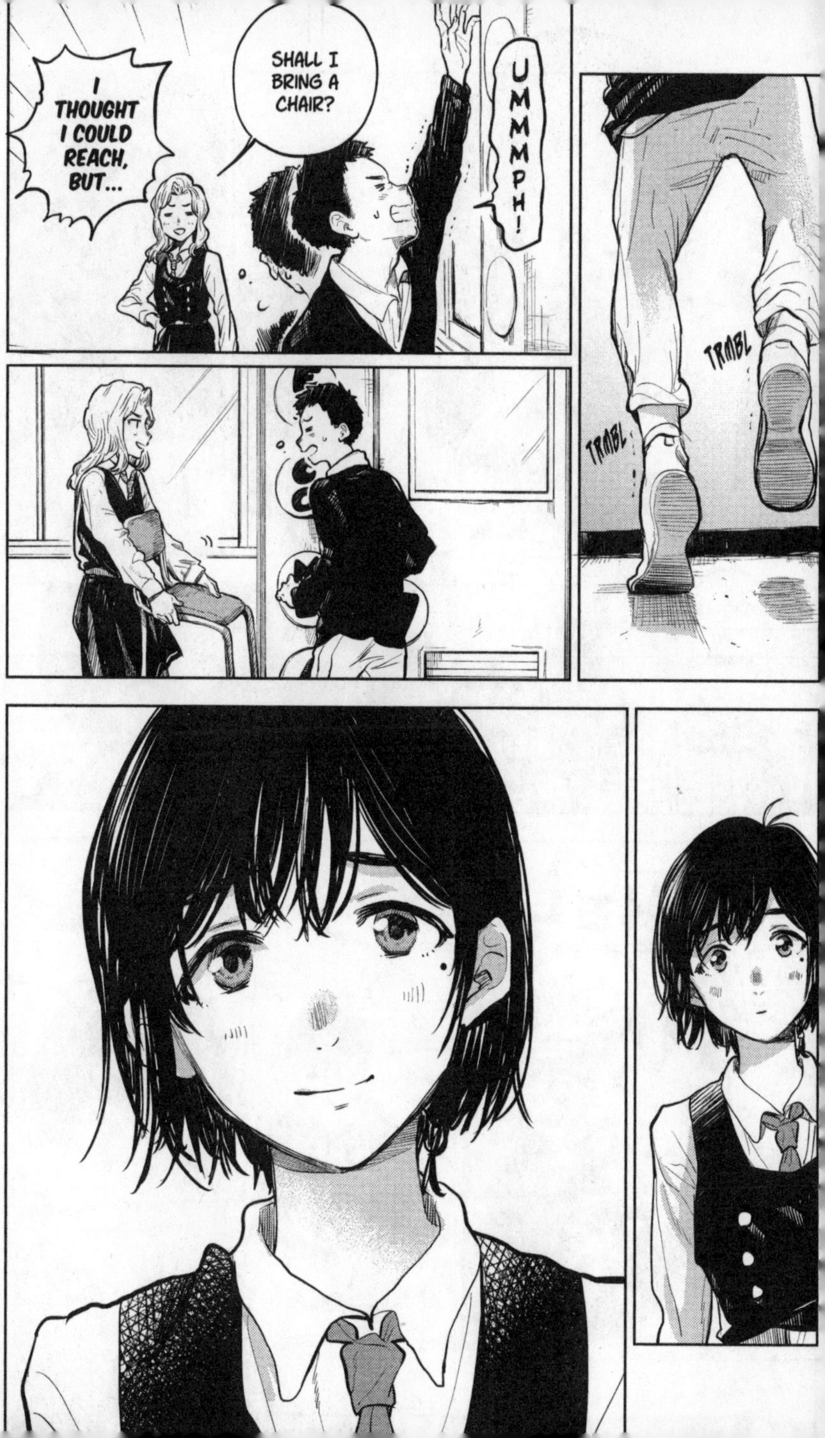
TRMBL
TRMBL
UMMMPH!
SHALL I BRING A CHAIR?
I THOUGHT I COULD REACH, BUT...

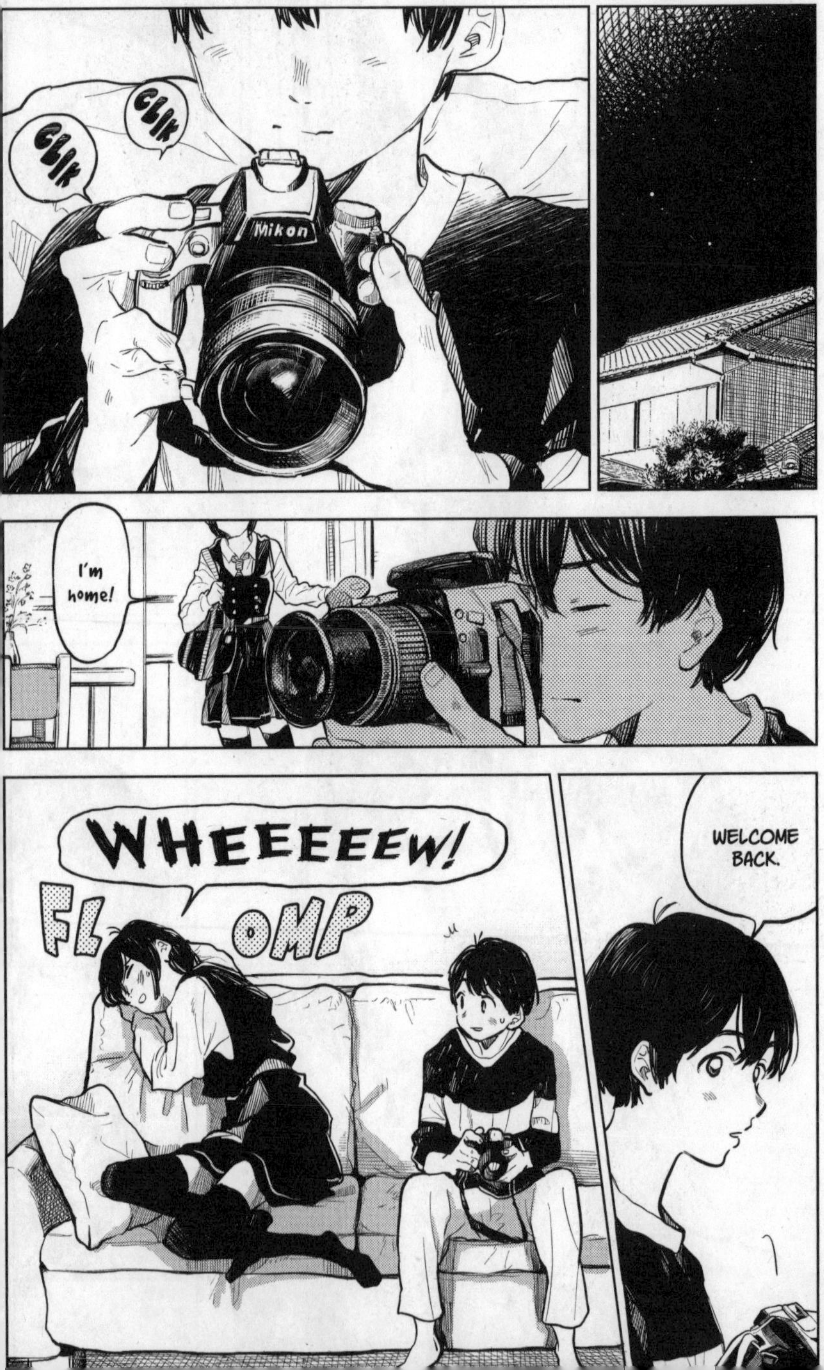
CLIK
CLIK
I'm home!
WELCOME BACK.
WHEEEEEW!
FL OMP

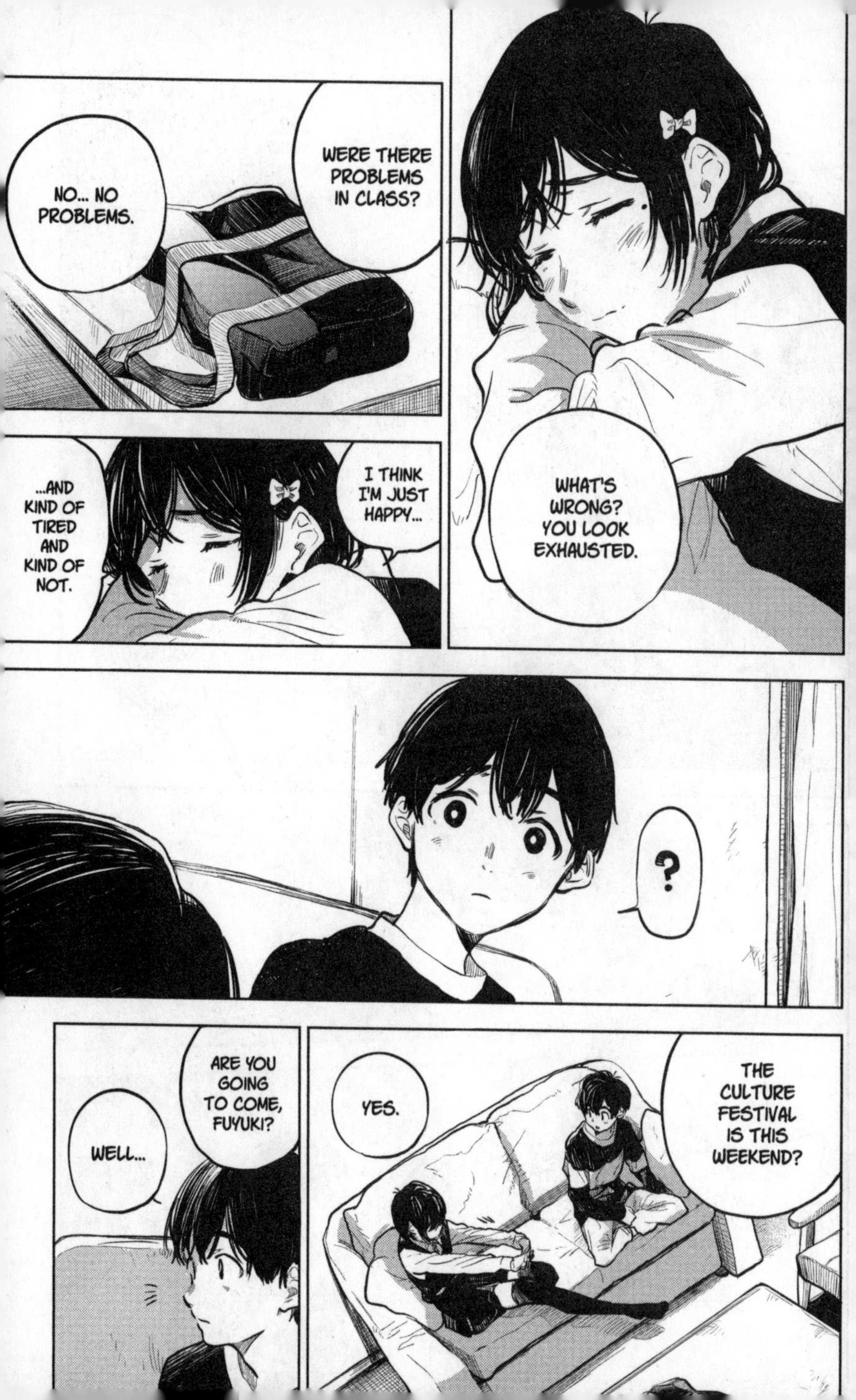
WHAT'S WRONG? YOU LOOK EXHAUSTED.
WERE THERE PROBLEMS IN CLASS?
NO... NO PROBLEMS.
I THINK I'M JUST HAPPY...
...AND KIND OF TIRED AND KIND OF NOT.
?
THE CULTURE FESTIVAL IS THIS WEEKEND?
YES.
ARE YOU GOING TO COME, FUYUKI?
WELL...

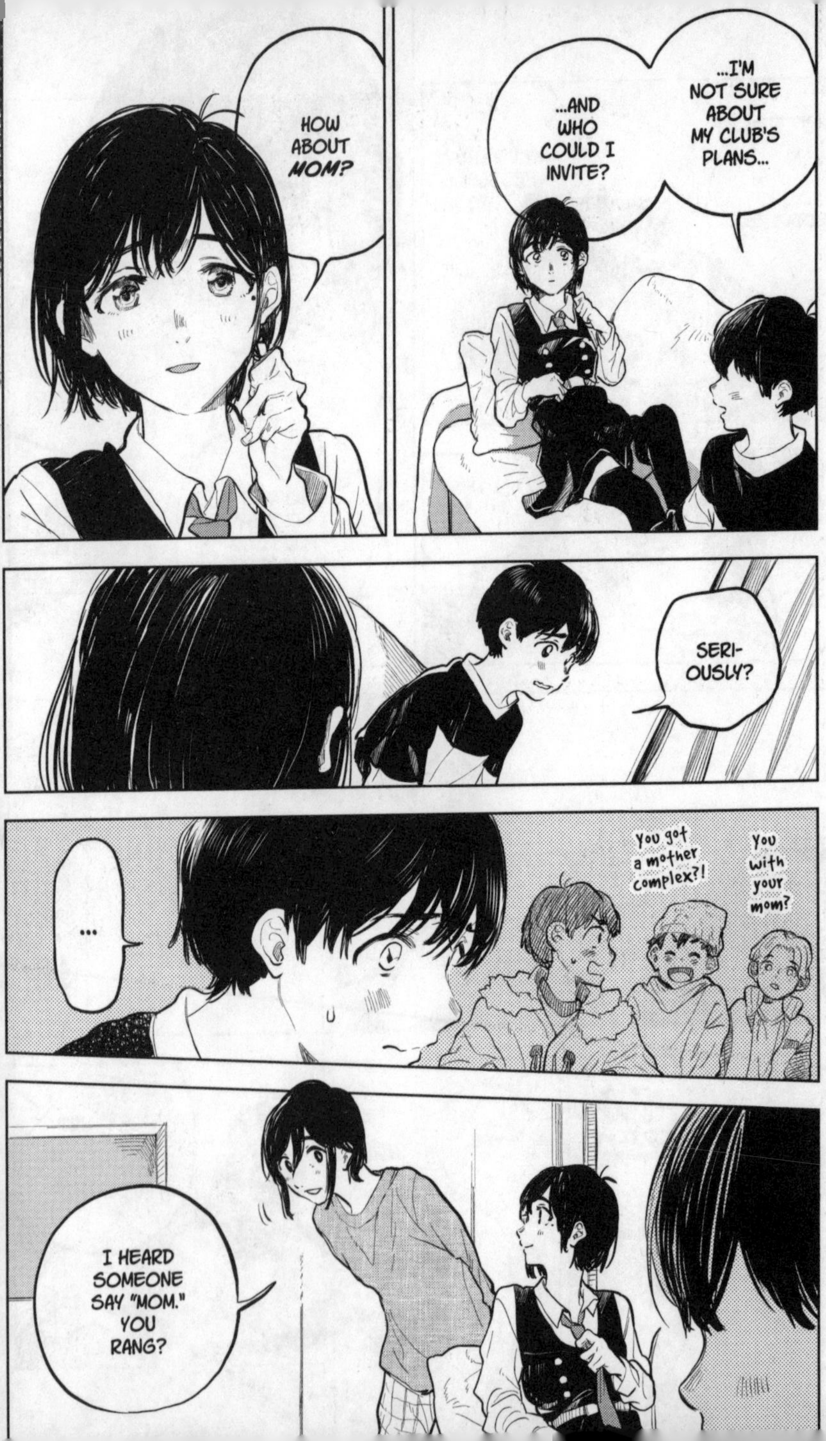
...I'M NOT SURE ABOUT MY CLUB'S PLANS...
...AND WHO COULD I INVITE?
HOW ABOUT *MOM?*
SERI-OUSLY?
You with your mom?
You got a mother complex?!
...
I HEARD SOMEONE SAY "MOM." YOU RANG?

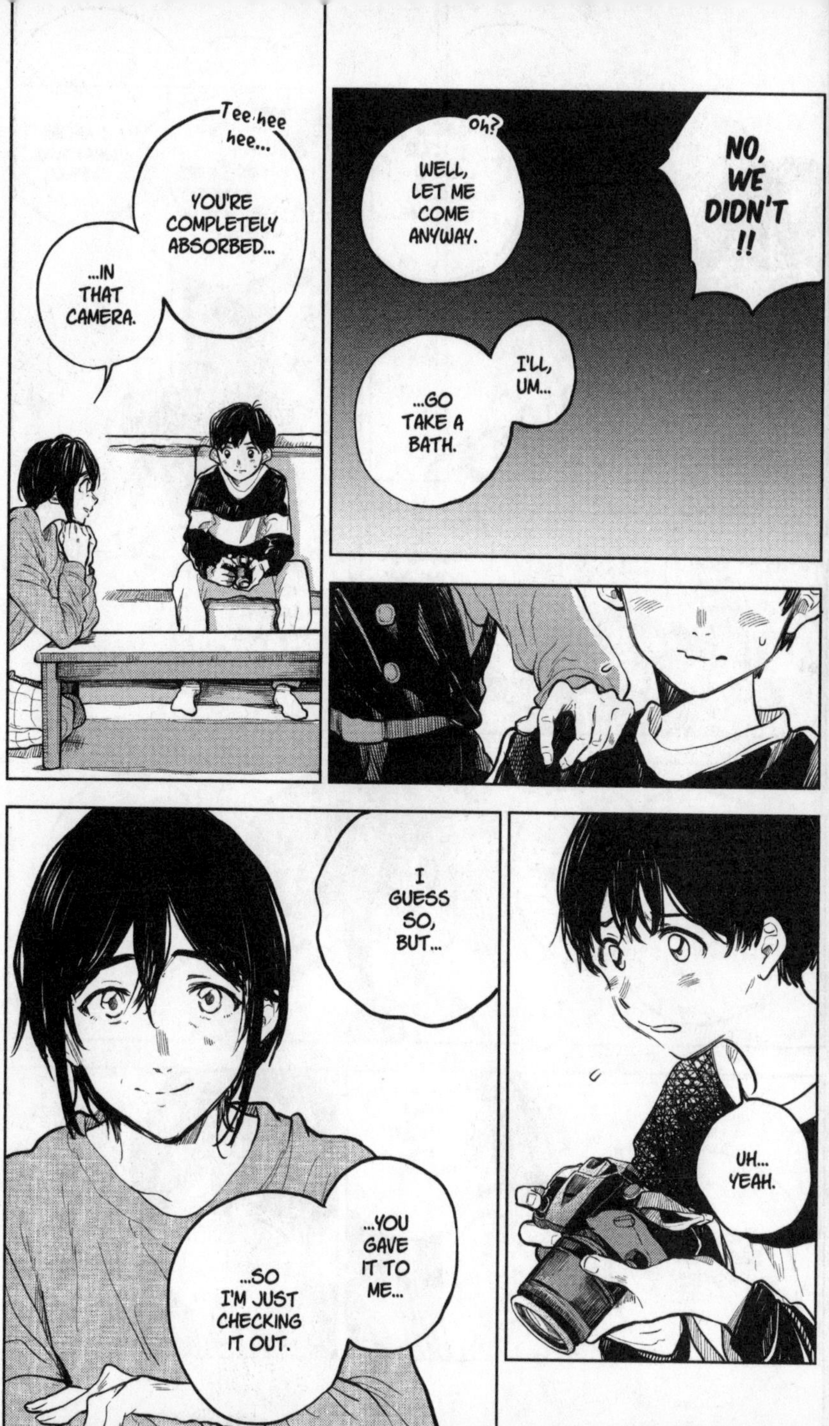
NO, WE DIDN'T!!
oh? WELL, LET ME COME ANYWAY.
I'LL, UM... ...GO TAKE A BATH.
Tee hee hee...
YOU'RE COMPLETELY ABSORBED...
...IN THAT CAMERA.
UH... YEAH.
I GUESS SO, BUT...
...YOU GAVE IT TO ME...
...SO I'M JUST CHECKING IT OUT.

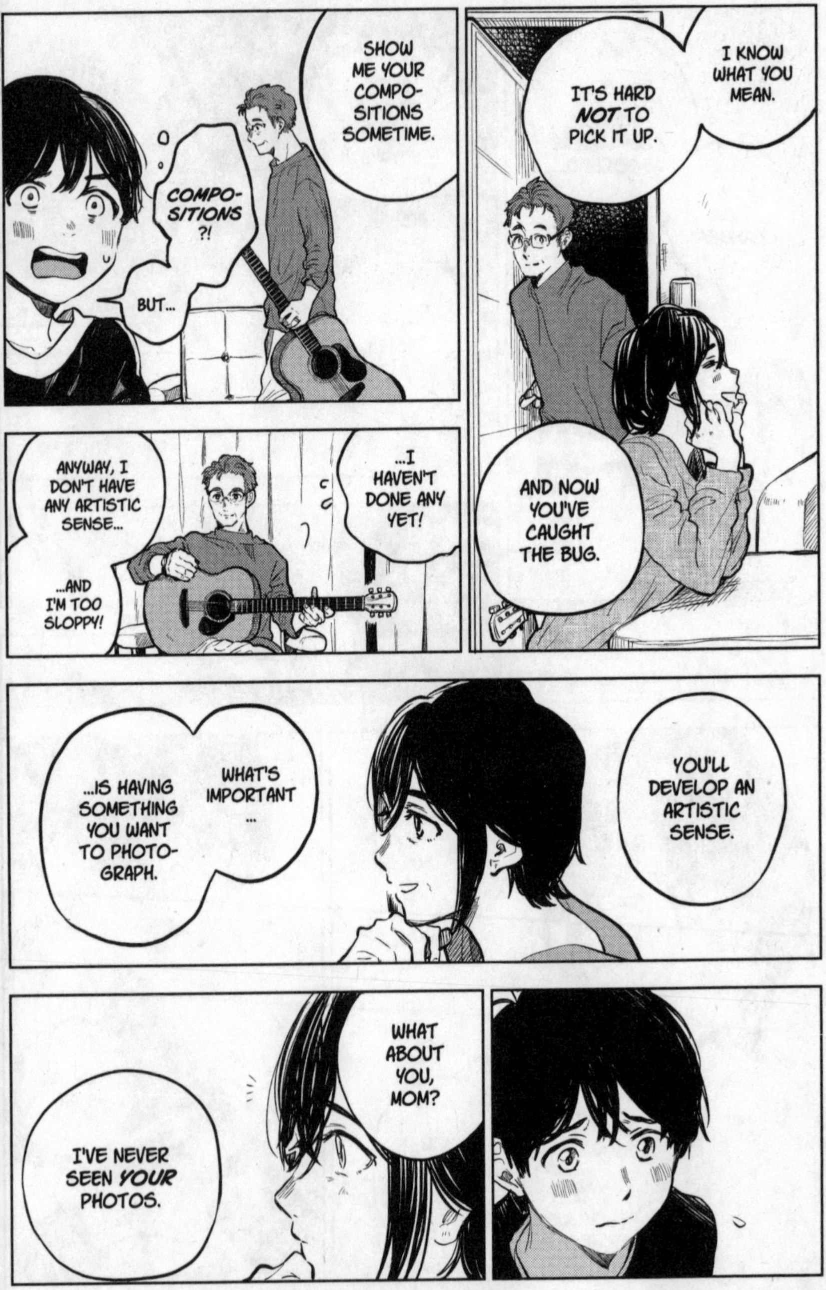
I KNOW WHAT YOU MEAN.
IT'S HARD *NOT* TO PICK IT UP.
AND NOW YOU'VE CAUGHT THE BUG.
SHOW ME YOUR COMPO-SITIONS SOMETIME.
COMPO-SITIONS ?!
BUT...
...I HAVEN'T DONE ANY YET!
ANYWAY, I DON'T HAVE ANY ARTISTIC SENSE...
...AND I'M TOO SLOPPY!
YOU'LL DEVELOP AN ARTISTIC SENSE.
WHAT'S IMPORTANT ...
...IS HAVING SOMETHING YOU WANT TO PHOTO-GRAPH.
WHAT ABOUT YOU, MOM?
I'VE NEVER SEEN *YOUR* PHOTOS.

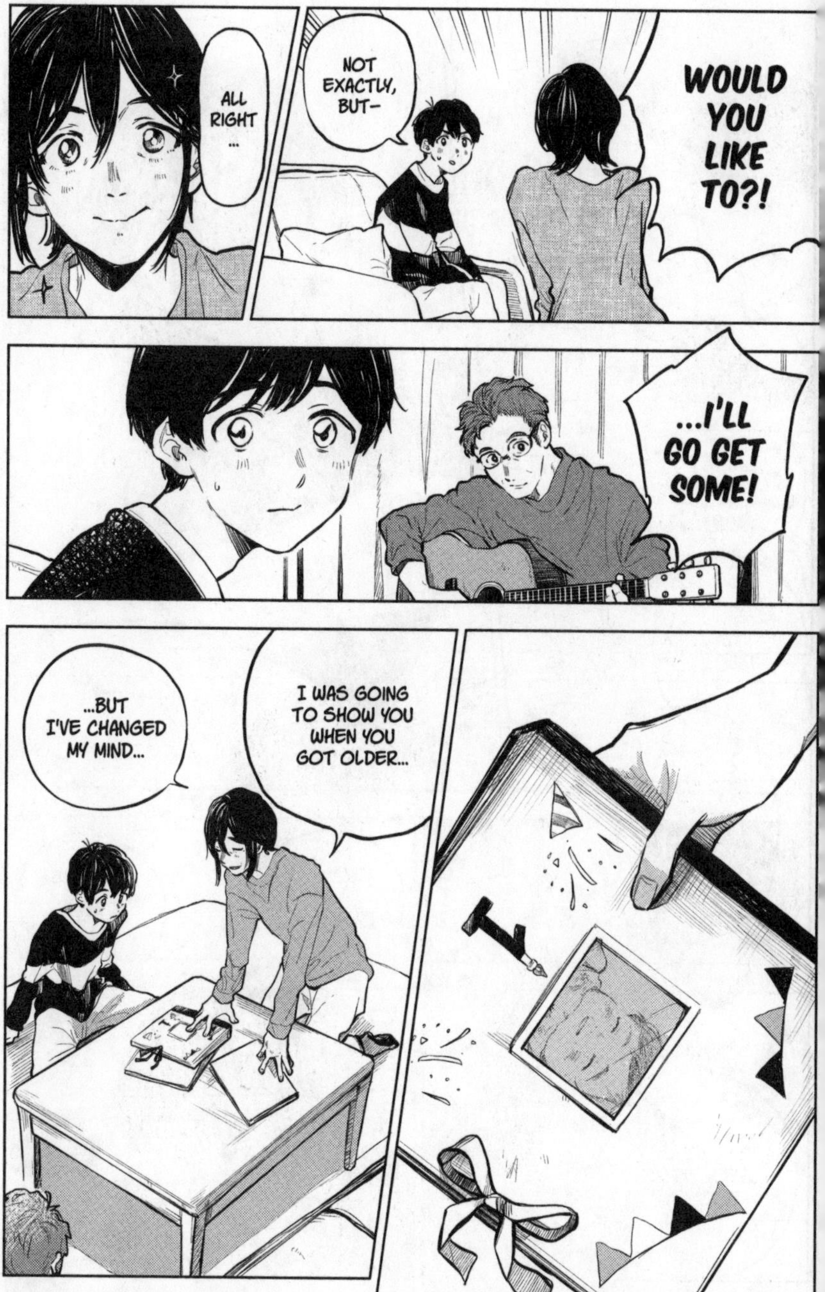
WOULD YOU LIKE TO?!
NOT EXACTLY, BUT-
ALL RIGHT ...
...I'LL GO GET SOME!
I WAS GOING TO SHOW YOU WHEN YOU GOT OLDER...
...BUT I'VE CHANGED MY MIND...

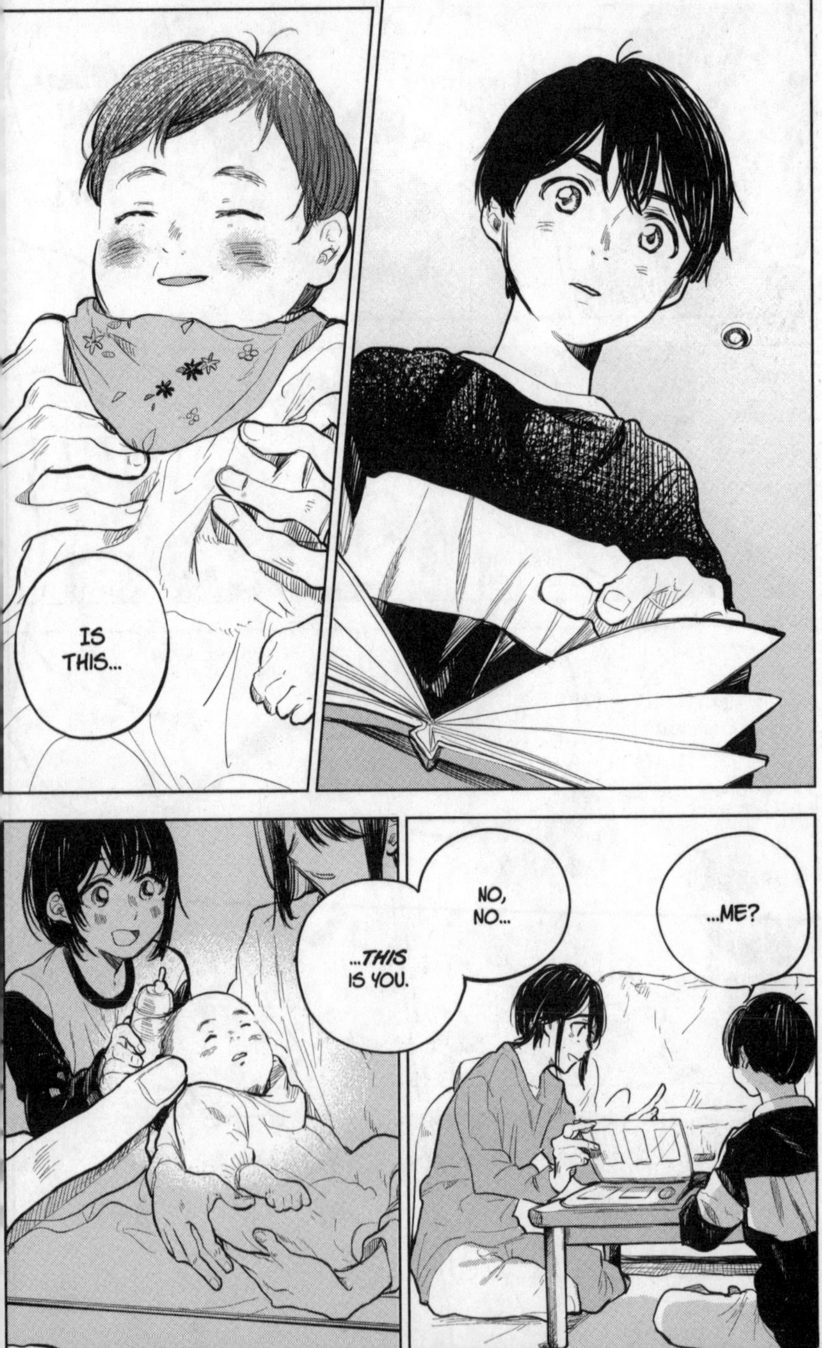
IS THIS...
...ME?
NO, NO...
...THIS IS YOU.

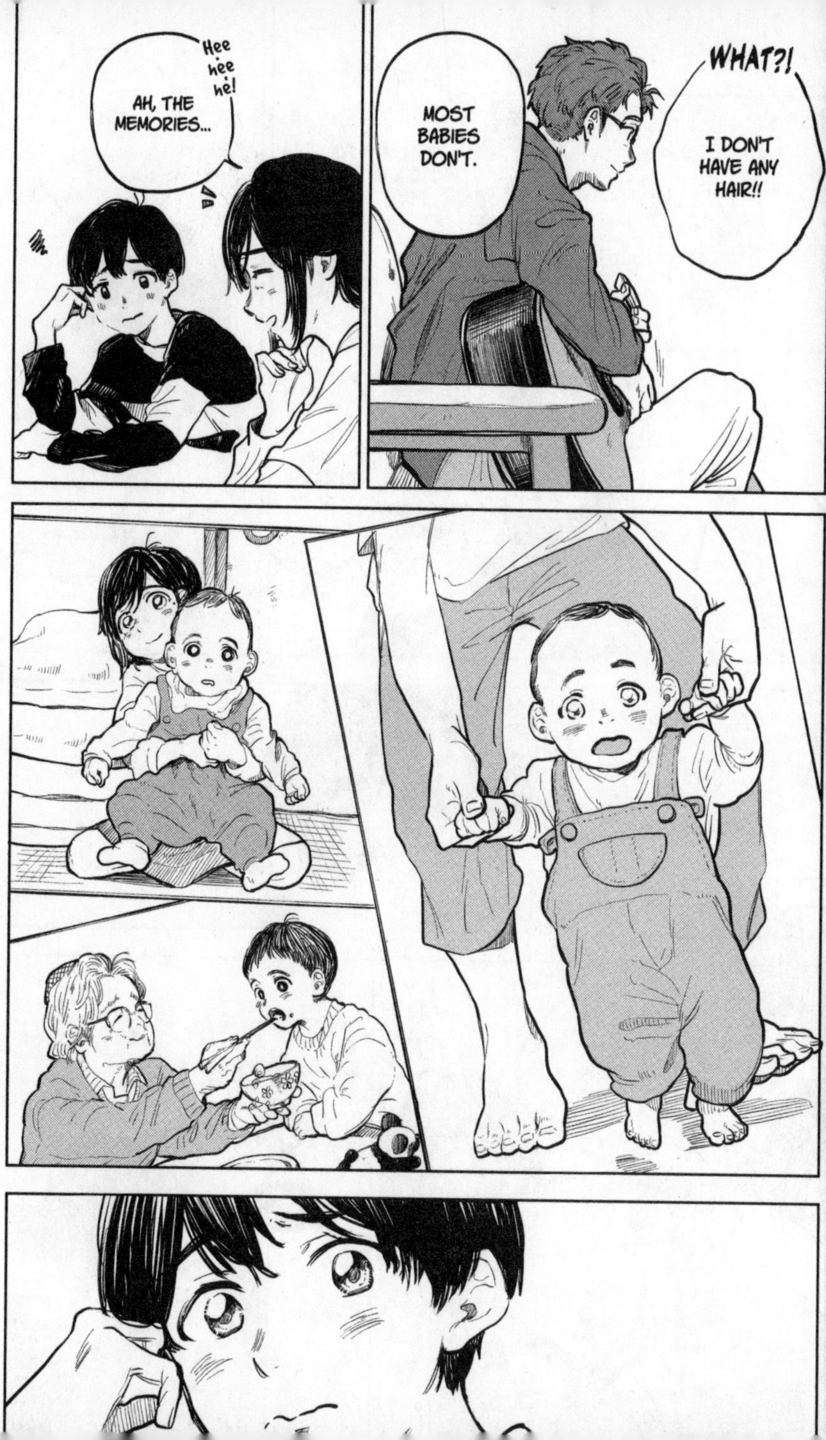
WHAT?!
I DON'T HAVE ANY HAIR!!
MOST BABIES DON'T.
AH, THE MEMORIES...
Hee hee he!

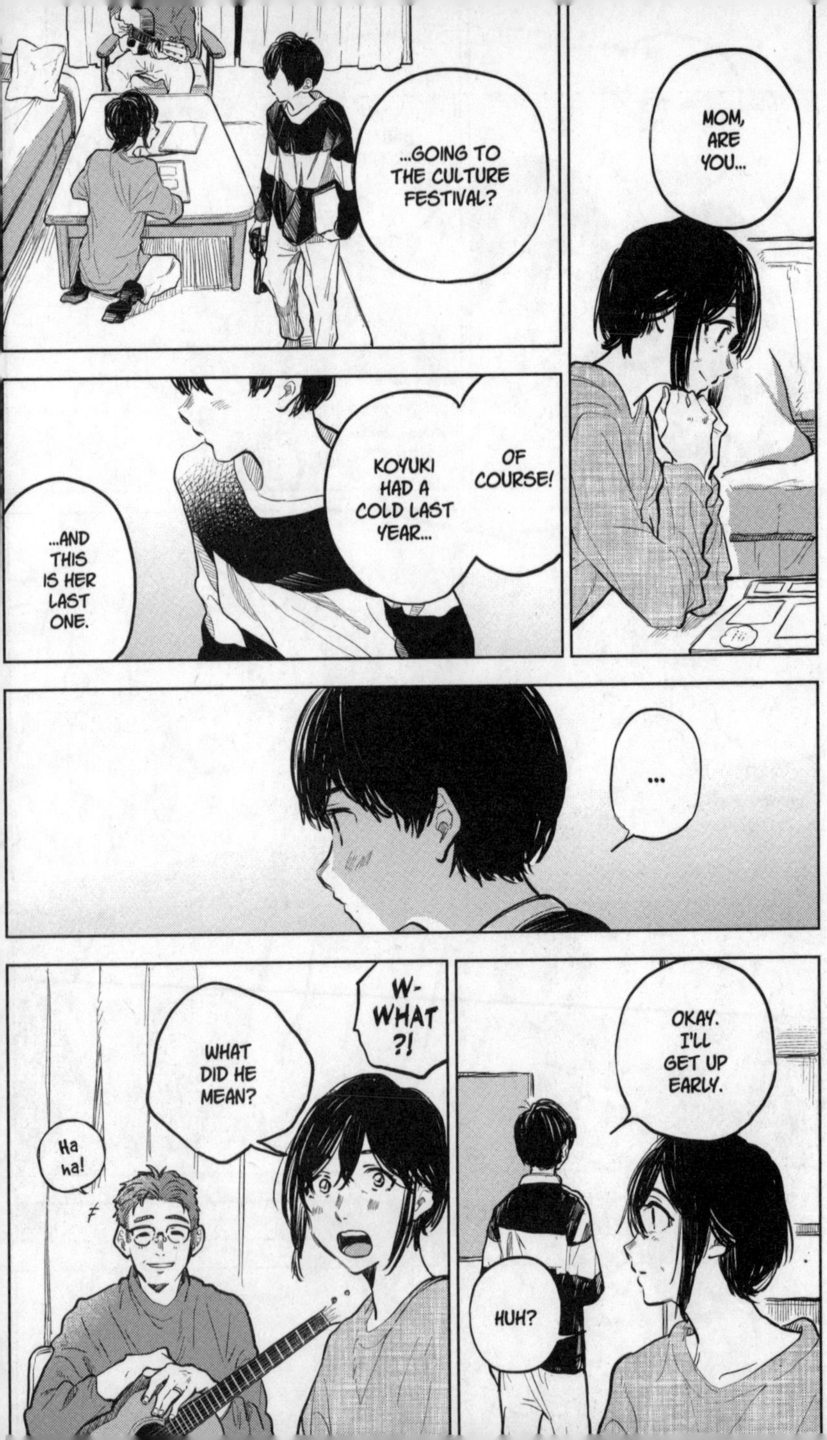
MOM, ARE YOU...
...GOING TO THE CULTURE FESTIVAL?
OF COURSE!
KOYUKI HAD A COLD LAST YEAR...
...AND THIS IS HER LAST ONE.
...
OKAY. I'LL GET UP EARLY.
HUH?
W-WHAT?!
WHAT DID HE MEAN?
Ha ha!

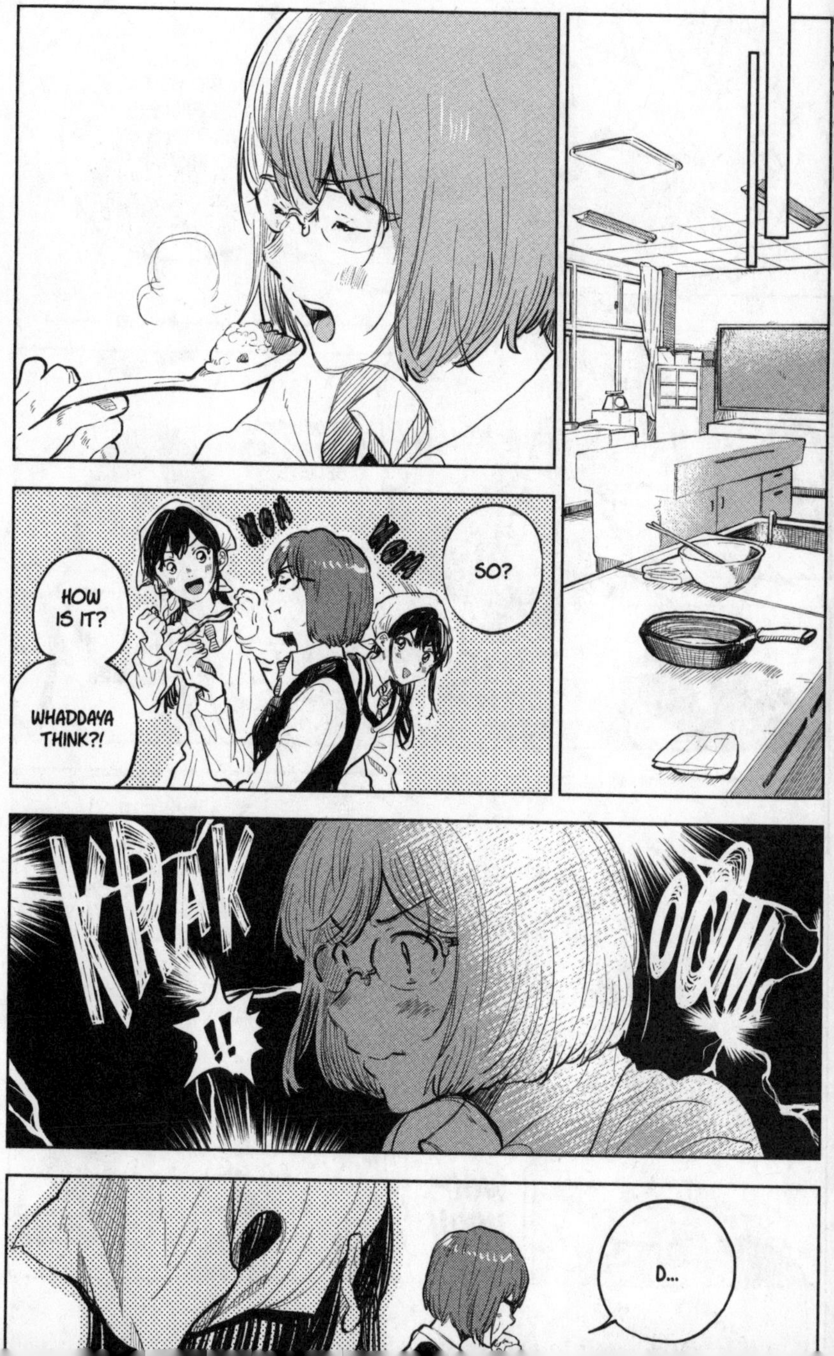
SO?
NOM
NOM
HOW IS IT?
WHADDAYA THINK?!
KRAK
!!
OOM
D...

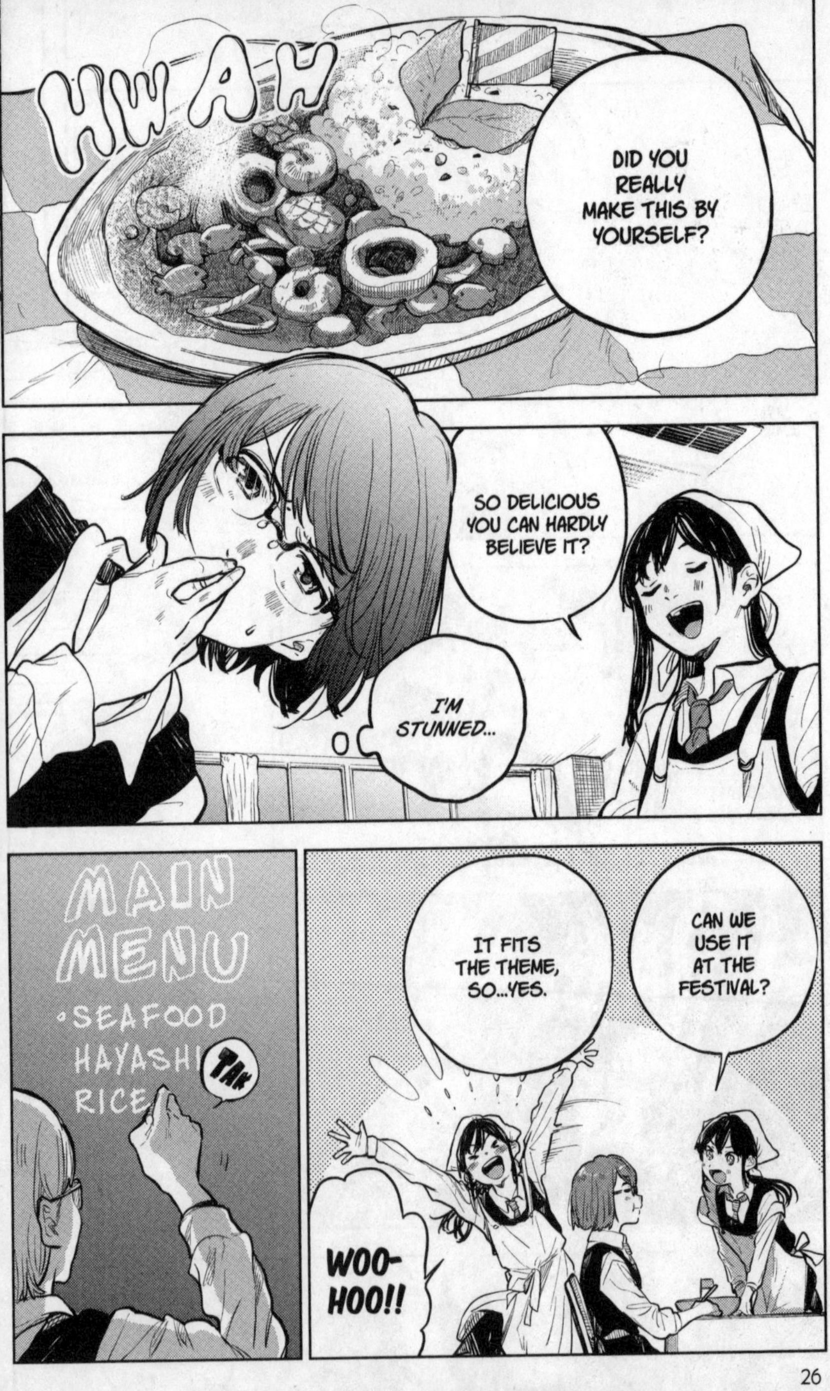
DID YOU REALLY MAKE THIS BY YOURSELF?
HWAH
SO DELICIOUS YOU CAN HARDLY BELIEVE IT?
I'M STUNNED...
CAN WE USE IT AT THE FESTIVAL?
IT FITS THE THEME, SO...YES.
WOO-HOO!!
MAIN MENU
•SEAFOOD HAYASHI RICE
TAK

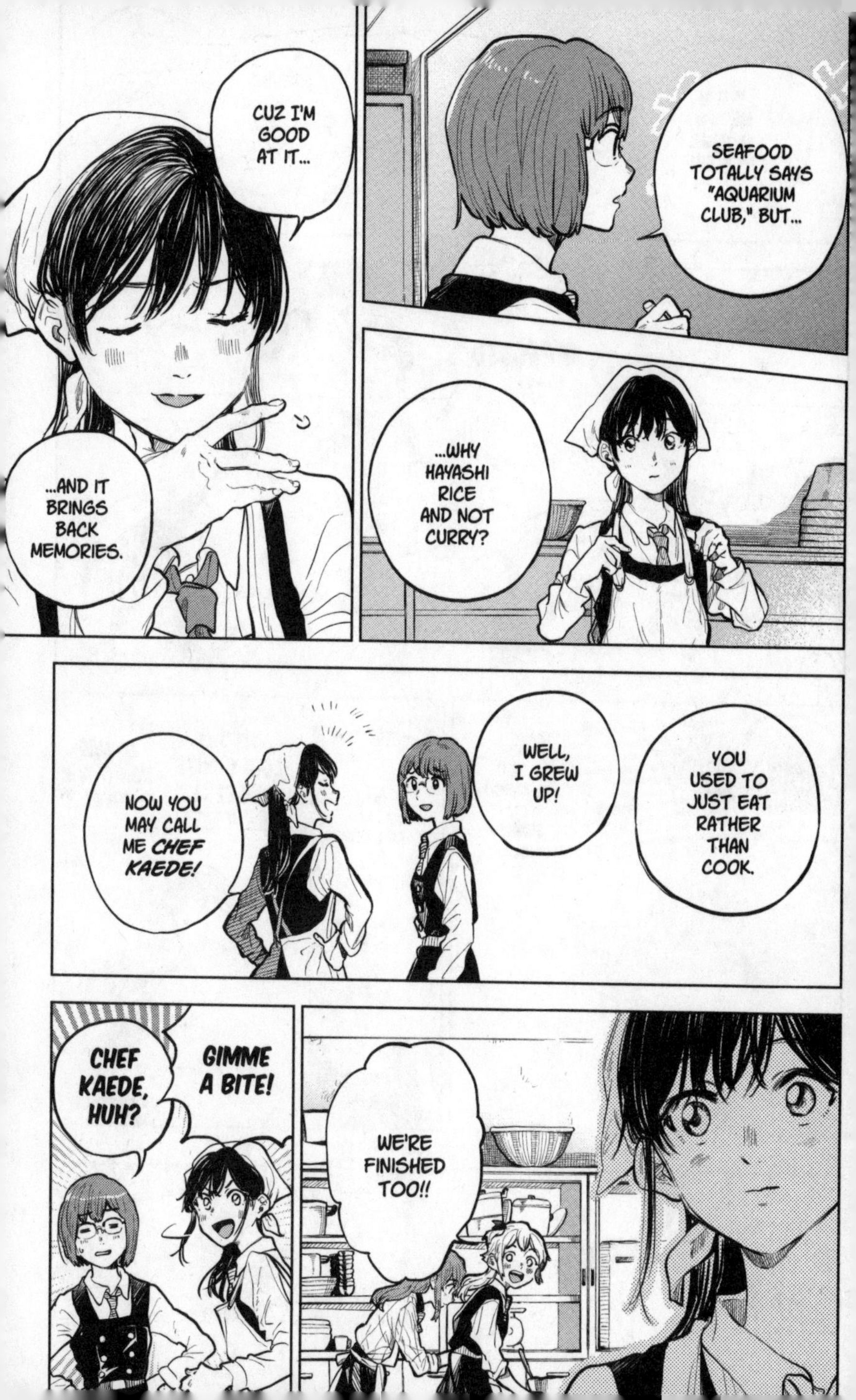
SEAFOOD TOTALLY SAYS "AQUARIUM CLUB," BUT...
...WHY HAYASHI RICE AND NOT CURRY?
CUZ I'M GOOD AT IT...
...AND IT BRINGS BACK MEMORIES.
YOU USED TO JUST EAT RATHER THAN COOK.
WELL, I GREW UP!
NOW YOU MAY CALL ME *CHEF KAEDE!*
WE'RE FINISHED TOO!!
GIMME A BITE!
CHEF KAEDE, HUH?

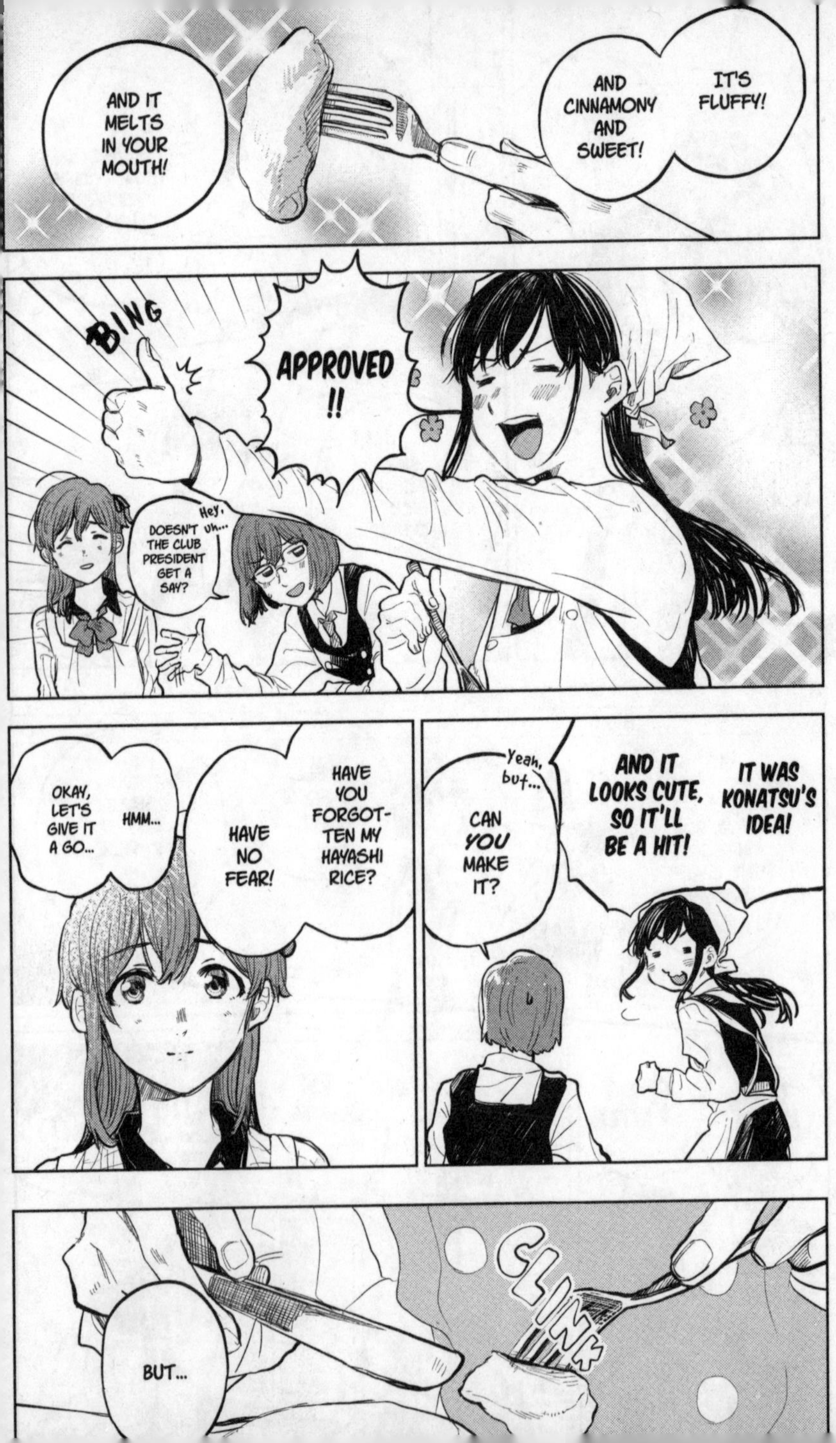
IT'S FLUFFY!
AND CINNAMONY AND SWEET!
AND IT MELTS IN YOUR MOUTH!
BING
APPROVED!!
Hey, DOESN'T uh... THE CLUB PRESIDENT GET A SAY?
IT WAS KONATSU'S IDEA!
AND IT LOOKS CUTE, SO IT'LL BE A HIT!
Yeah, but...
CAN *YOU* MAKE IT?
HAVE YOU FORGOT-TEN MY HAYASHI RICE?
HAVE NO FEAR!
HMM...
OKAY, LET'S GIVE IT A GO...
CLINK
BUT...

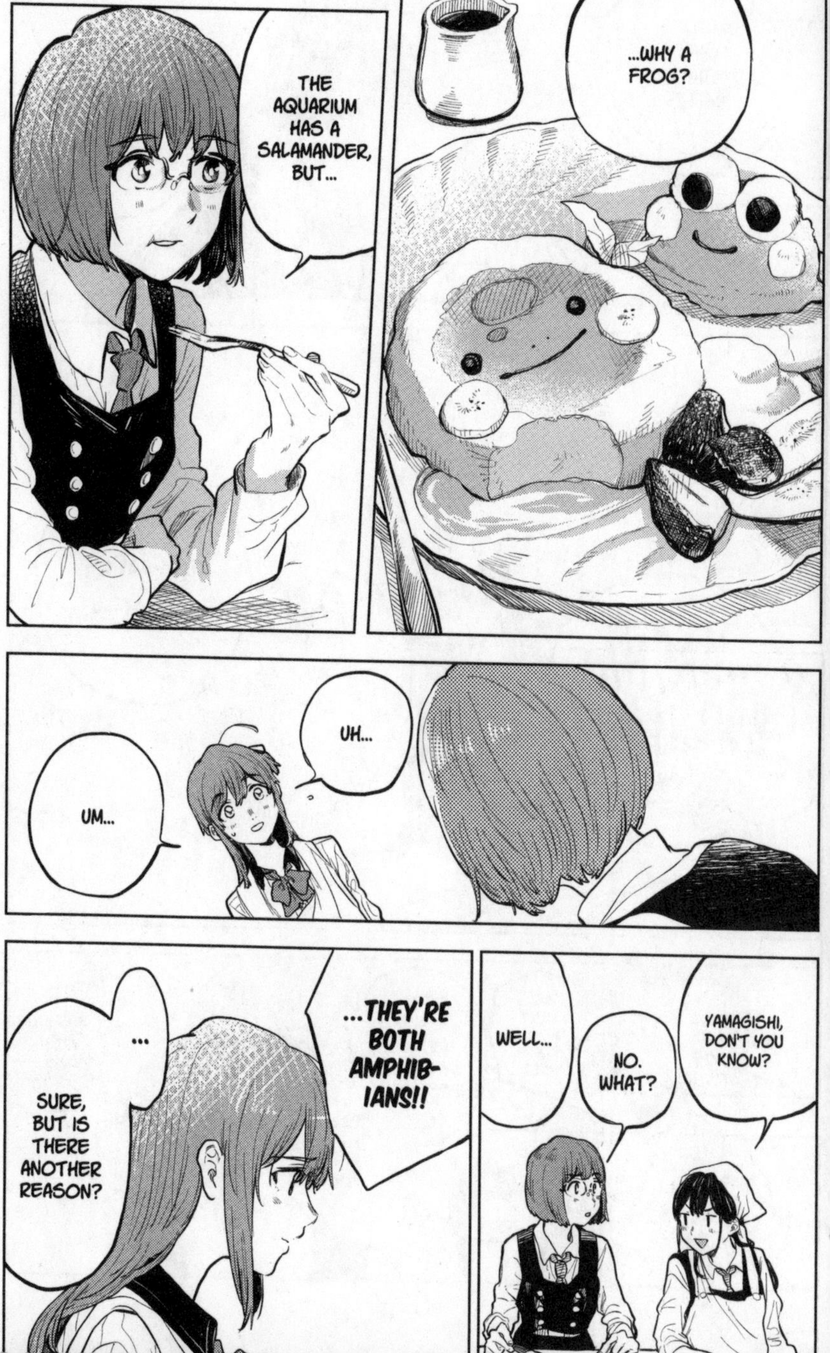
...WHY A FROG?
THE AQUARIUM HAS A SALAMANDER, BUT...
UH...
UM...
YAMAGISHI, DON'T YOU KNOW?
NO. WHAT?
WELL...
...THEY'RE BOTH AMPHIB-IANS!!
...
SURE, BUT IS THERE ANOTHER REASON?

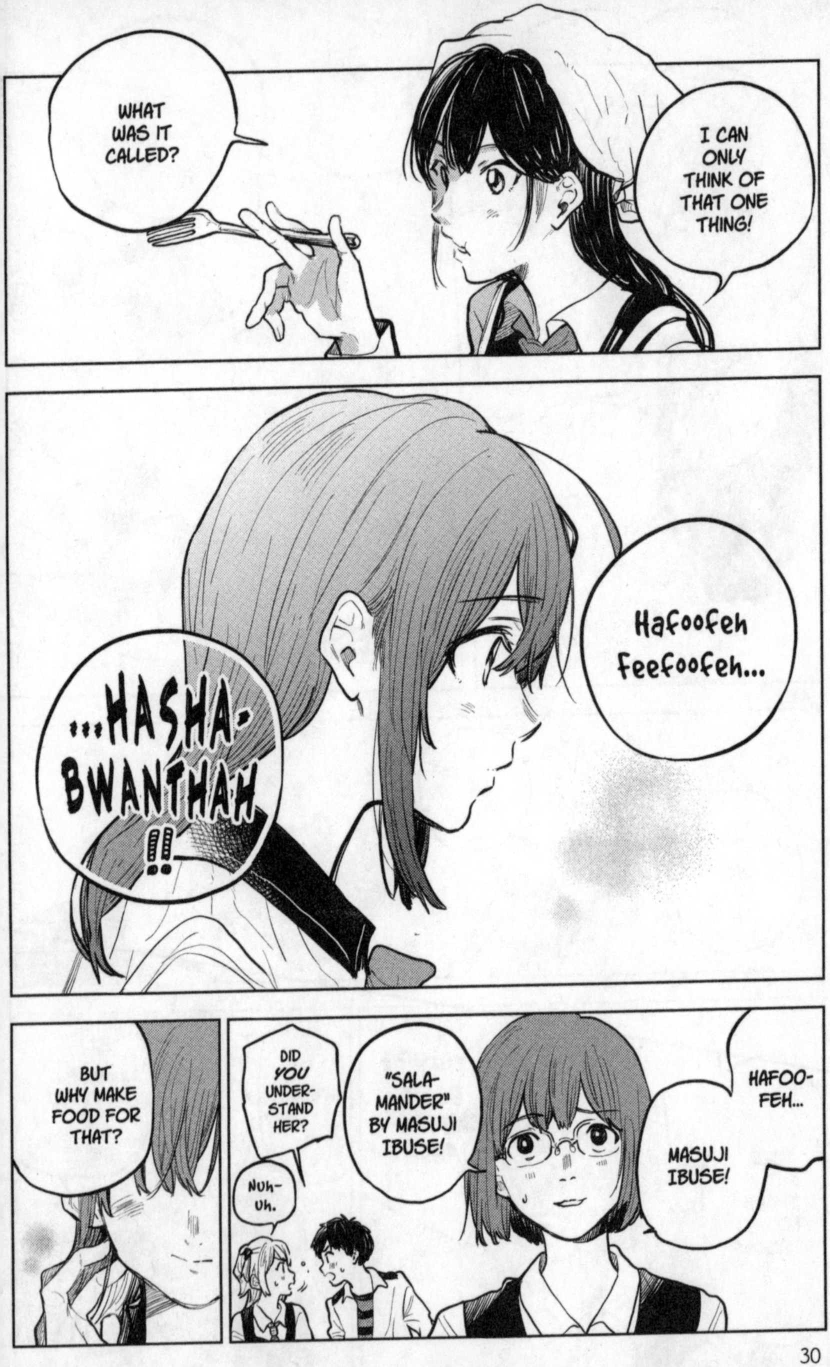
I CAN ONLY THINK OF THAT ONE THING!
WHAT WAS IT CALLED?
Hafoofeh feefoofeh...
...HASHA-BWANTHAH!!
HAFOO-FEH...
MASUJI IBUSE!
"SALAMANDER" BY MASUJI IBUSE!
DID YOU UNDERSTAND HER?
Nuh-uh.
BUT WHY MAKE FOOD FOR THAT?

...IT'S A **SECRET!!**

THERE IS A REASON, BUT...

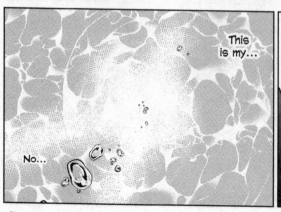

This is my...

No...

what?!
NOW I GOTTA KNOW!!

- SEAFOOD HAYASHI RICE
- SALAMANDER & FROG SOUFFLÉ PANCAKE SET

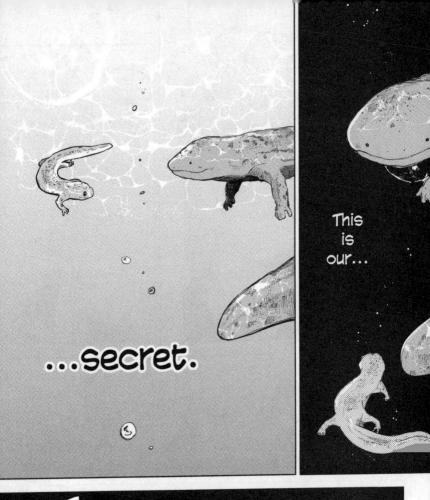

This
is
our...

...secret.

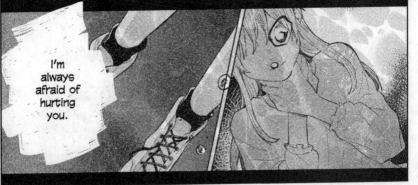

I'm
always
afraid of
hurting
you.

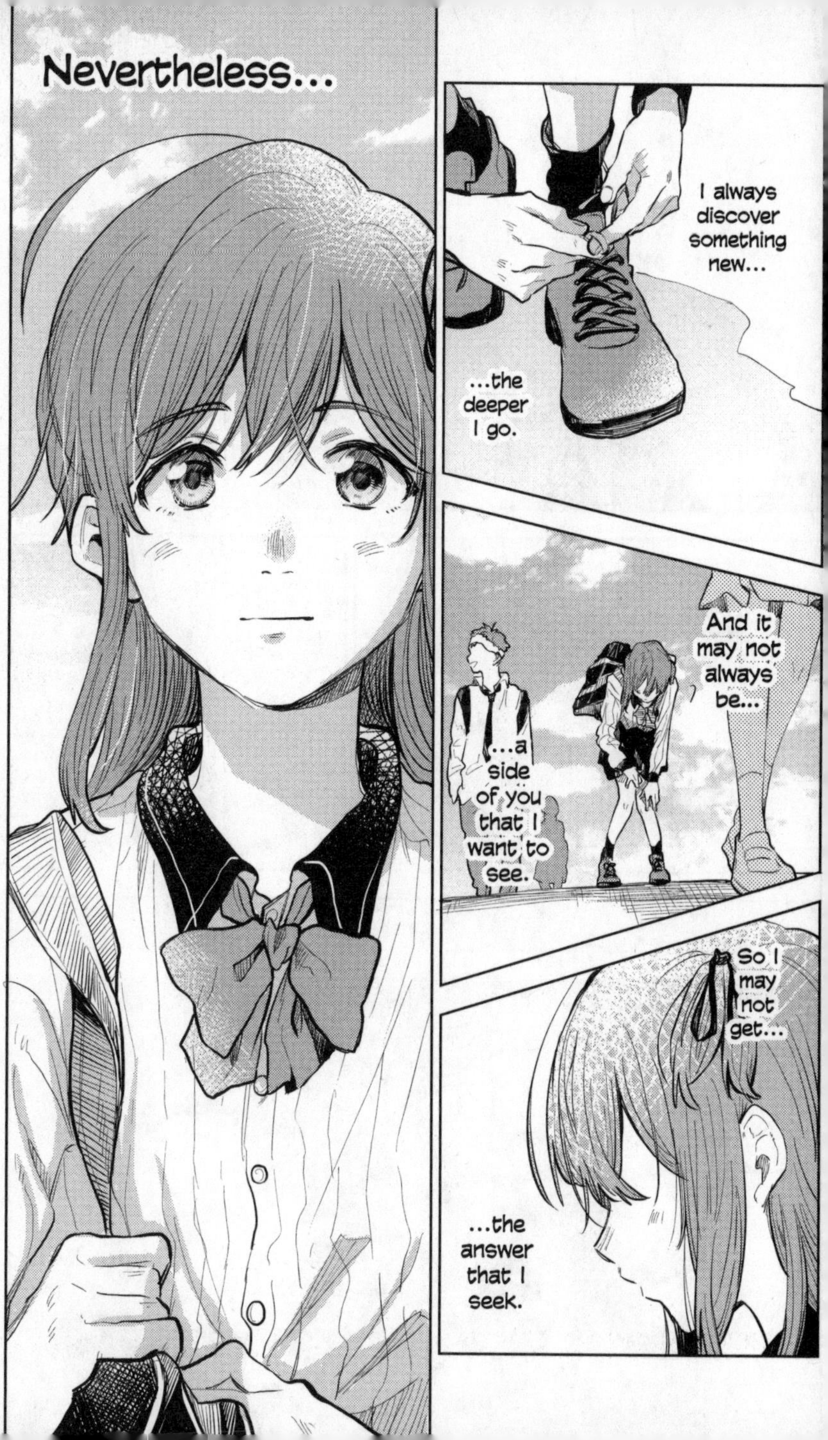
I always discover something new...
...the deeper I go.
And it may not always be...
...a side of you that I want to see.
So I may not get...
...the answer that I seek.
Nevertheless...

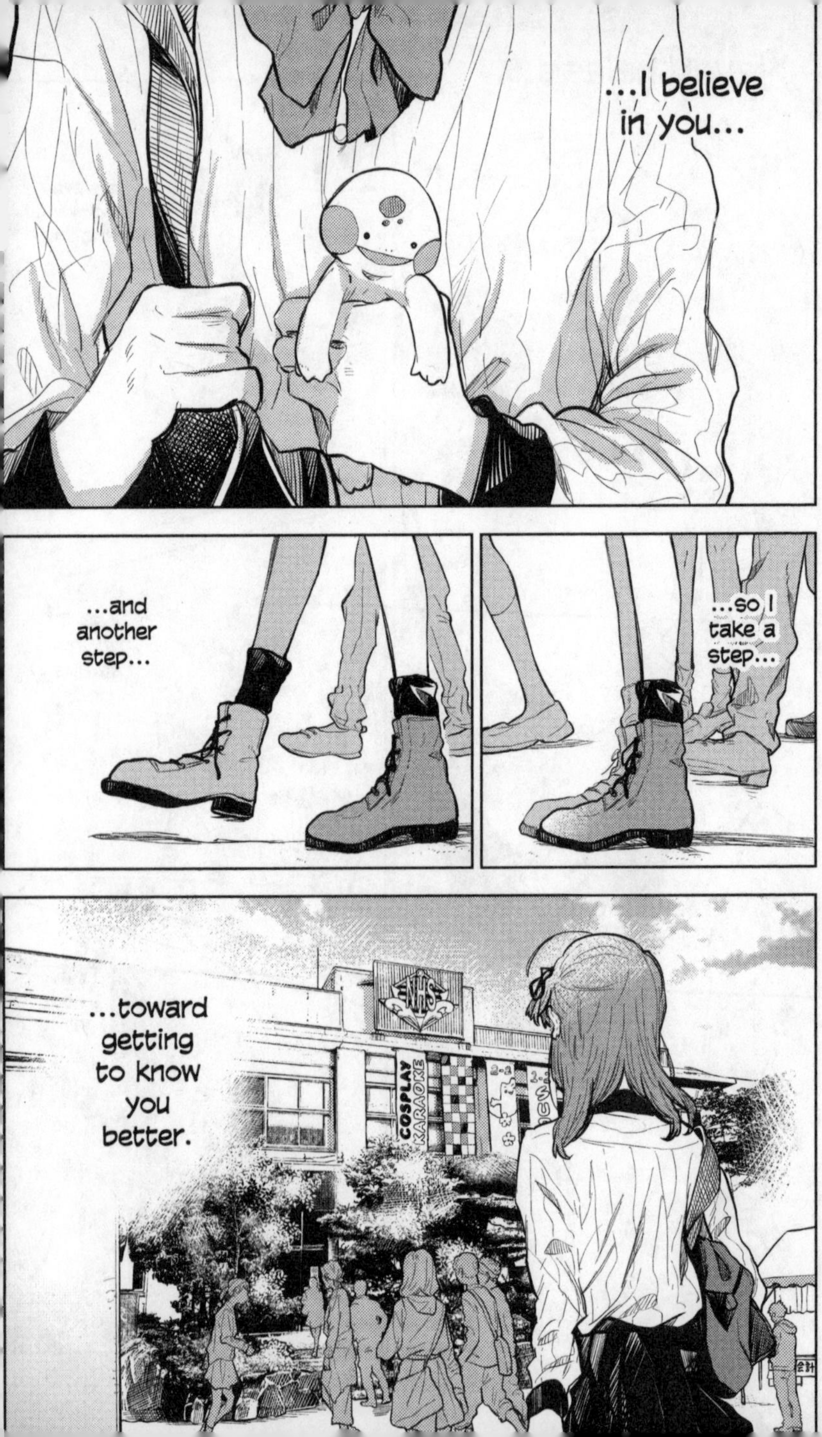
...I believe in you...
...so I take a step...
...and another step...
...toward getting to know you better.
NHS
COSPLAY
KARAOKE

A Tropical Fish
Yearns for Snow

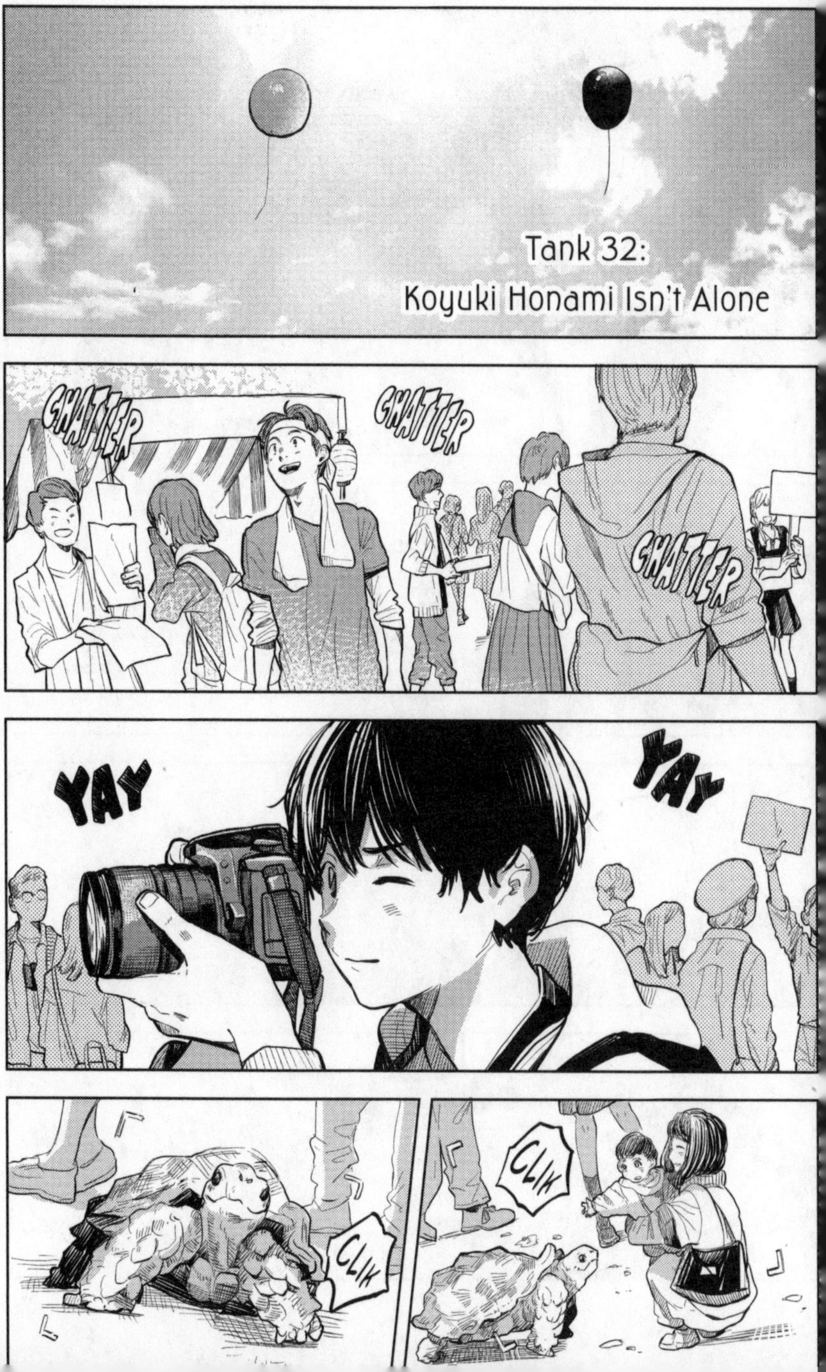
Tank 32:
Koyuki Honami Isn't Alone
CHATTER
CHATTER
CHATTER
YAY
YAY
CLIK
CLIK

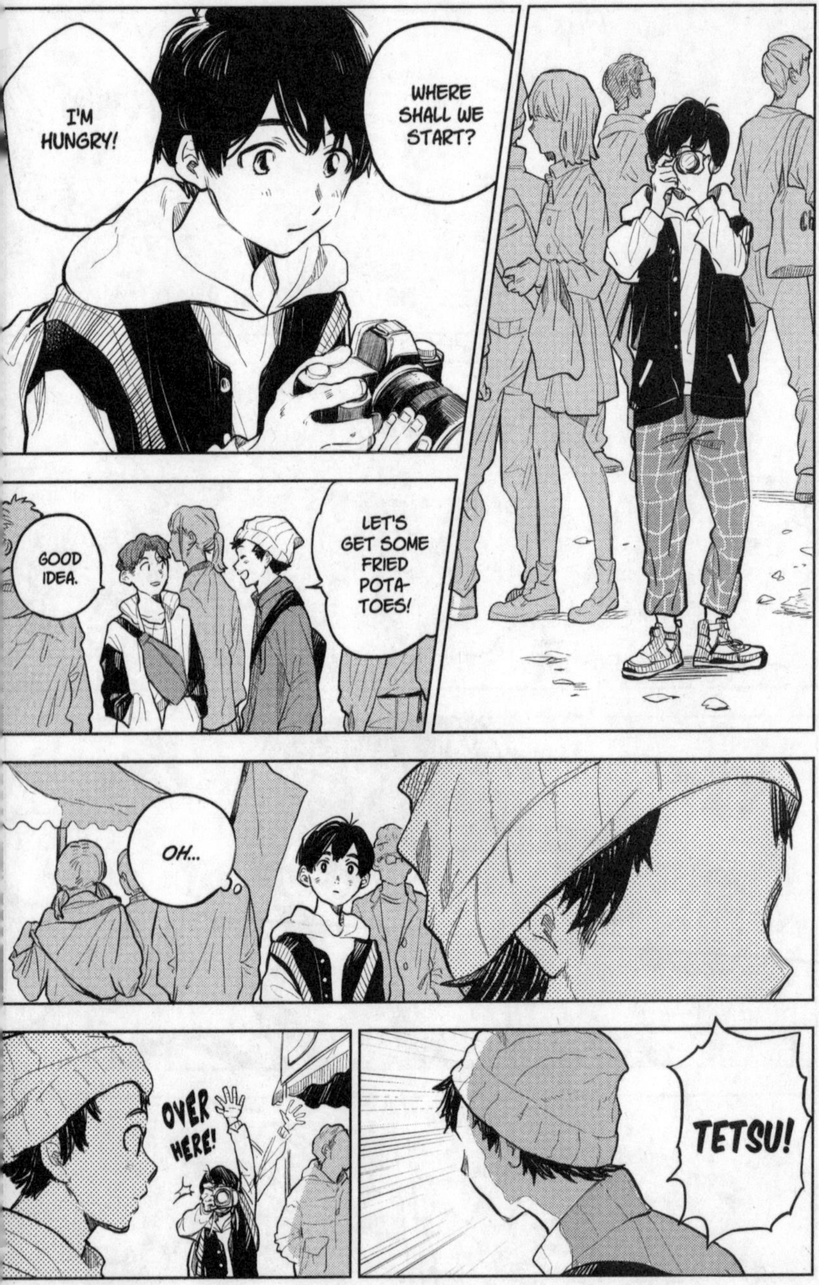
WHERE SHALL WE START?
I'M HUNGRY!
LET'S GET SOME FRIED POTA-TOES!
GOOD IDEA.
OH...
TETSU!
OVER HERE!

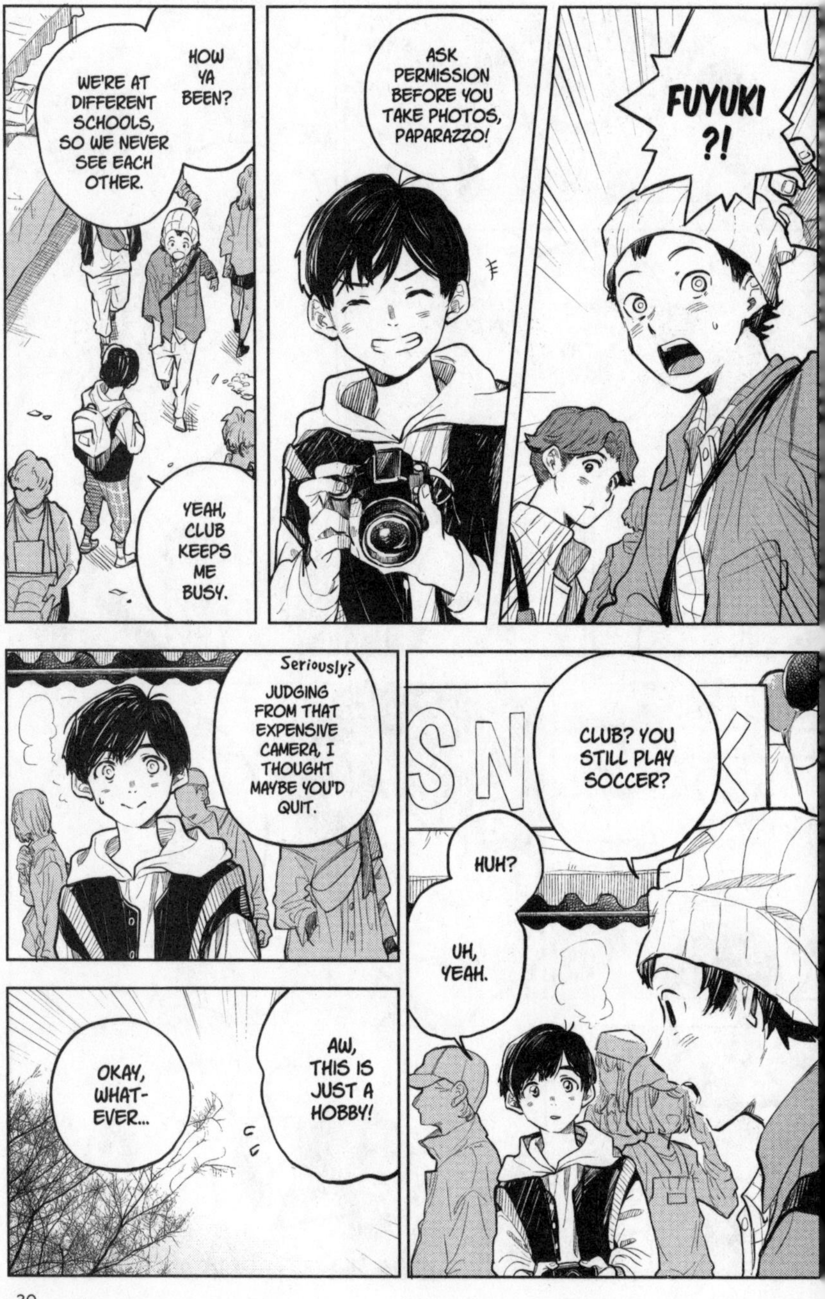
FUYUKI?!
ASK PERMISSION BEFORE YOU TAKE PHOTOS, PAPARAZZO!
HOW YA BEEN?
WE'RE AT DIFFERENT SCHOOLS, SO WE NEVER SEE EACH OTHER.
YEAH, CLUB KEEPS ME BUSY.
CLUB? YOU STILL PLAY SOCCER?
HUH?
UH, YEAH.
Seriously?
JUDGING FROM THAT EXPENSIVE CAMERA, I THOUGHT MAYBE YOU'D QUIT.
AW, THIS IS JUST A HOBBY!
OKAY, WHAT-EVER...

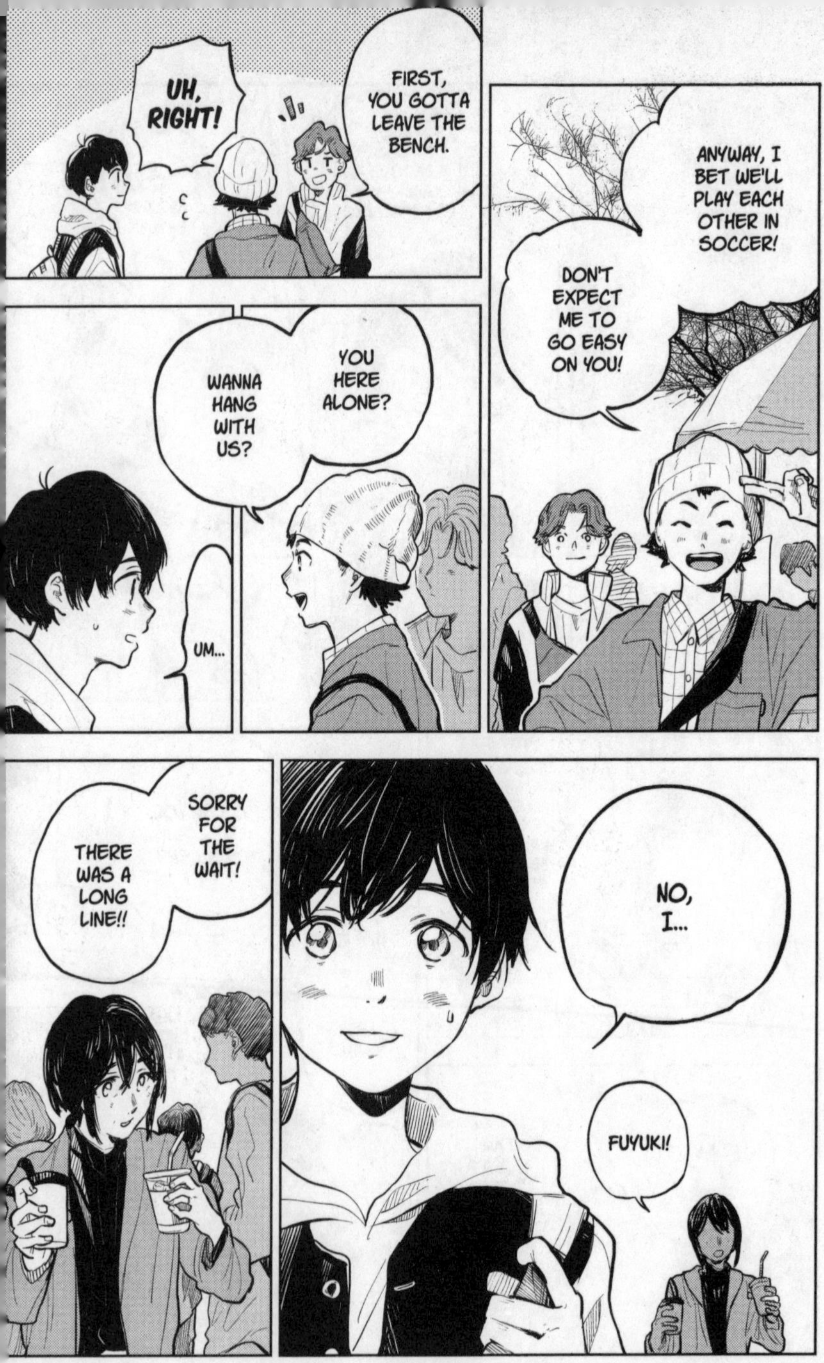
FIRST, YOU GOTTA LEAVE THE BENCH.
UH, RIGHT!
ANYWAY, I BET WE'LL PLAY EACH OTHER IN SOCCER!
DON'T EXPECT ME TO GO EASY ON YOU!
YOU HERE ALONE?
WANNA HANG WITH US?
UM...
NO, I...
FUYUKI!
SORRY FOR THE WAIT!
THERE WAS A LONG LINE!!

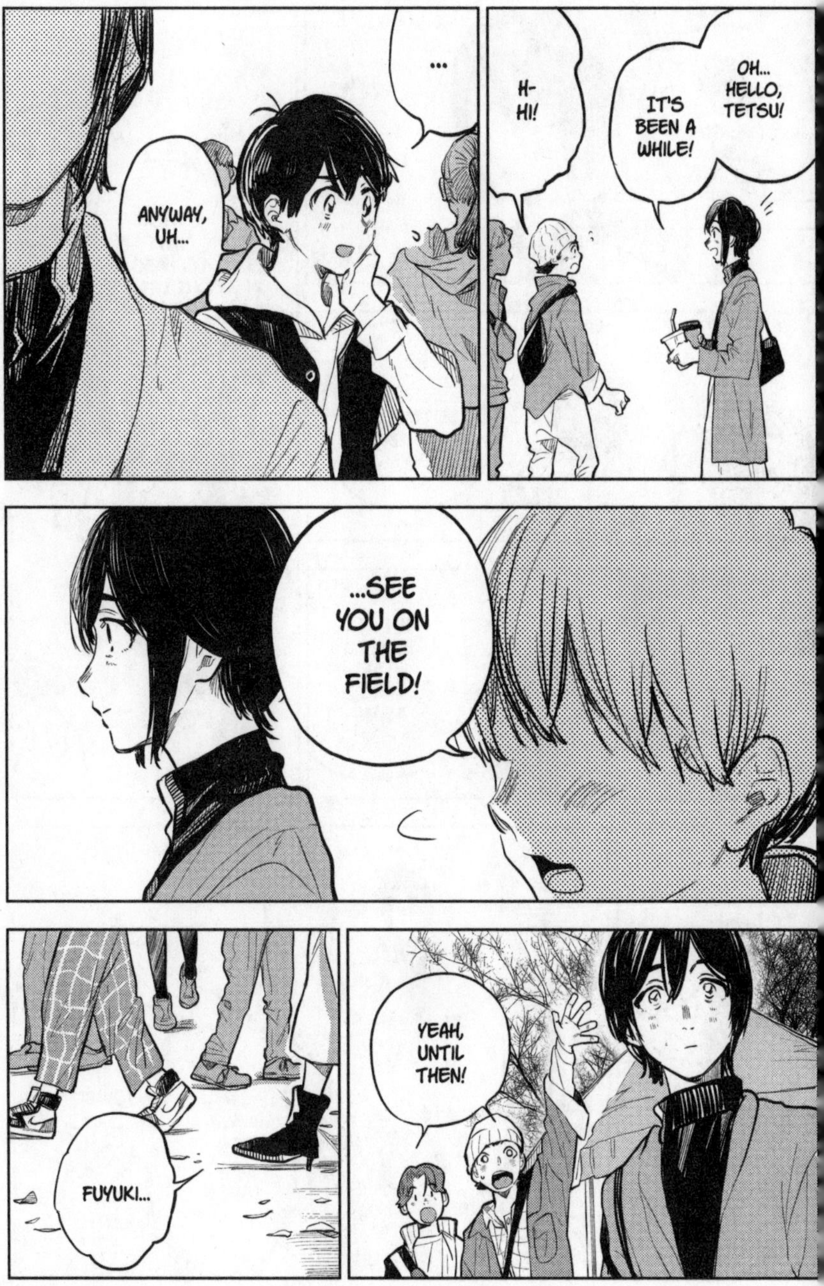
OH... HELLO, TETSU!
IT'S BEEN A WHILE!
H-HI!
...
ANYWAY, UH...
...SEE YOU ON THE FIELD!
YEAH, UNTIL THEN!
FUYUKI...

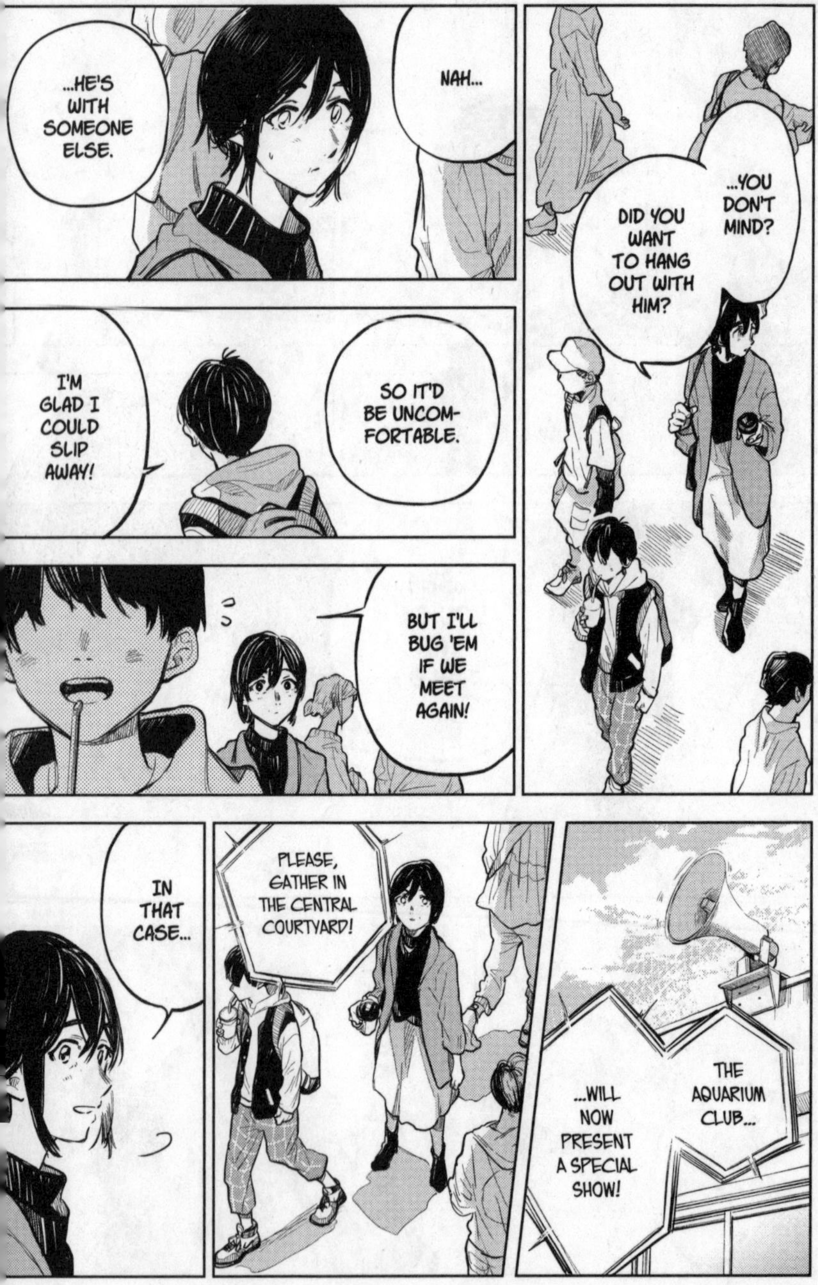
...YOU DON'T MIND?
DID YOU WANT TO HANG OUT WITH HIM?
NAH...
...HE'S WITH SOMEONE ELSE.
SO IT'D BE UNCOMFORTABLE.
I'M GLAD I COULD SLIP AWAY!
BUT I'LL BUG 'EM IF WE MEET AGAIN!
THE AQUARIUM CLUB...
...WILL NOW PRESENT A SPECIAL SHOW!
PLEASE, GATHER IN THE CENTRAL COURTYARD!
IN THAT CASE...

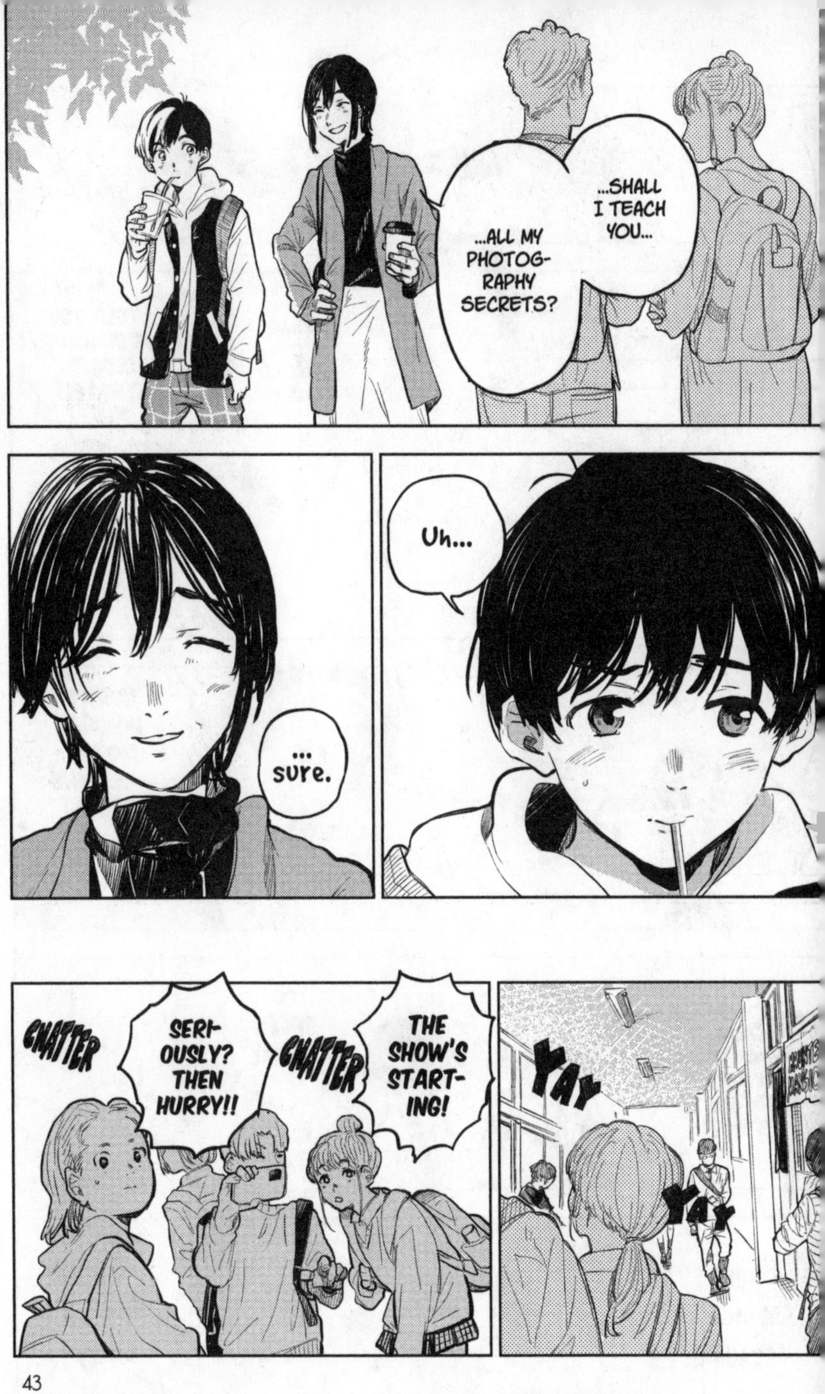
...SHALL I TEACH YOU...
...ALL MY PHOTOGRAPHY SECRETS?
Uh...
...sure.
YAY
YAY
THE SHOW'S STARTING!
CHATTER
SERIOUSLY? THEN HURRY!!
CHATTER

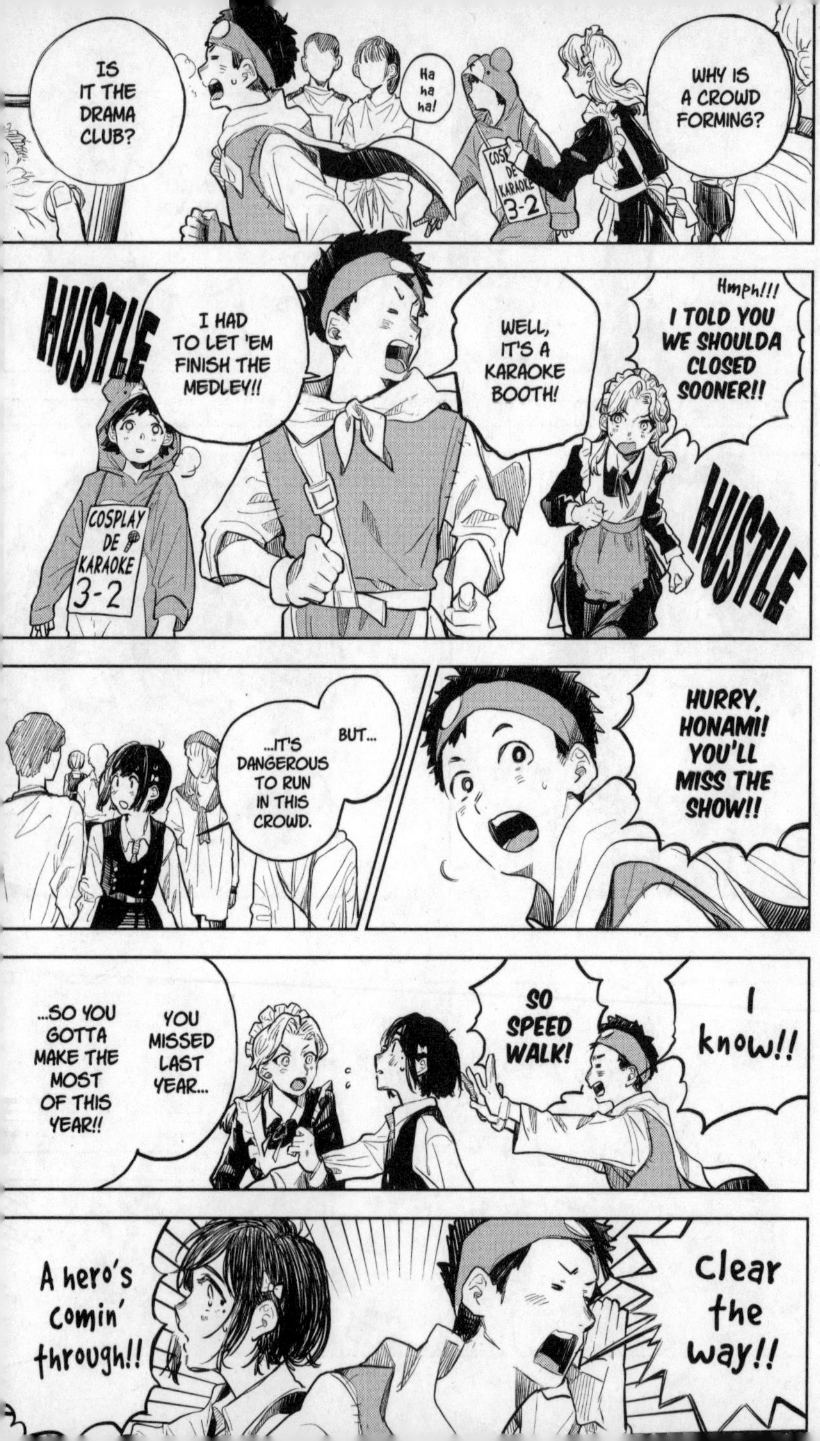
WHY IS A CROWD FORMING?
COSPLAY DE KARAOKE 3-2
Ha ha ha!
IS IT THE DRAMA CLUB?
Hmph!!! I TOLD YOU WE SHOULDA CLOSED SOONER!!
HUSTLE
WELL, IT'S A KARAOKE BOOTH!
I HAD TO LET 'EM FINISH THE MEDLEY!!
HUSTLE
COSPLAY DE KARAOKE 3-2
HURRY, HONAMI! YOU'LL MISS THE SHOW!!
BUT...
...IT'S DANGEROUS TO RUN IN THIS CROWD.
I know!!
SO SPEED WALK!
YOU MISSED LAST YEAR...
...SO YOU GOTTA MAKE THE MOST OF THIS YEAR!!
Clear the way!!
A hero's comin' through!!

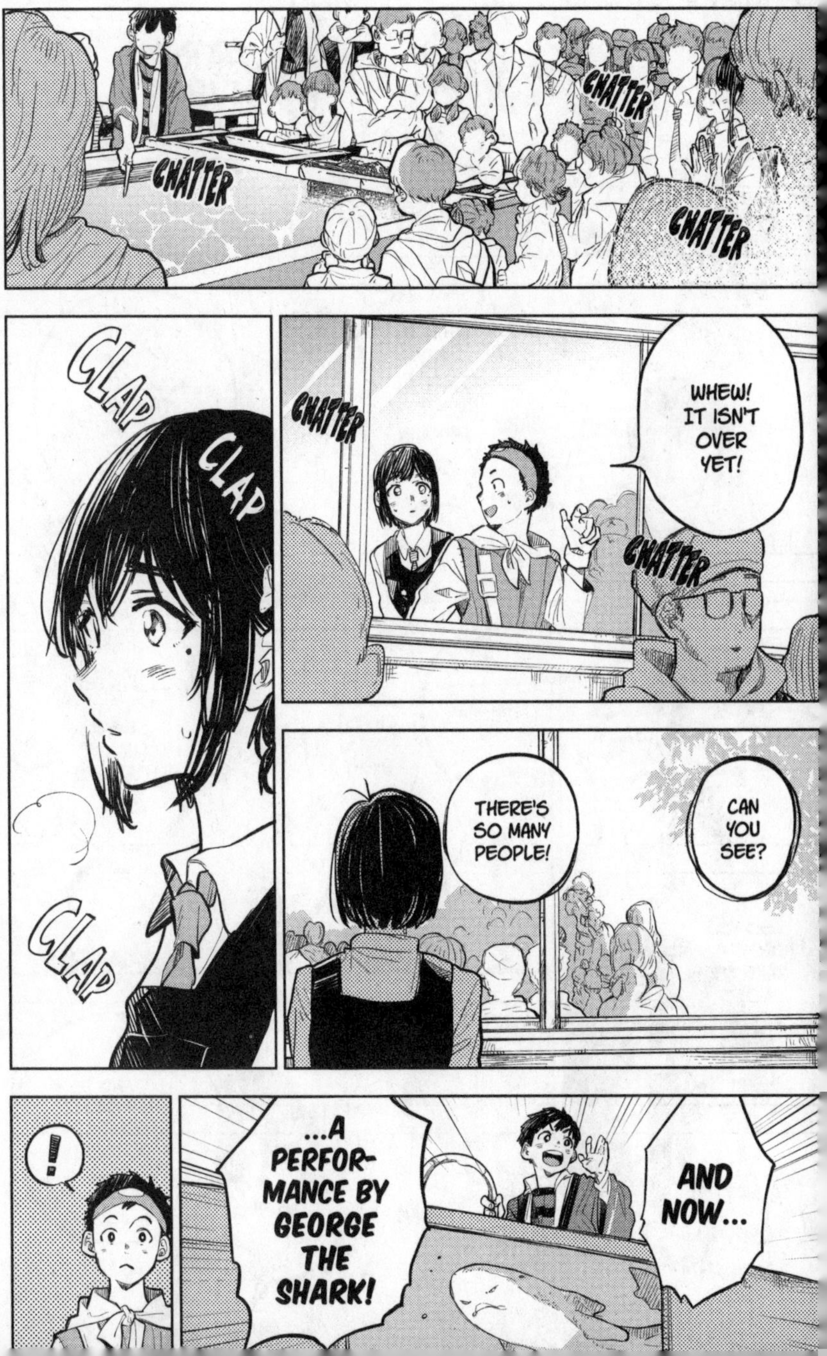
CHATTER
CHATTER
CHATTER
WHEW! IT ISN'T OVER YET!
CHATTER
CHATTER
CAN YOU SEE?
THERE'S SO MANY PEOPLE!
CLAP
CLAP
CLAP
AND NOW...
...A PERFORMANCE BY GEORGE THE SHARK!
!

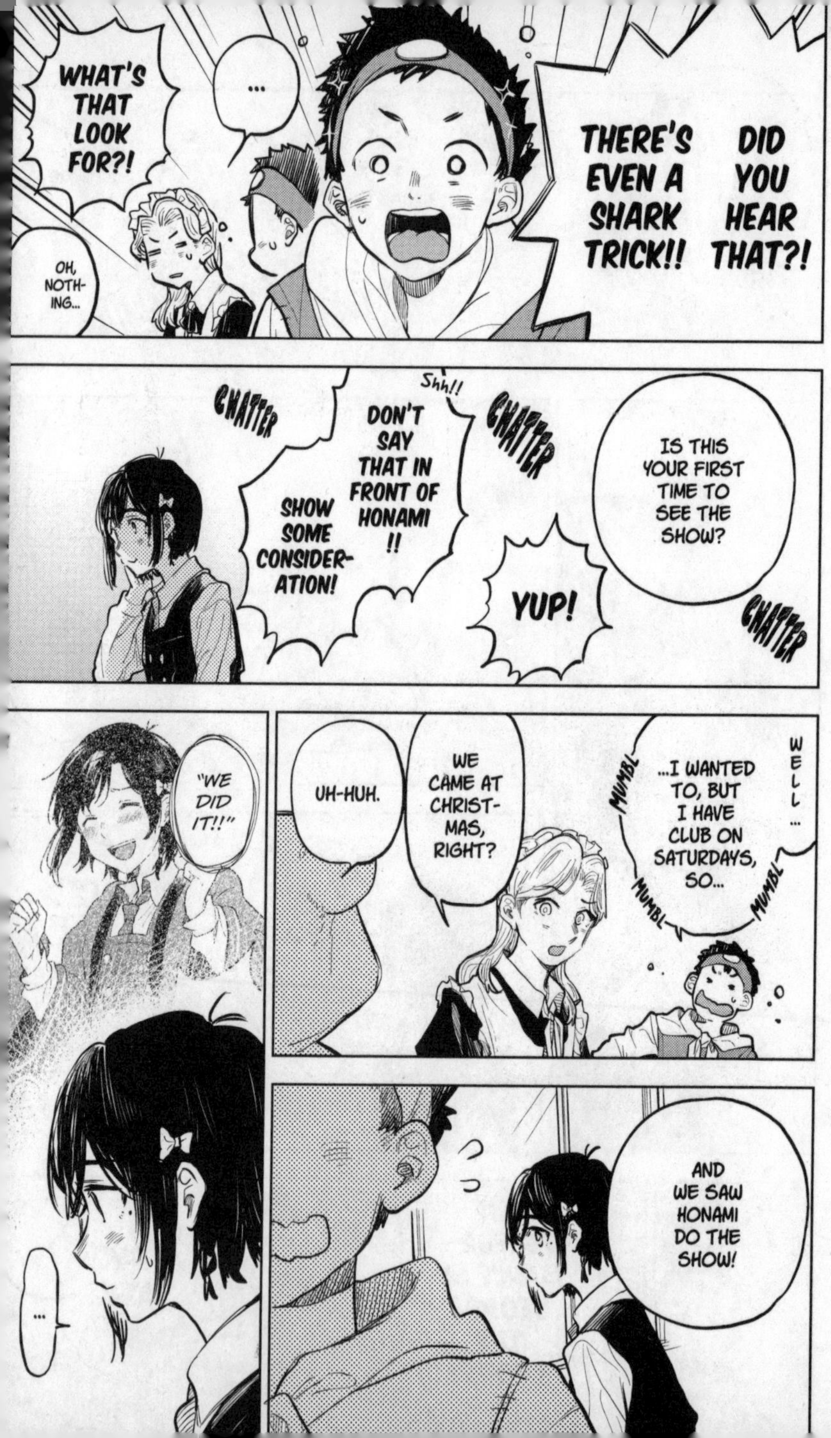
DID YOU HEAR THAT?!
THERE'S EVEN A SHARK TRICK!!
...
WHAT'S THAT LOOK FOR?!
OH, NOTHING...
IS THIS YOUR FIRST TIME TO SEE THE SHOW?
CHATTER
YUP!
CHATTER
Shh!!
DON'T SAY THAT IN FRONT OF HONAMI!!
SHOW SOME CONSIDERATION!
CHATTER
WELL...
...I WANTED TO, BUT I HAVE CLUB ON SATURDAYS, SO...
MUMBL
MUMBL
MUMBL
WE CAME AT CHRISTMAS, RIGHT?
UH-HUH.
AND WE SAW HONAMI DO THE SHOW!
"WE DID IT!!"
...

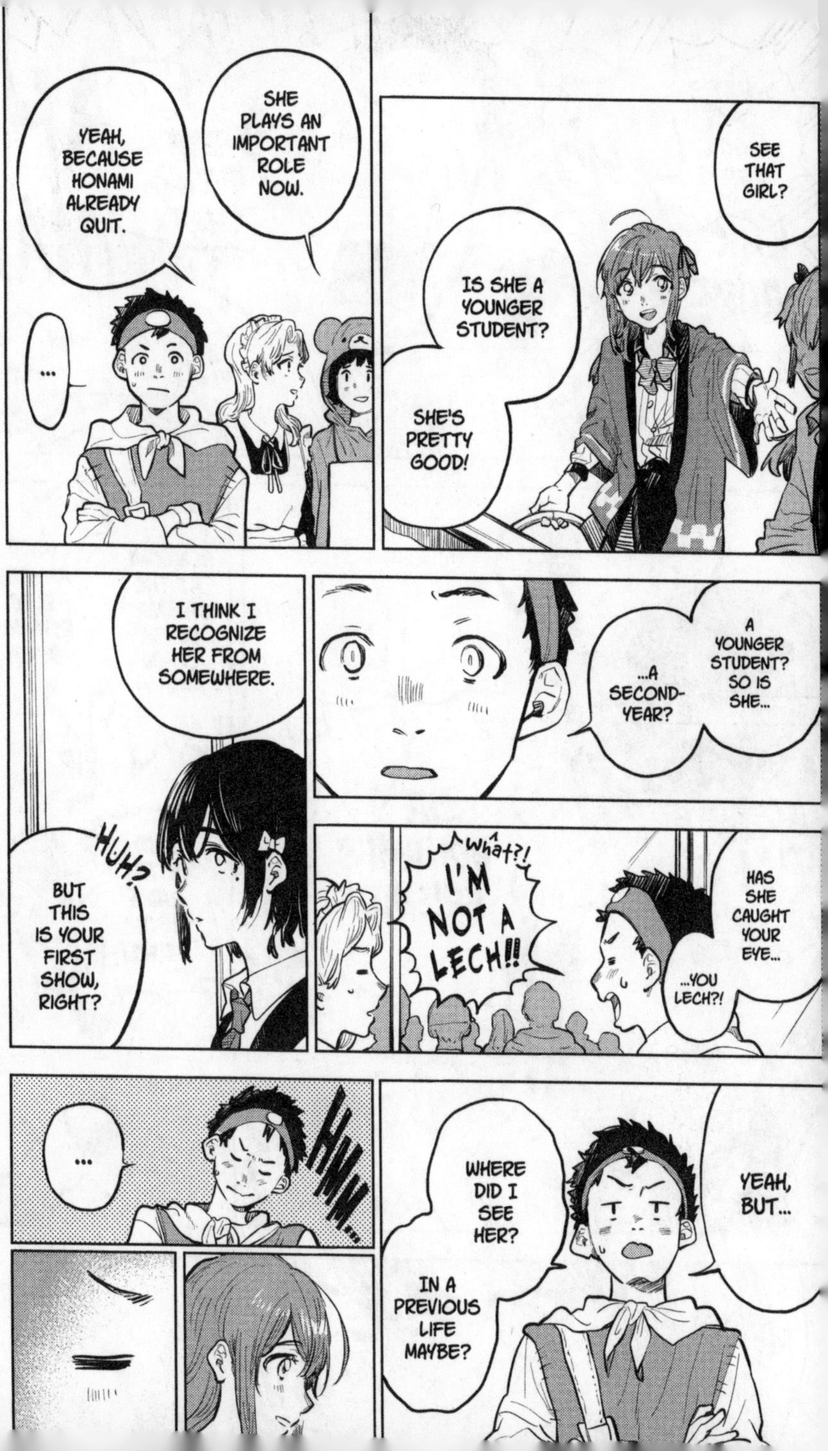
SEE THAT GIRL?
IS SHE A YOUNGER STUDENT?
SHE'S PRETTY GOOD!
SHE PLAYS AN IMPORTANT ROLE NOW.
YEAH, BECAUSE HONAMI ALREADY QUIT.
...
A YOUNGER STUDENT? SO IS SHE...
...A SECOND-YEAR?
I THINK I RECOGNIZE HER FROM SOMEWHERE.
HAS SHE CAUGHT YOUR EYE...
...YOU LECH?!
What?!
I'M NOT A LECH!!
HUH?
BUT THIS IS YOUR FIRST SHOW, RIGHT?
YEAH, BUT...
WHERE DID I SEE HER?
IN A PREVIOUS LIFE MAYBE?
HMM...
...

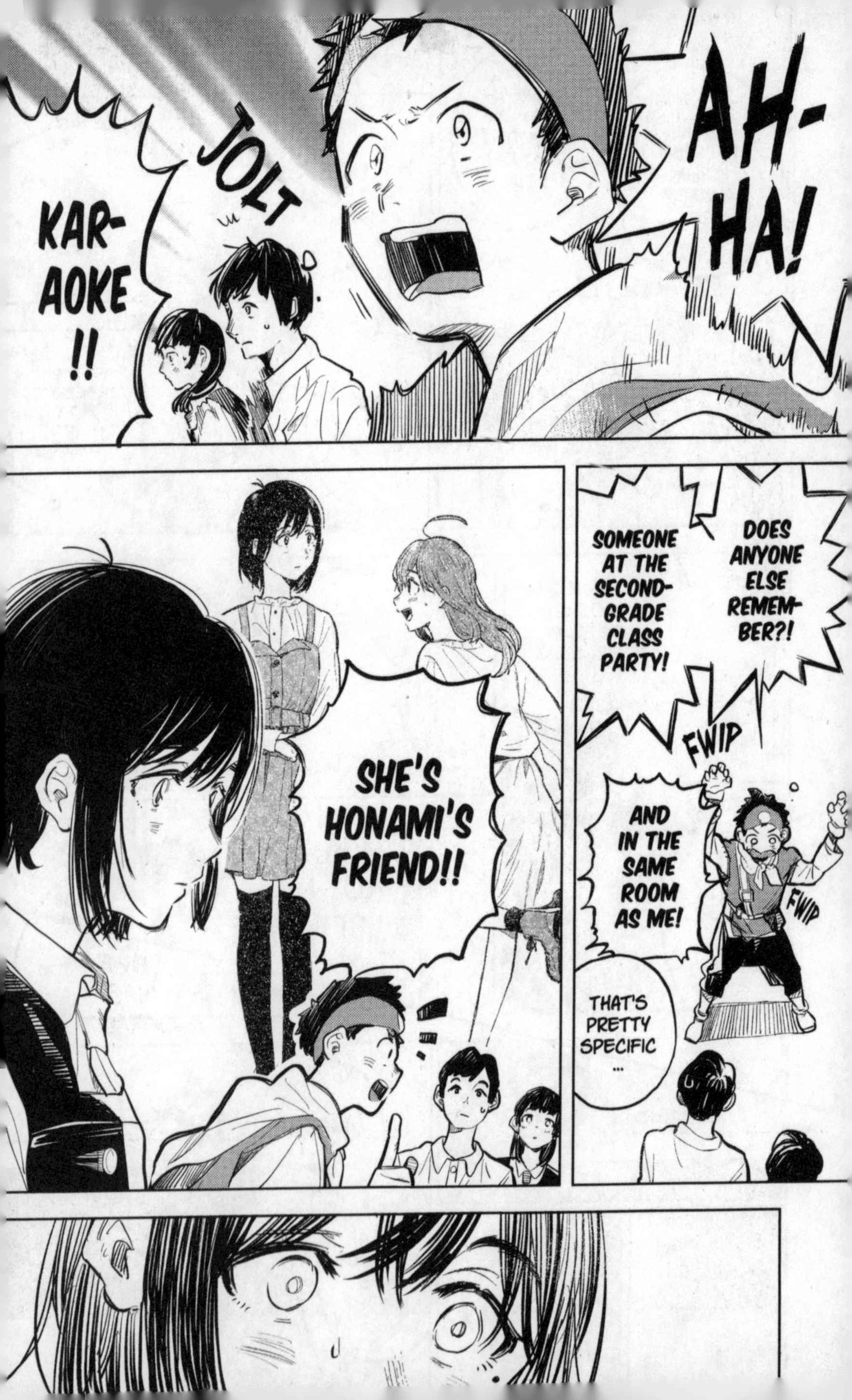
AH-HA!
JOLT
KAR-AOKE!!
DOES ANYONE ELSE REMEM-BER?!
SOMEONE AT THE SECOND-GRADE CLASS PARTY!
FWIP
AND IN THE SAME ROOM AS ME!
FWIP
THAT'S PRETTY SPECIFIC...
SHE'S HONAMI'S FRIEND!!

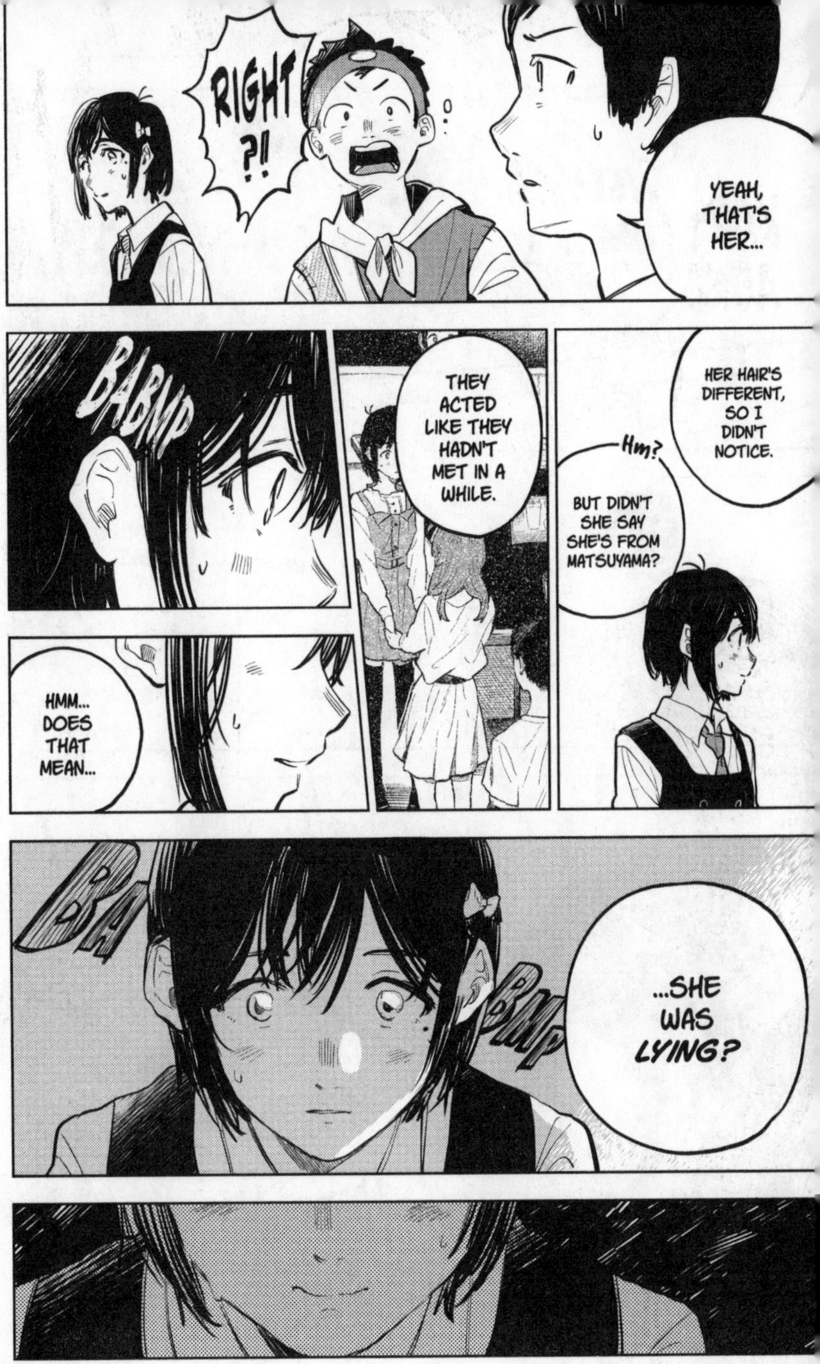
YEAH, THAT'S HER...
RIGHT ?!
HER HAIR'S DIFFERENT, SO I DIDN'T NOTICE.
Hm?
BUT DIDN'T SHE SAY SHE'S FROM MATSUYAMA?
THEY ACTED LIKE THEY HADN'T MET IN A WHILE.
BABMP
HMM... DOES THAT MEAN...
...SHE WAS LYING?
BMP

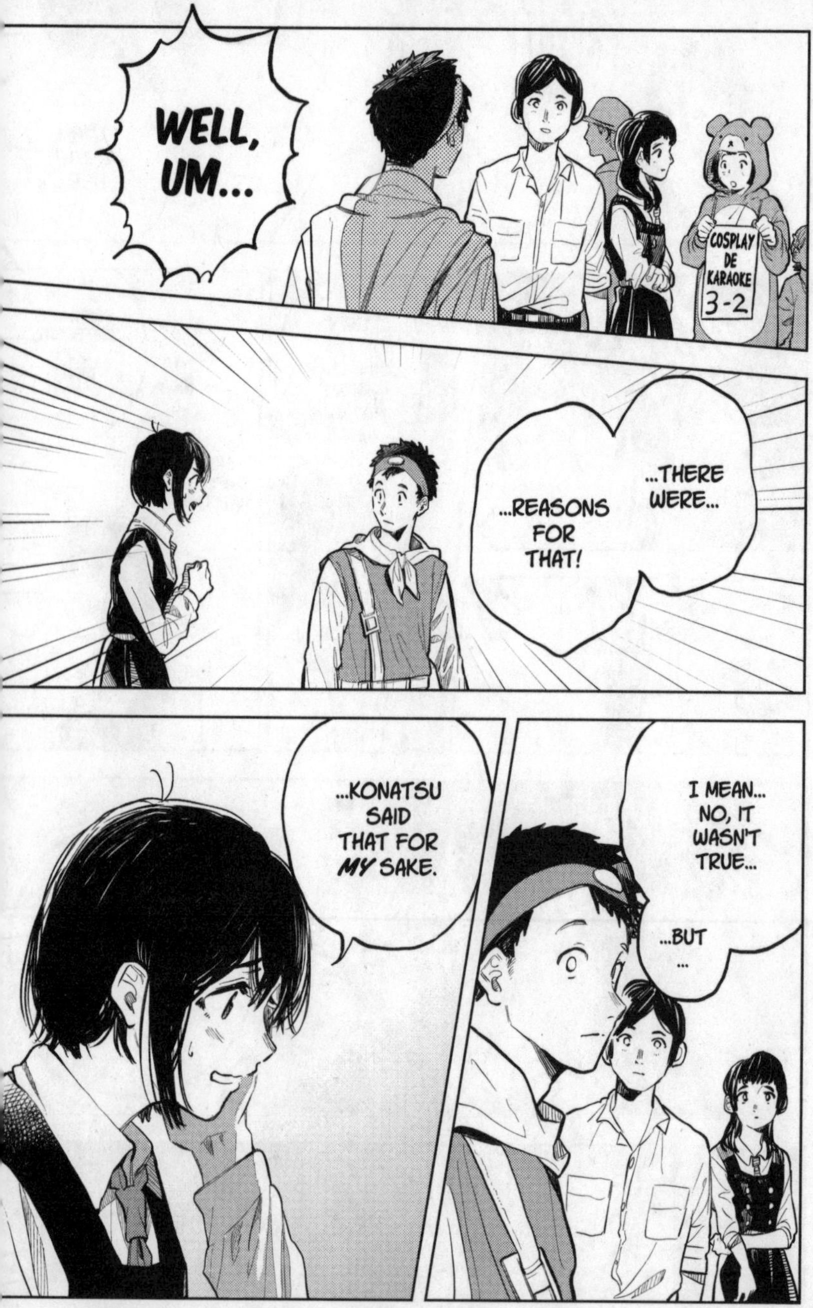
WELL, UM...
COSPLAY DE KARAOKE 3-2
...THERE WERE...
...REASONS FOR THAT!
I MEAN... NO, IT WASN'T TRUE...
...BUT ...
...KONATSU SAID THAT FOR MY SAKE.

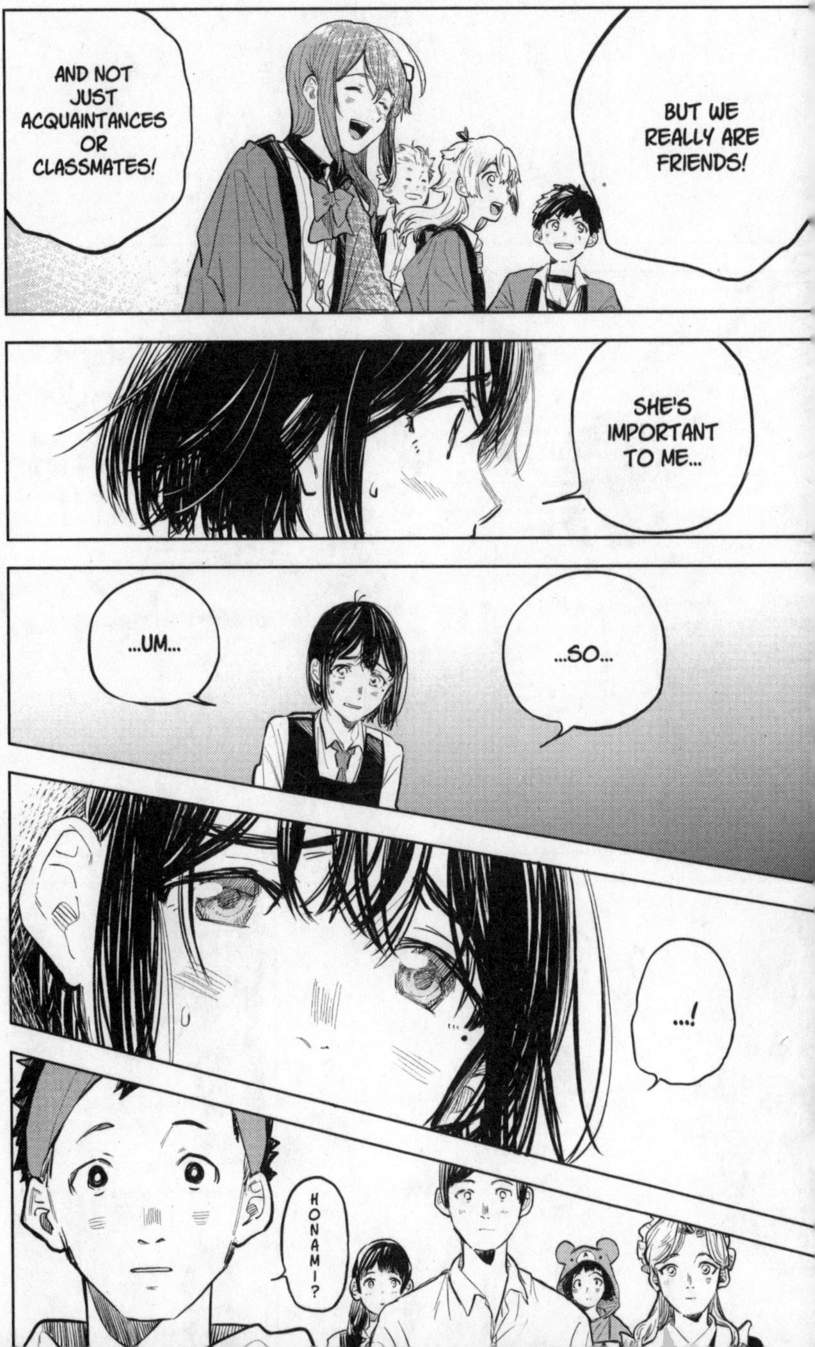
BUT WE REALLY ARE FRIENDS!
AND NOT JUST ACQUAINTANCES OR CLASSMATES!
SHE'S IMPORTANT TO ME...
...SO...
...UM...
...!
HONAMI?

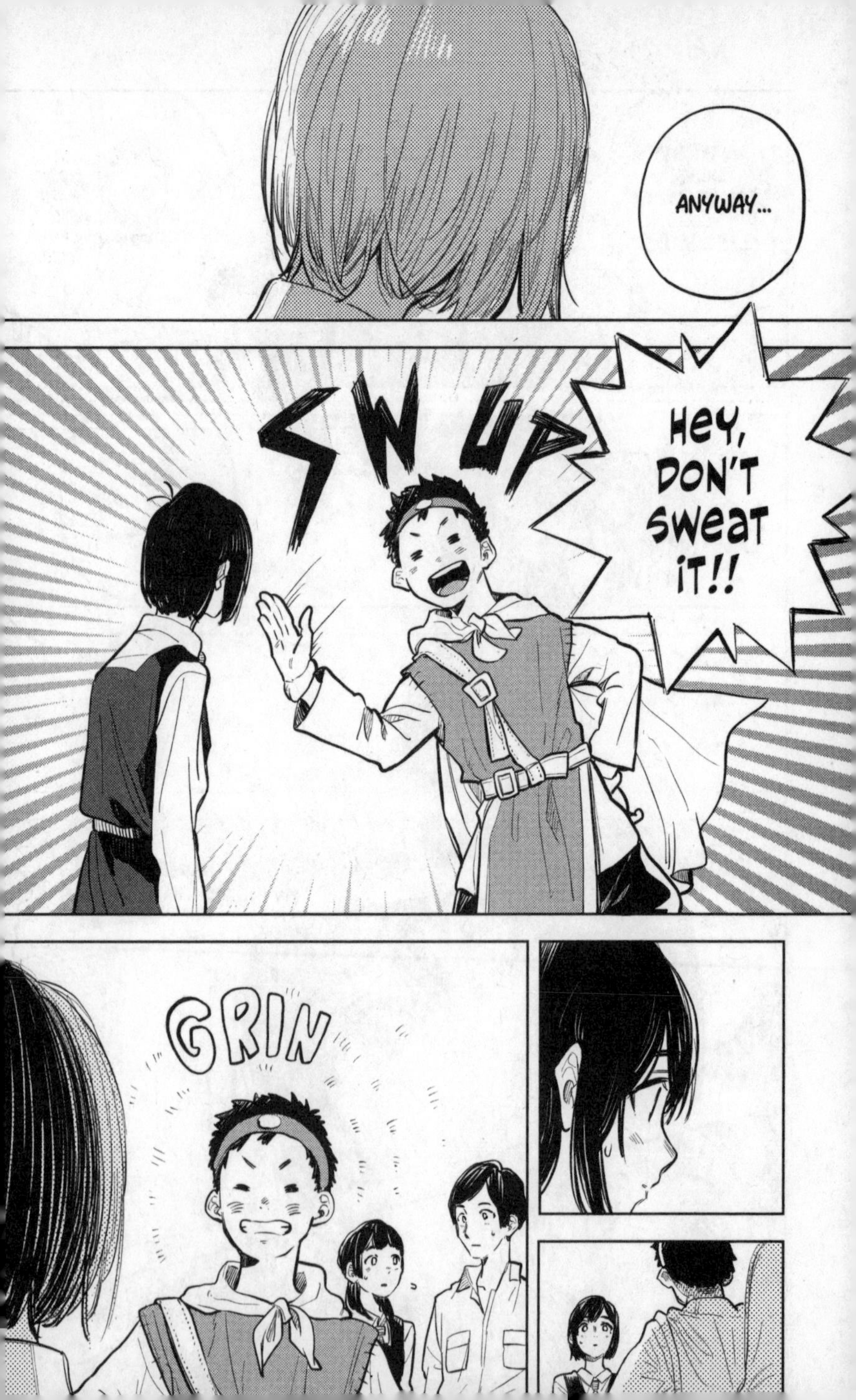
ANYWAY...
SWUP
HEY, DON'T SWEAT IT!!
GRIN

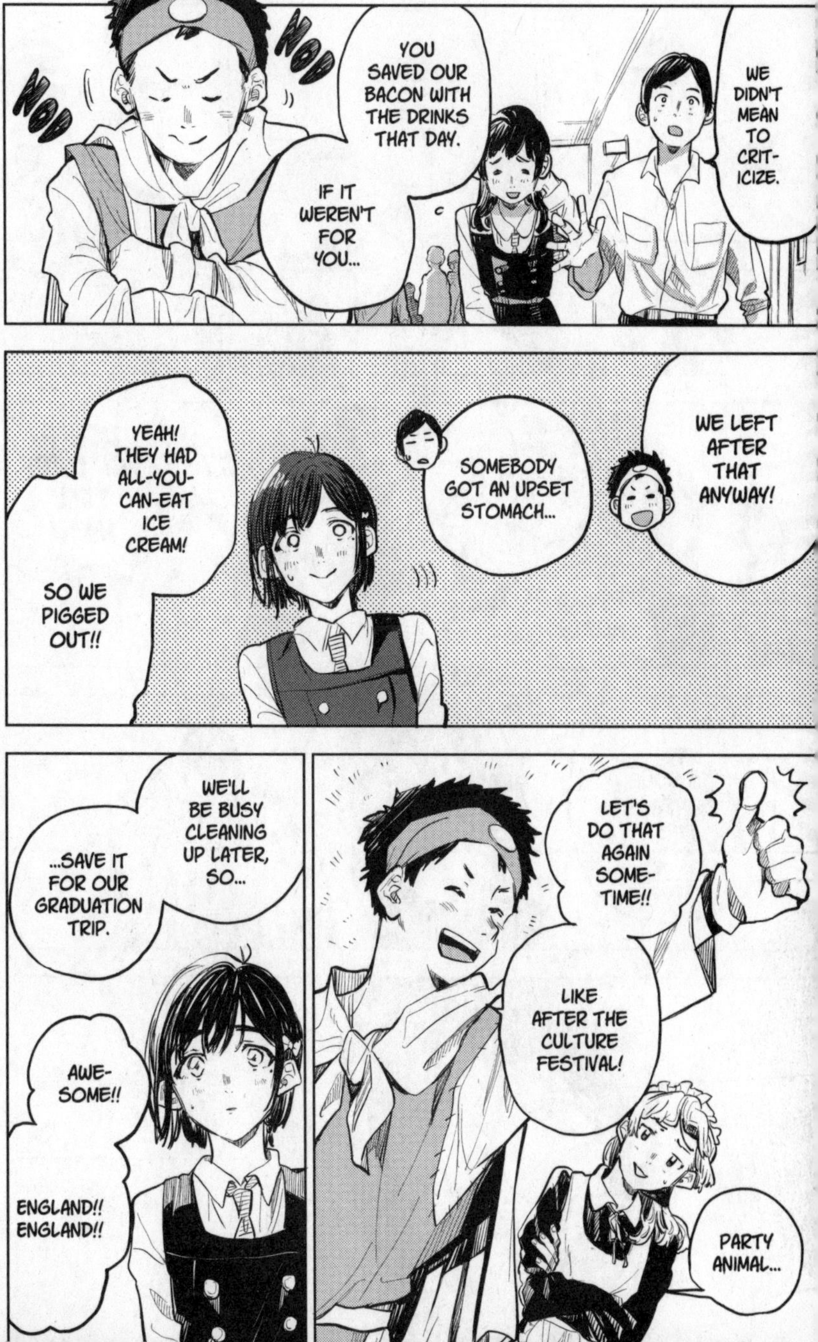
WE DIDN'T MEAN TO CRIT-ICIZE.
YOU SAVED OUR BACON WITH THE DRINKS THAT DAY.
NOD
NOD
IF IT WEREN'T FOR YOU...
WE LEFT AFTER THAT ANYWAY!
SOMEBODY GOT AN UPSET STOMACH...
YEAH! THEY HAD ALL-YOU-CAN-EAT ICE CREAM!
SO WE PIGGED OUT!!
LET'S DO THAT AGAIN SOME-TIME!!
LIKE AFTER THE CULTURE FESTIVAL!
PARTY ANIMAL...
WE'LL BE BUSY CLEANING UP LATER, SO...
...SAVE IT FOR OUR GRADUATION TRIP.
AWE-SOME!!
ENGLAND!! ENGLAND!!

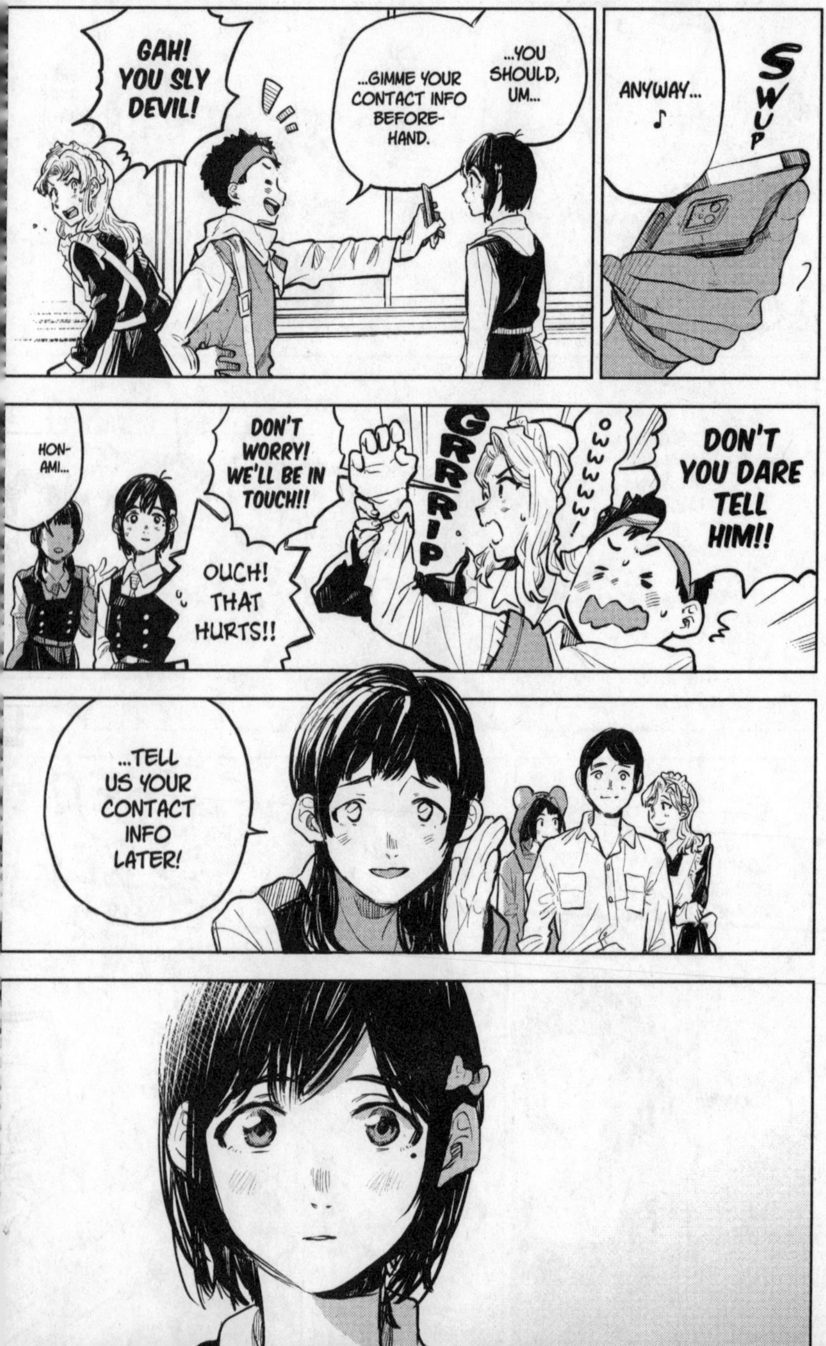
SWUP
ANYWAY... ♪
...YOU SHOULD, UM...
...GIMME YOUR CONTACT INFO BEFORE-HAND.
GAH! YOU SLY DEVIL!
DON'T YOU DARE TELL HIM!!
OWWWWW!
GRRRIP
DON'T WORRY! WE'LL BE IN TOUCH!!
OUCH! THAT HURTS!!
HON-AMI...
...TELL US YOUR CONTACT INFO LATER!

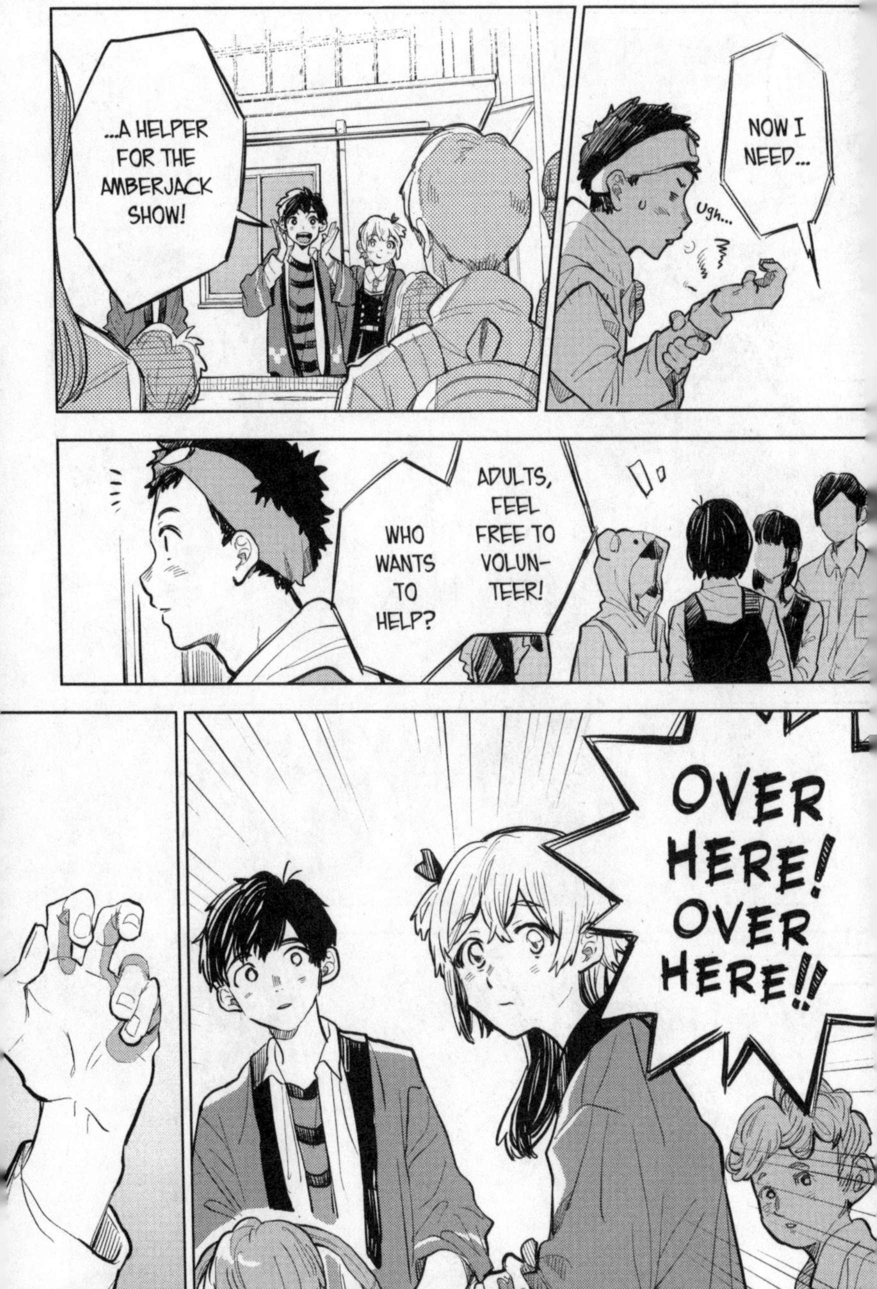
NOW I NEED...
Ugh...
...A HELPER FOR THE AMBERJACK SHOW!
ADULTS, FEEL FREE TO VOLUNTEER!
WHO WANTS TO HELP?
OVER HERE! OVER HERE!!

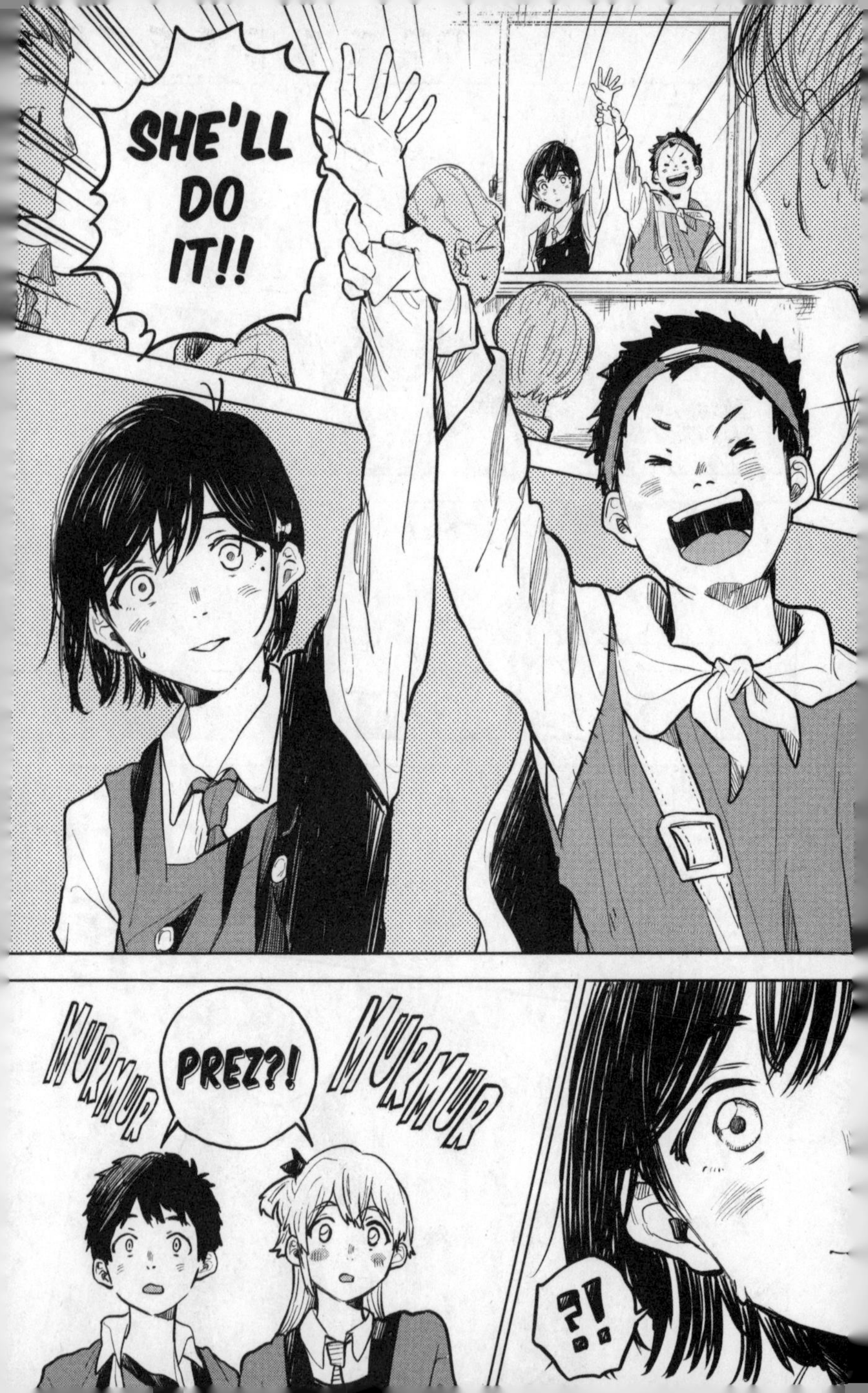
SHE'LL DO IT!!
?!
MURMUR
PREZ?!
MURMUR

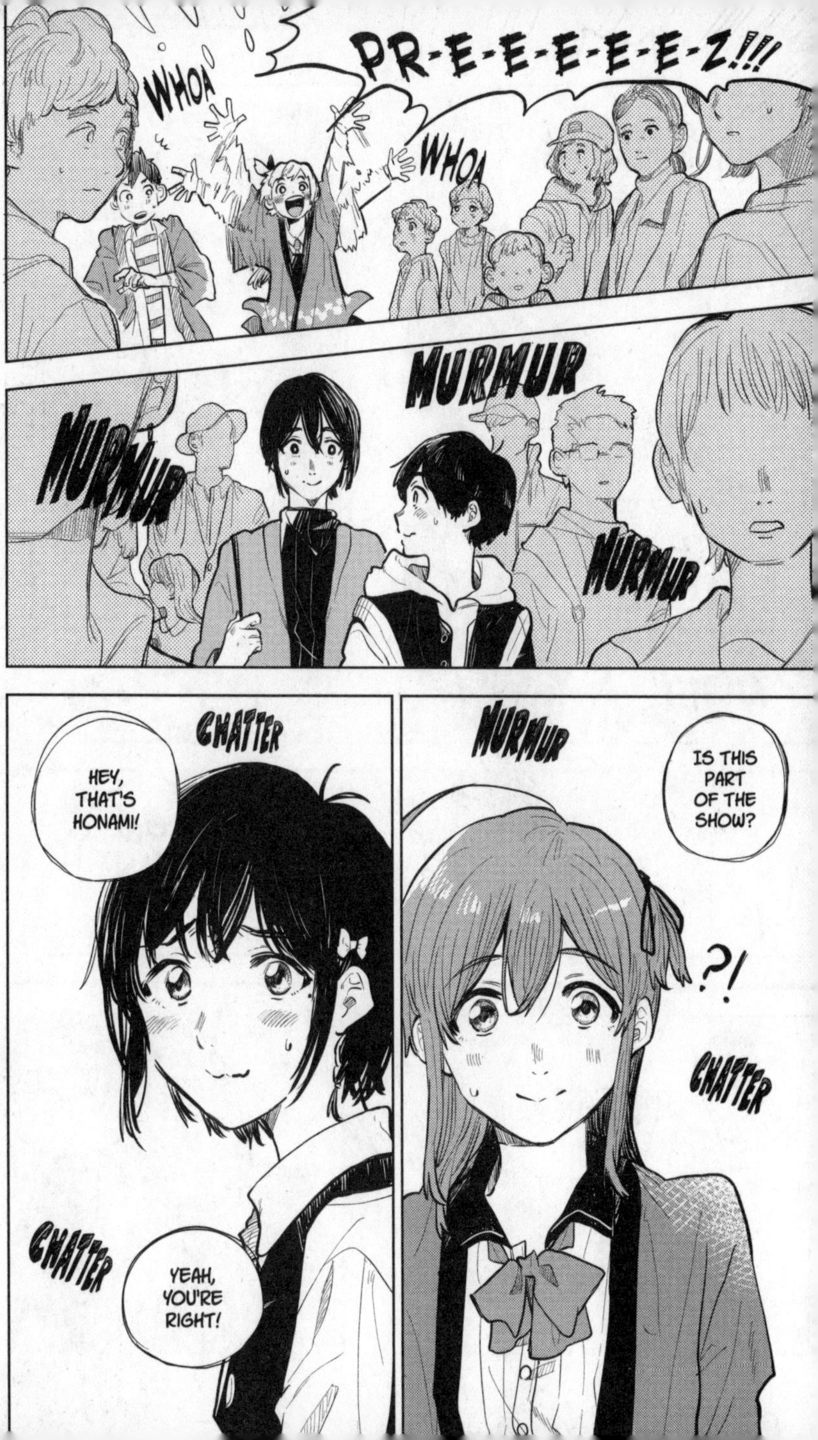
PR-E-E-E-E-E-Z!!!
WHOA
WHOA
MURMUR
MURMUR
MURMUR
MURMUR
IS THIS PART OF THE SHOW?
?!
CHATTER
CHATTER
HEY, THAT'S HONAMI!
CHATTER
YEAH, YOU'RE RIGHT!

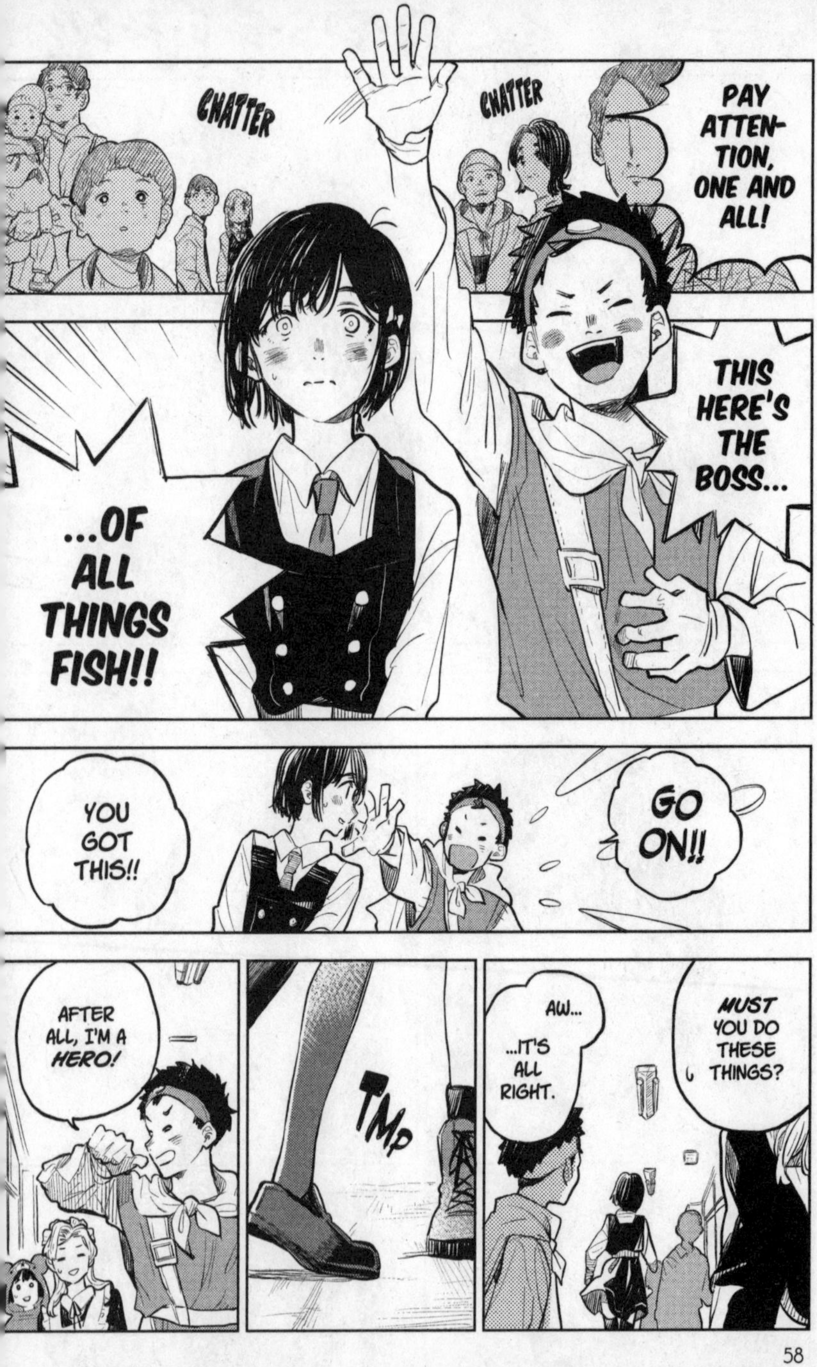
PAY ATTENTION, ONE AND ALL!
CHATTER
CHATTER
THIS HERE'S THE BOSS...
...OF ALL THINGS FISH!!
GO ON!!
YOU GOT THIS!!
MUST YOU DO THESE THINGS?
AW...
...IT'S ALL RIGHT.
TMP
AFTER ALL, I'M A HERO!

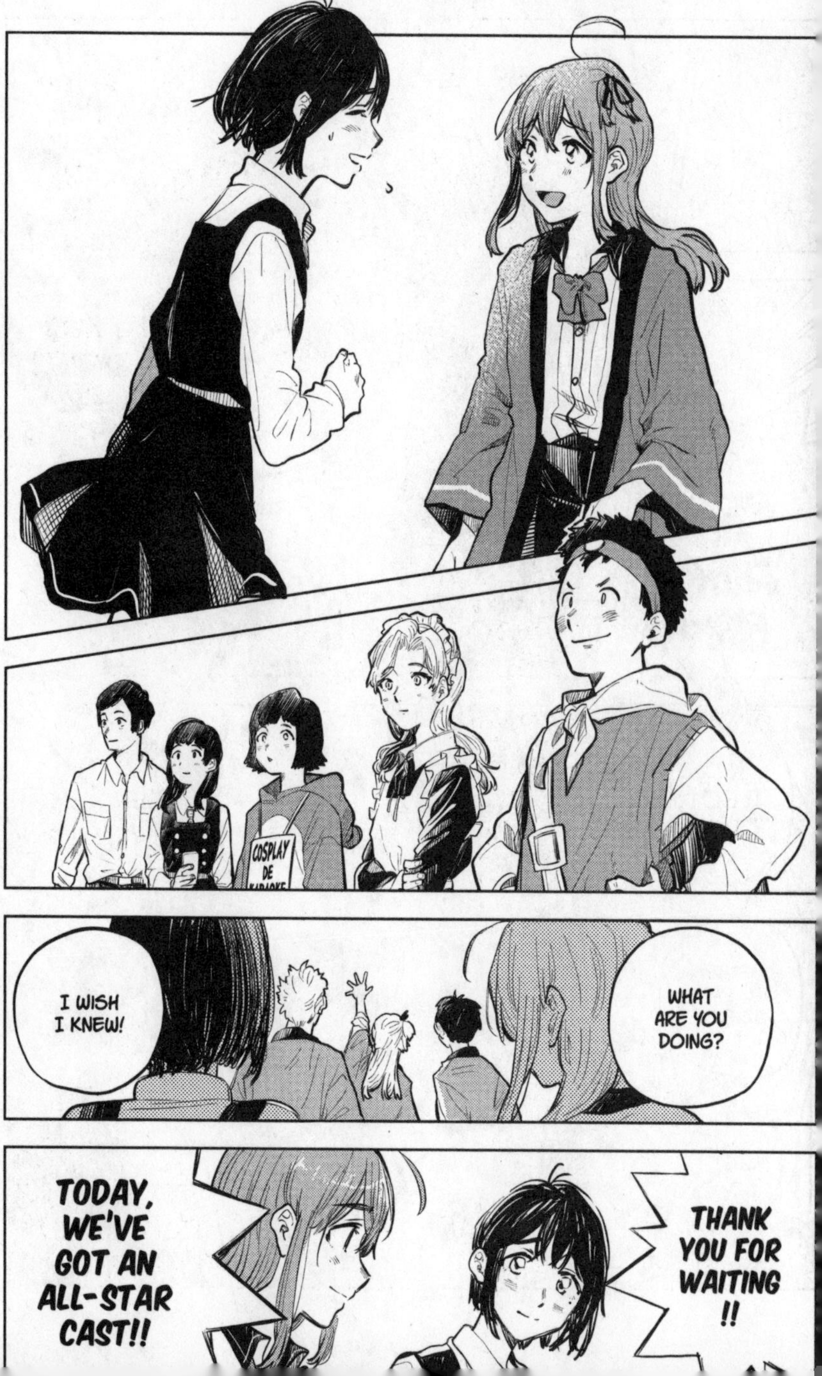
COSPLAY
DE
WHAT ARE YOU DOING?
I WISH I KNEW!
THANK YOU FOR WAITING!!
TODAY, WE'VE GOT AN ALL-STAR CAST!!

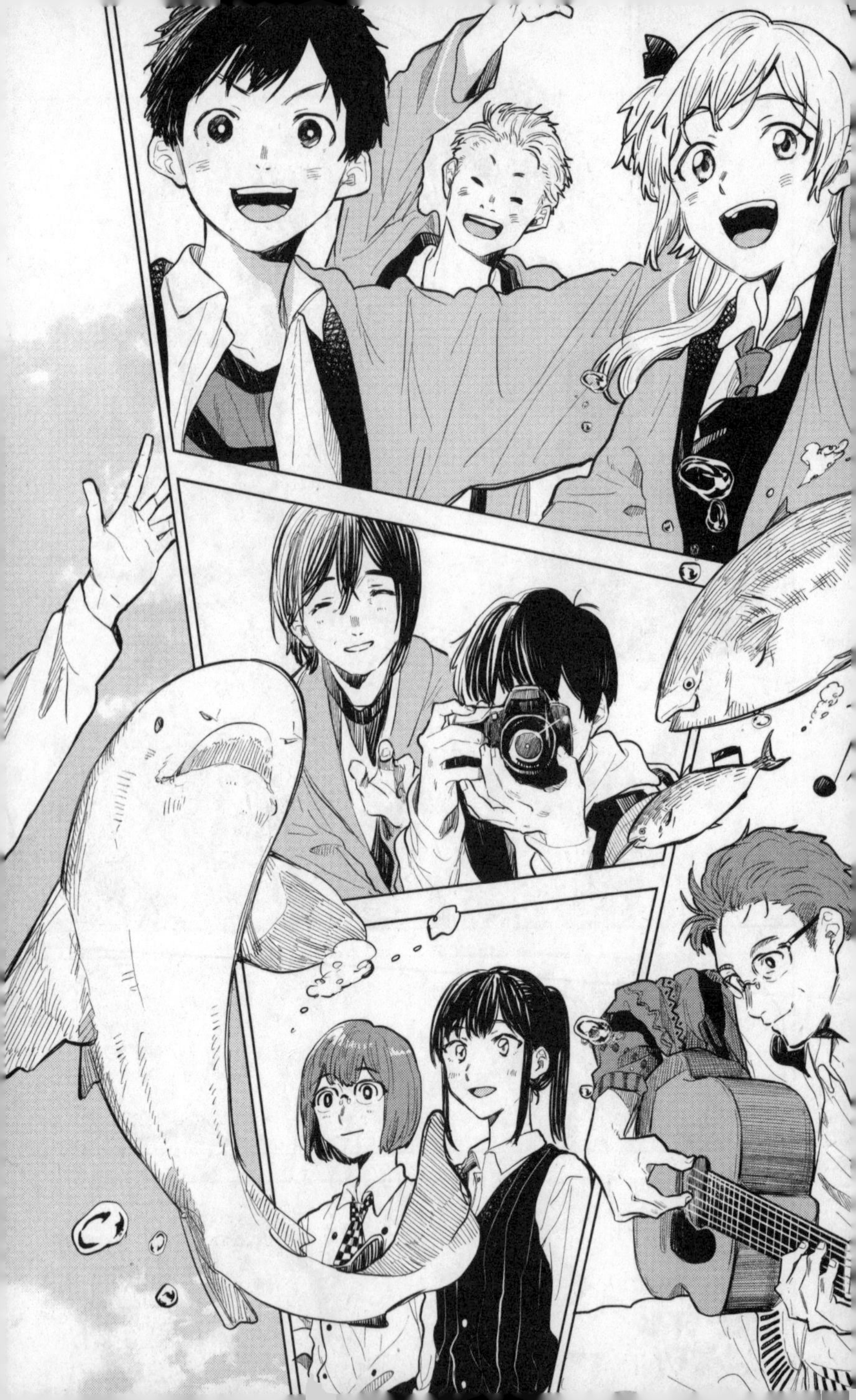

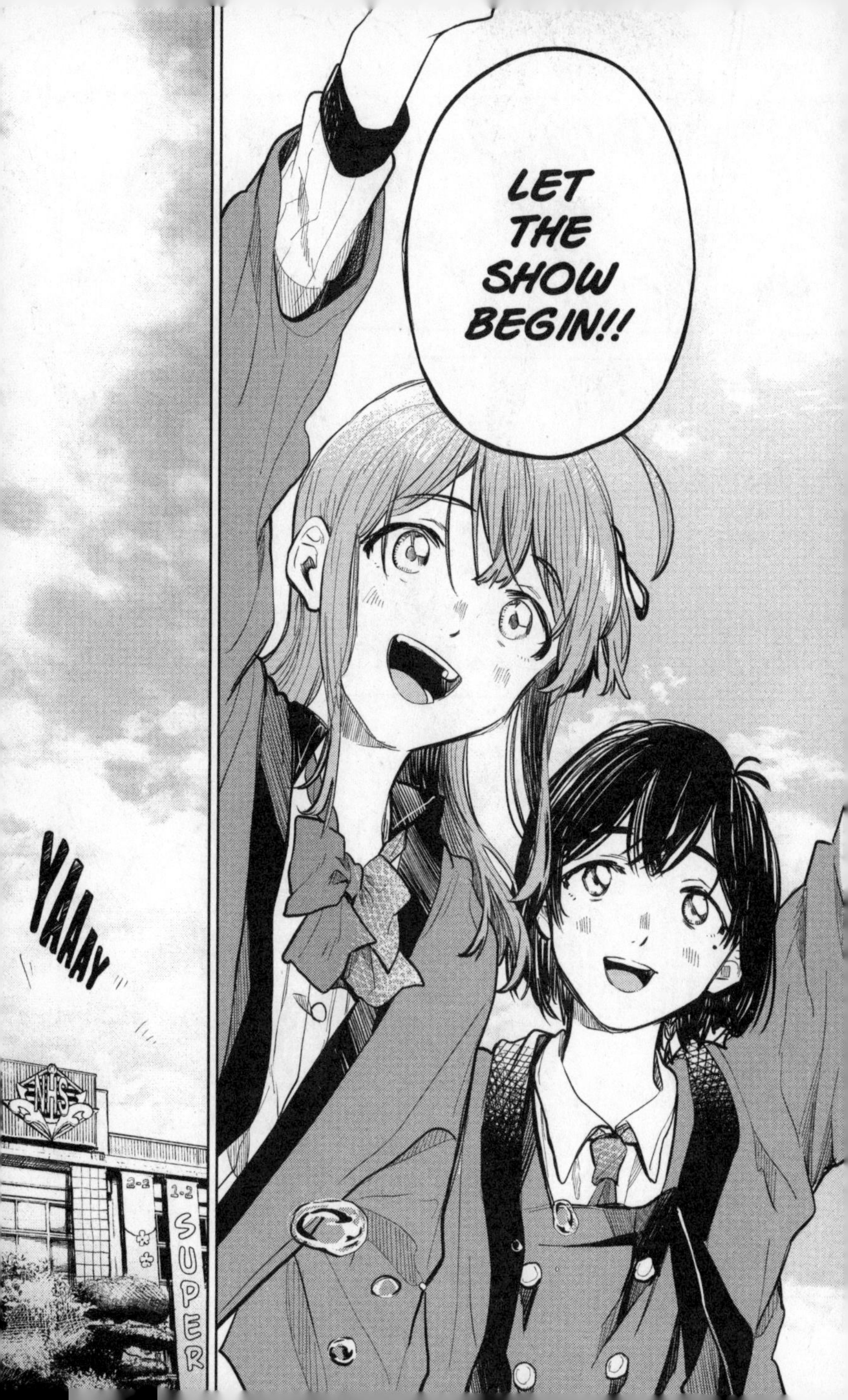
LET THE SHOW BEGIN!!
YAAAY
NHS
2-2
1-2
SUPER

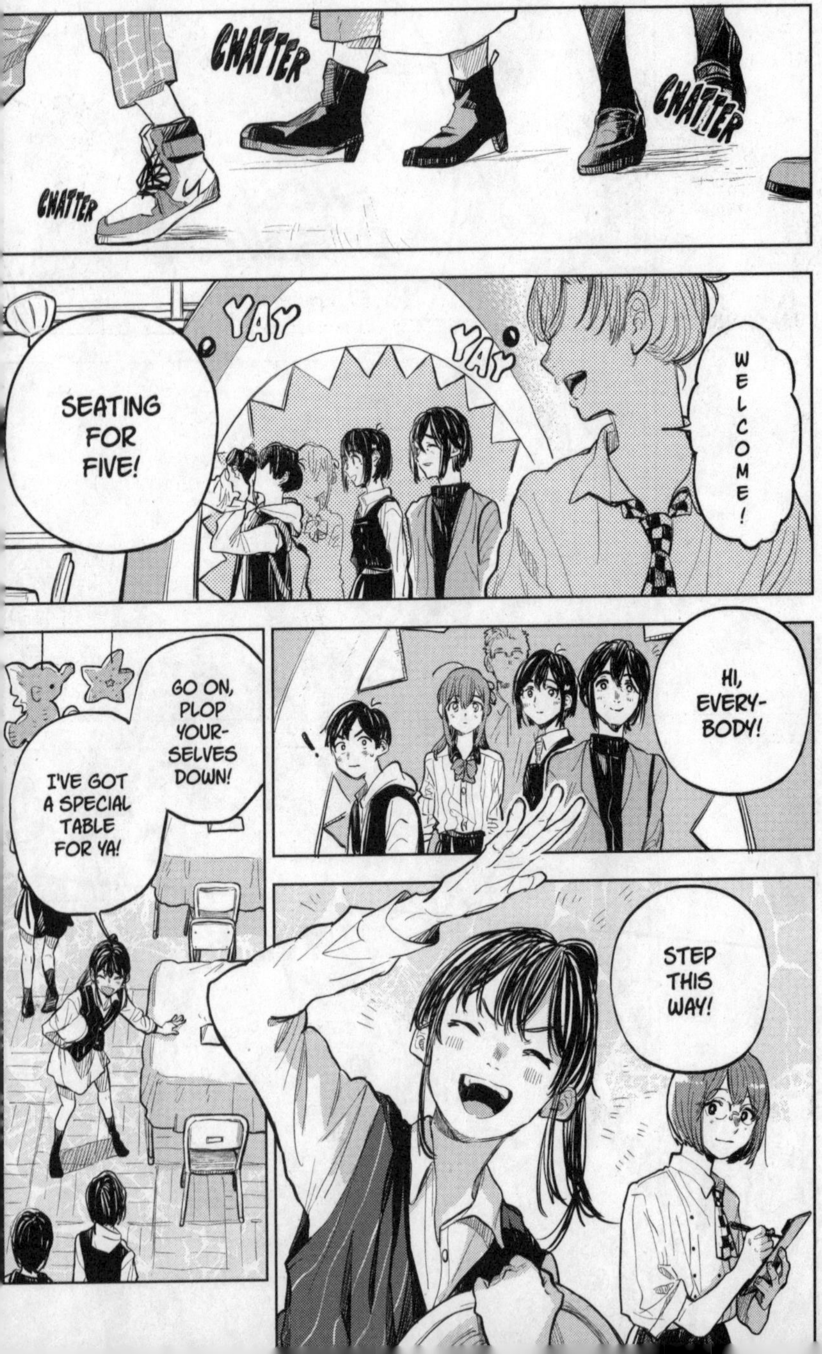
CHATTER
CHATTER
CHATTER
WELCOME!
YAY
YAY
SEATING FOR FIVE!
HI, EVERY-BODY!
STEP THIS WAY!
GO ON, PLOP YOUR-SELVES DOWN!
I'VE GOT A SPECIAL TABLE FOR YA!

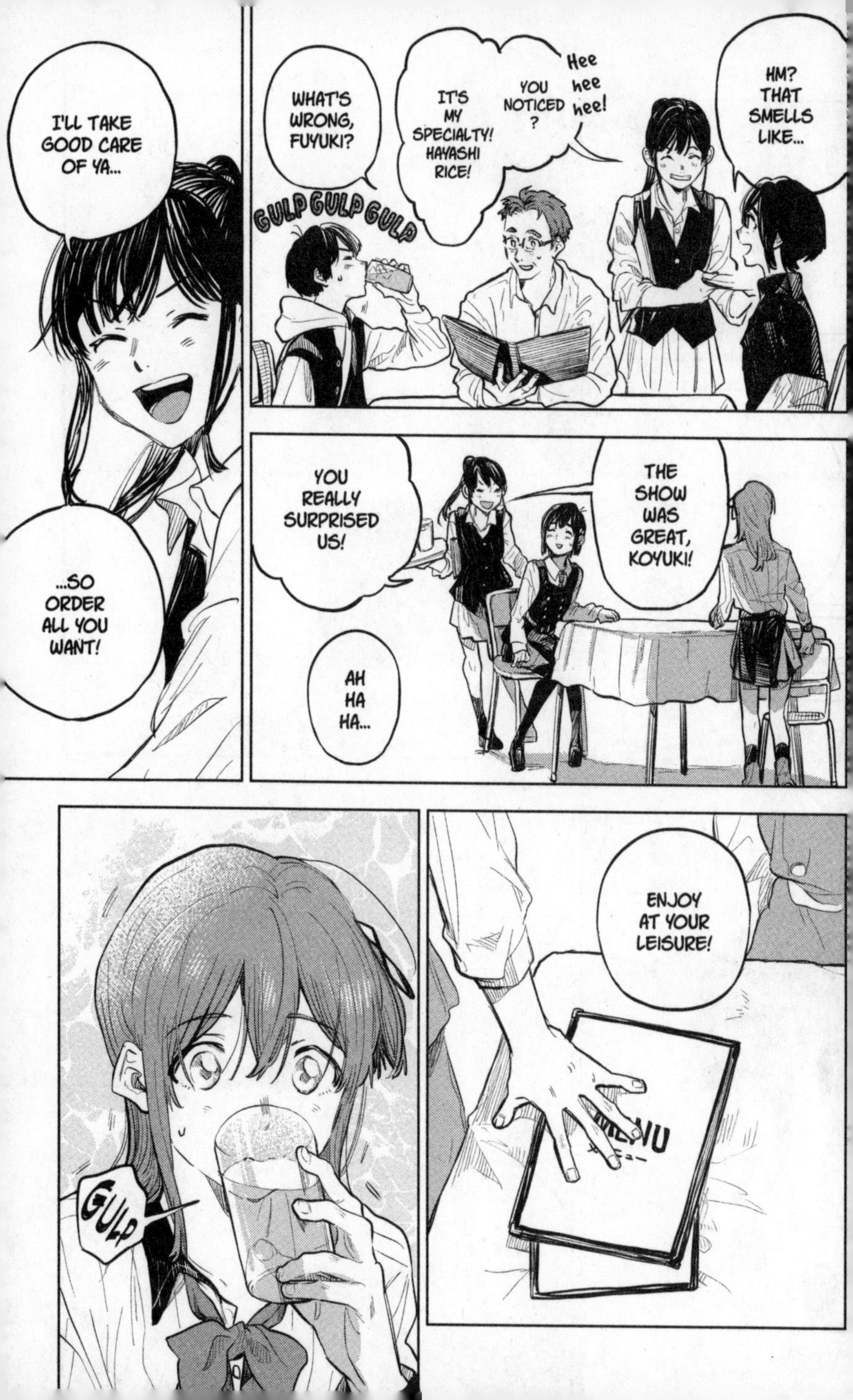
HM? THAT SMELLS LIKE...
Hee hee hee!
YOU NOTICED?
IT'S MY SPECIALTY! HAYASHI RICE!
WHAT'S WRONG, FUYUKI?
GULP GULP GULP
THE SHOW WAS GREAT, KOYUKI!
YOU REALLY SURPRISED US!
AH HA HA...
I'LL TAKE GOOD CARE OF YA...
...SO ORDER ALL YOU WANT!
ENJOY AT YOUR LEISURE!
GULP

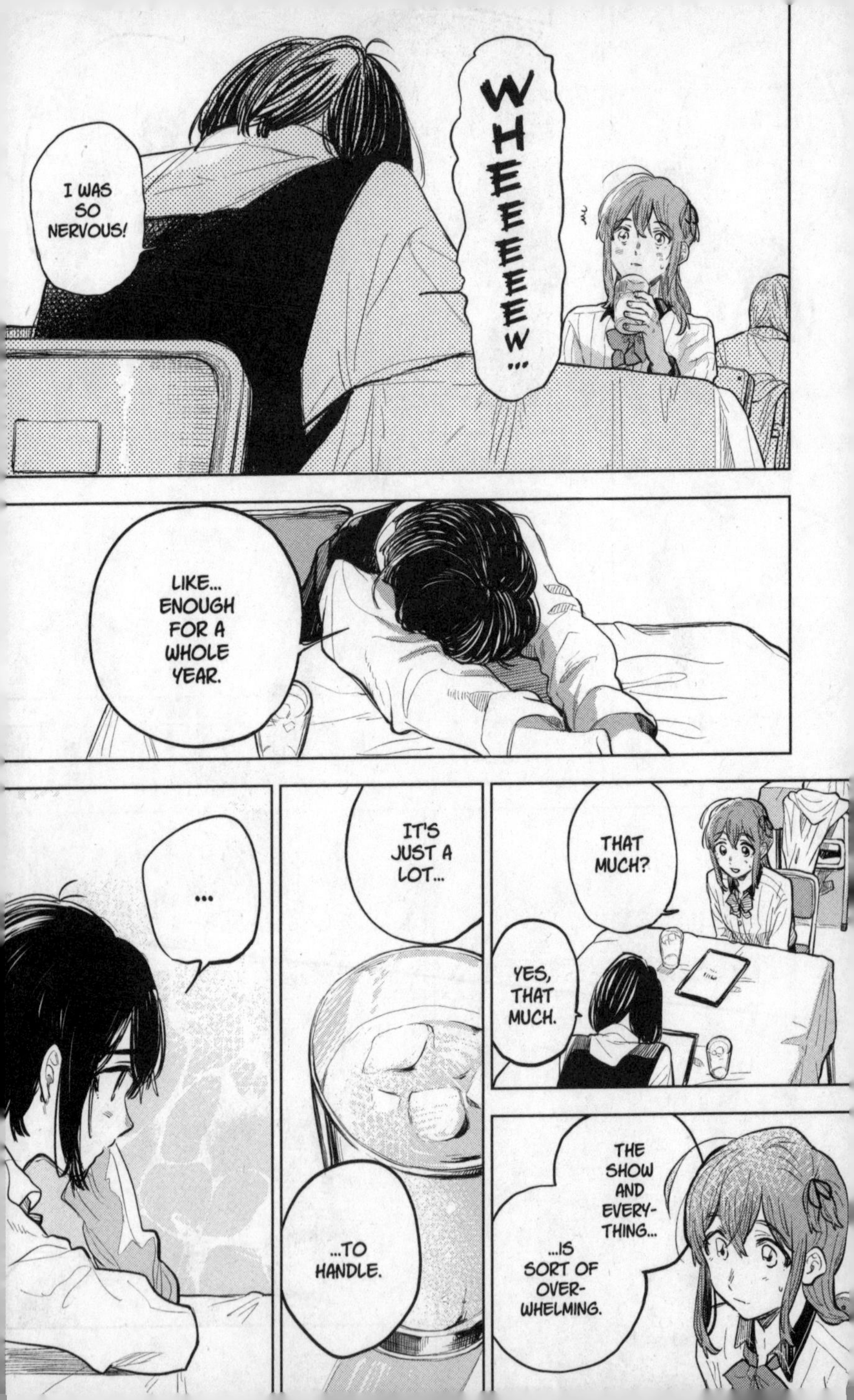
WHEEEEEEW...
I WAS SO NERVOUS!
LIKE... ENOUGH FOR A WHOLE YEAR.
THAT MUCH?
YES, THAT MUCH.
THE SHOW AND EVERY-THING...
...IS SORT OF OVER-WHELMING.
IT'S JUST A LOT...
...TO HANDLE.
...

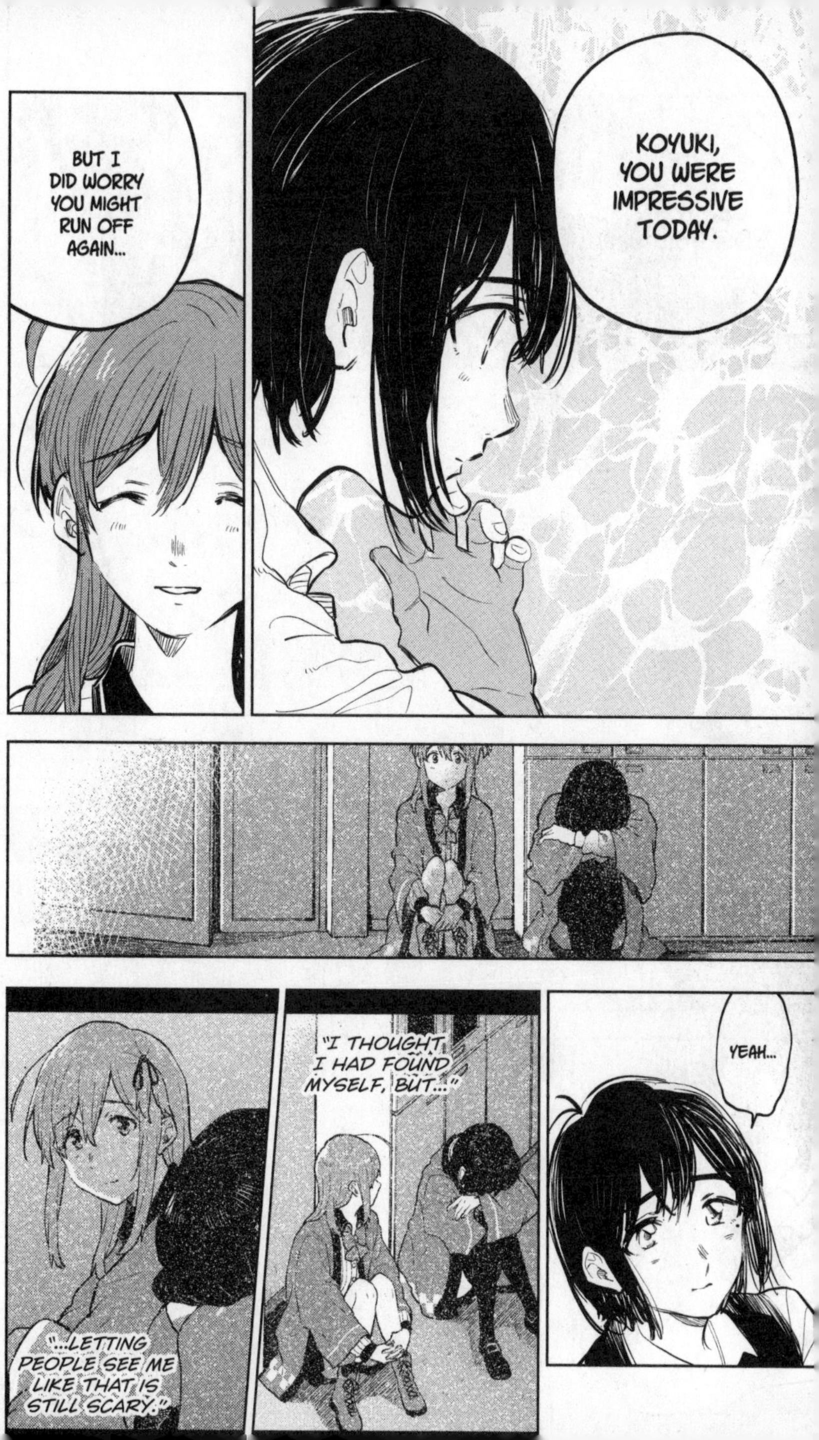
KOYUKI, YOU WERE IMPRESSIVE TODAY.
BUT I DID WORRY YOU MIGHT RUN OFF AGAIN...
YEAH...
"I THOUGHT I HAD FOUND MYSELF, BUT..."
"...LETTING PEOPLE SEE ME LIKE THAT IS STILL SCARY."

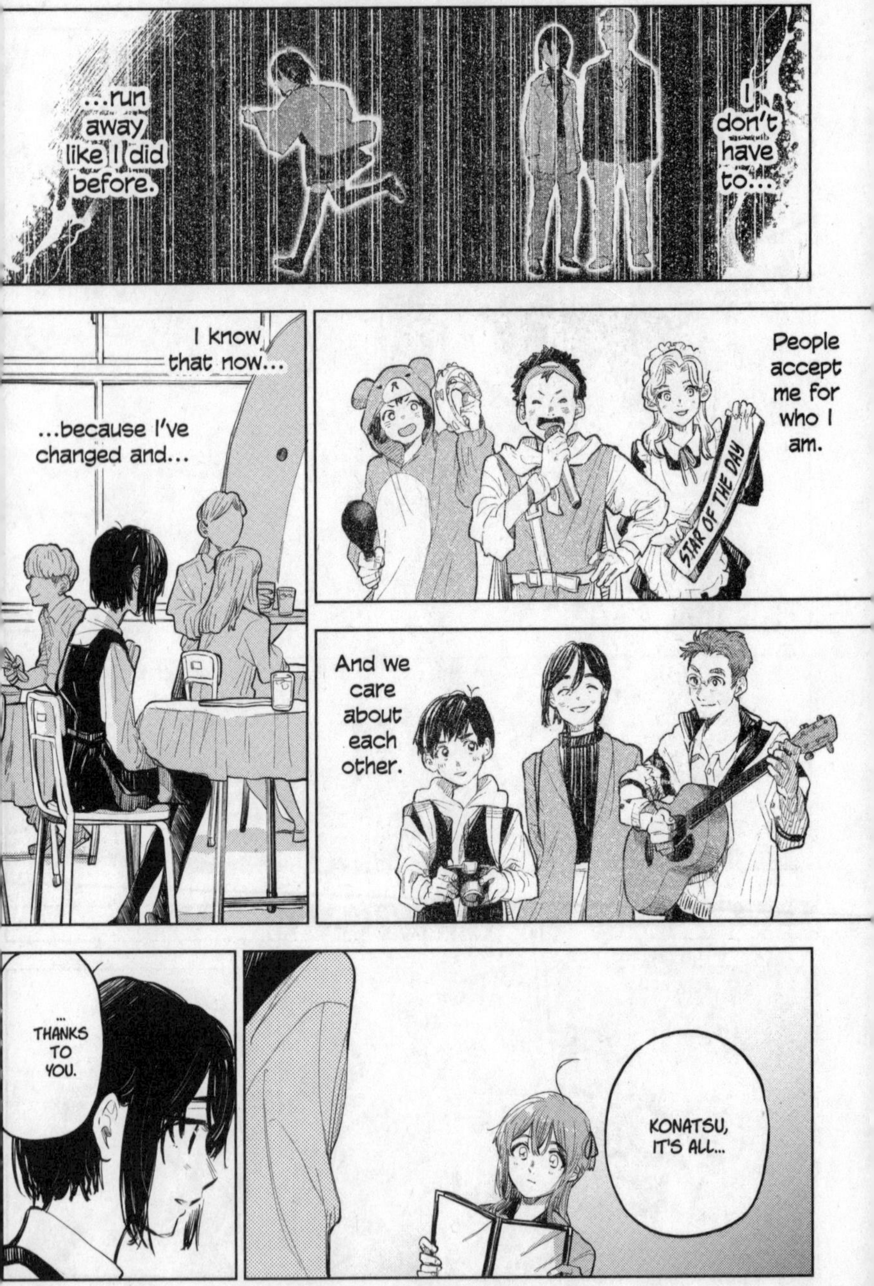
I don't have to...
...run away like I did before.
People accept me for who I am.
And we care about each other.
I know that now...
...because I've changed and...
STAR OF THE DAY
KONATSU, IT'S ALL...
...THANKS TO YOU.

...

I'm able to be who I am...

...because Konatsu stayed by my side.

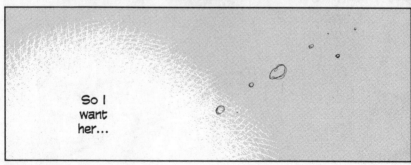

So I want her...

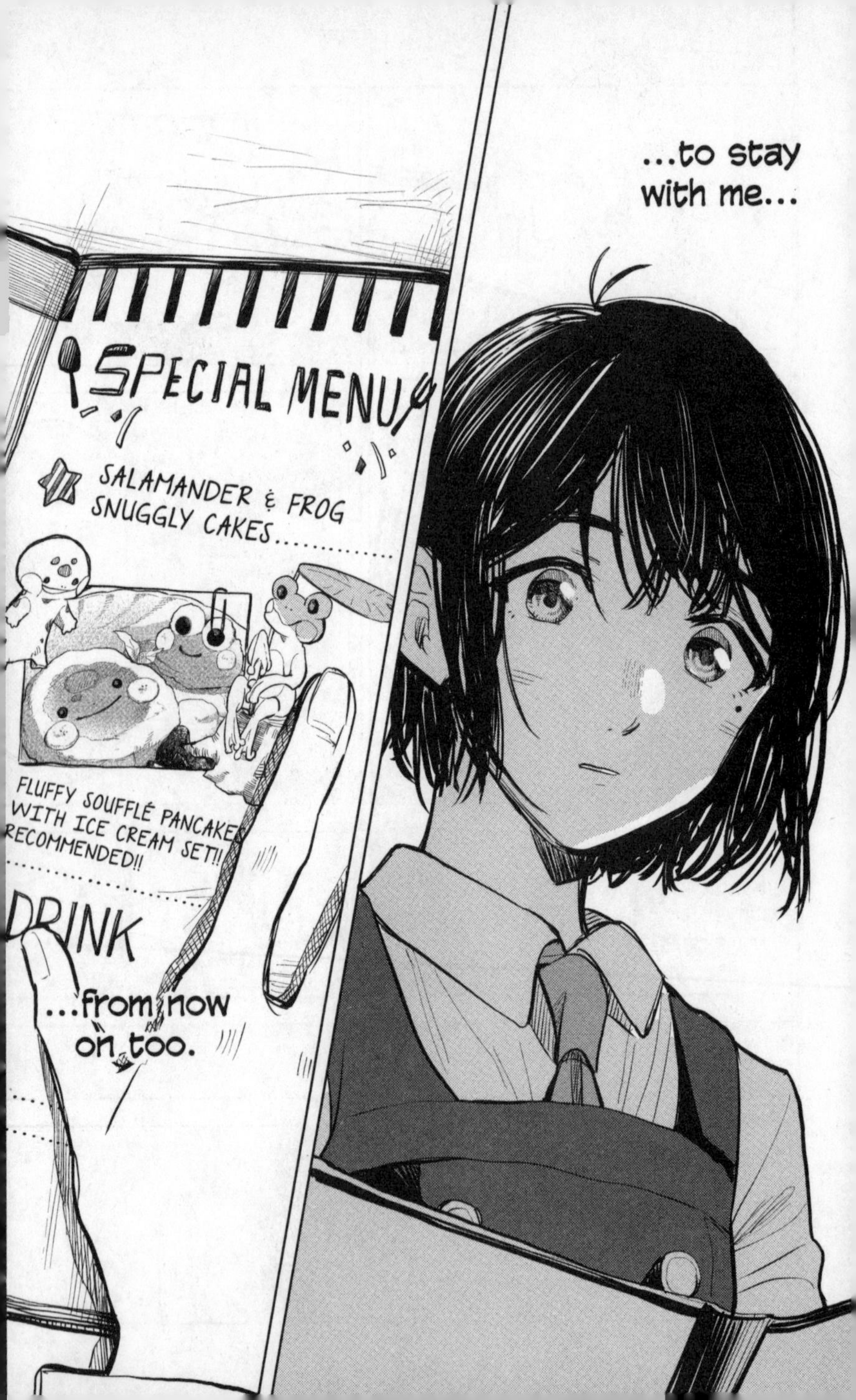
...to stay with me...
SPECIAL MENU
SALAMANDER & FROG SNUGGLY CAKES
FLUFFY SOUFFLÉ PANCAKE WITH ICE CREAM SET!! RECOMMENDED!!
DRINK
...from now on too.

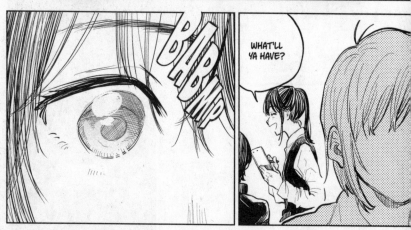

BABMP

WHAT'LL YA HAVE?

BABMP

THAT LOOKS LIKE...

BABMP

...

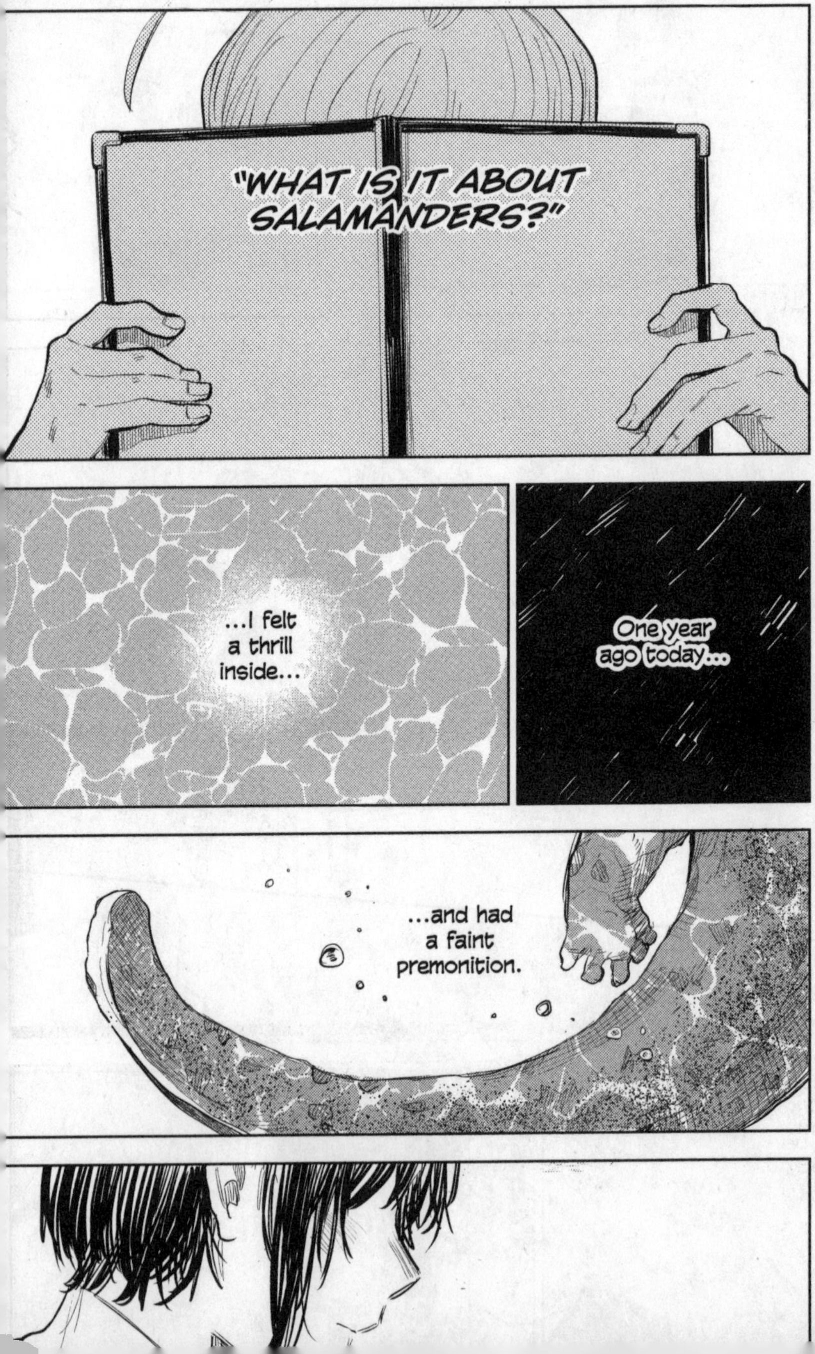
"WHAT IS IT ABOUT SALAMANDERS?"
One year ago today...
...I felt a thrill inside...
...and had a faint premonition.

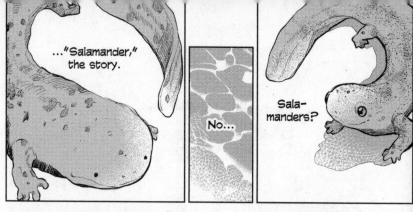

..."Salamander," the story.

No...

Sala-manders?

"I CAN'T TAKE IT ANYMORE."

"THEN LET'S ST[...]
TOGETHER FOREVE[...]"

...I would like that.

If that's true...

THIS MENU MUST'VE BEEN KONATSU'S IDEA.

...

YES, THAT'S RIGHT.

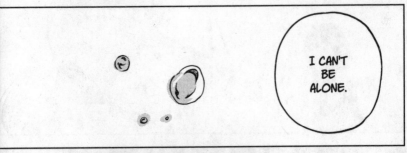

I CAN'T BE ALONE.

A SALAMANDER NEEDS A FROG.

I
WANT
...

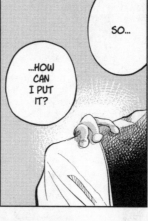

SO...

...HOW
CAN
I PUT
IT?

...

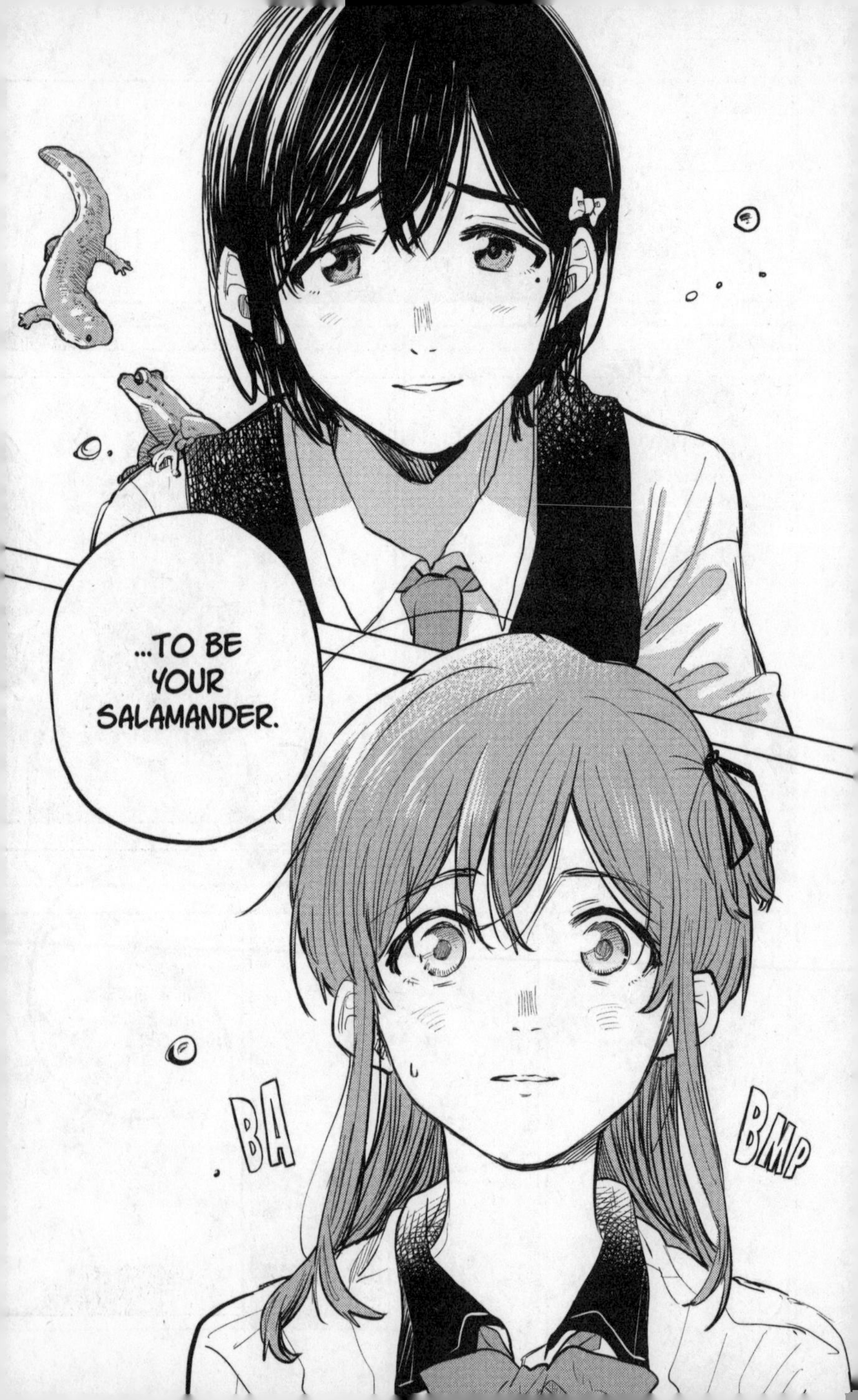
...TO BE YOUR SALAMANDER.
BA BMP

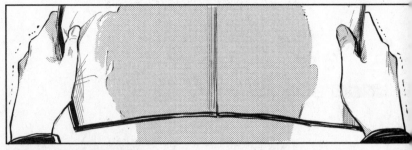

UH...

...YEAH, UM...

HAVE YOU DECIDED?

AND YOU, KONATSU?

...I'LL HAVE THE SALAMANDER AND FROG SET.

OKAY, GOT IT!!

UM, KONATSU?

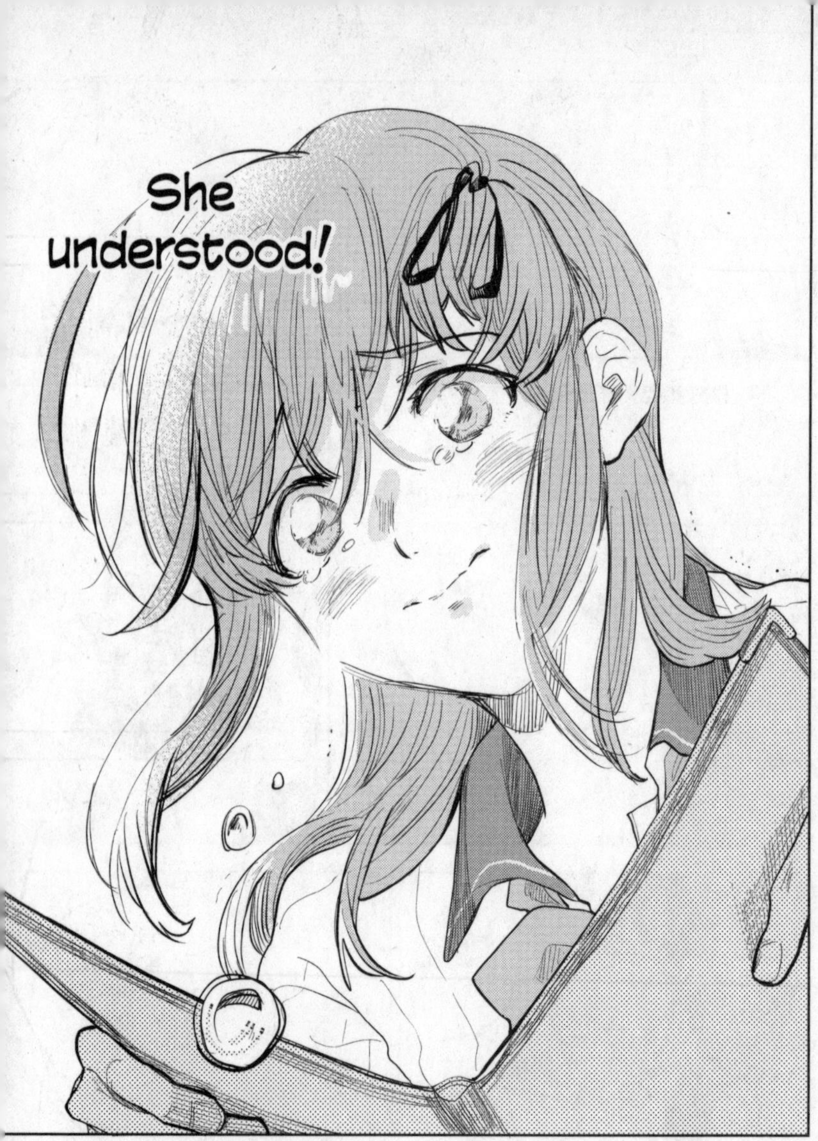
She understood!
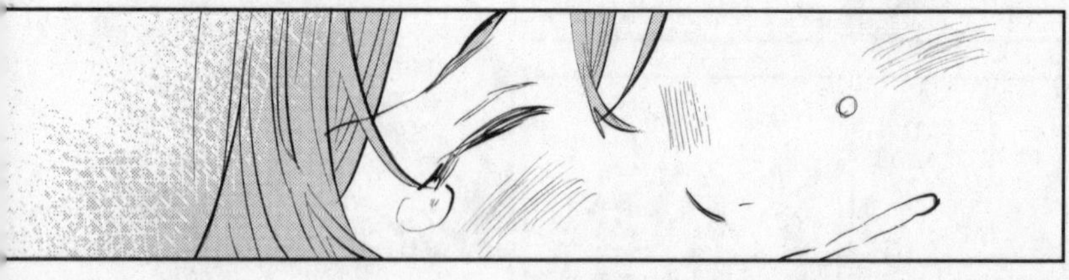

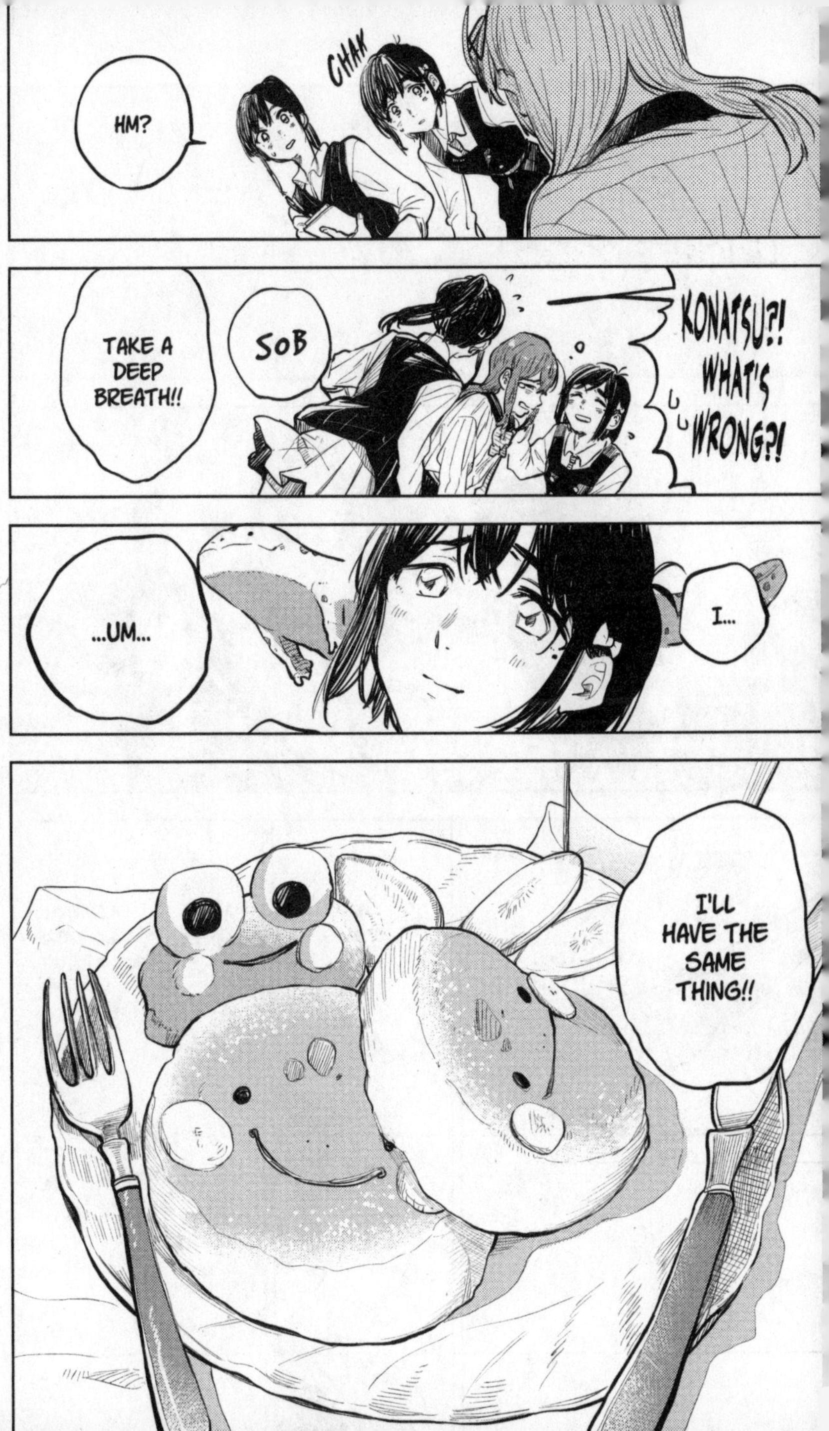
CHAK
HM?
KONATSU?! WHAT'S WRONG?!
SOB
TAKE A DEEP BREATH!!
I...
...UM...
I'LL HAVE THE SAME THING!!

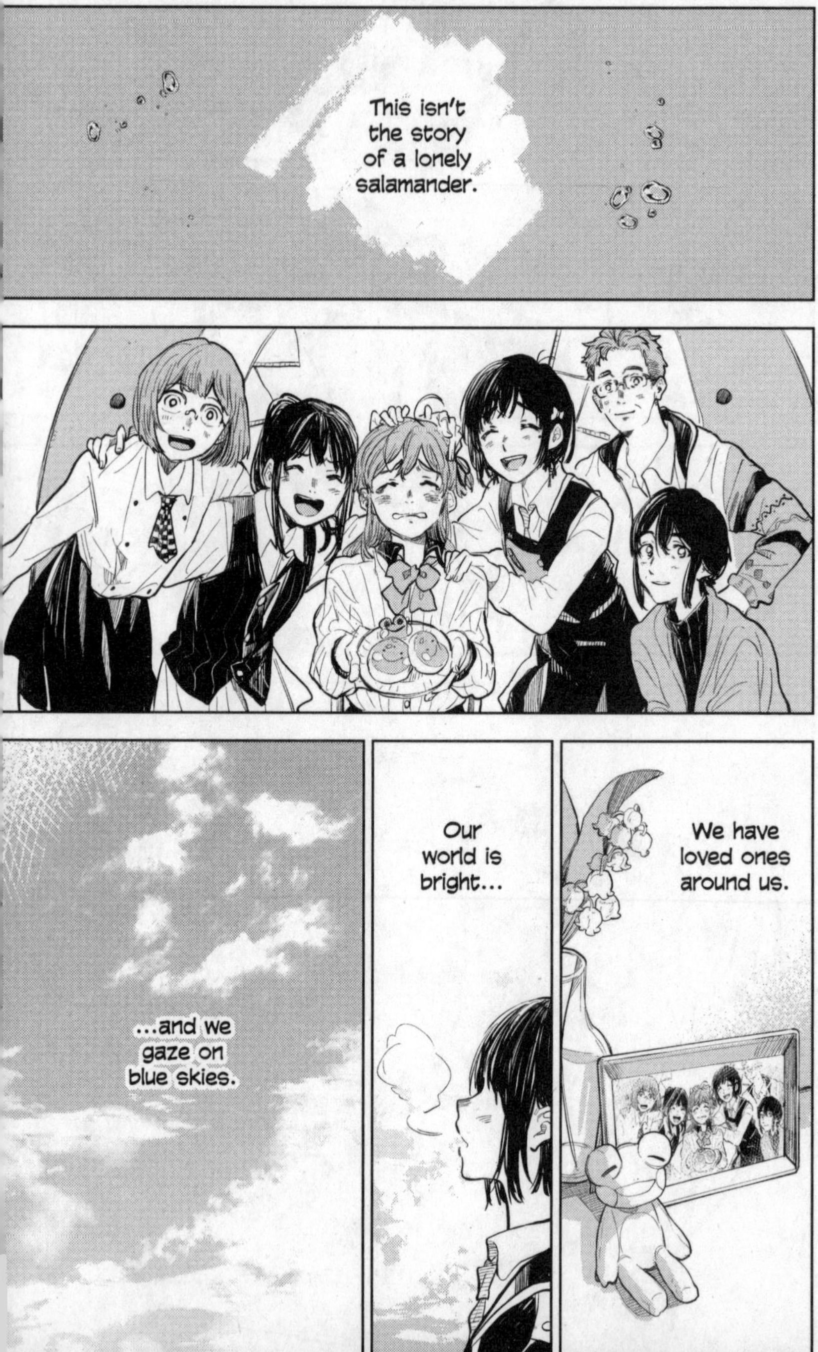
This isn't the story of a lonely salamander.
We have loved ones around us.
Our world is bright...
...and we gaze on blue skies.

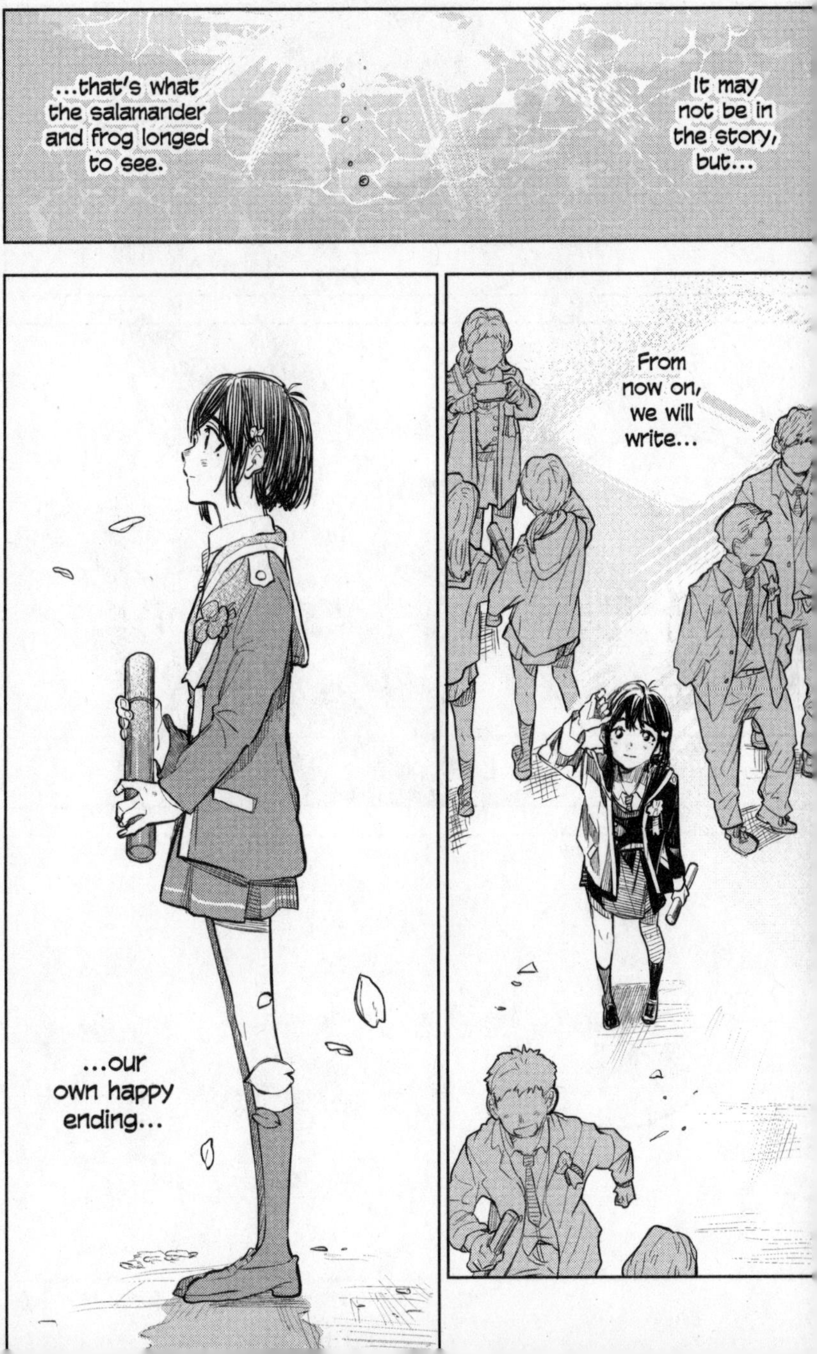
It may not be in the story, but...
...that's what the salamander and frog longed to see.
From now on, we will write...
...our own happy ending...

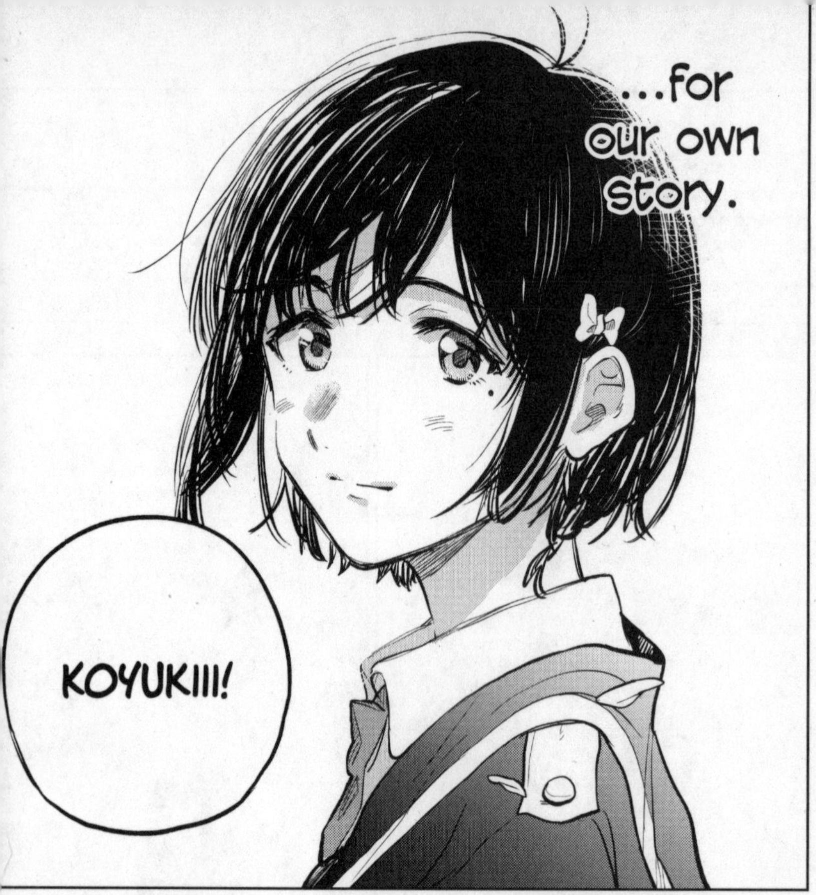
...for our own story.
KOYUKIIII!
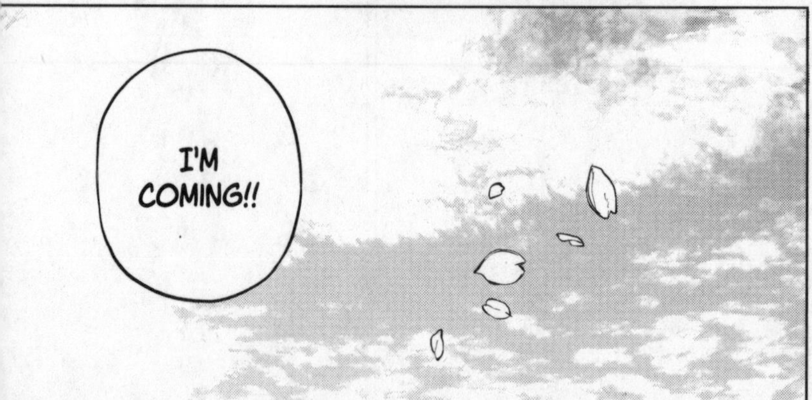
I'M COMING!!

A Tropical Fish
Yearns for Snow

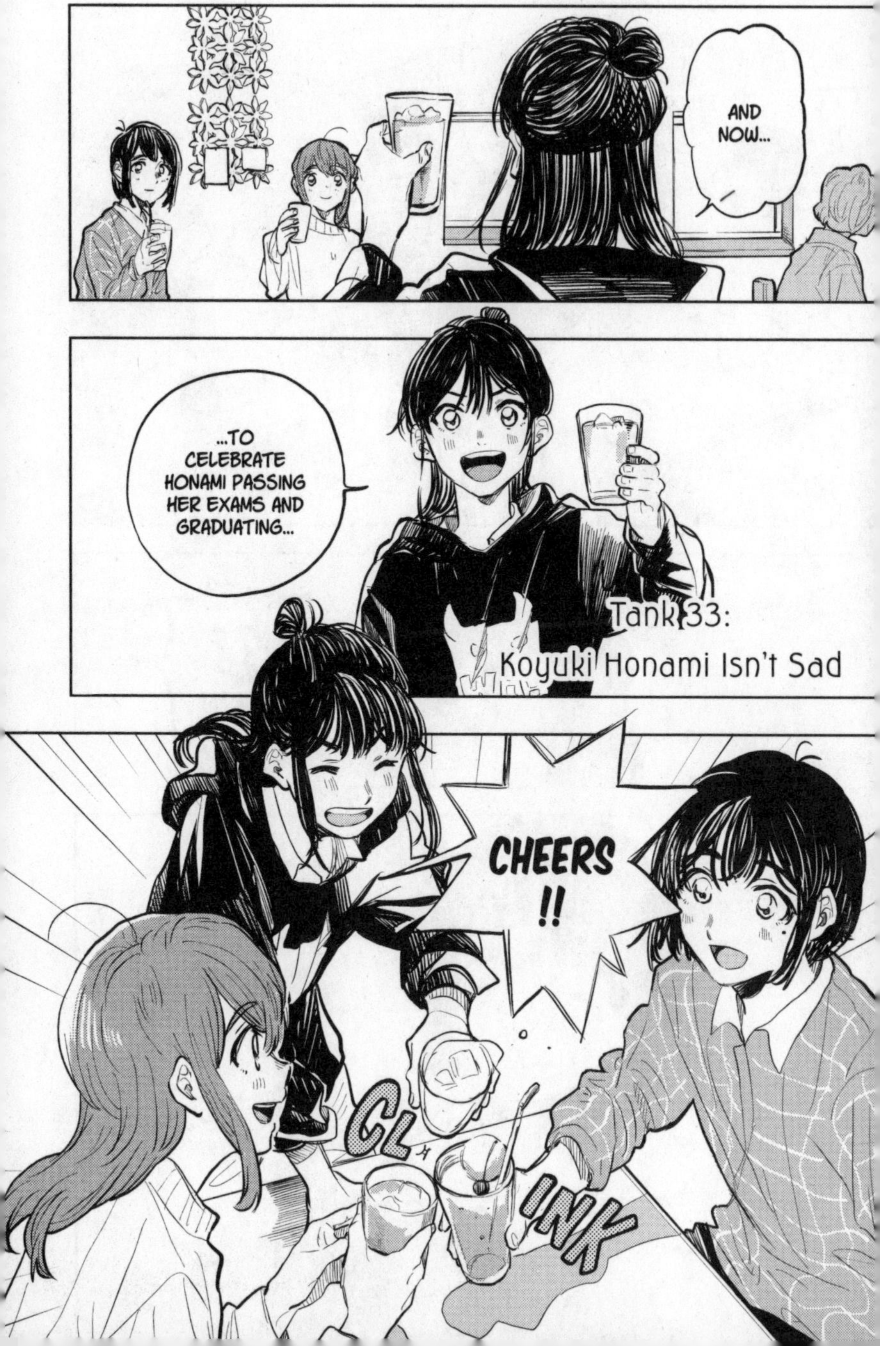
AND NOW...
...TO CELEBRATE HONAMI PASSING HER EXAMS AND GRADUATING...
Tank 33:
Koyuki Honami Isn't Sad
CHEERS !!
CLINK

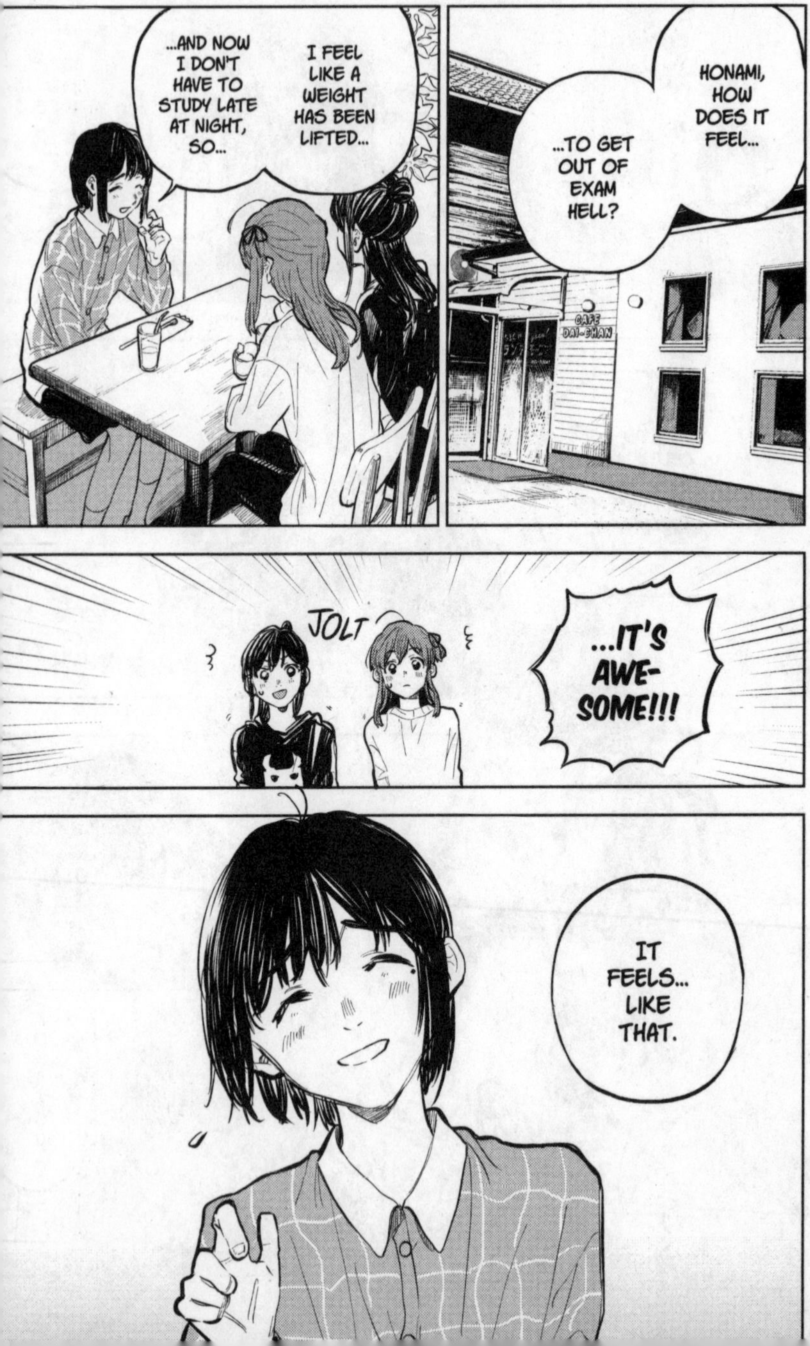
HONAMI, HOW DOES IT FEEL...
...TO GET OUT OF EXAM HELL?
CAFE DAI-CHAN
I FEEL LIKE A WEIGHT HAS BEEN LIFTED...
...AND NOW I DON'T HAVE TO STUDY LATE AT NIGHT, SO...
...IT'S AWESOME!!!
JOLT
IT FEELS... LIKE THAT.

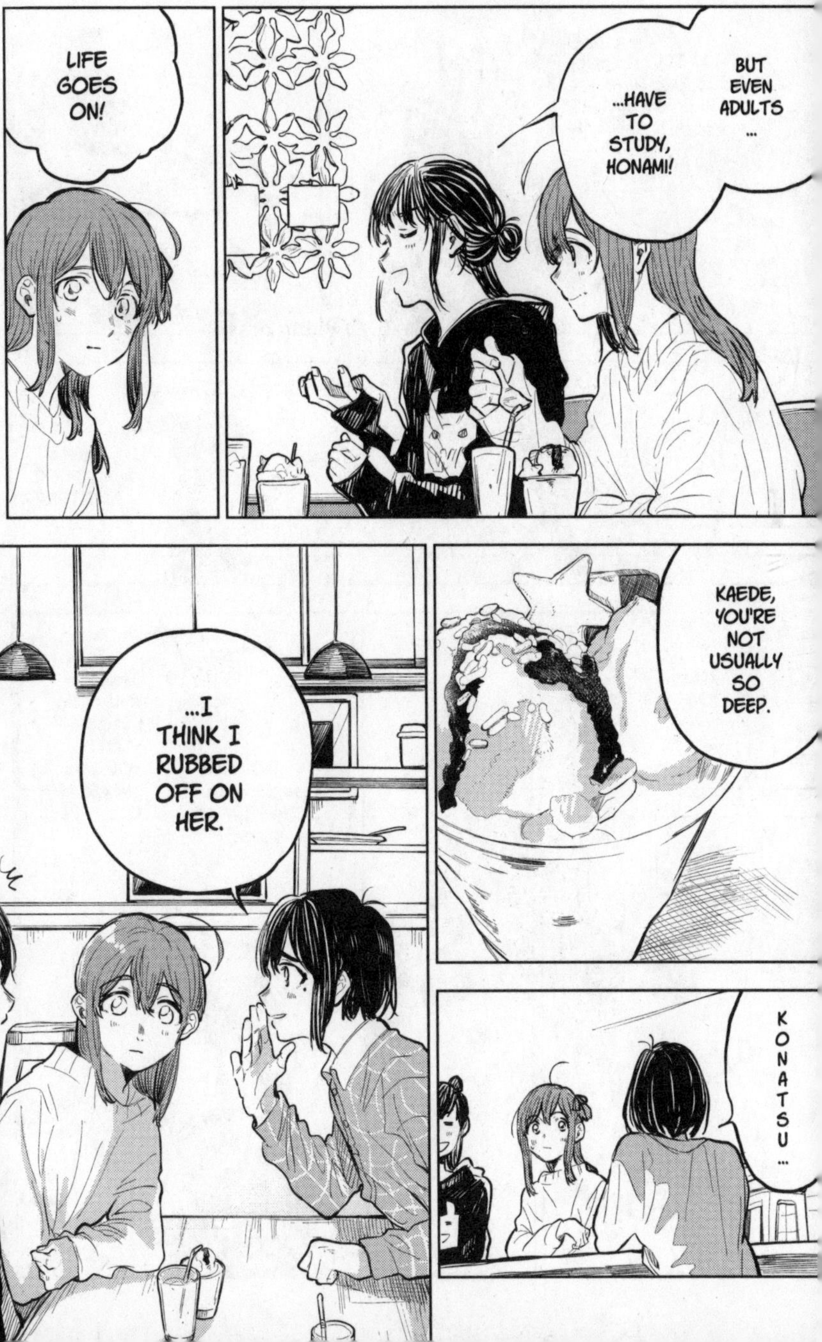
BUT EVEN ADULTS ...
...HAVE TO STUDY, HONAMI!
LIFE GOES ON!
KAEDE, YOU'RE NOT USUALLY SO DEEP.
KONATSU ...
...I THINK I RUBBED OFF ON HER.

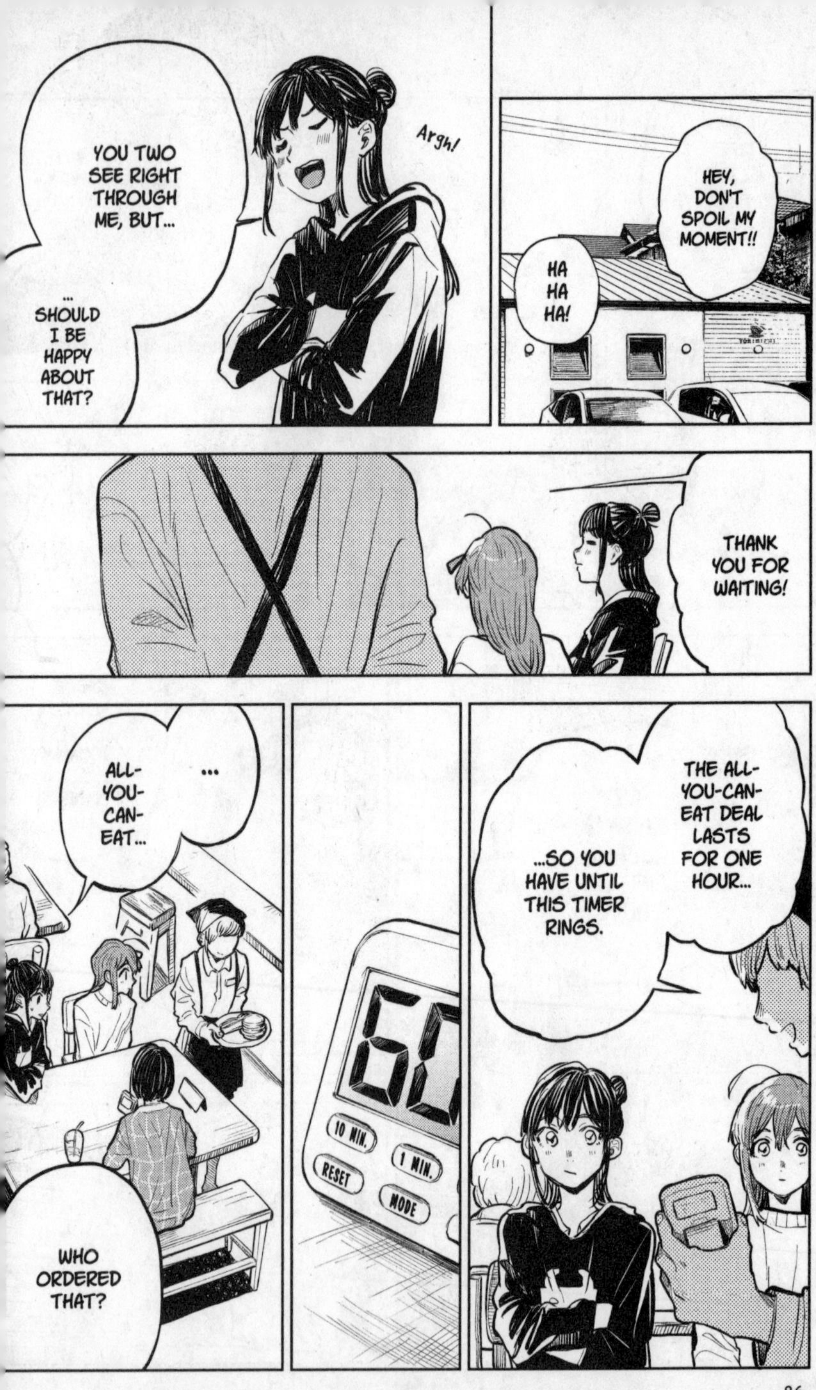
HEY, DON'T SPOIL MY MOMENT!!
HA HA HA!
YOU TWO SEE RIGHT THROUGH ME, BUT...
Argh!
...SHOULD I BE HAPPY ABOUT THAT?
THANK YOU FOR WAITING!
THE ALL-YOU-CAN-EAT DEAL LASTS FOR ONE HOUR...
...SO YOU HAVE UNTIL THIS TIMER RINGS.
10 MIN.
1 MIN.
RESET
MODE
...
ALL-YOU-CAN-EAT...
WHO ORDERED THAT?

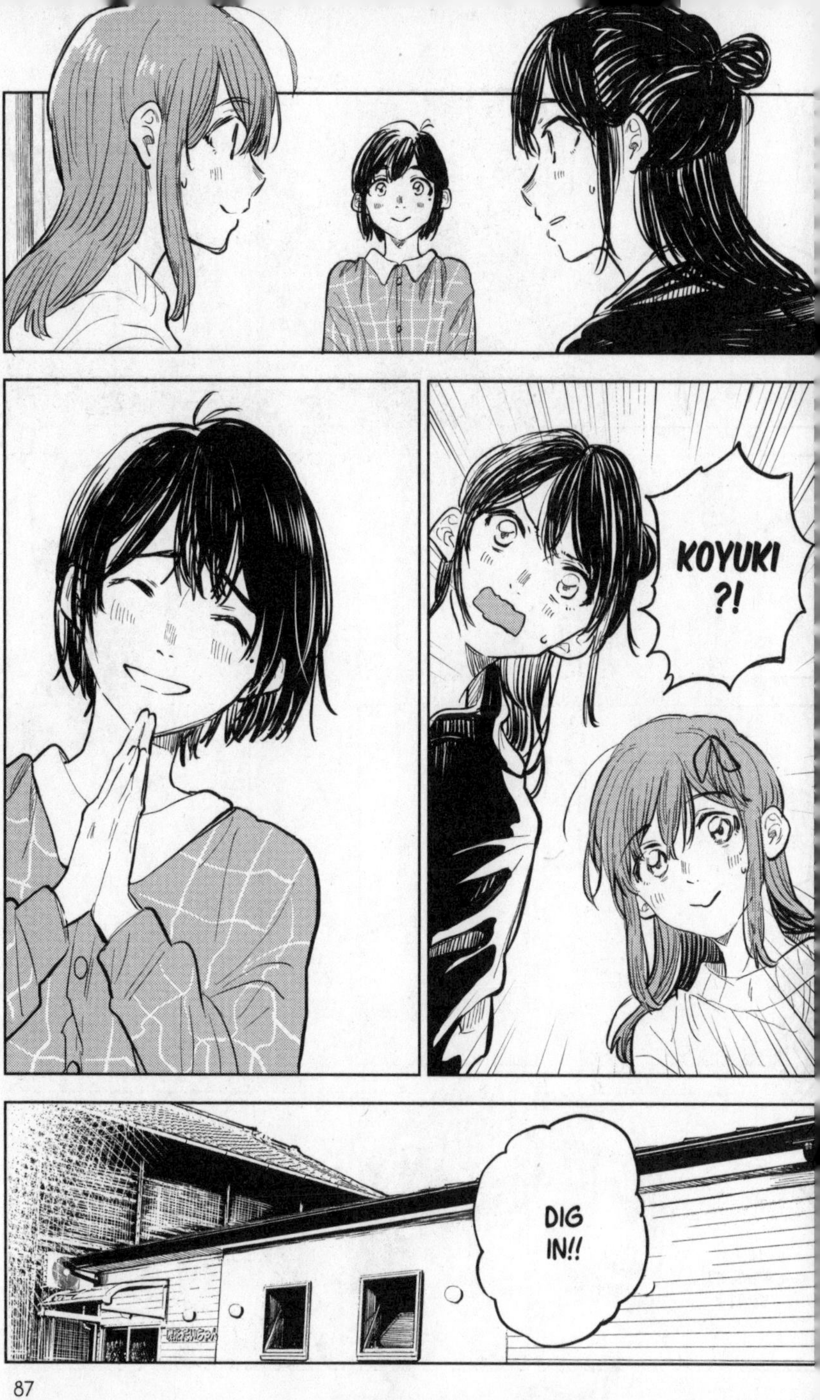
KOYUKI ?!
DIG IN!!

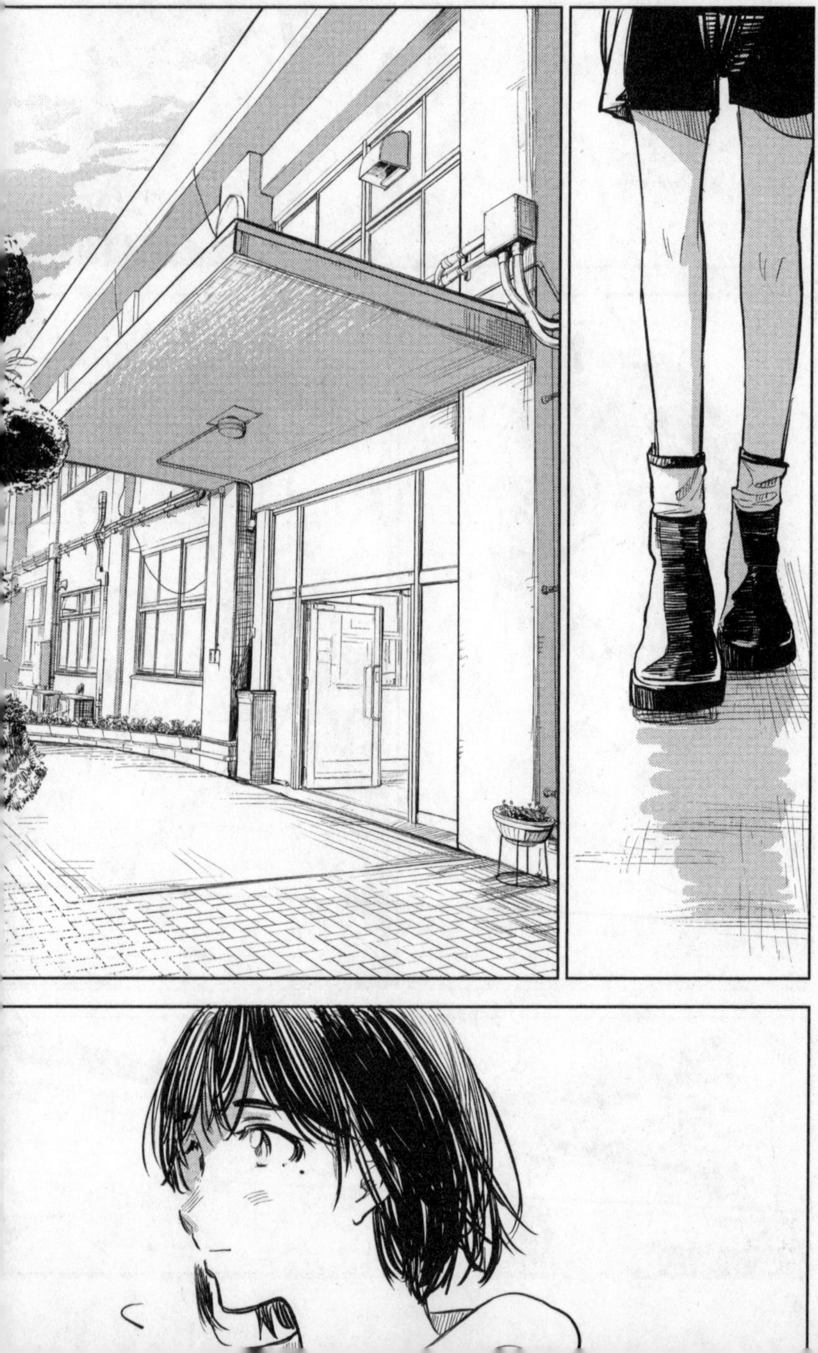

...LET'S TAKE A WALK AGAIN SOME-TIME...

...AND HAVE FUN WITH EVERY-BODY.

RIKU...

...I HAVE TO GO NOW.

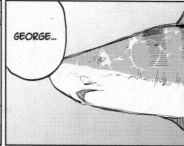

GEORGE...

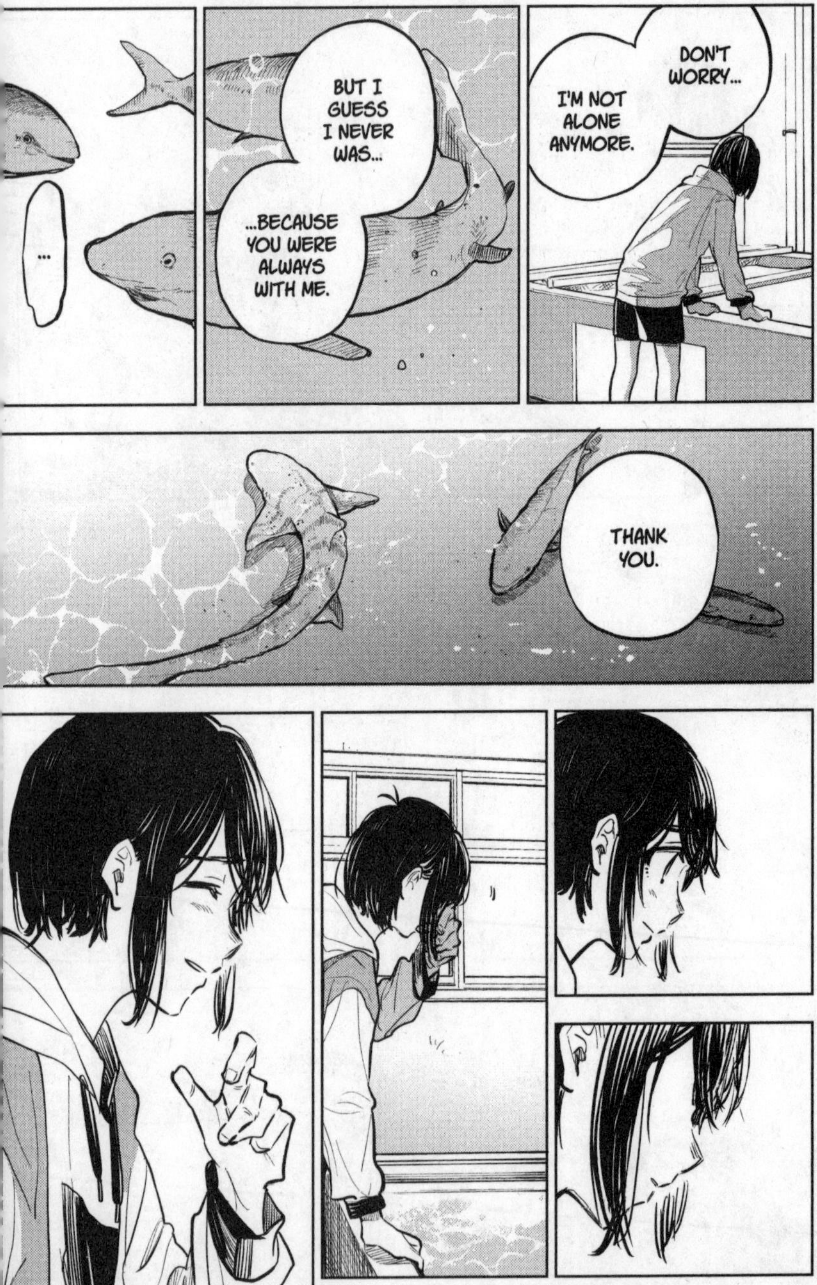
DON'T WORRY...
I'M NOT ALONE ANYMORE.
BUT I GUESS I NEVER WAS...
...BECAUSE YOU WERE ALWAYS WITH ME.
...
THANK YOU.

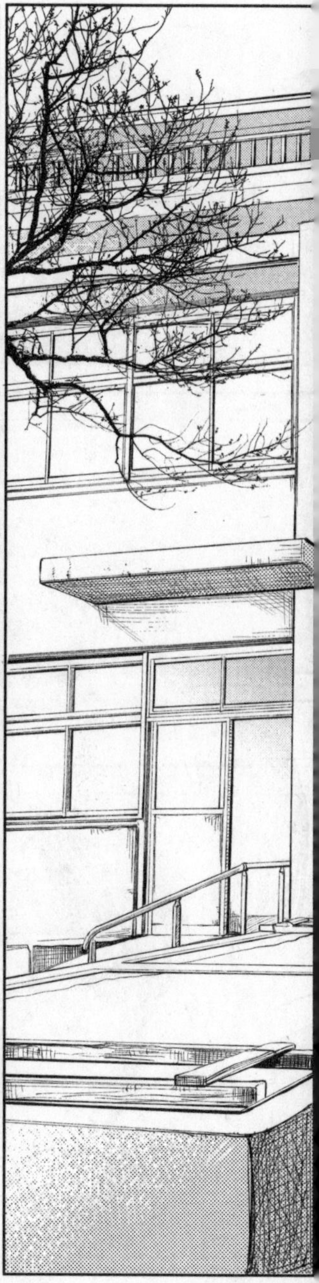

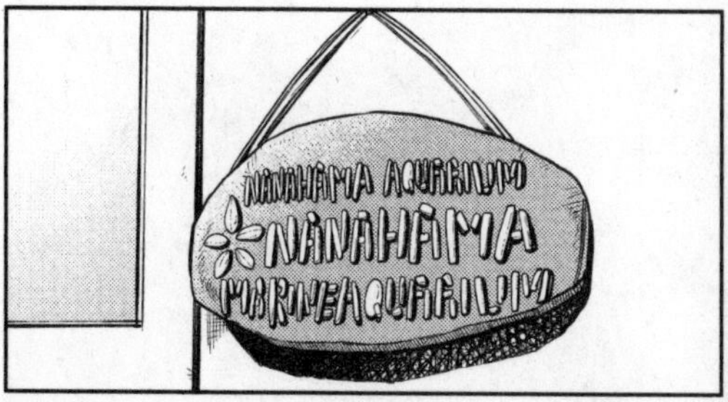
NANAHAMA AQUARIUM
NANAHAMA
MARINE AQUARIUM

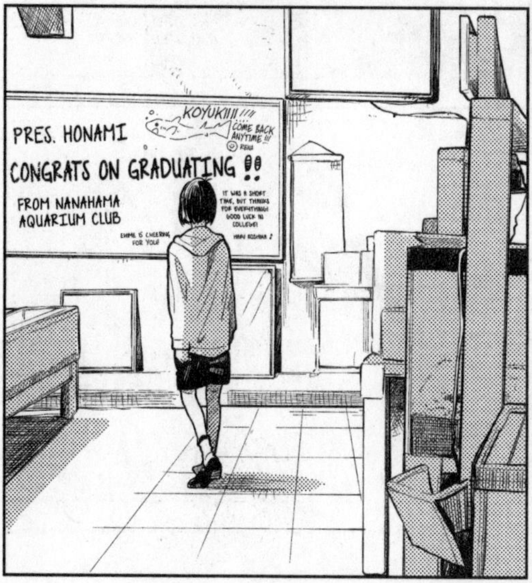
PRES. HONAMI
CONGRATS ON GRADUATING !!
FROM NANAHAMA AQUARIUM CLUB
KOYUKI!!!
COME BACK ANYTIME !!!
IT WAS A SHORT TIME, BUT THANKS FOR EVERYTHING!! GOOD LUCK IN COLLEGE!!
EHIME IS CHEERING FOR YOU!

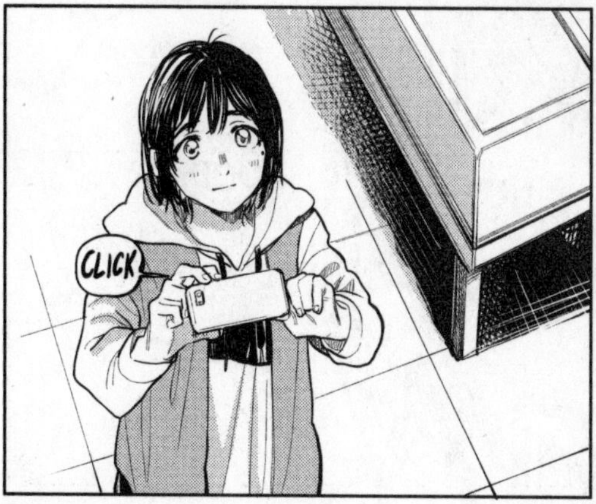
CLICK

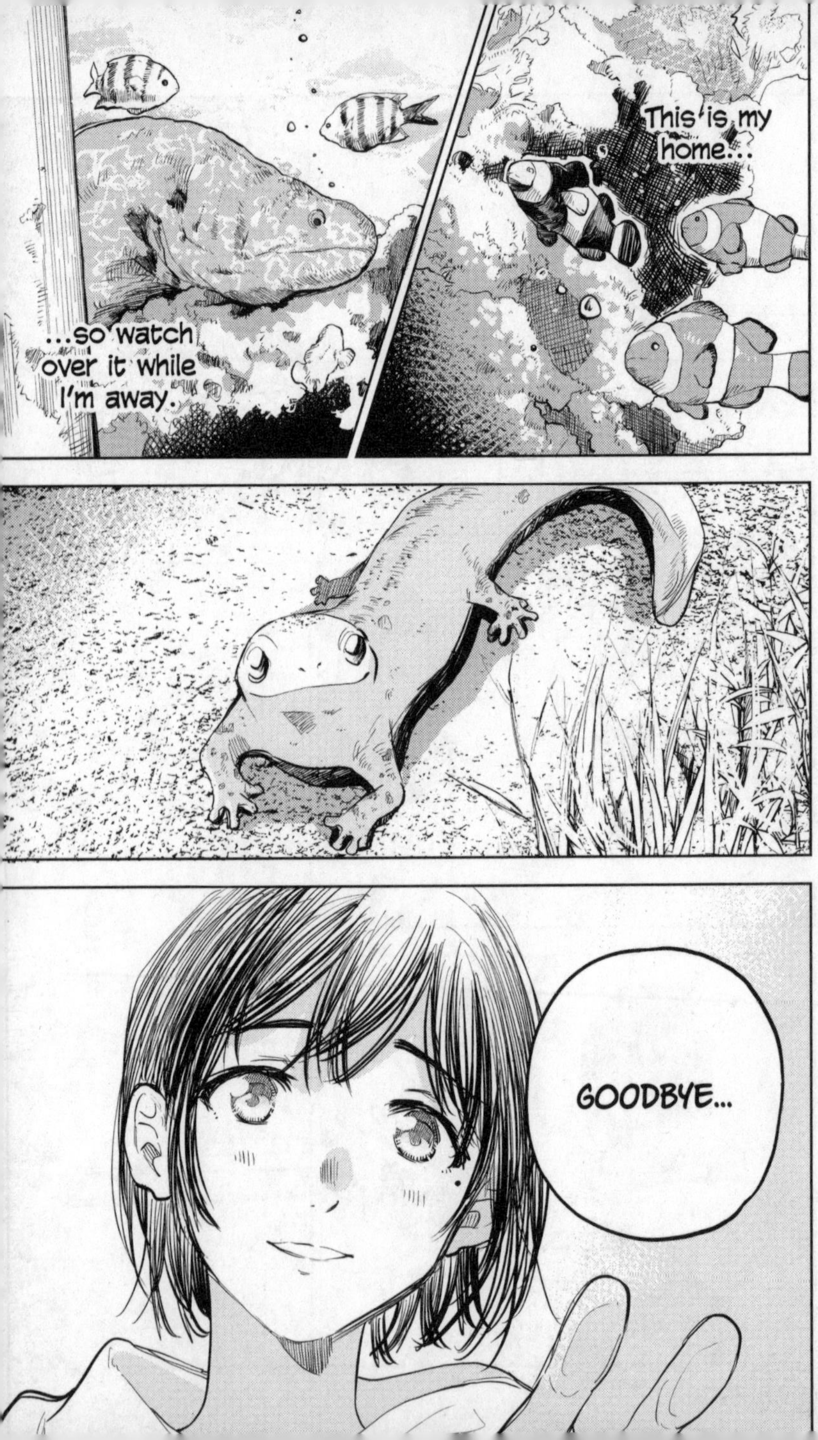
This is my home...
...so watch over it while I'm away.
GOODBYE...

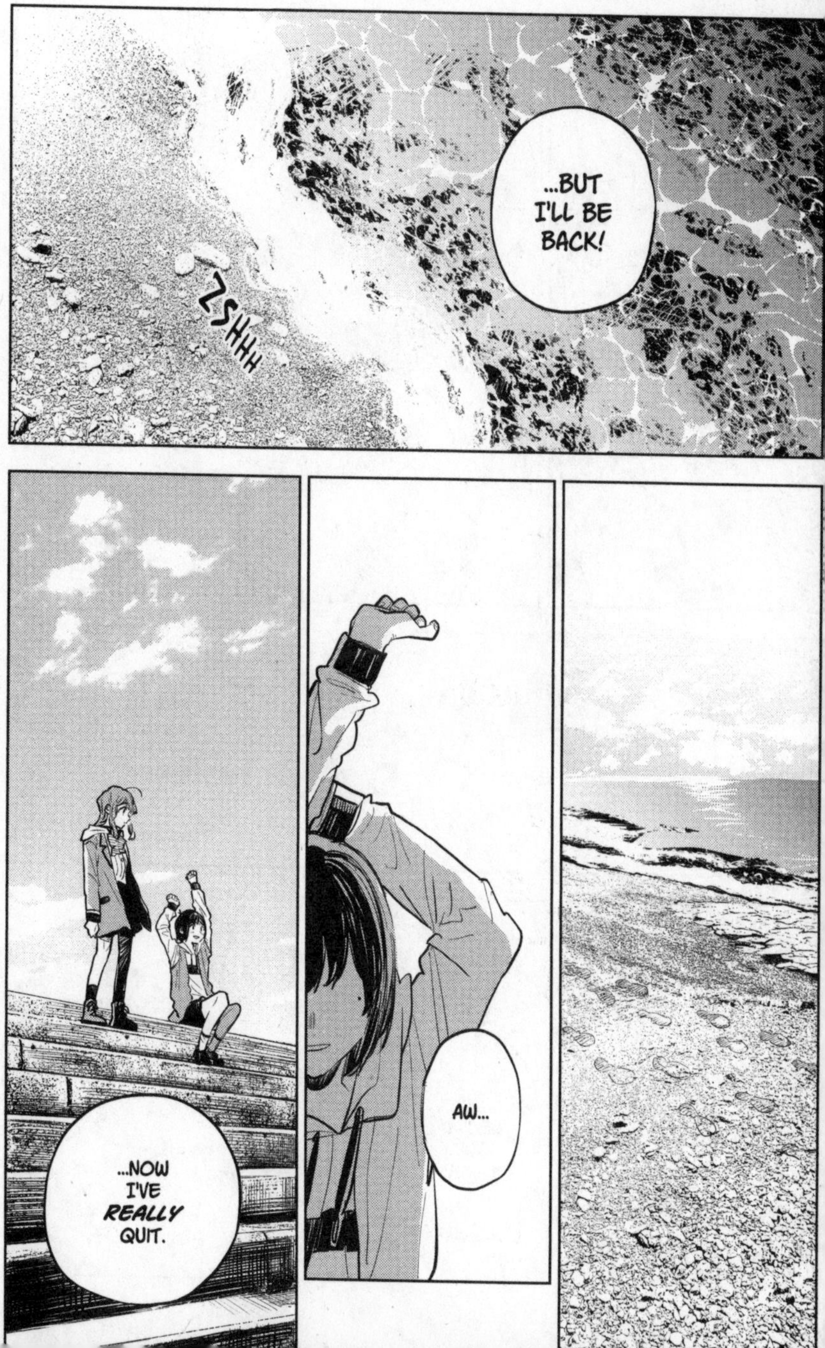
...BUT I'LL BE BACK!
ZSHHH
AW...
...NOW I'VE REALLY QUIT.

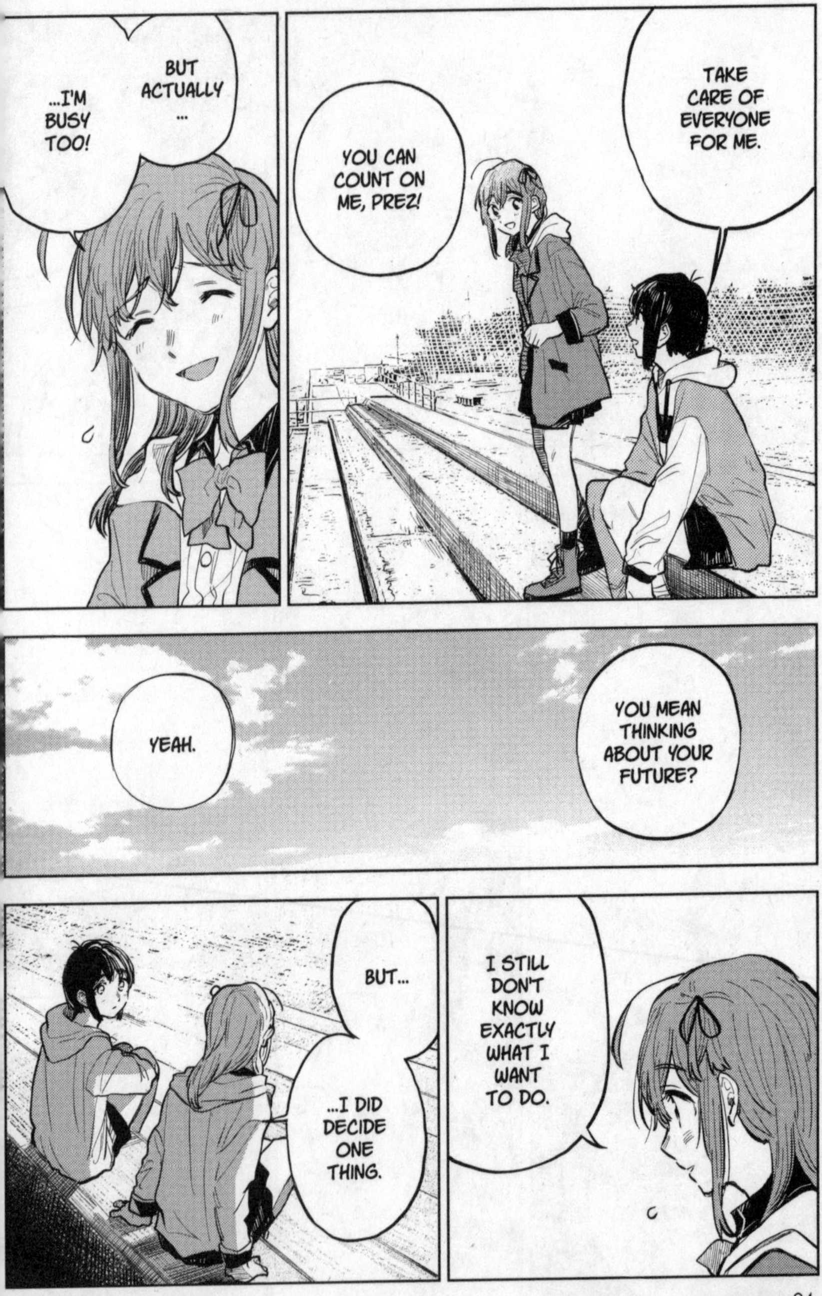
TAKE CARE OF EVERYONE FOR ME.
YOU CAN COUNT ON ME, PREZ!
BUT ACTUALLY ...
...I'M BUSY TOO!
YOU MEAN THINKING ABOUT YOUR FUTURE?
YEAH.
I STILL DON'T KNOW EXACTLY WHAT I WANT TO DO.
BUT...
...I DID DECIDE ONE THING.

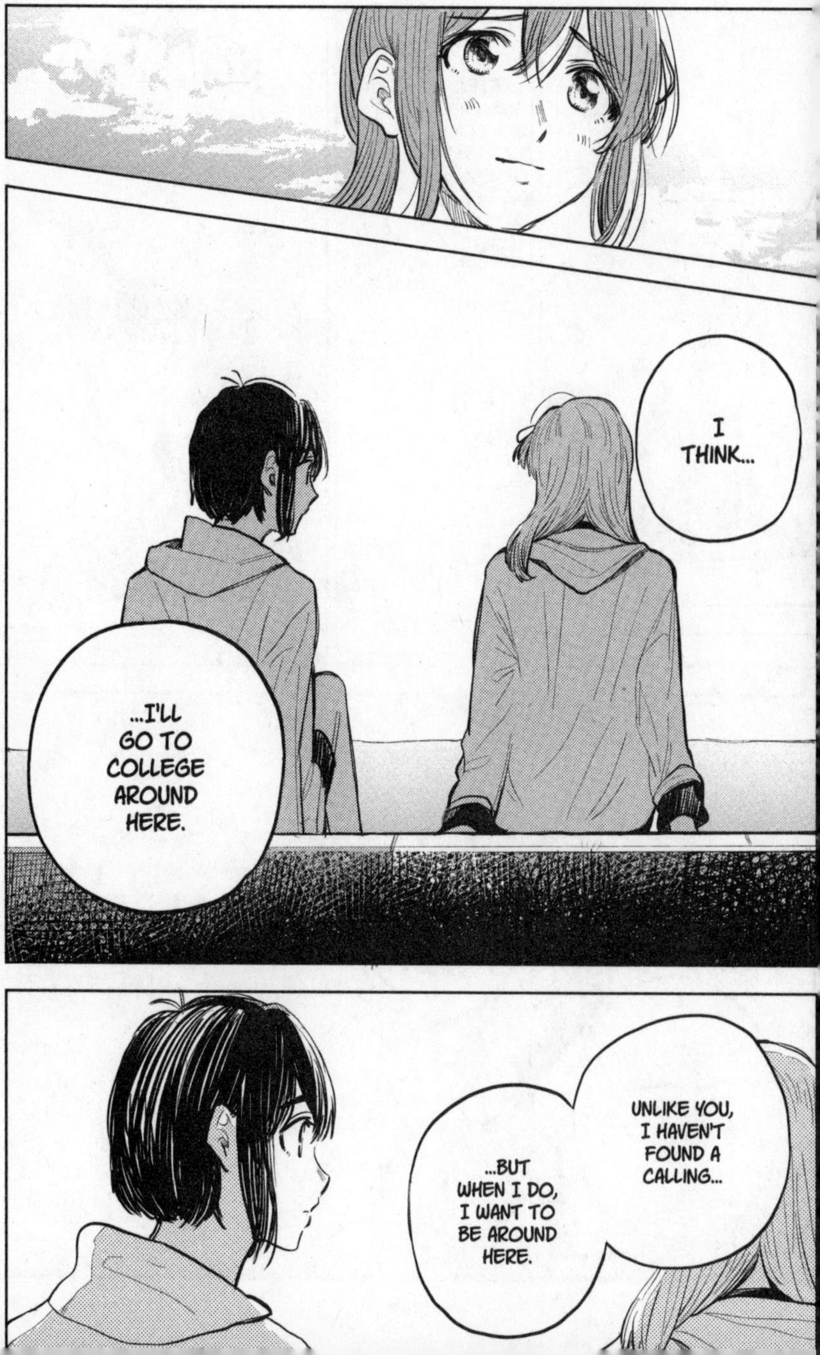
I THINK...
...I'LL GO TO COLLEGE AROUND HERE.
UNLIKE YOU, I HAVEN'T FOUND A CALLING...
...BUT WHEN I DO, I WANT TO BE AROUND HERE.

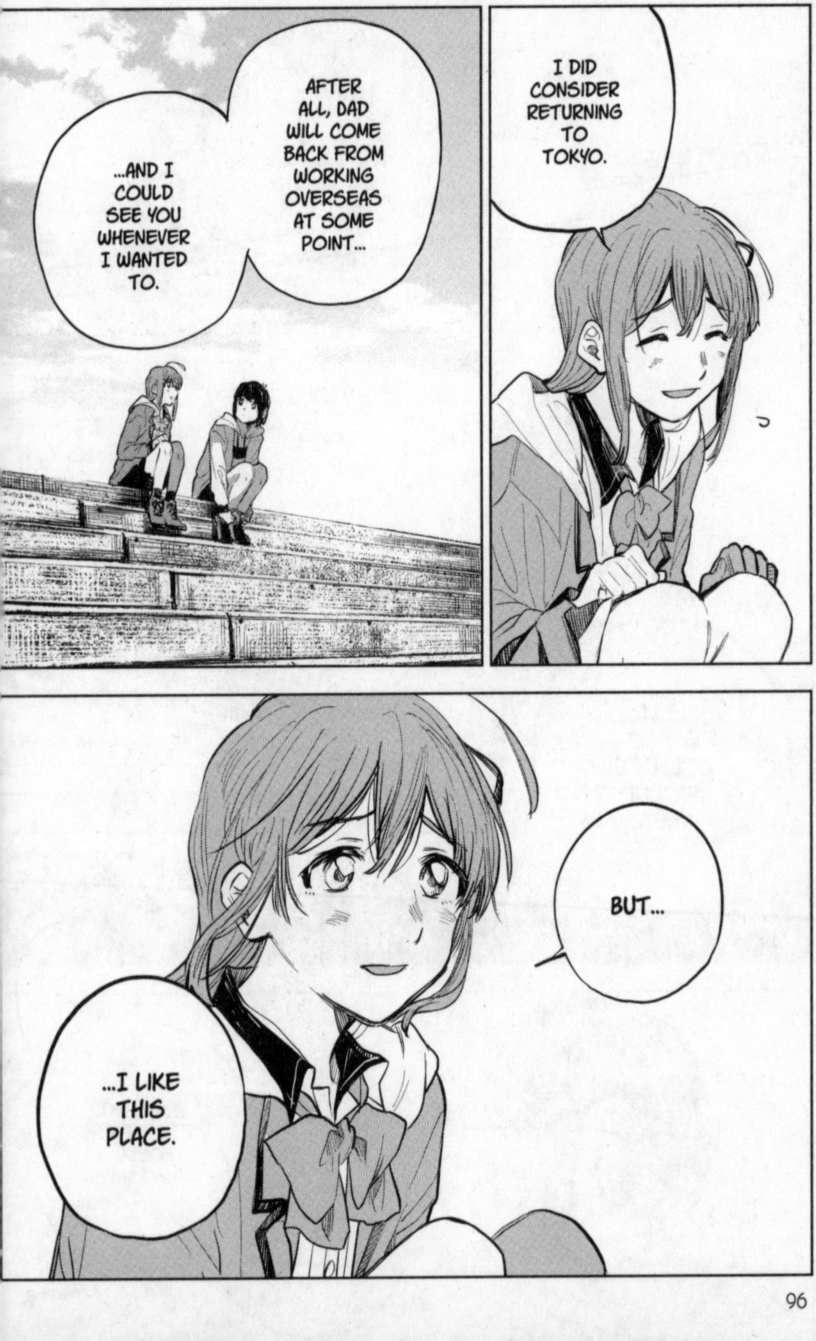
I DID CONSIDER RETURNING TO TOKYO.
AFTER ALL, DAD WILL COME BACK FROM WORKING OVERSEAS AT SOME POINT...
...AND I COULD SEE YOU WHENEVER I WANTED TO.
BUT...
...I LIKE THIS PLACE.

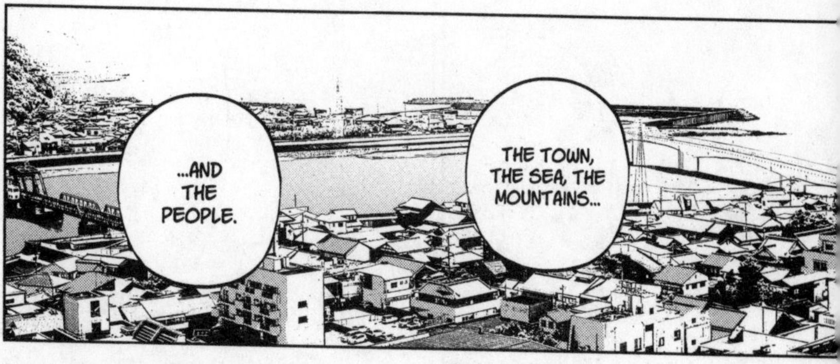
THE TOWN, THE SEA, THE MOUNTAINS...
...AND THE PEOPLE.

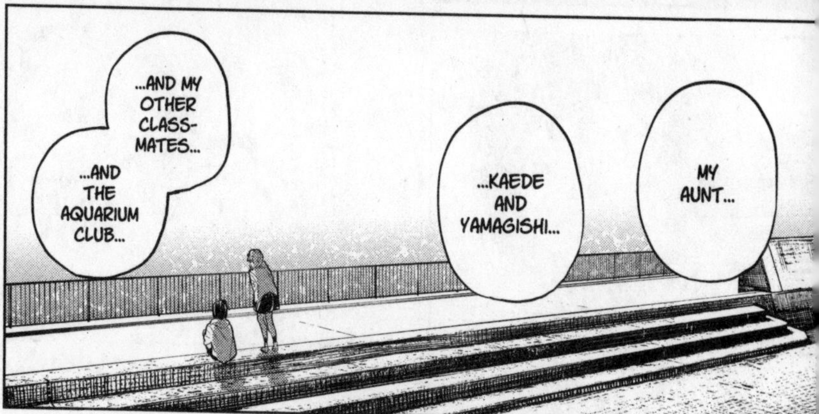
MY AUNT...
...KAEDE AND YAMAGISHI...
...AND MY OTHER CLASSMATES...
...AND THE AQUARIUM CLUB...

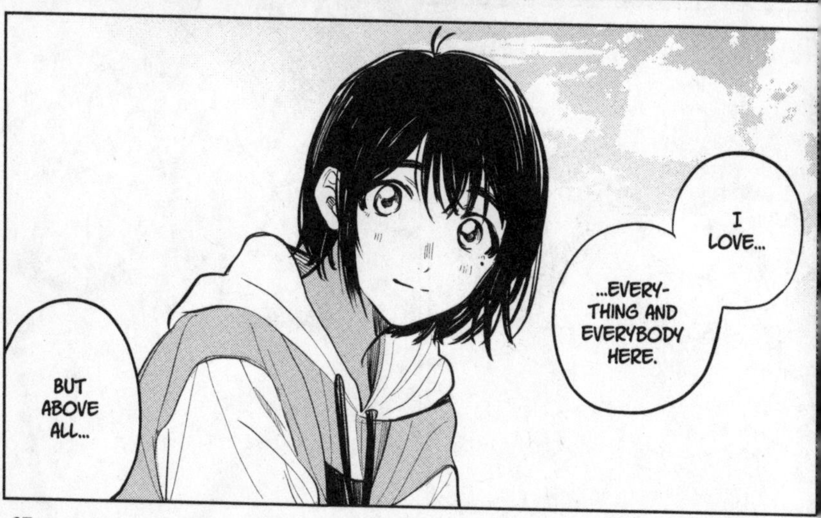
I LOVE...
...EVERYTHING AND EVERYBODY HERE.
BUT ABOVE ALL...

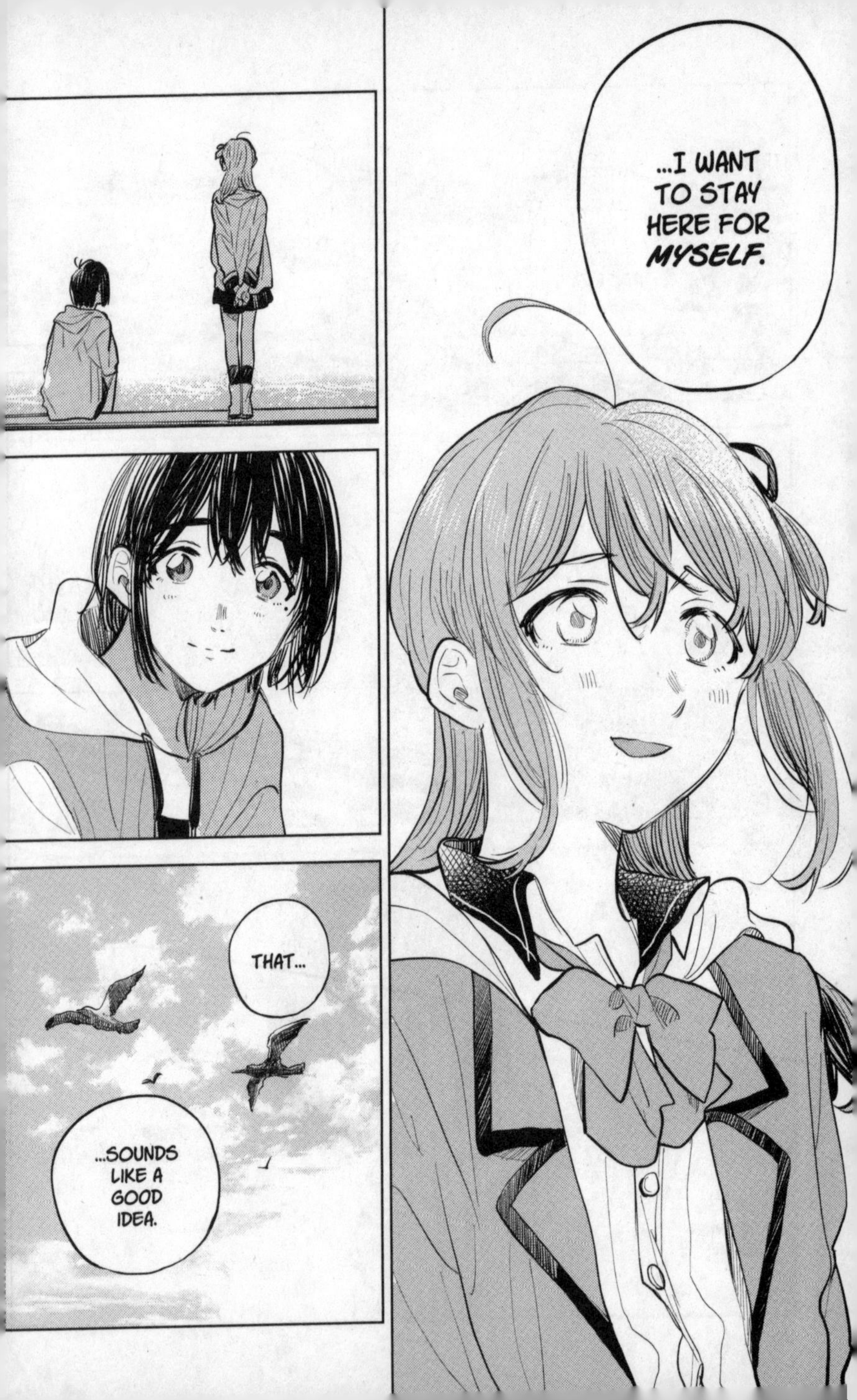
...I WANT TO STAY HERE FOR MYSELF.
THAT...
...SOUNDS LIKE A GOOD IDEA.

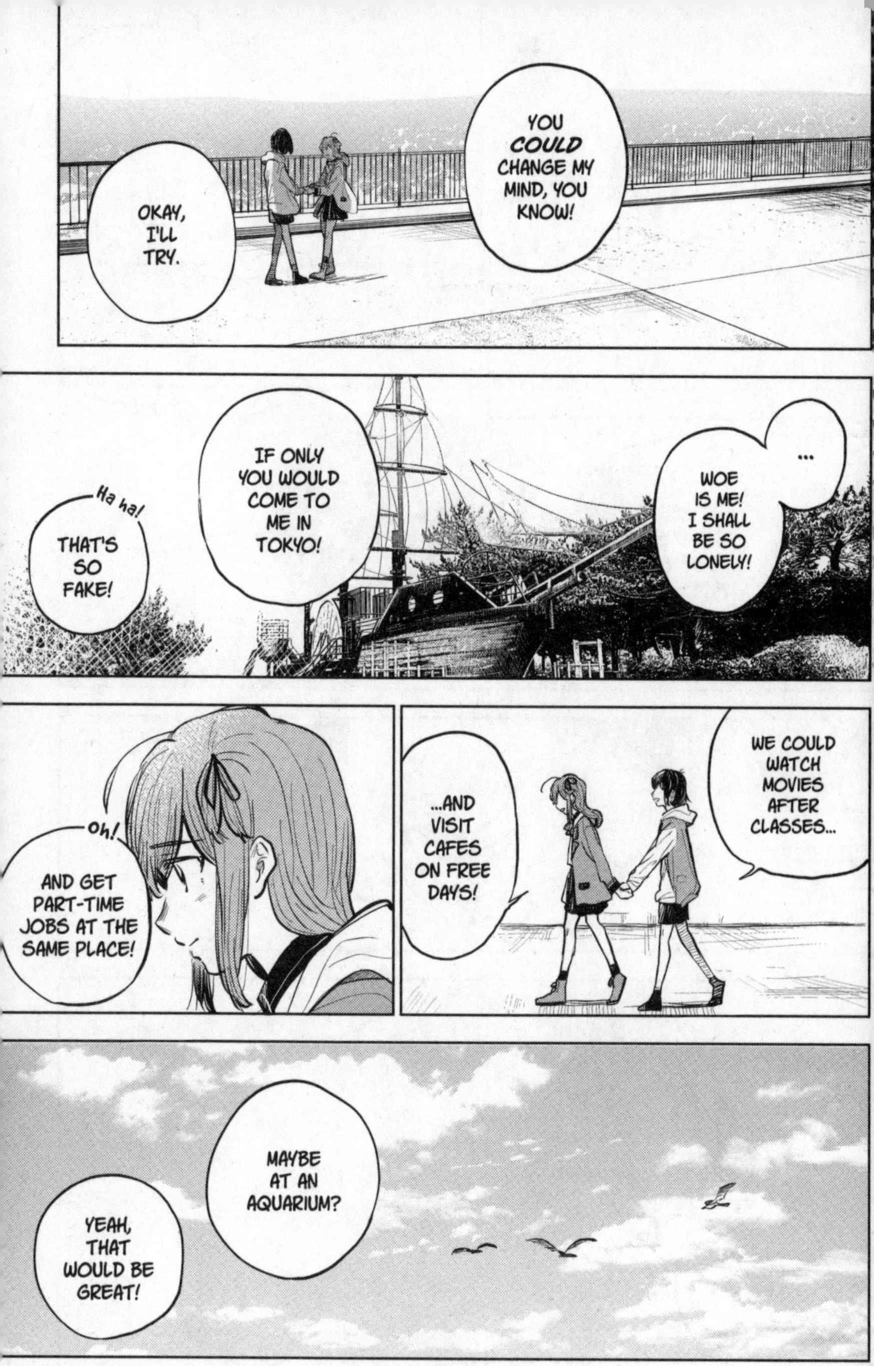
YOU COULD CHANGE MY MIND, YOU KNOW!
OKAY, I'LL TRY.
...
WOE IS ME! I SHALL BE SO LONELY!
IF ONLY YOU WOULD COME TO ME IN TOKYO!
Ha ha!
THAT'S SO FAKE!
WE COULD WATCH MOVIES AFTER CLASSES...
...AND VISIT CAFES ON FREE DAYS!
Oh!
AND GET PART-TIME JOBS AT THE SAME PLACE!
MAYBE AT AN AQUARIUM?
YEAH, THAT WOULD BE GREAT!

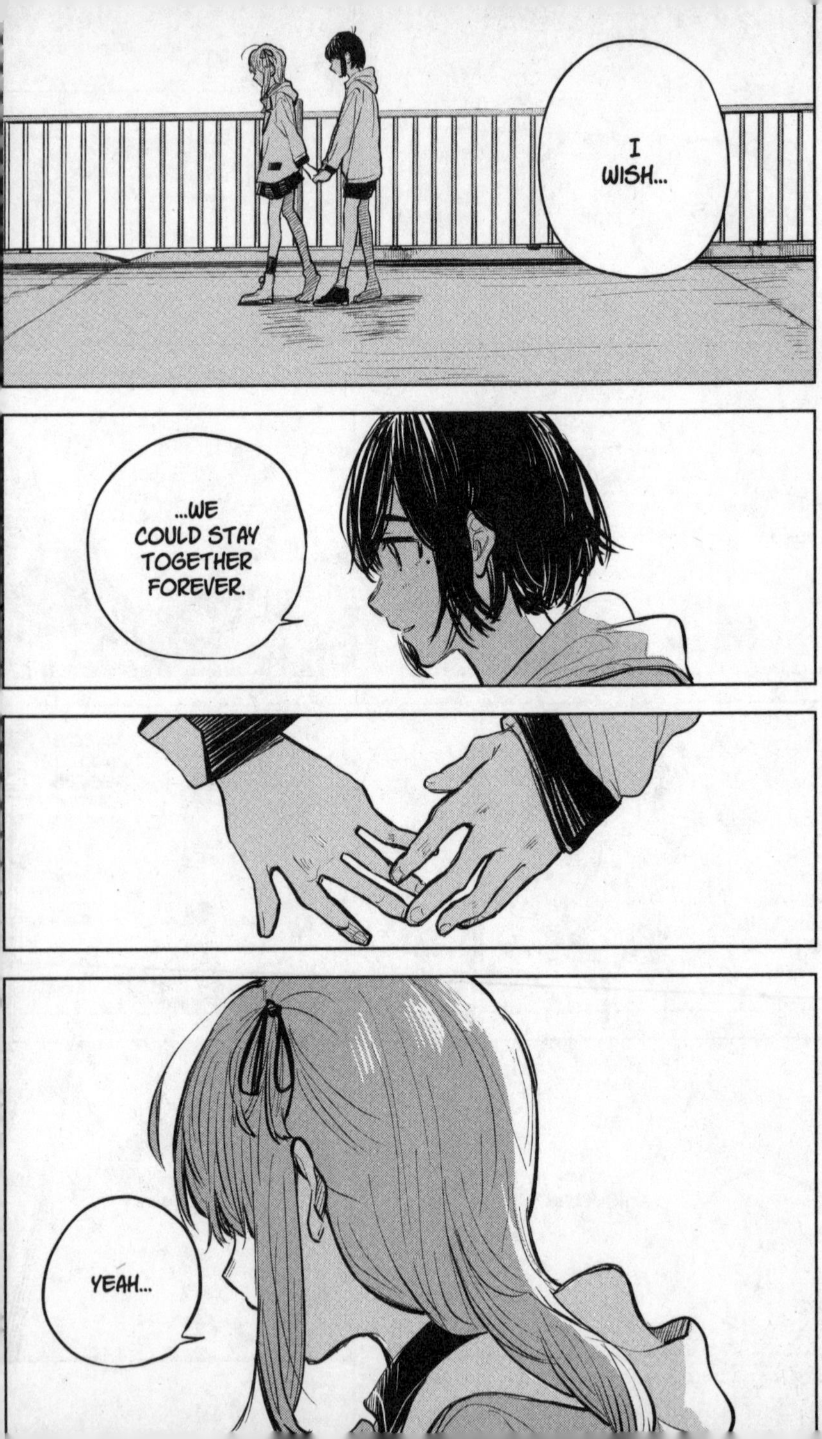
I WISH...
...WE COULD STAY TOGETHER FOREVER.
YEAH...

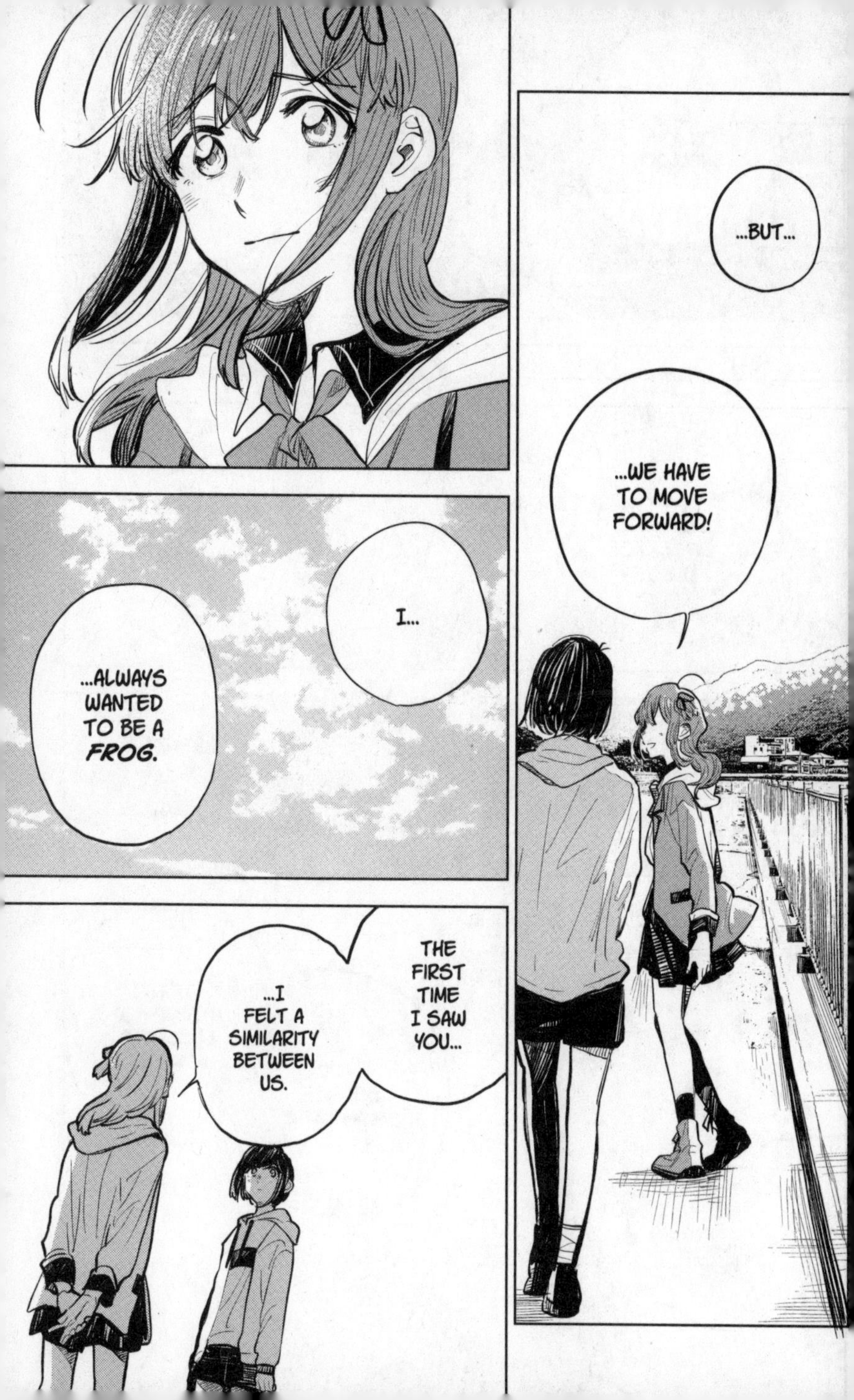
...BUT...
...WE HAVE TO MOVE FORWARD!
I...
...ALWAYS WANTED TO BE A *FROG.*
THE FIRST TIME I SAW YOU...
...I FELT A SIMILARITY BETWEEN US.

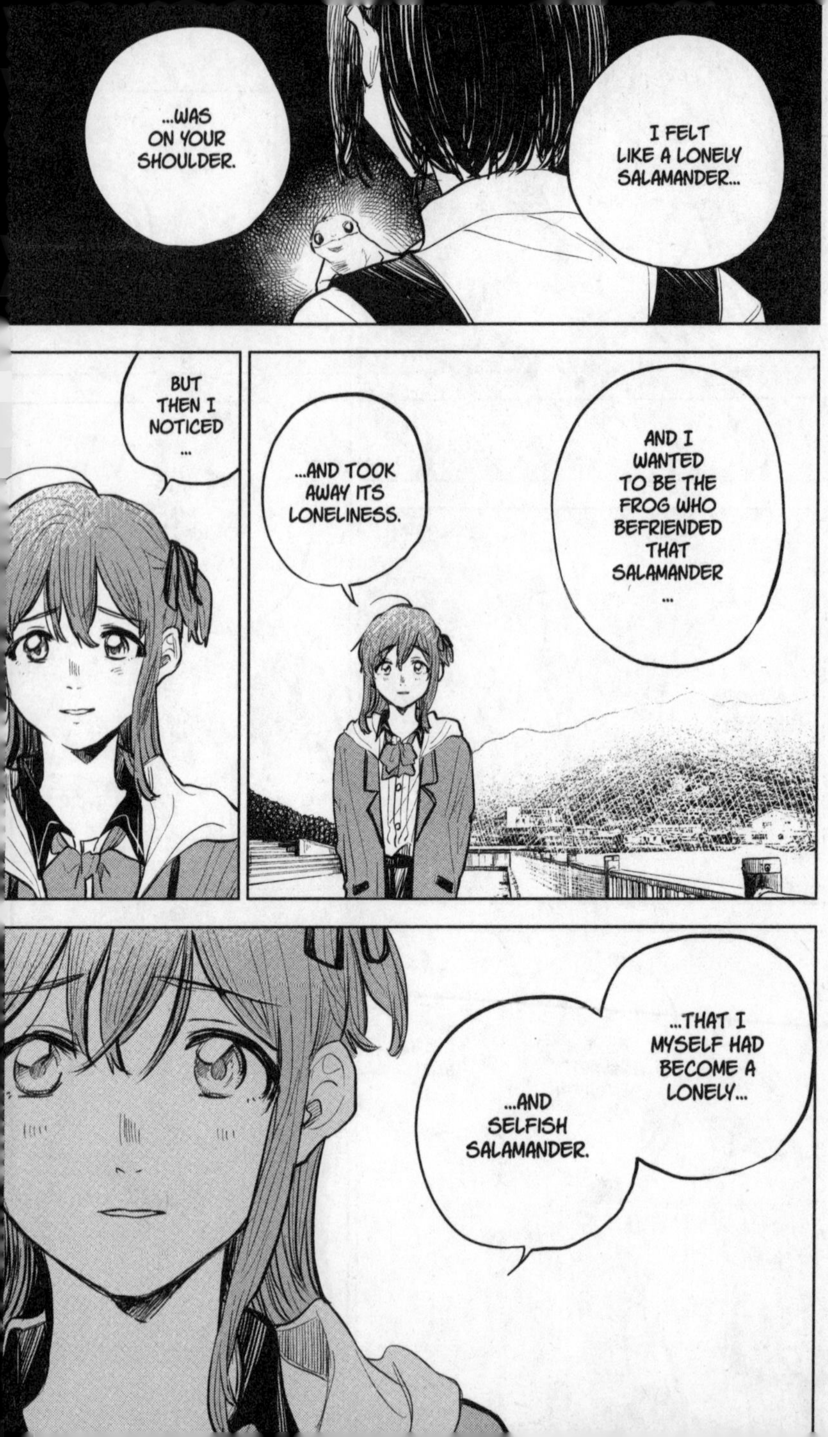
I FELT LIKE A LONELY SALAMANDER...
...WAS ON YOUR SHOULDER.
AND I WANTED TO BE THE FROG WHO BEFRIENDED THAT SALAMANDER ...
...AND TOOK AWAY ITS LONELINESS.
BUT THEN I NOTICED ...
...THAT I MYSELF HAD BECOME A LONELY...
...AND SELFISH SALAMANDER.

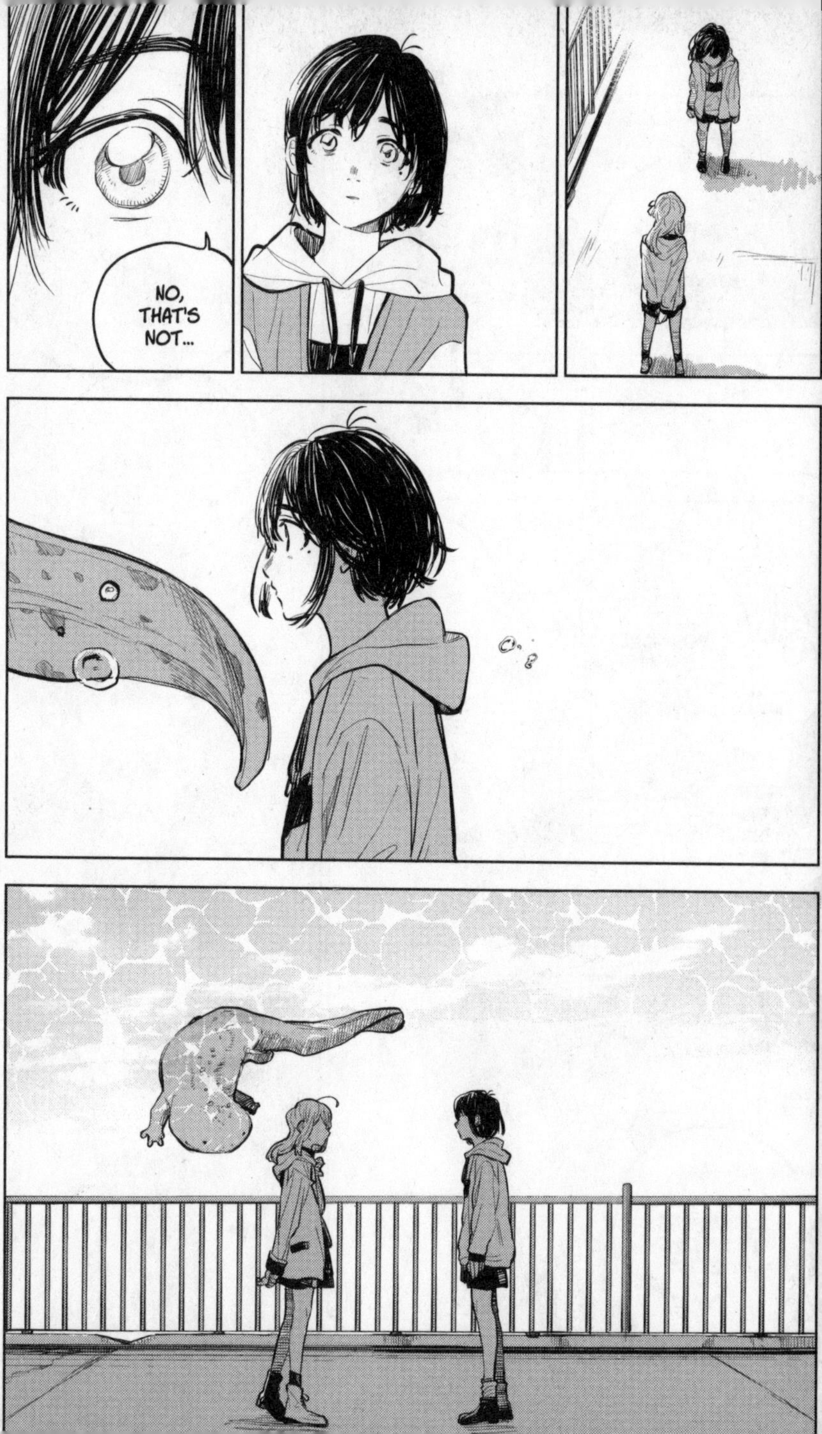
NO, THAT'S NOT...

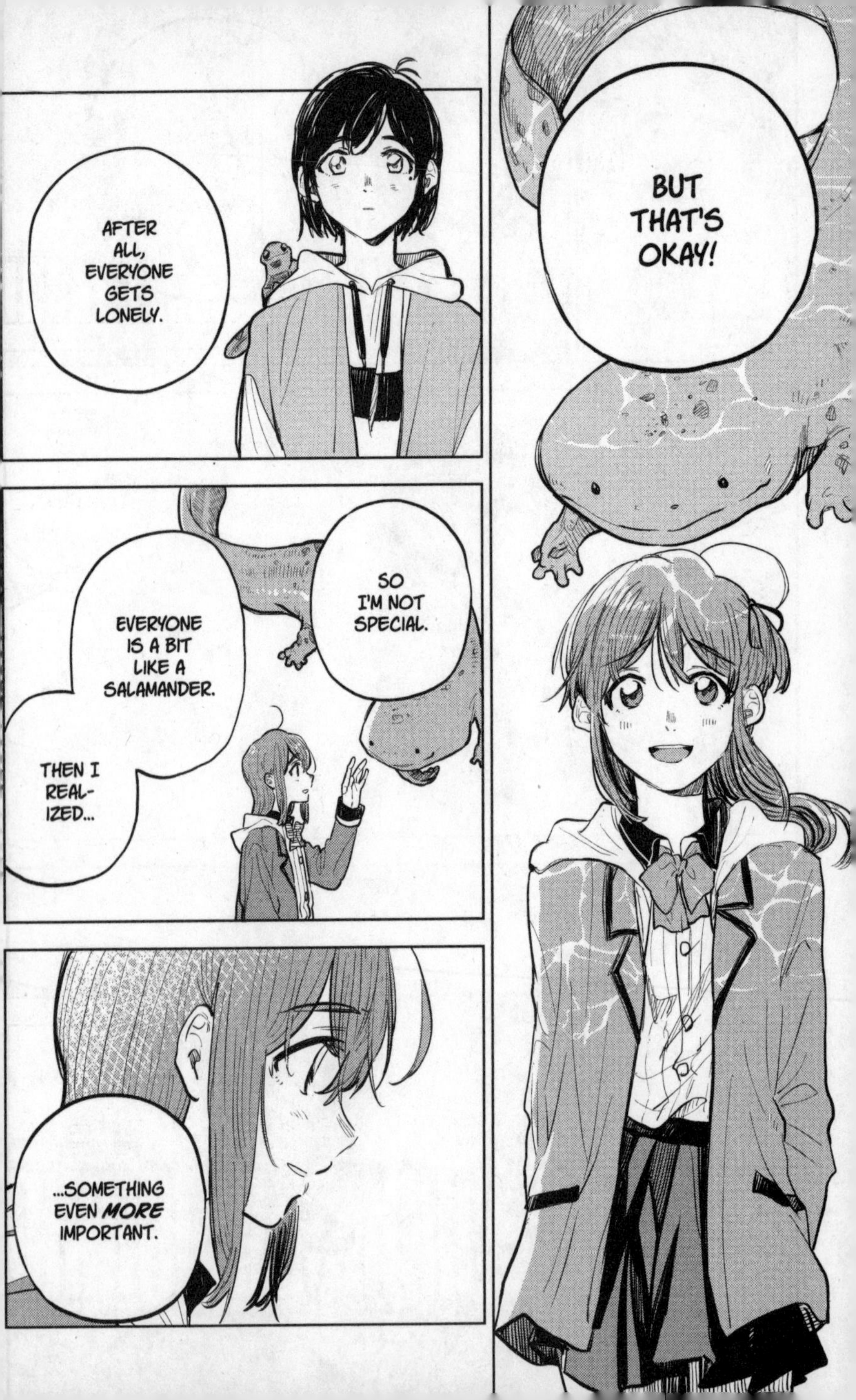
AFTER ALL, EVERYONE GETS LONELY.
THEN I REAL-IZED...
EVERYONE IS A BIT LIKE A SALAMANDER.
SO I'M NOT SPECIAL.
...SOMETHING EVEN *MORE* IMPORTANT.
BUT THAT'S OKAY!

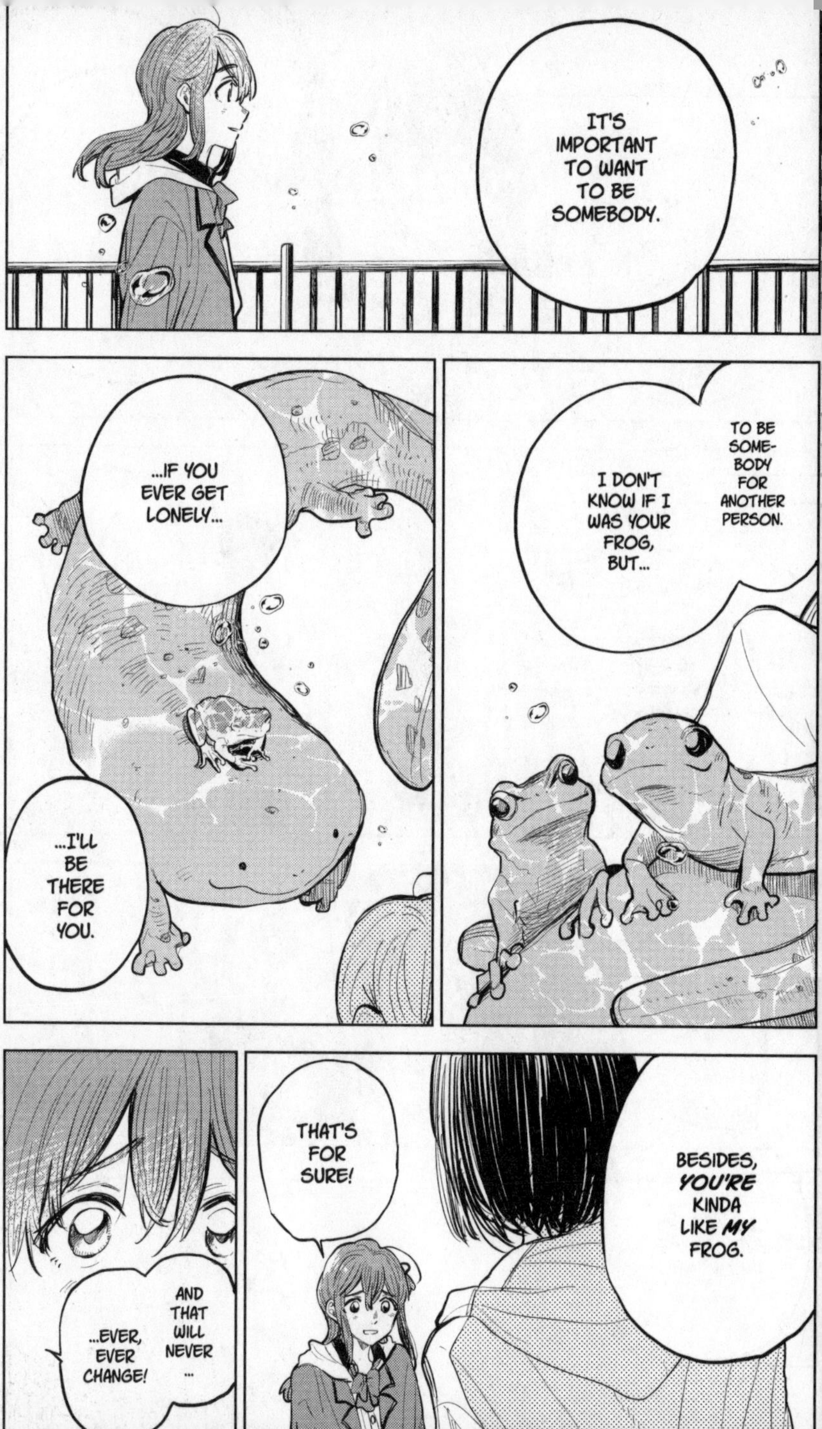
IT'S IMPORTANT TO WANT TO BE SOMEBODY.
TO BE SOME-BODY FOR ANOTHER PERSON.
I DON'T KNOW IF I WAS YOUR FROG, BUT...
...IF YOU EVER GET LONELY...
...I'LL BE THERE FOR YOU.
BESIDES, *YOU'RE* KINDA LIKE *MY* FROG.
THAT'S FOR SURE!
AND THAT WILL NEVER ...
...EVER, EVER CHANGE!

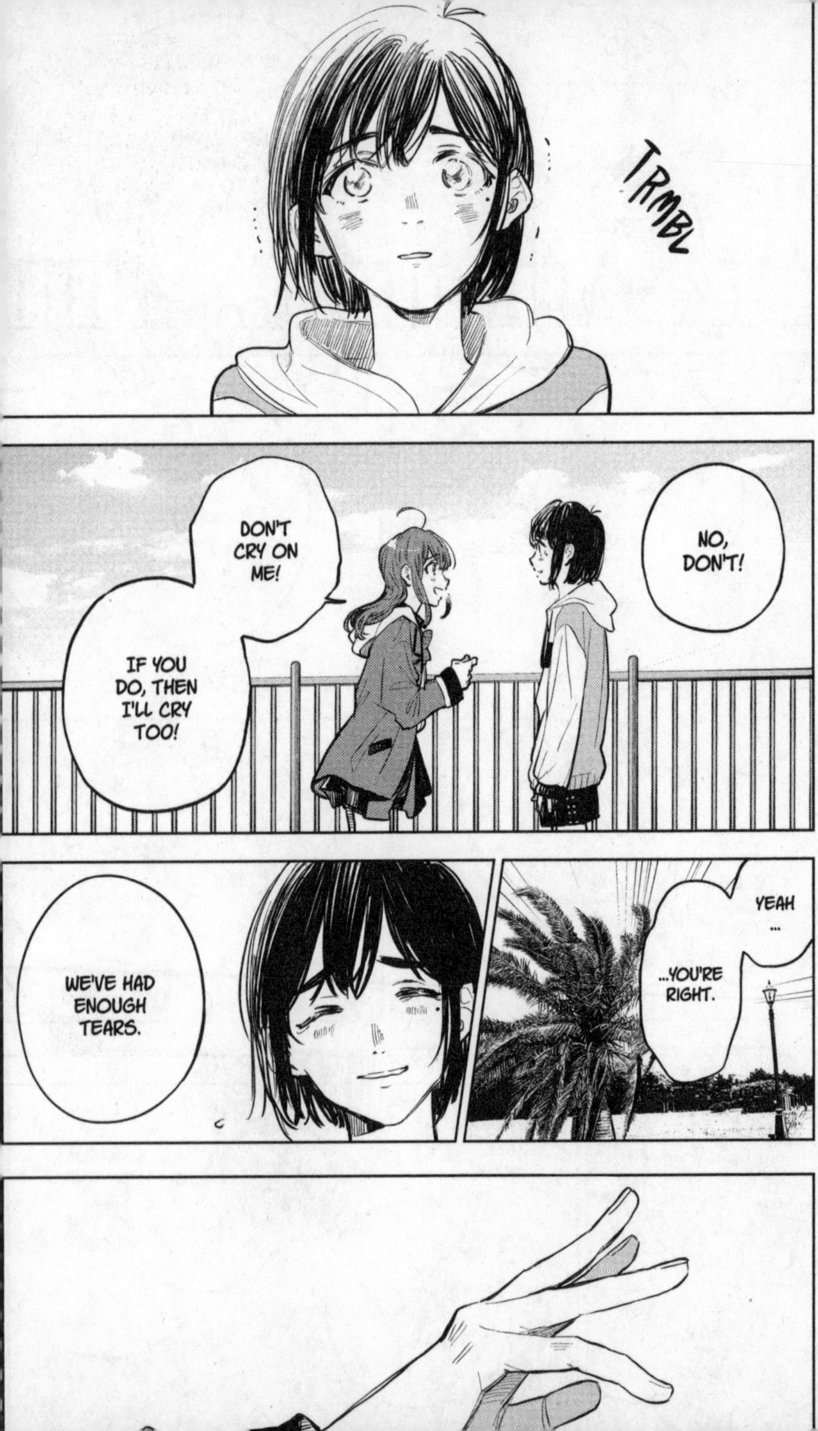
TRMBL
NO, DON'T!
DON'T CRY ON ME!
IF YOU DO, THEN I'LL CRY TOO!
YEAH ...
...YOU'RE RIGHT.
WE'VE HAD ENOUGH TEARS.

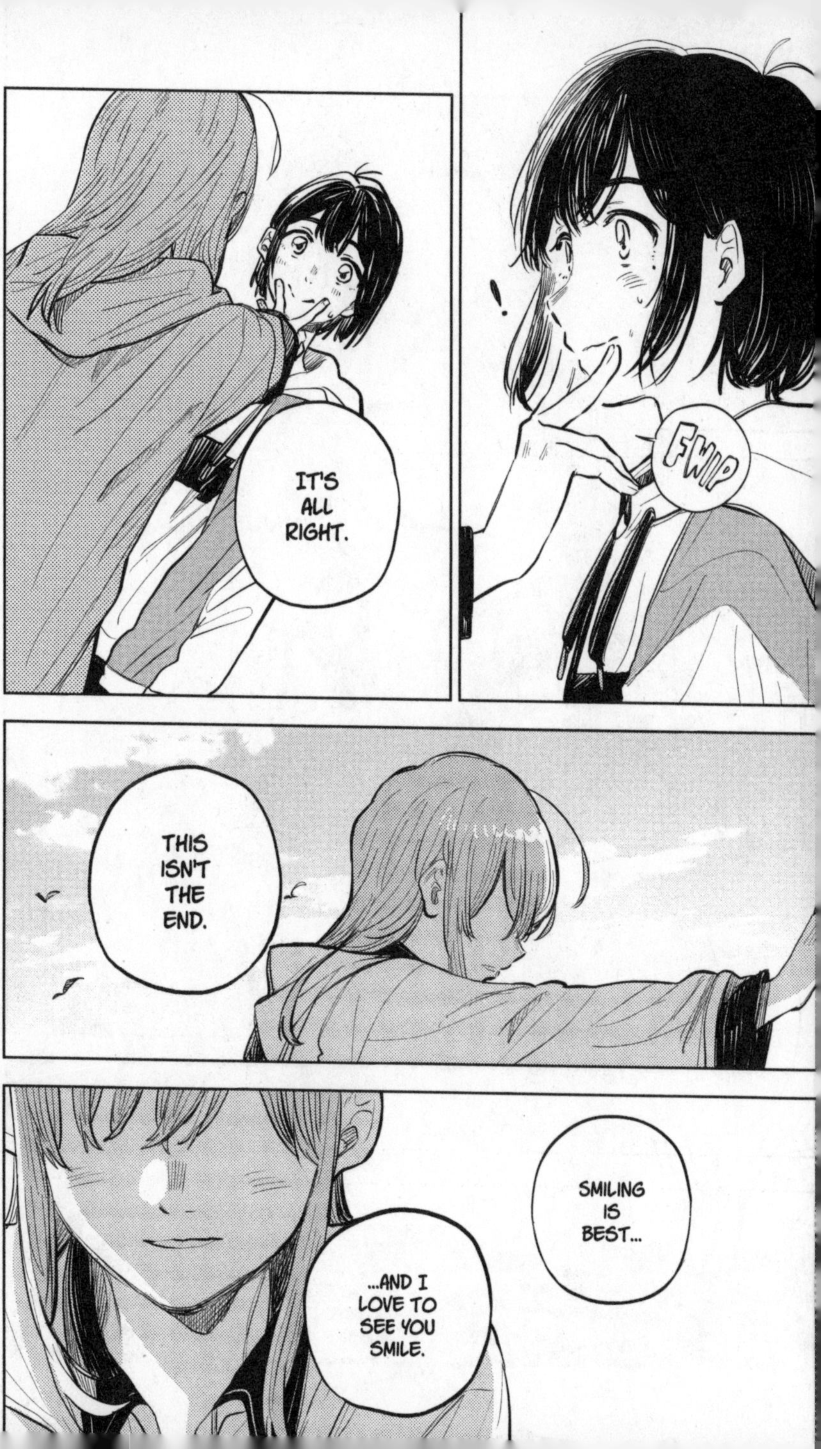
!
FWIP
IT'S ALL RIGHT.
THIS ISN'T THE END.
SMILING IS BEST...
...AND I LOVE TO SEE YOU SMILE.

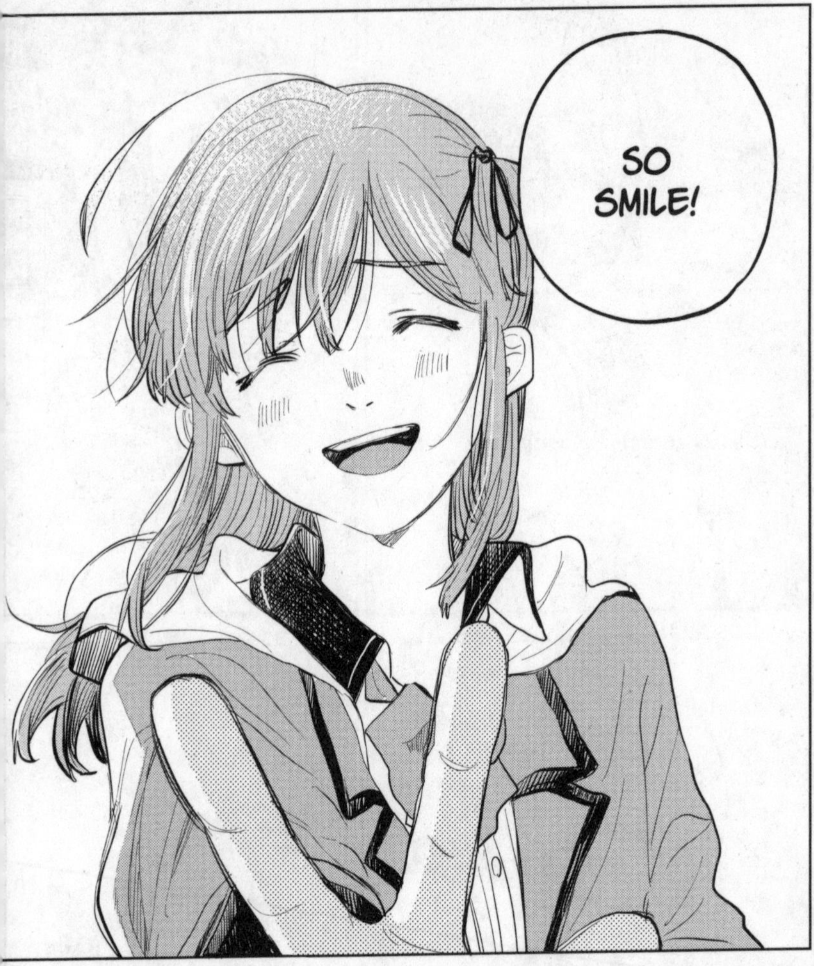
SO SMILE!

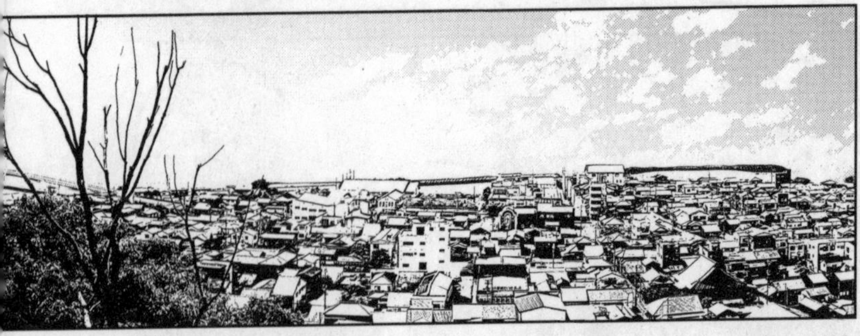

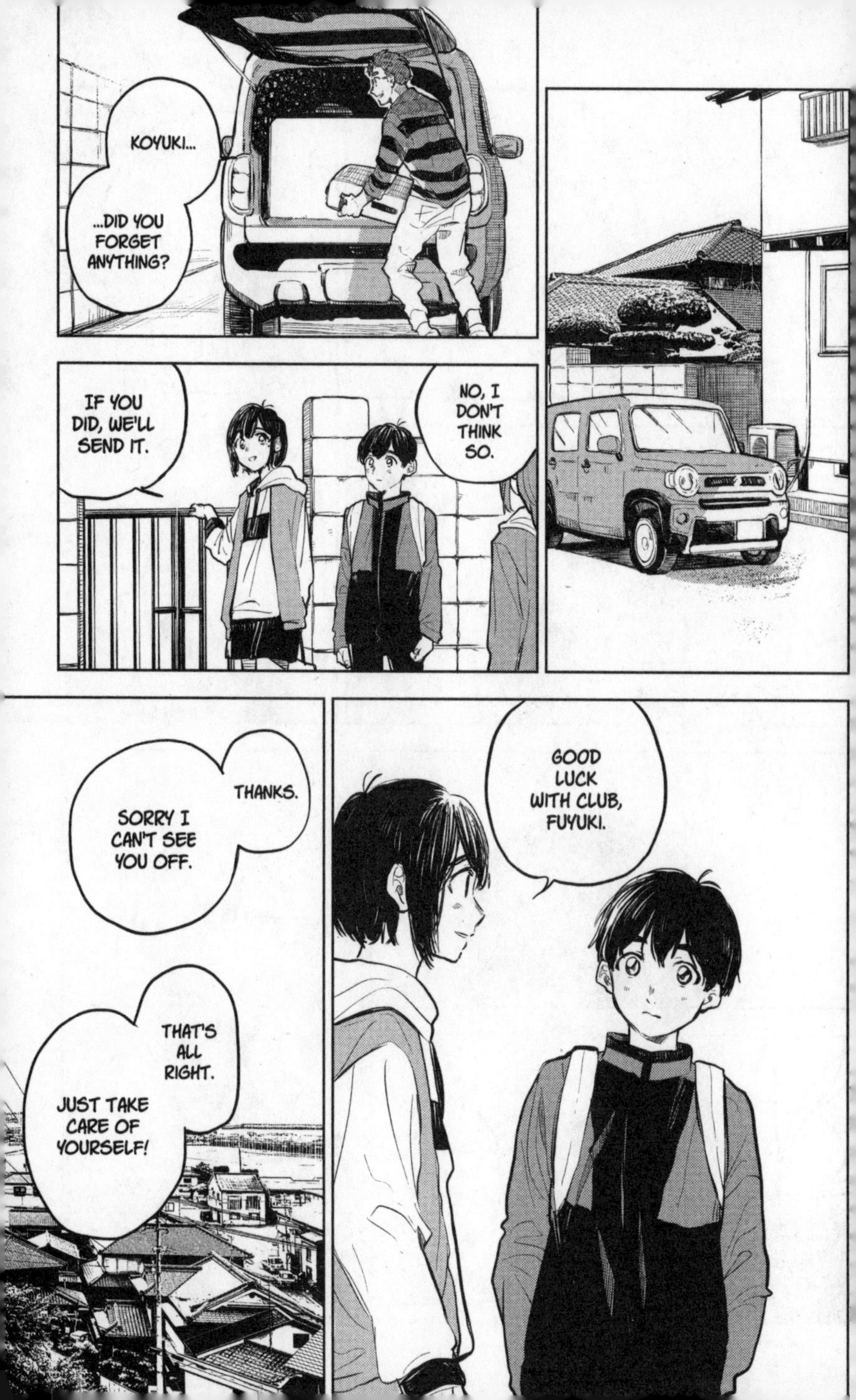
KOYUKI...
...DID YOU FORGET ANYTHING?
NO, I DON'T THINK SO.
IF YOU DID, WE'LL SEND IT.
GOOD LUCK WITH CLUB, FUYUKI.
THANKS.
SORRY I CAN'T SEE YOU OFF.
THAT'S ALL RIGHT.
JUST TAKE CARE OF YOURSELF!

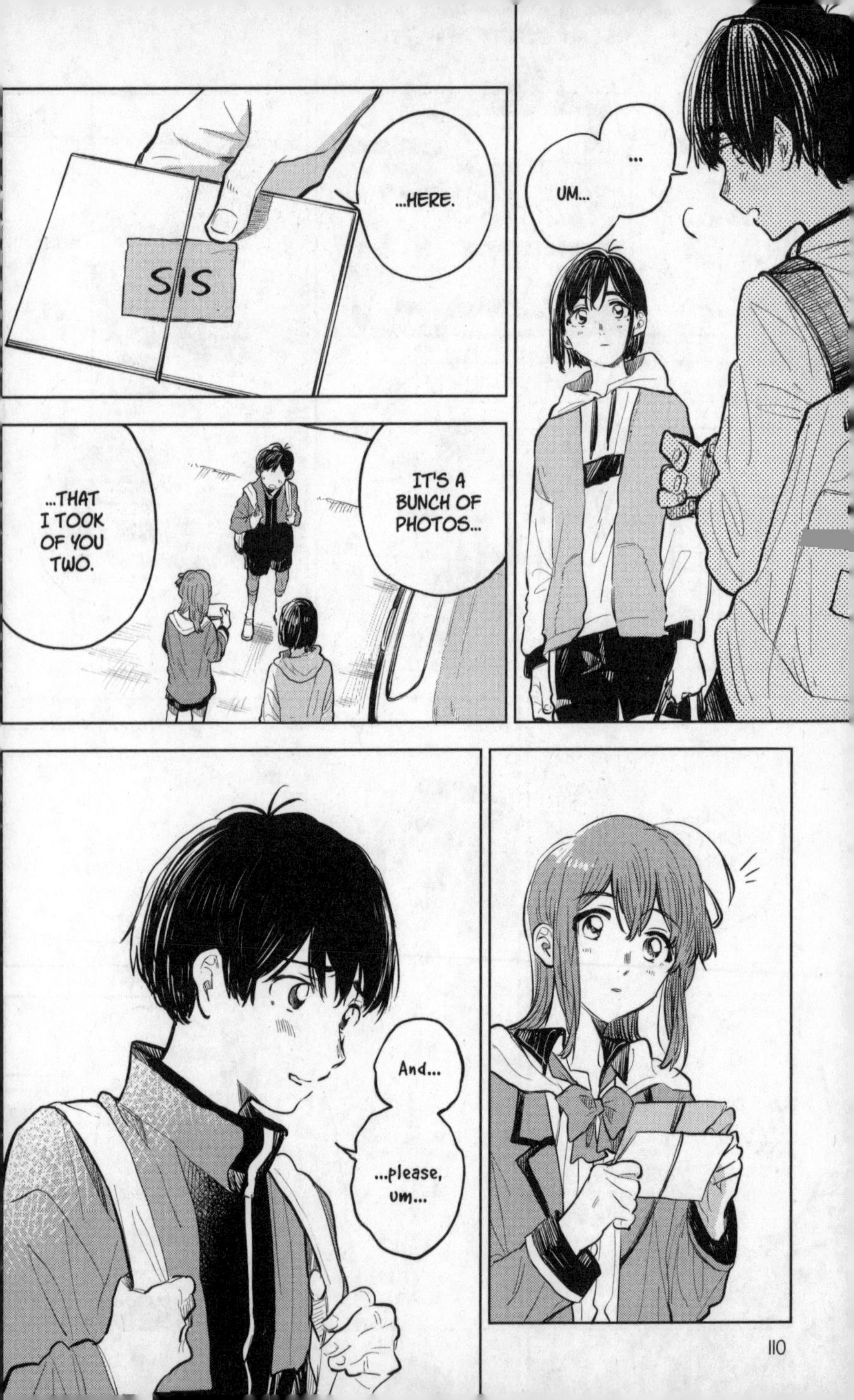
...
UM...
...HERE.
IT'S A BUNCH OF PHOTOS...
...THAT I TOOK OF YOU TWO.
SIS
And...
...please, um...

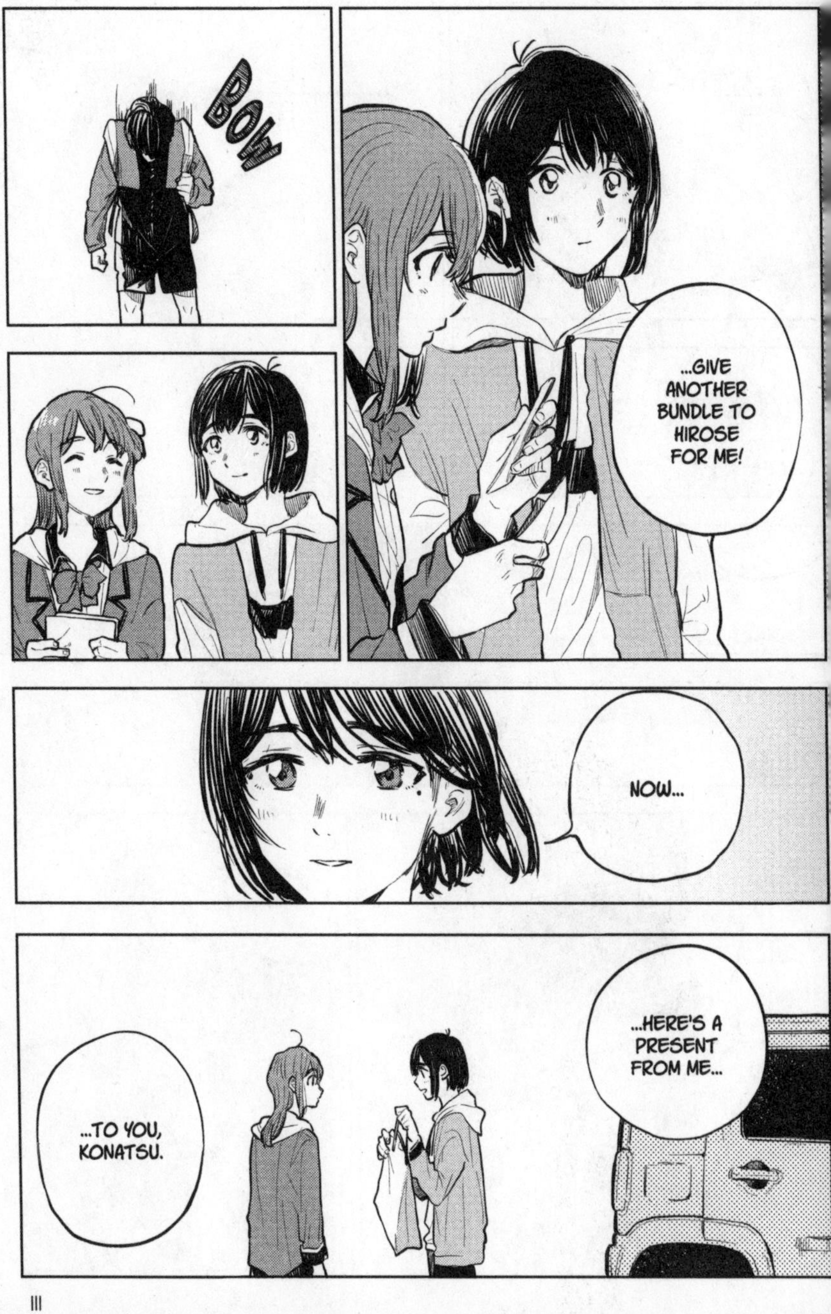
...GIVE ANOTHER BUNDLE TO HIROSE FOR ME!
BOW
NOW...
...HERE'S A PRESENT FROM ME...
...TO YOU, KONATSU.

WHAT'S INSIDE?

IT'S KINDA HEAVY.

Heh heh...

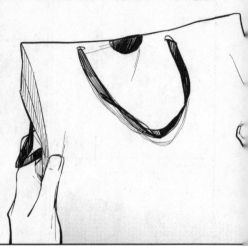

KOYUKI!

YOU'LL MISS YOUR PLANE!

DON'T LOOK YET!

WELL, I BETTER GO.

OKAY, COMING!

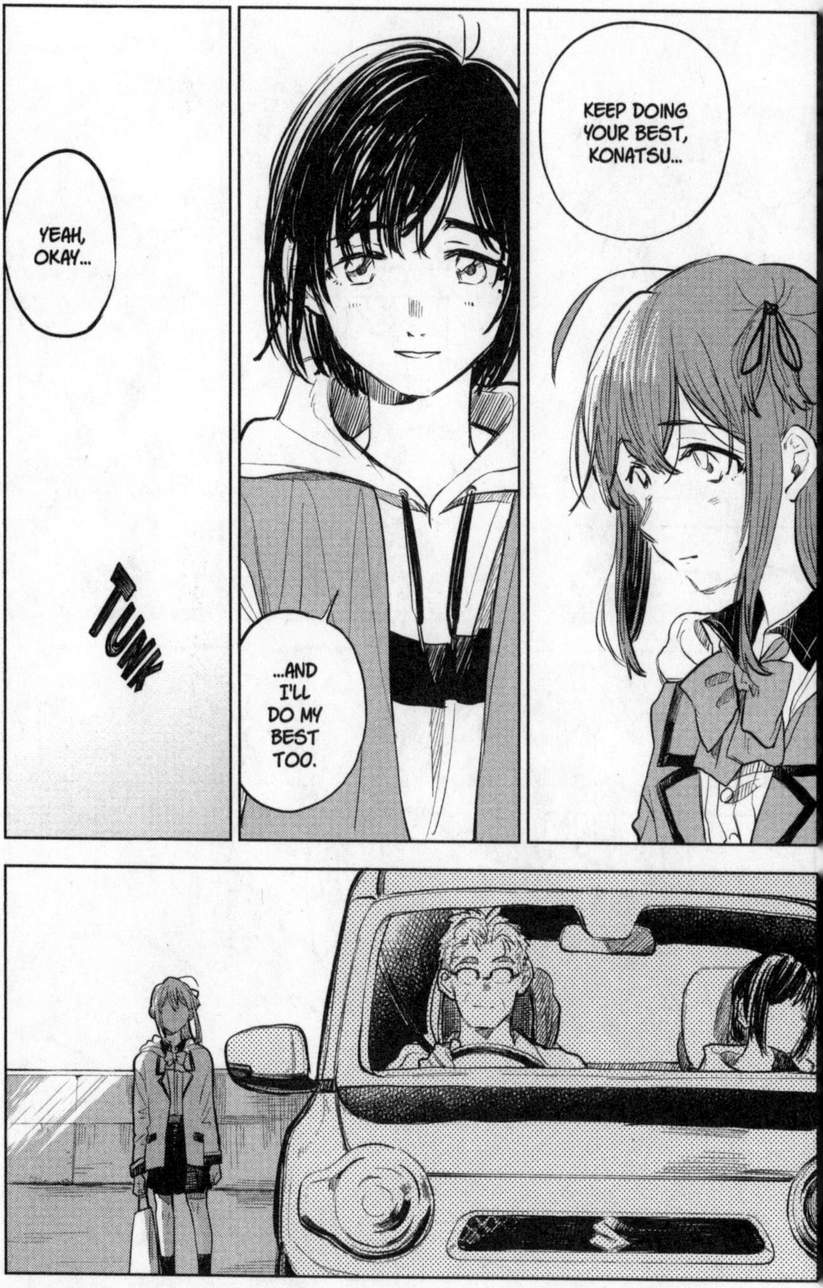
KEEP DOING YOUR BEST, KONATSU...
...AND I'LL DO MY BEST TOO.
YEAH, OKAY...
TUNK

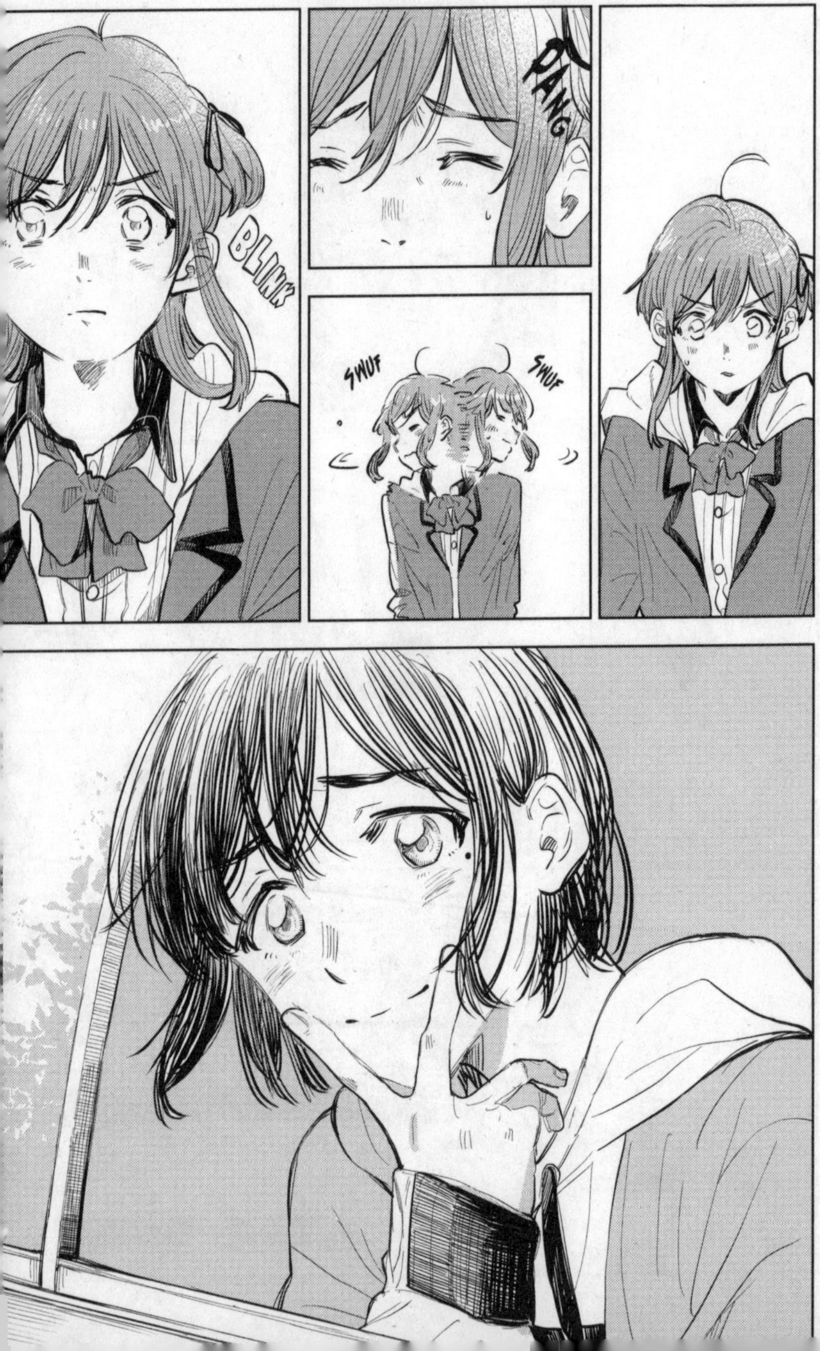
DANG
SWUF
SWUF
BLINK

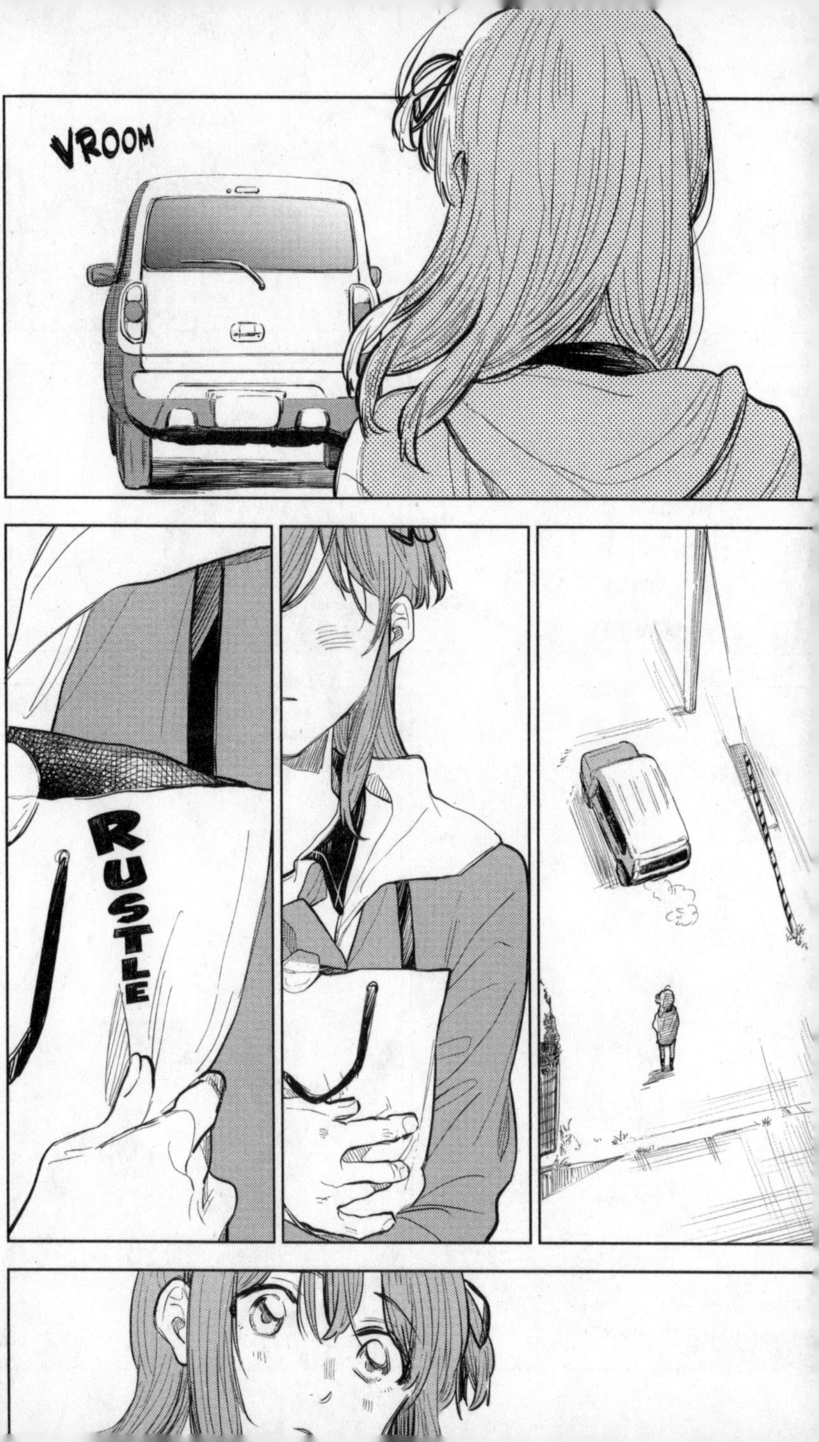
VROOM
RUSTLE

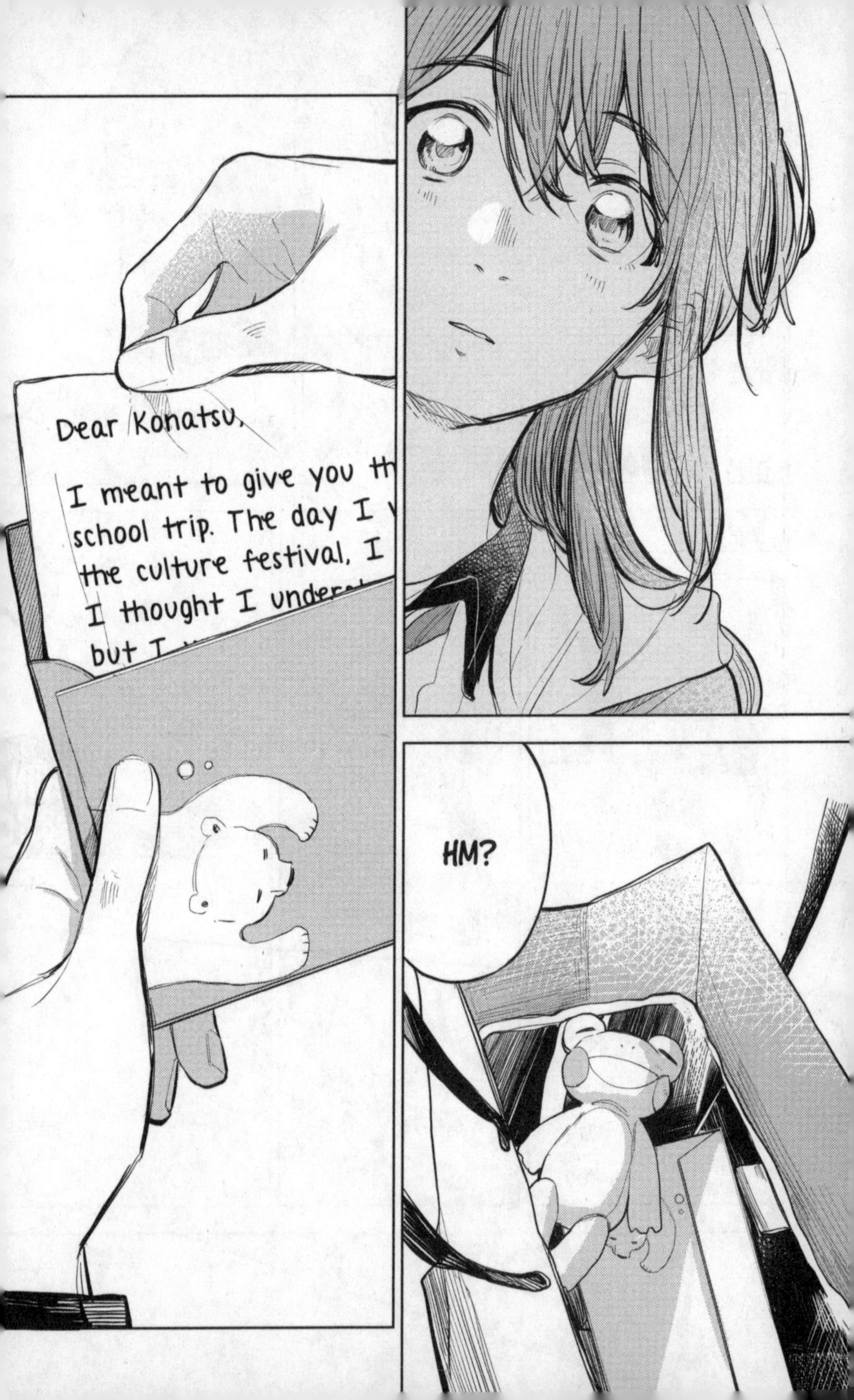
HM?
Dear Konatsu,
I meant to give you
school trip. The day I
the culture festival, I
I thought I
but I

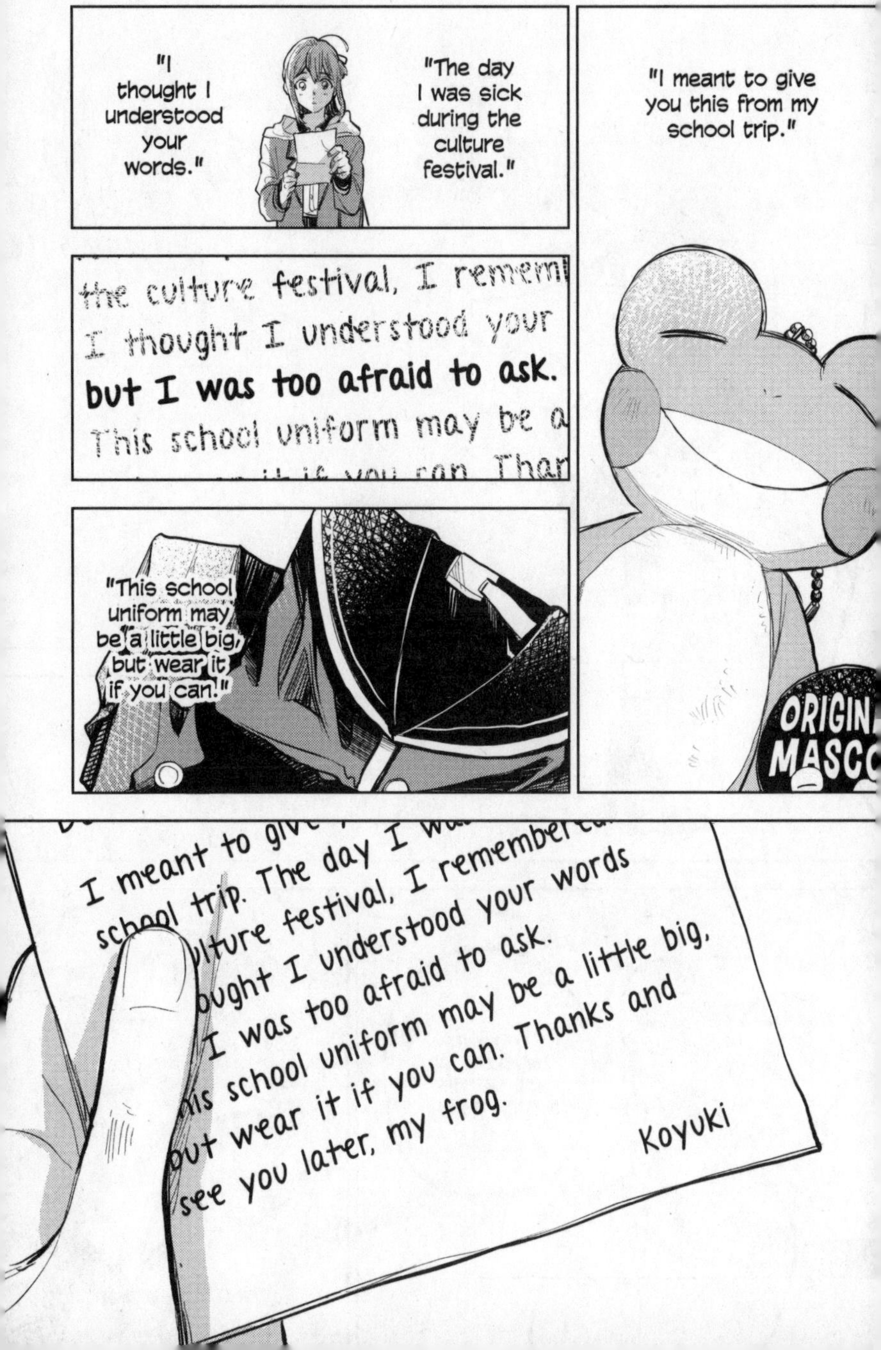
"I meant to give you this from my school trip."
"The day I was sick during the culture festival."
"I thought I understood your words."
the culture festival, I rememl
I thought I understood your
but I was too afraid to ask.
This school uniform may be a
"This school uniform may be a little big, but wear it if you can."
ORIGIN
MASCO
I meant to give
school trip. The day I wa
ulture festival, I remembered
ought I understood your words
I was too afraid to ask.
is school uniform may be a little big,
out wear it if you can. Thanks and
see you later, my frog.
Koyuki

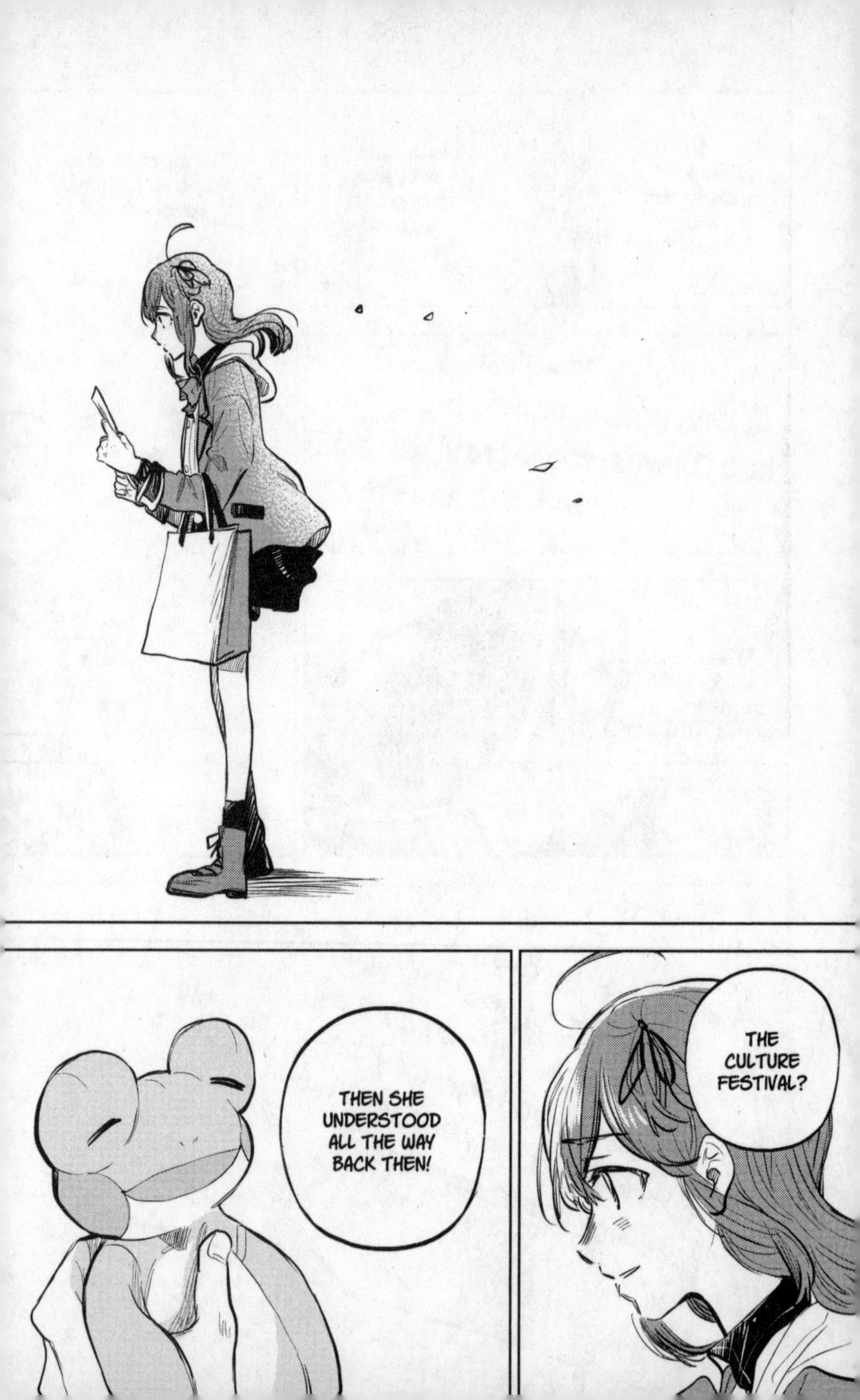
THE CULTURE FESTIVAL?
THEN SHE UNDERSTOOD ALL THE WAY BACK THEN!

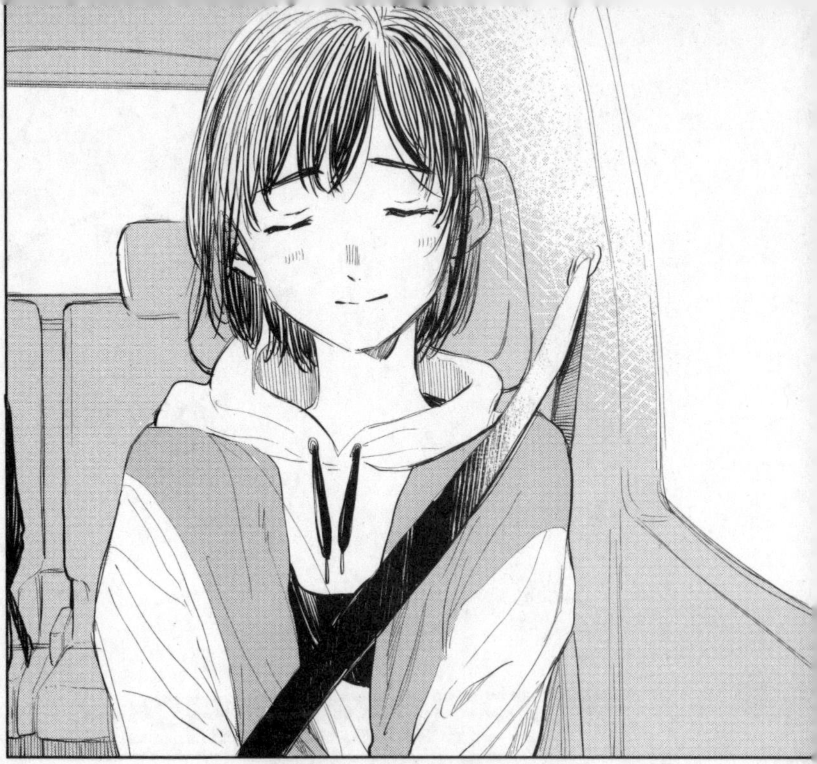
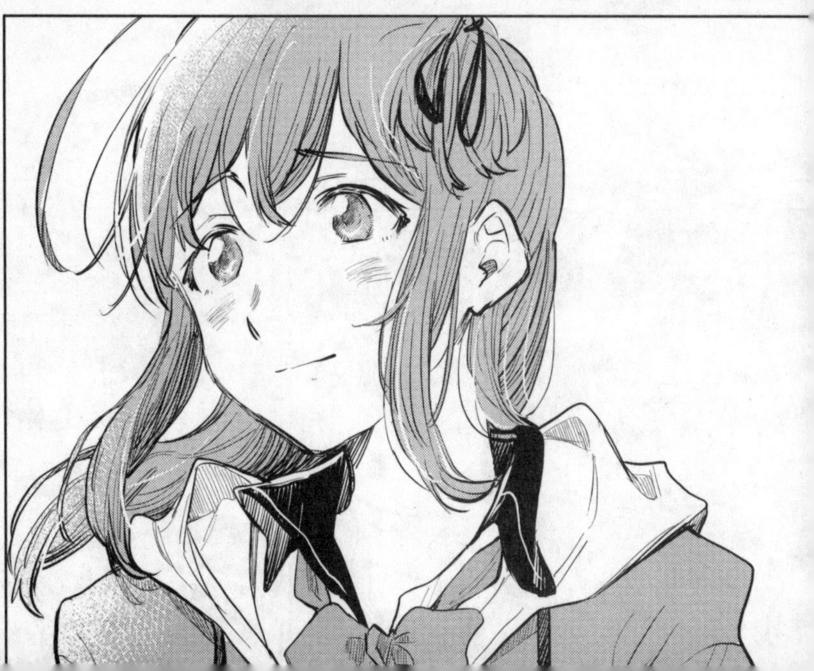

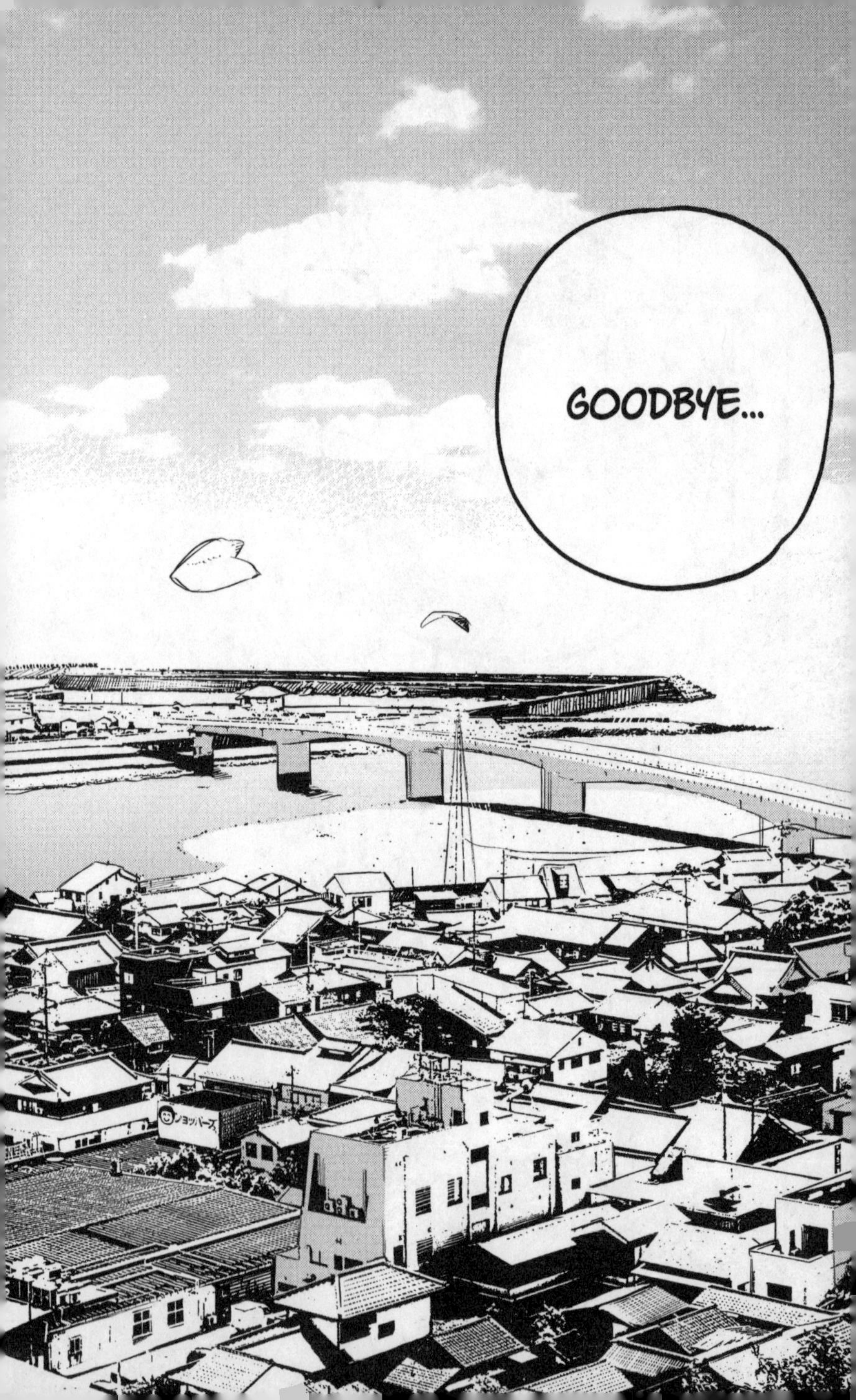
GOODBYE...
ショッパーズ

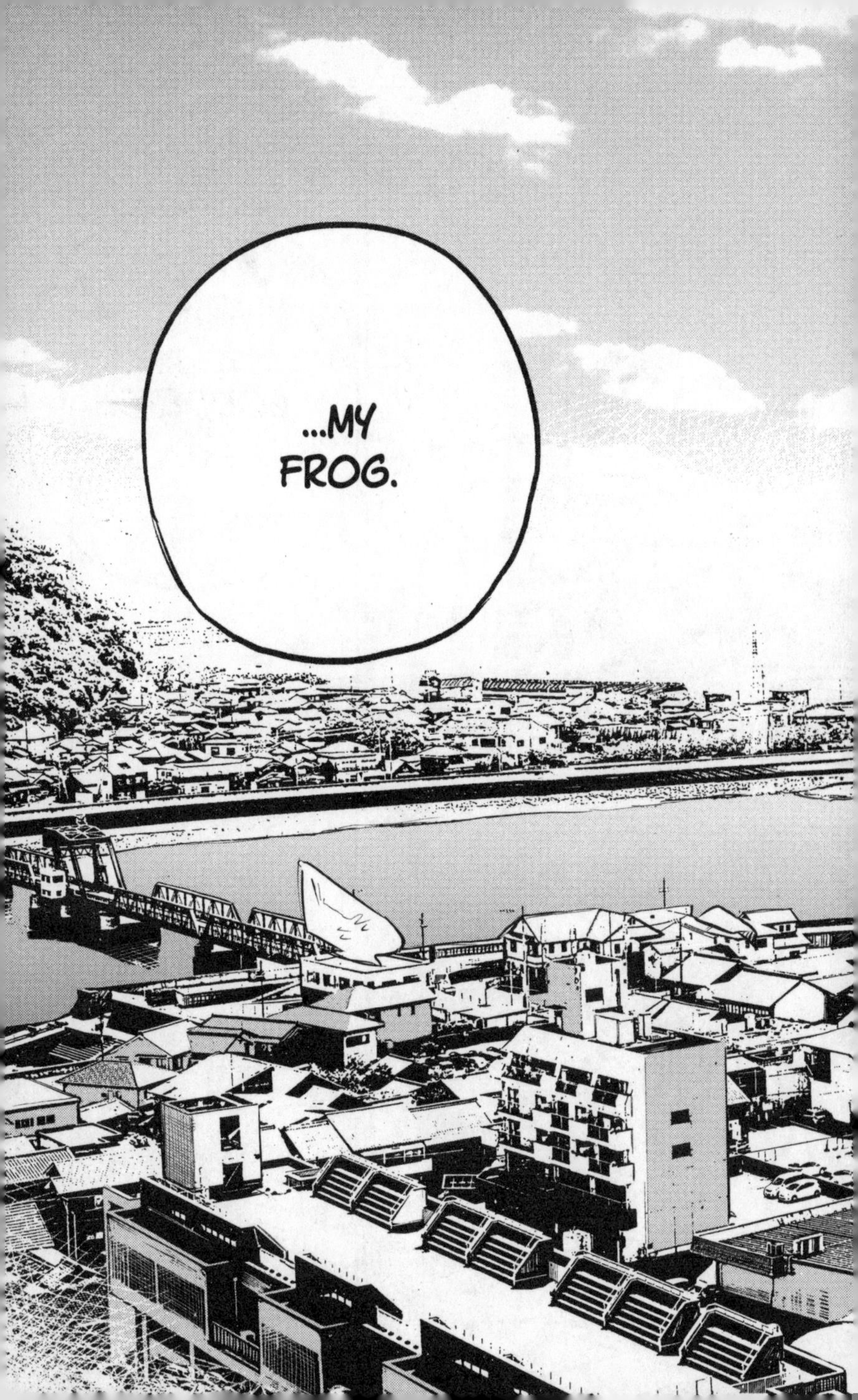
...MY FROG.

Good morning!

CHATTER

CHATTER

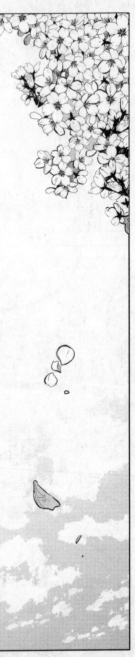

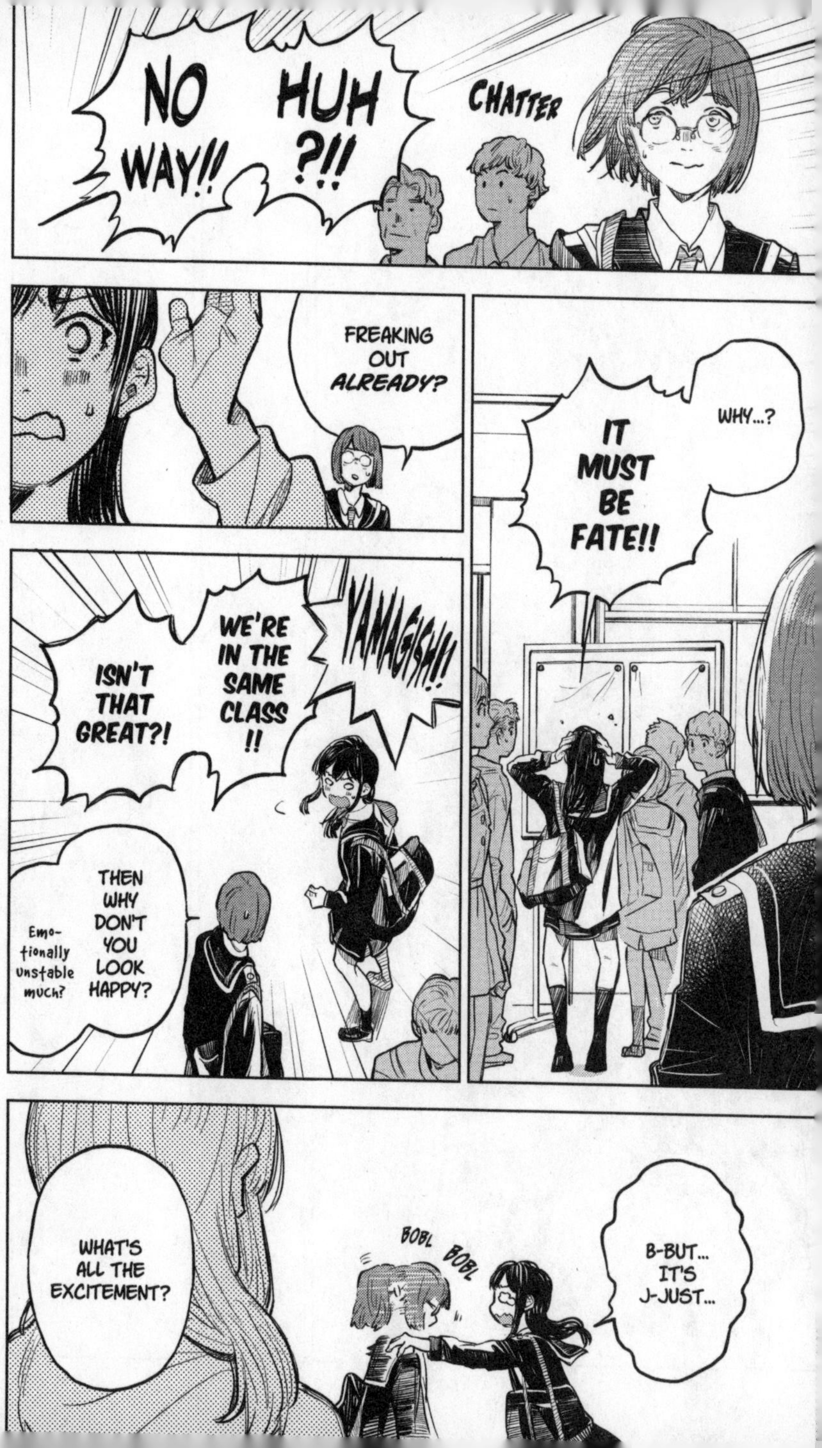
CHATTER
HUH ?!!
NO WAY!!
WHY...?
IT MUST BE FATE!!
FREAKING OUT ALREADY?
YAMAGISHI!!
WE'RE IN THE SAME CLASS !!
ISN'T THAT GREAT?!
THEN WHY DON'T YOU LOOK HAPPY?
Emo-tionally unstable much?
B-BUT... IT'S J-JUST...
BOBL BOBL
WHAT'S ALL THE EXCITEMENT?

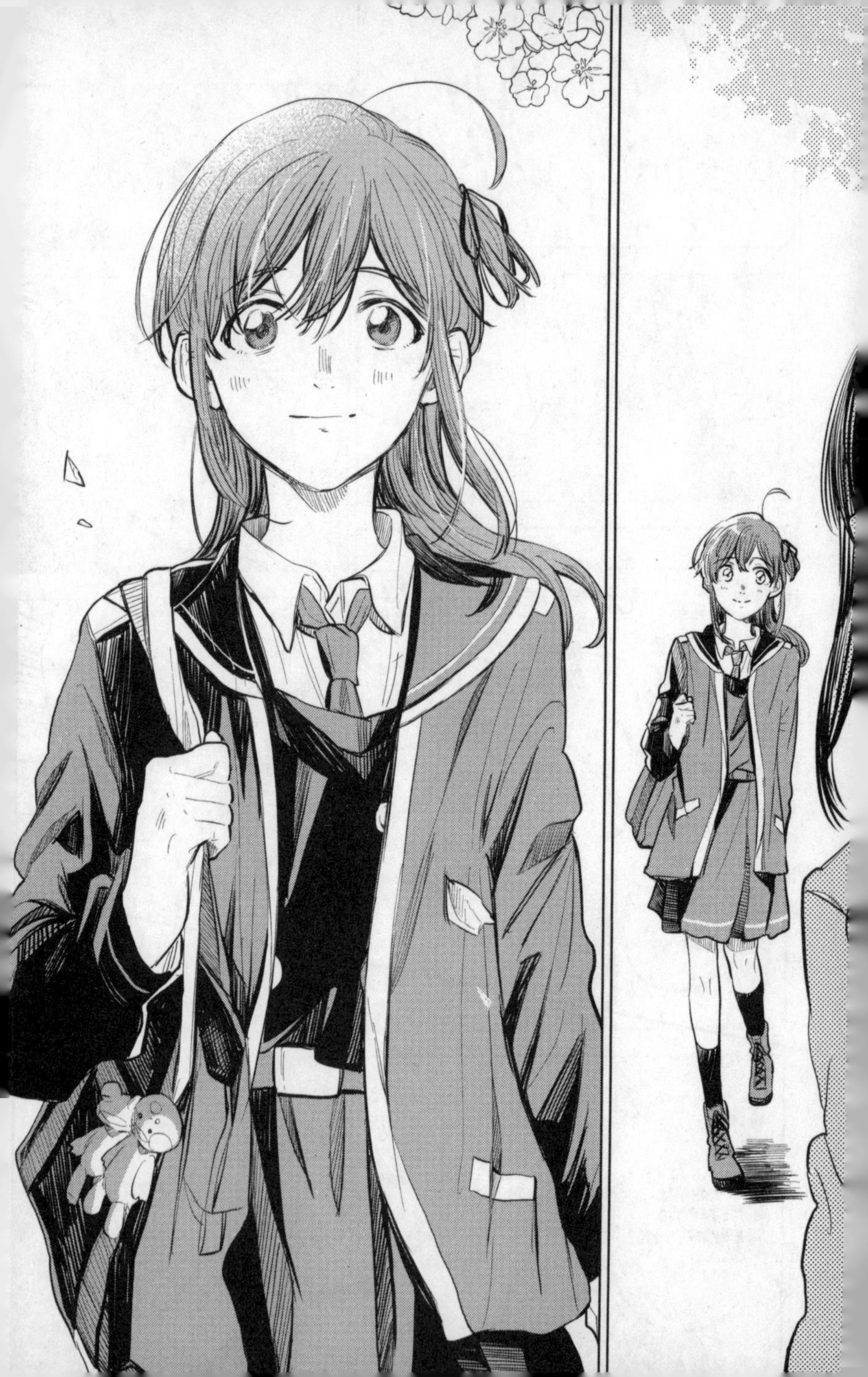

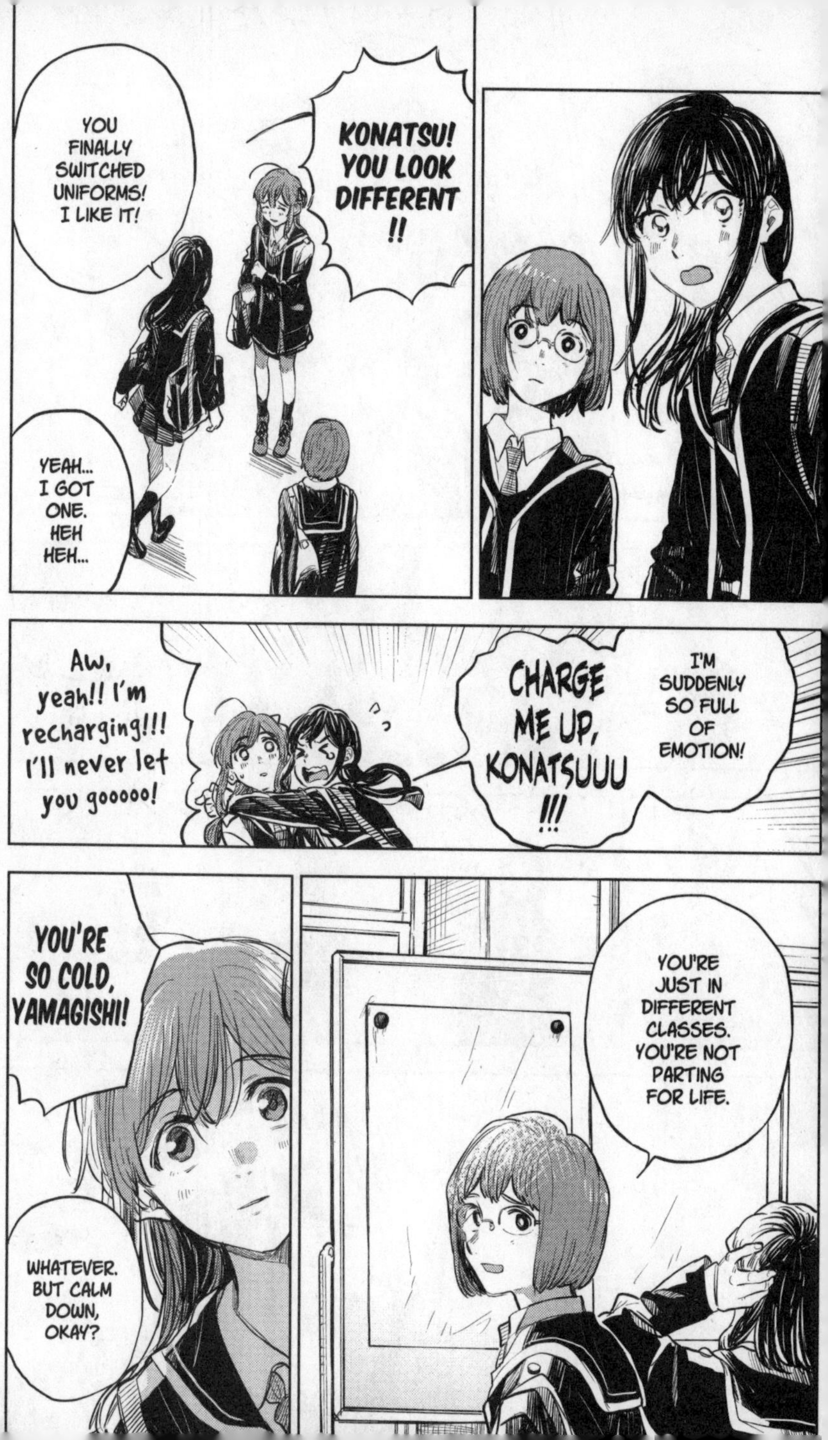
KONATSU! YOU LOOK DIFFERENT !!
YOU FINALLY SWITCHED UNIFORMS! I LIKE IT!
YEAH... I GOT ONE. HEH HEH...
I'M SUDDENLY SO FULL OF EMOTION!
CHARGE ME UP, KONATSUUU !!!
Aw, yeah!! I'm recharging!!! I'll never let you gooooo!
YOU'RE JUST IN DIFFERENT CLASSES. YOU'RE NOT PARTING FOR LIFE.
YOU'RE SO COLD, YAMAGISHI!
WHATEVER. BUT CALM DOWN, OKAY?

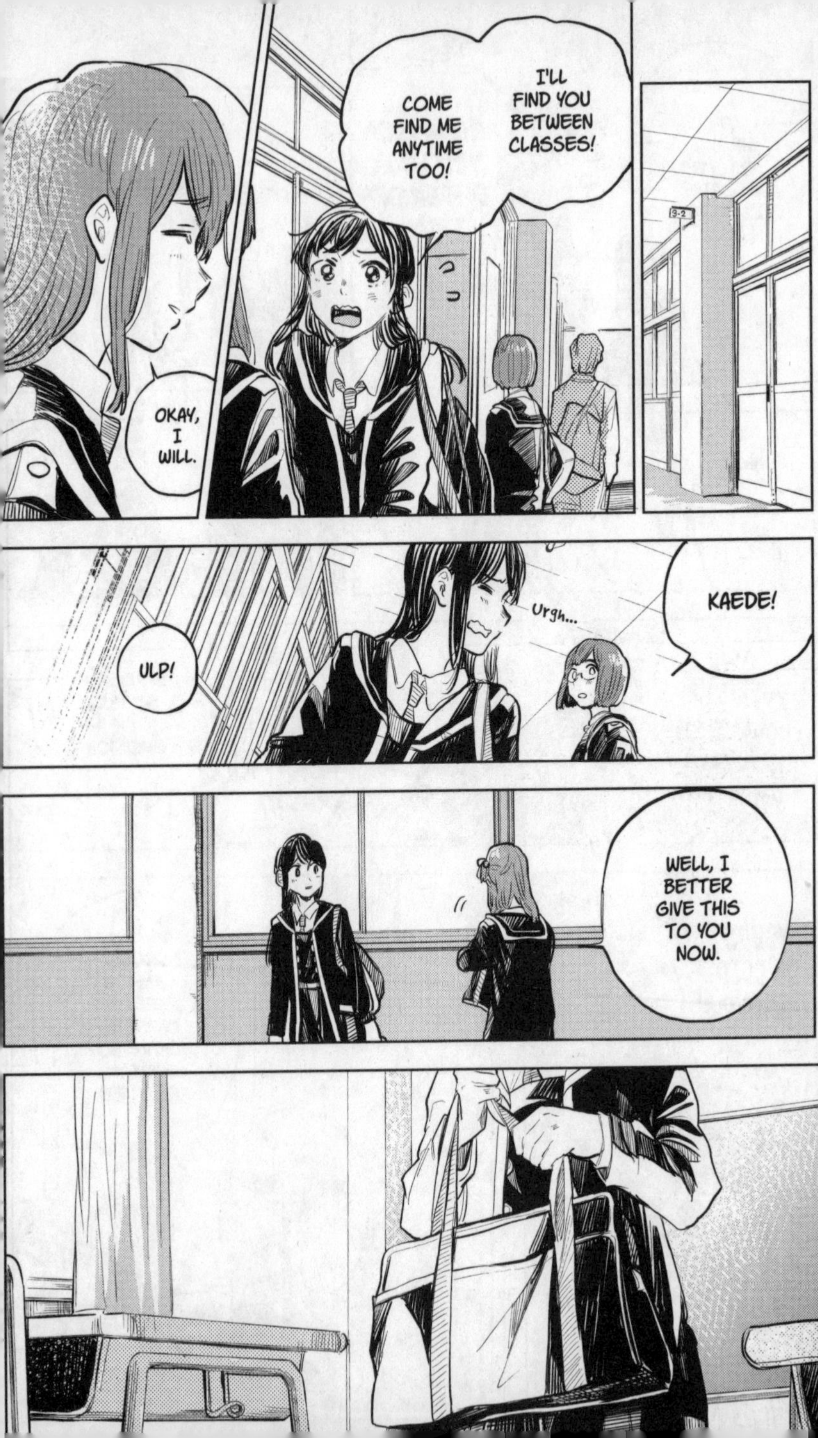
I'LL FIND YOU BETWEEN CLASSES!
COME FIND ME ANYTIME TOO!
OKAY, I WILL.
KAEDE!
Urgh...
ULP!
WELL, I BETTER GIVE THIS TO YOU NOW.

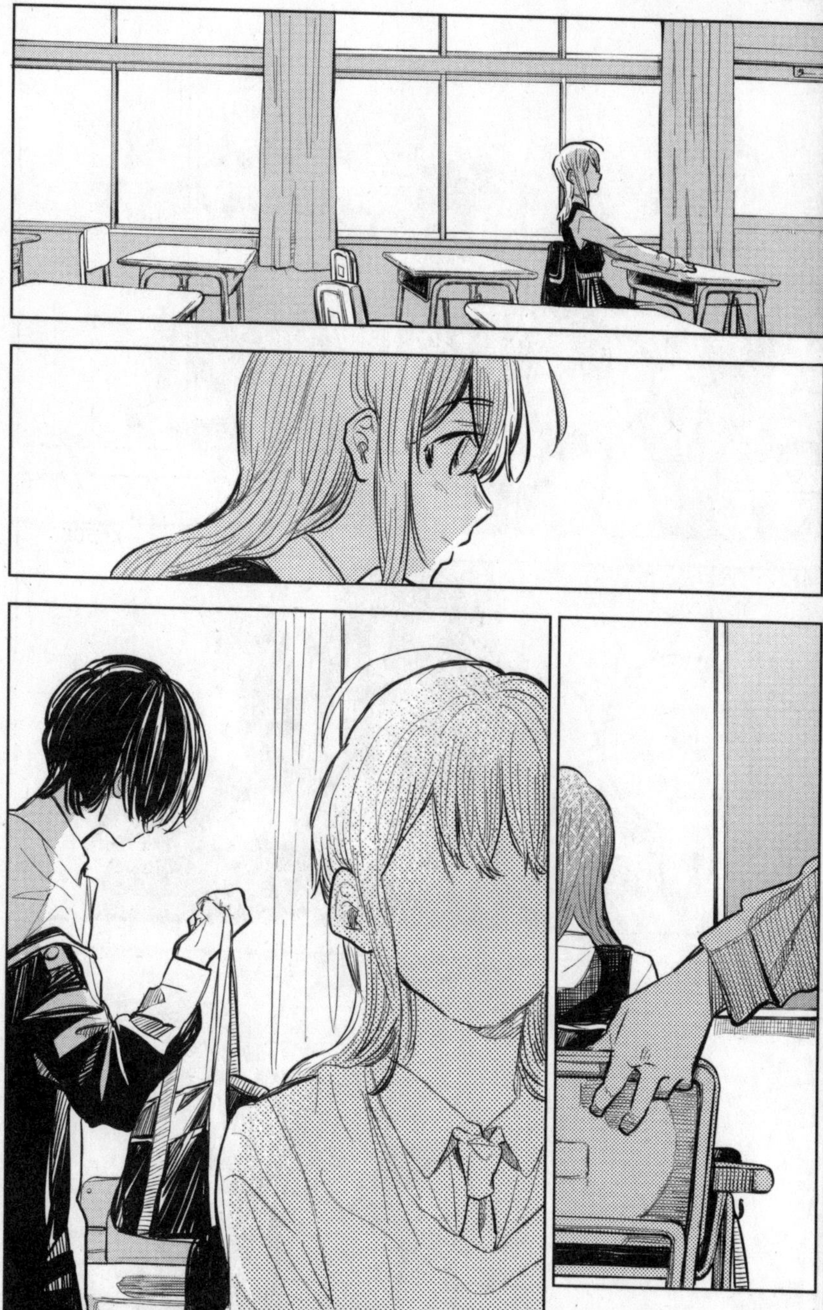

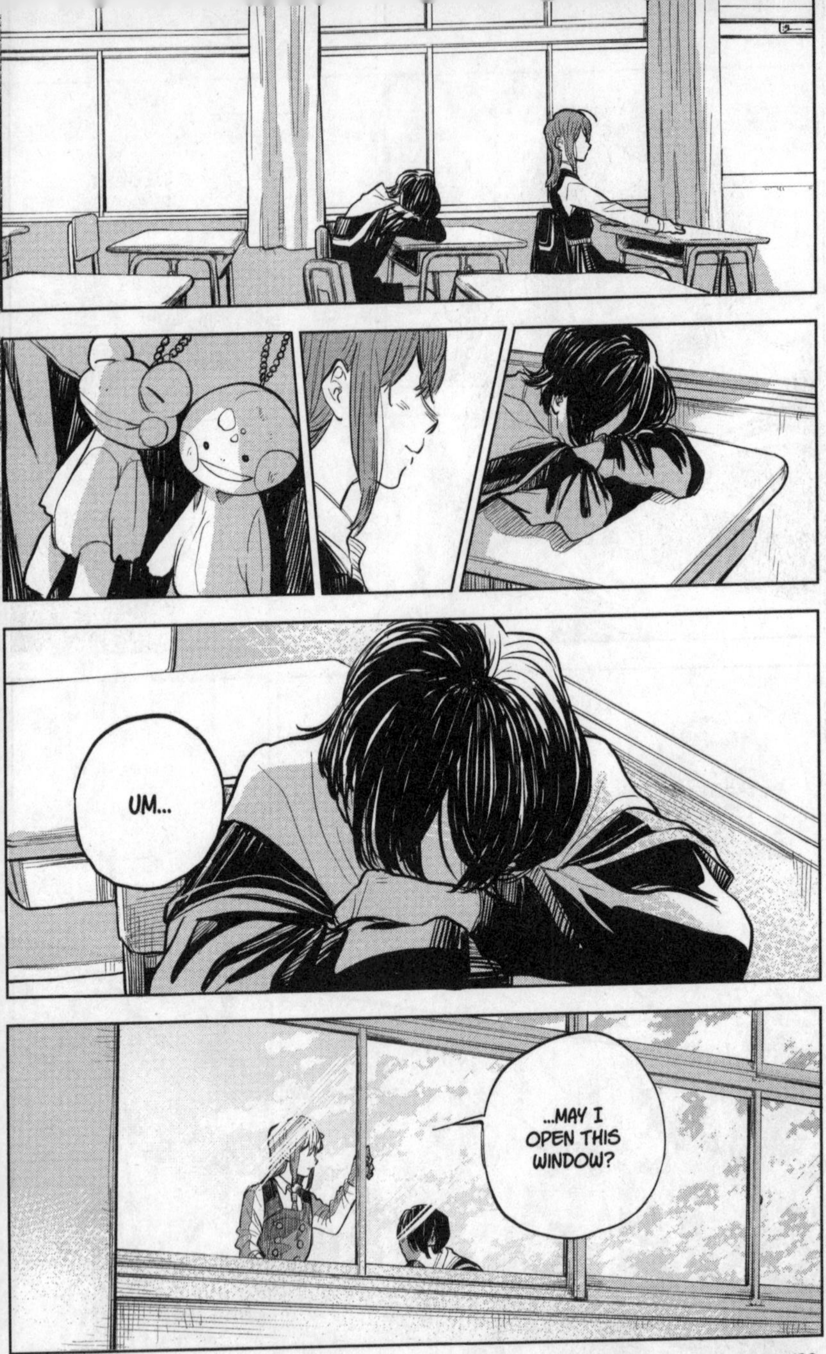
UM...
...MAY I OPEN THIS WINDOW?

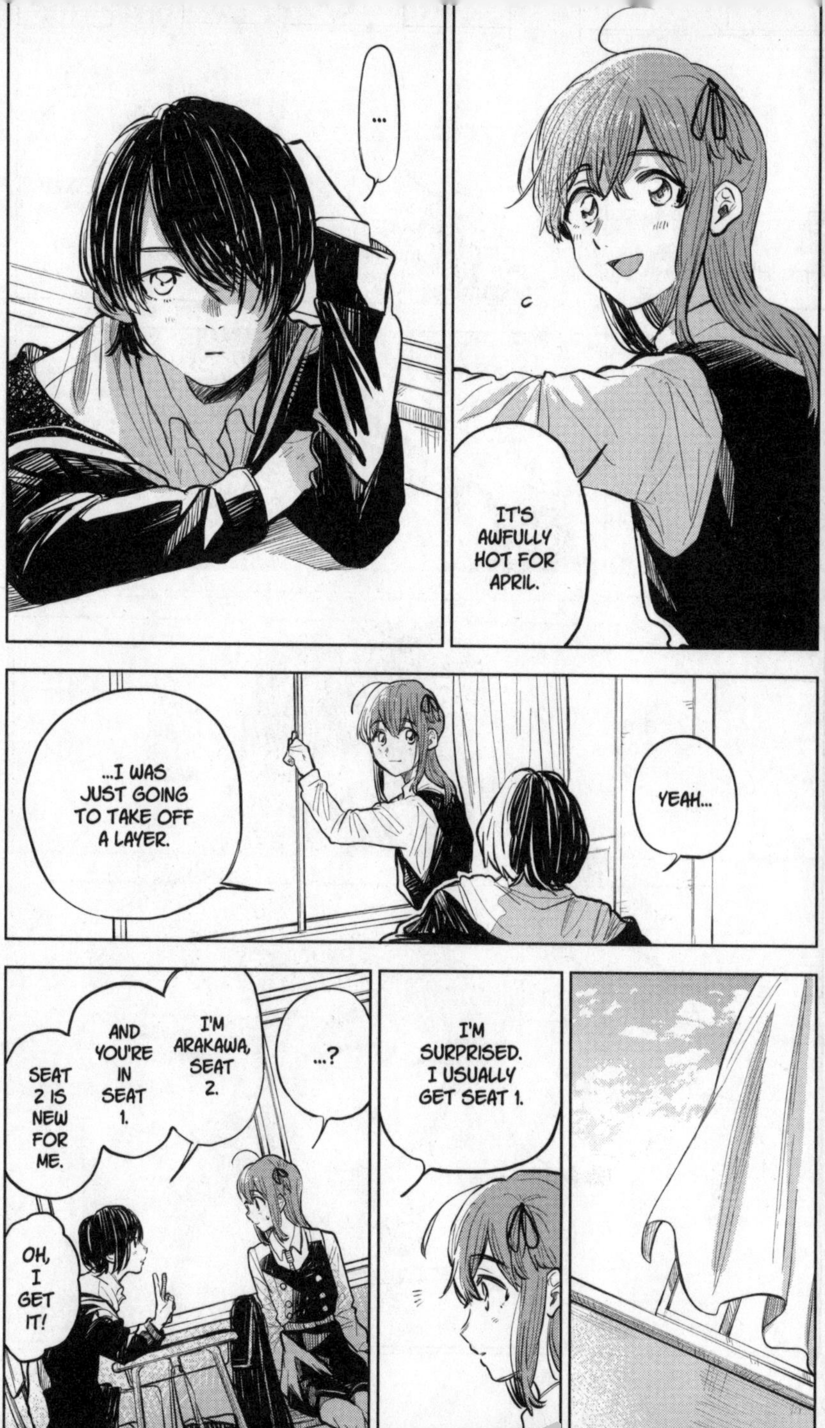
IT'S AWFULLY HOT FOR APRIL.
...
YEAH...
...I WAS JUST GOING TO TAKE OFF A LAYER.
I'M SURPRISED. I USUALLY GET SEAT 1.
...?
I'M ARAKAWA, SEAT 2. AND YOU'RE IN SEAT 1. SEAT 2 IS NEW FOR ME.
OH, I GET IT!

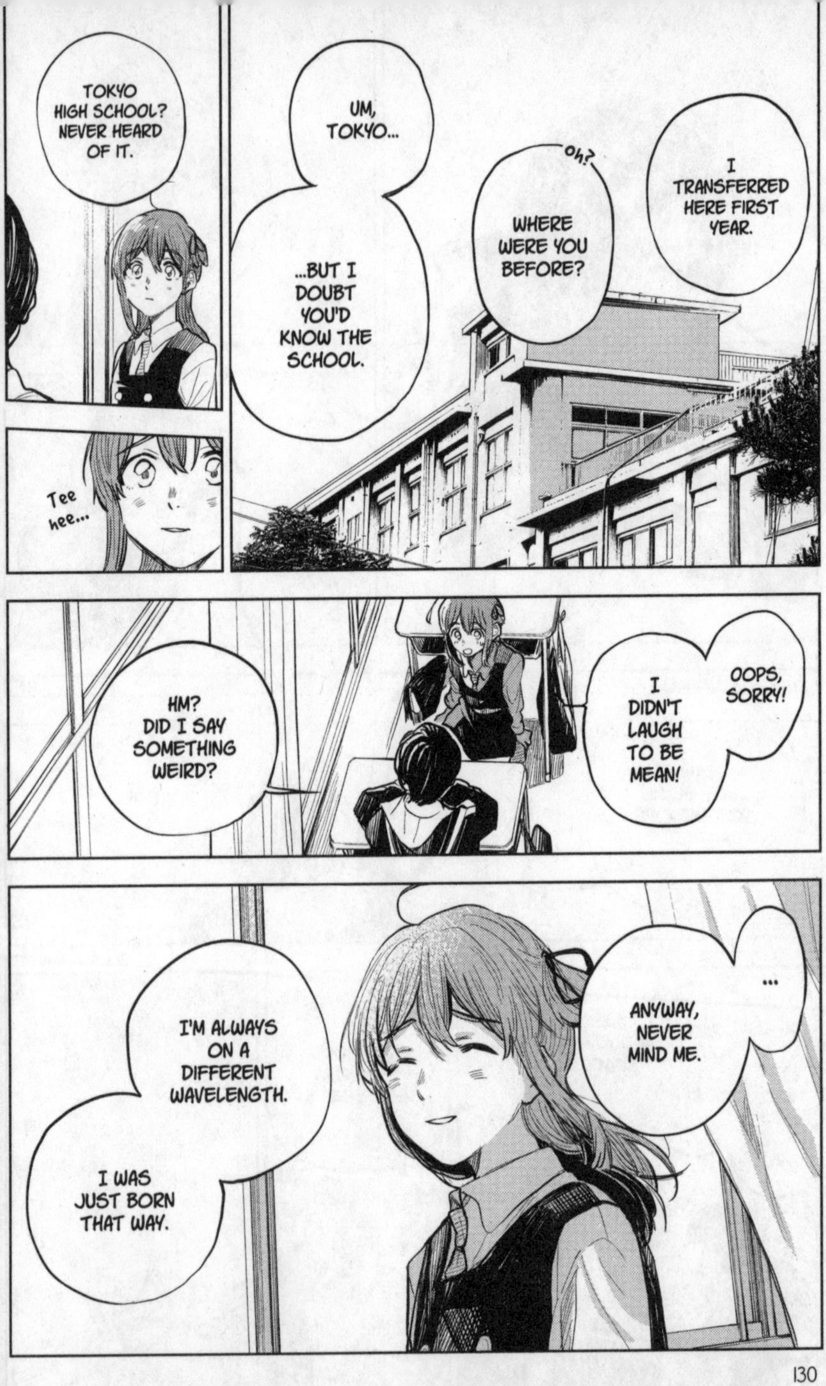
I TRANSFERRED HERE FIRST YEAR.
Oh?
WHERE WERE YOU BEFORE?
UM, TOKYO... ...BUT I DOUBT YOU'D KNOW THE SCHOOL.
TOKYO HIGH SCHOOL? NEVER HEARD OF IT.
Tee hee...
OOPS, SORRY! I DIDN'T LAUGH TO BE MEAN!
HM? DID I SAY SOMETHING WEIRD?
... ANYWAY, NEVER MIND ME.
I'M ALWAYS ON A DIFFERENT WAVELENGTH. I WAS JUST BORN THAT WAY.

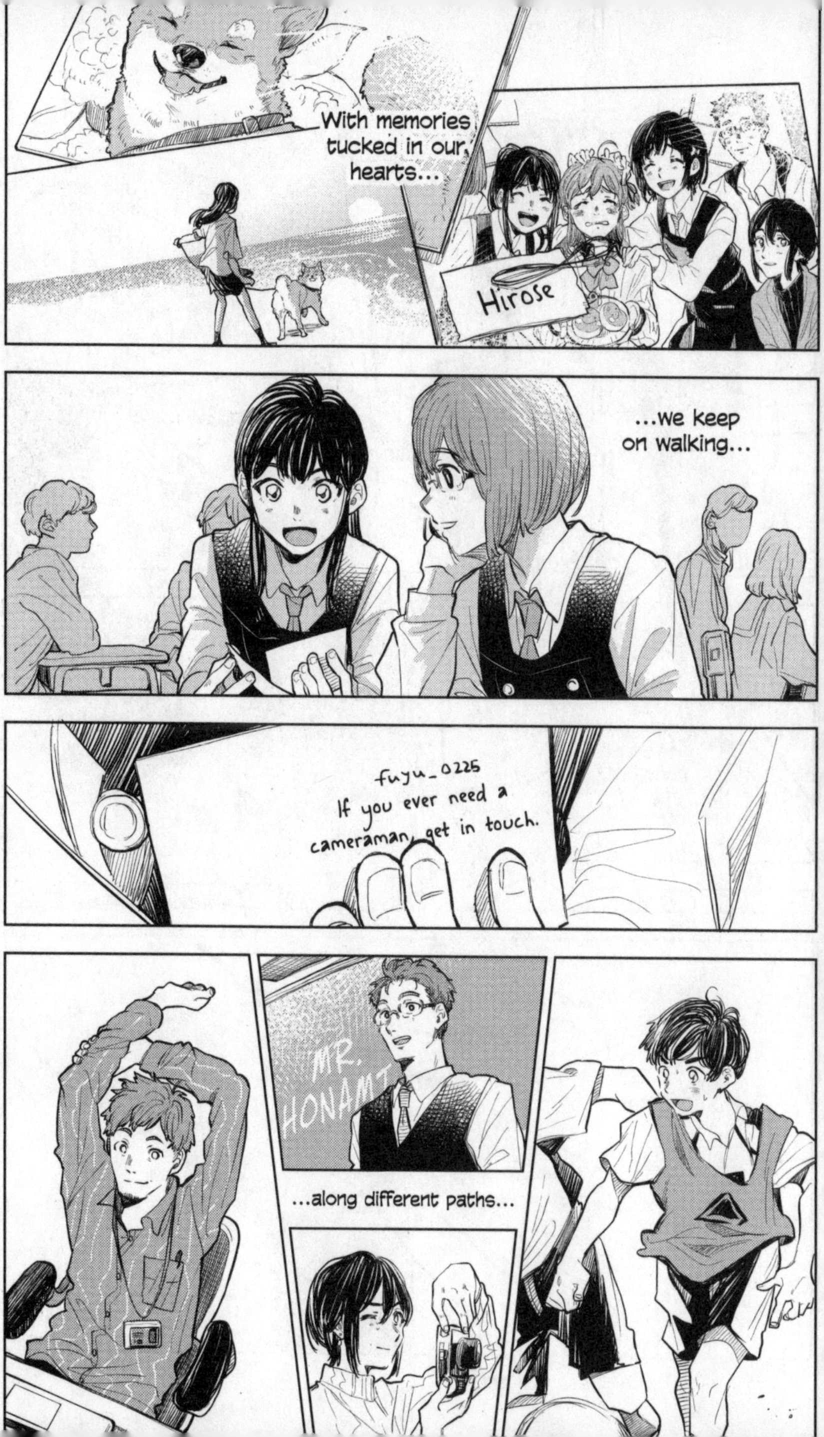
With memories tucked in our hearts...
Hirose
...we keep on walking...
fuyu_0225
If you ever need a cameraman, get in touch.
MR. HONAMI
...along different paths...

...each heading toward a unique future.

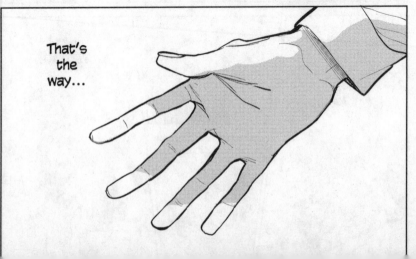

That's the way...

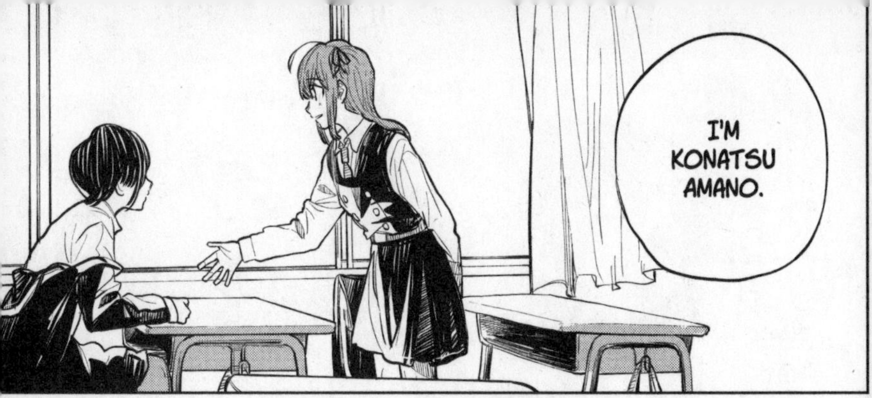
I'M KONATSU AMANO.
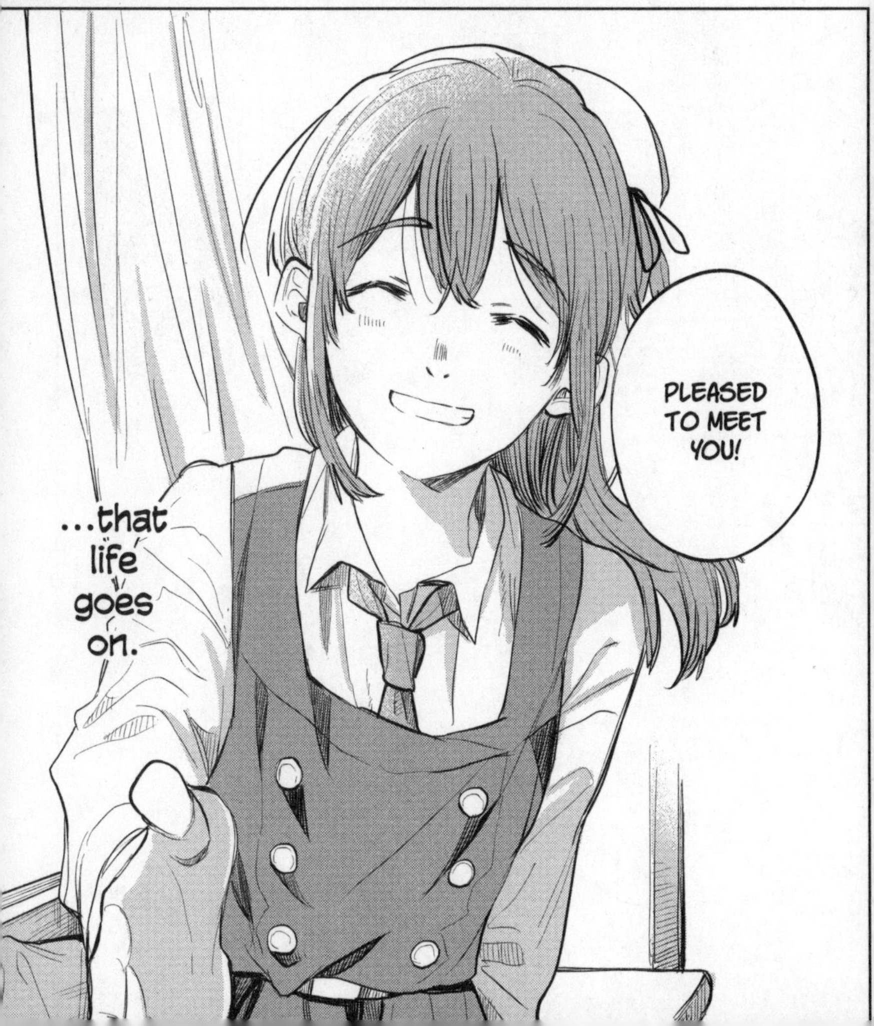
PLEASED TO MEET YOU!
...that life goes on.

A Tropical Fish
Yearns for Snow

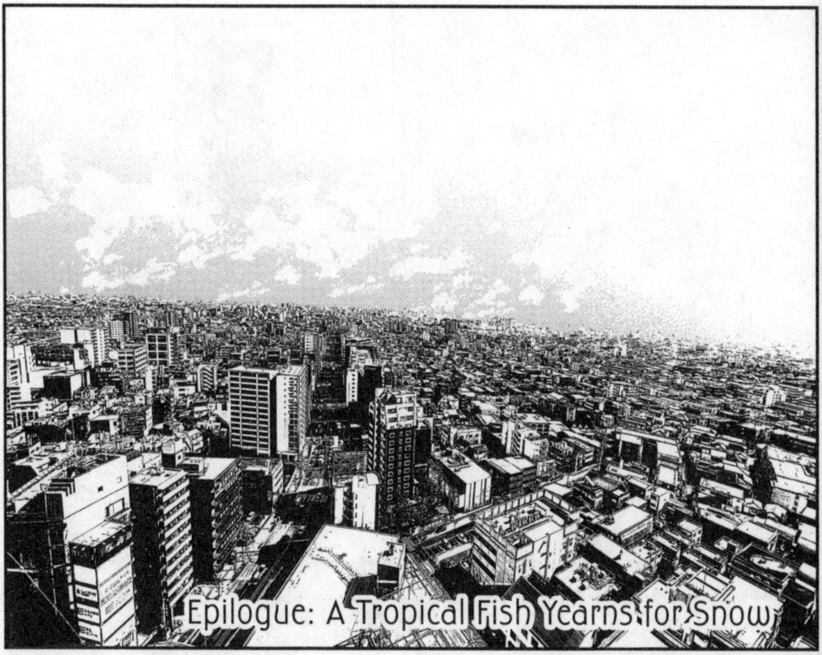
Epilogue: A Tropical Fish Yearns for Snow

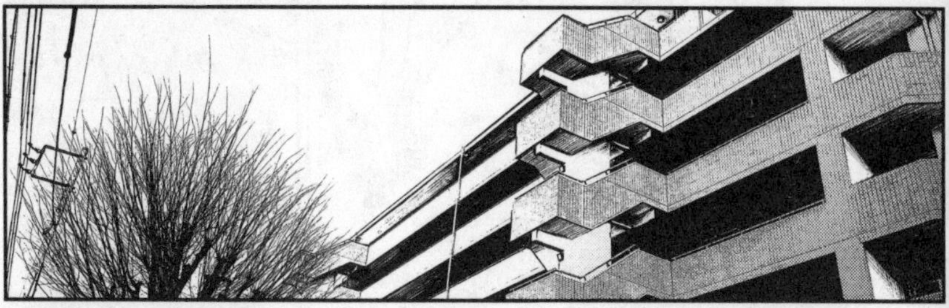

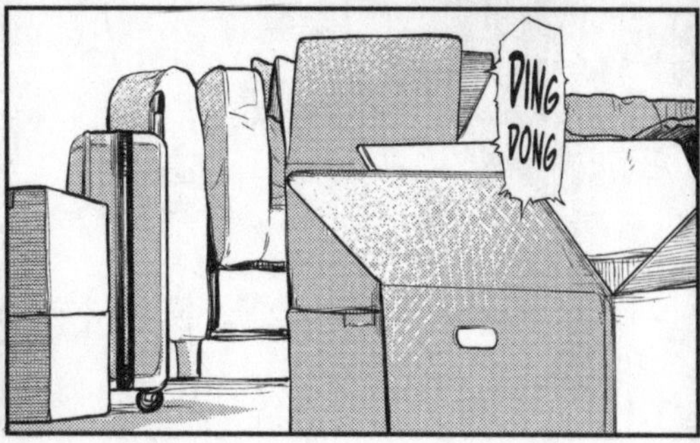
DING DONG

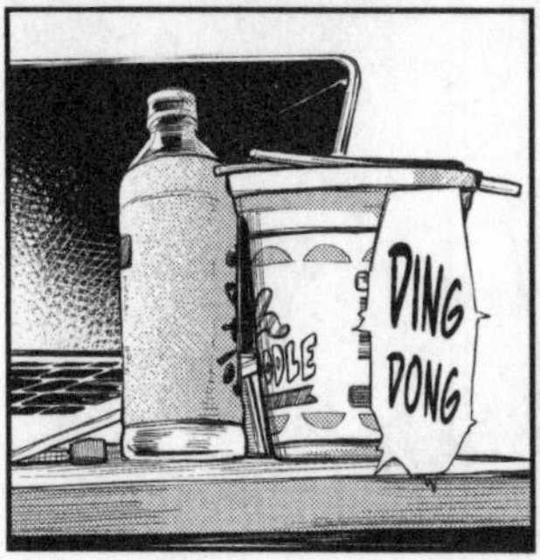
DING DONG

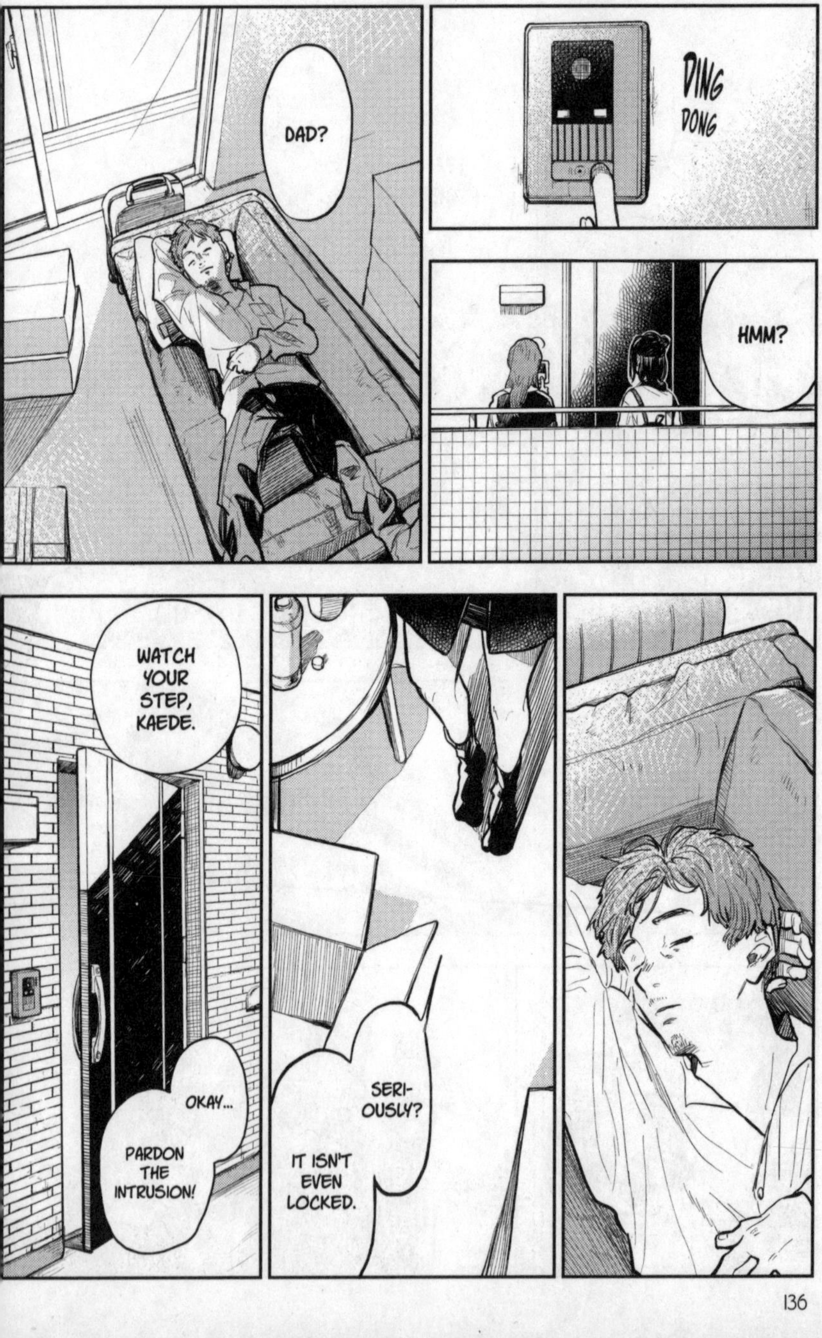
DING DONG
HMM?
DAD?
SERI-OUSLY?
IT ISN'T EVEN LOCKED.
WATCH YOUR STEP, KAEDE.
OKAY...
PARDON THE INTRUSION!

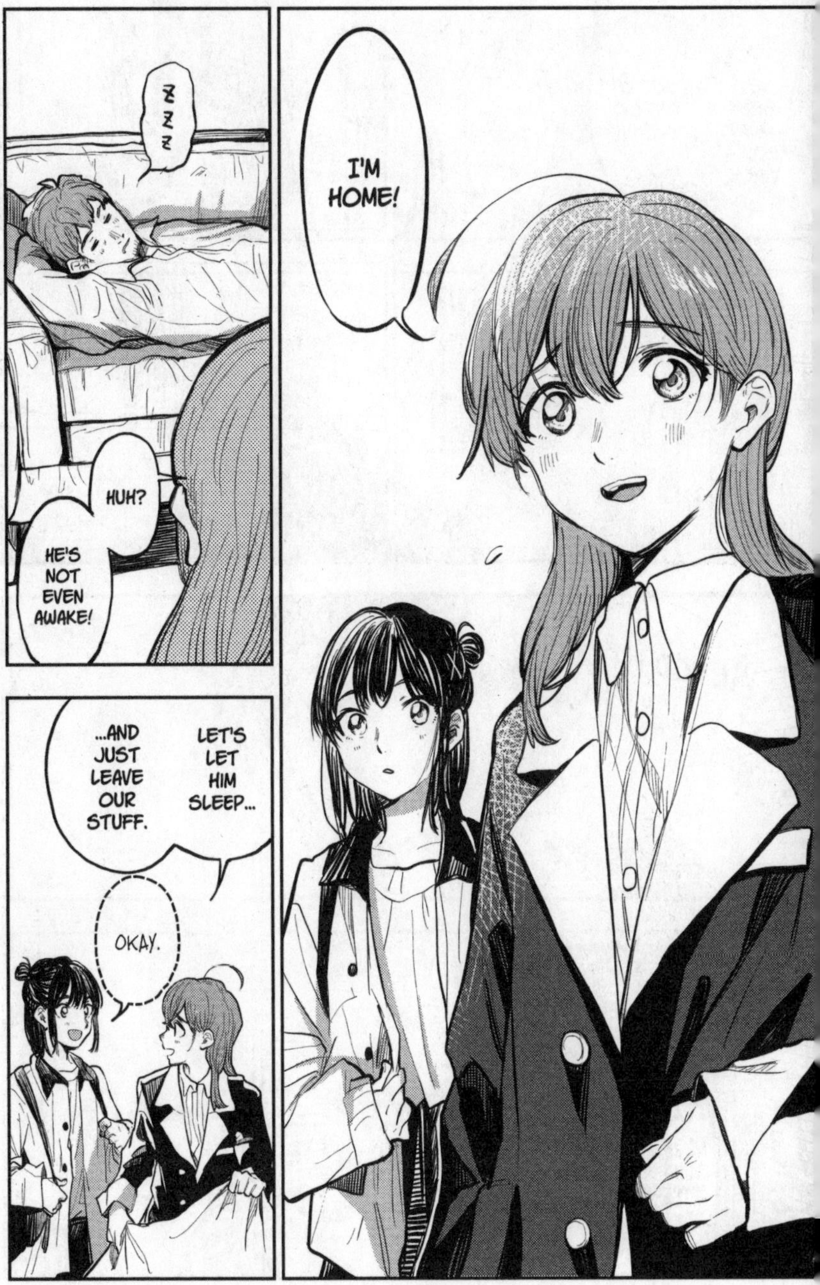
I'M HOME!
Z Z Z
HUH?
HE'S NOT EVEN AWAKE!
LET'S LET HIM SLEEP...
...AND JUST LEAVE OUR STUFF.
OKAY.

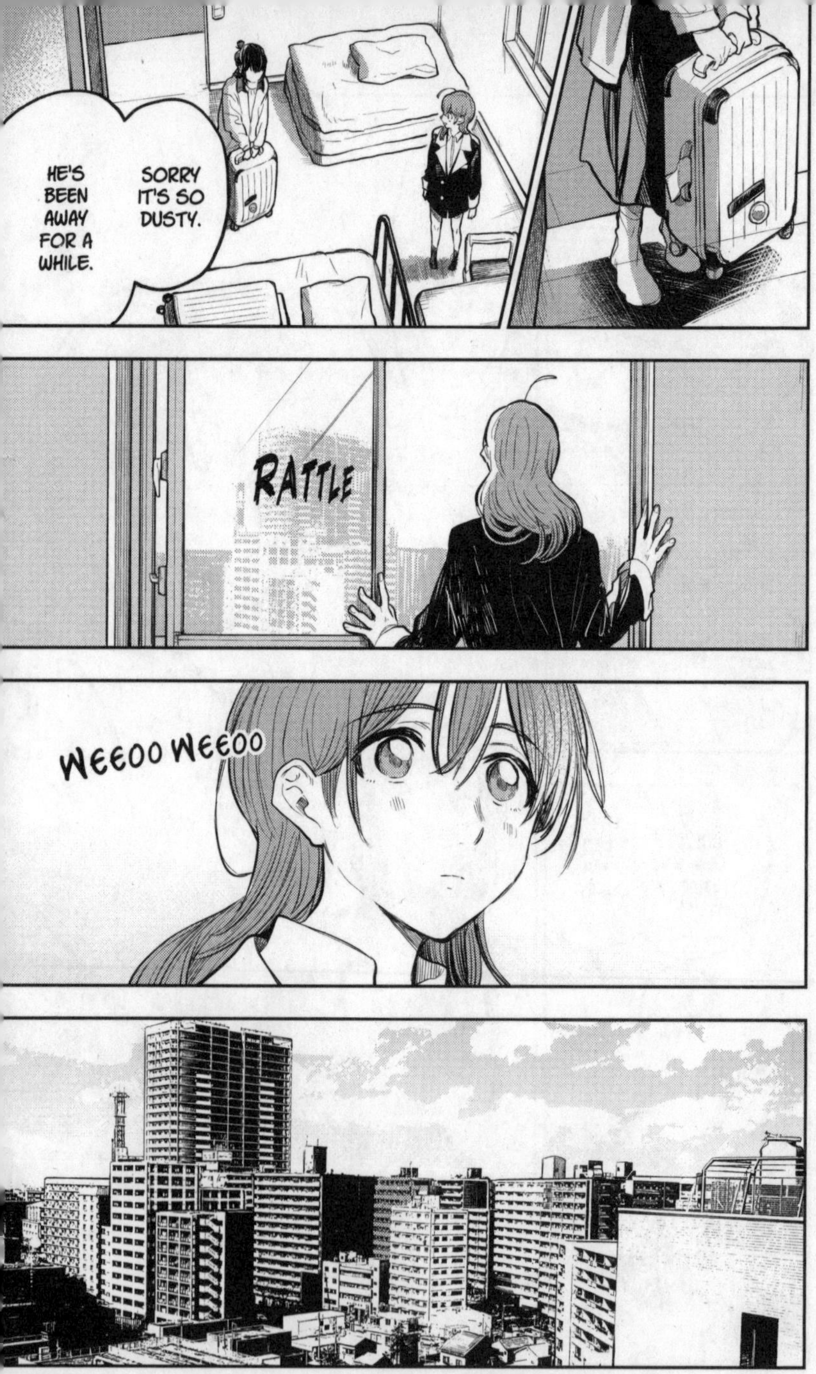
SORRY IT'S SO DUSTY.
HE'S BEEN AWAY FOR A WHILE.
RATTLE
WEEOO WEEOO

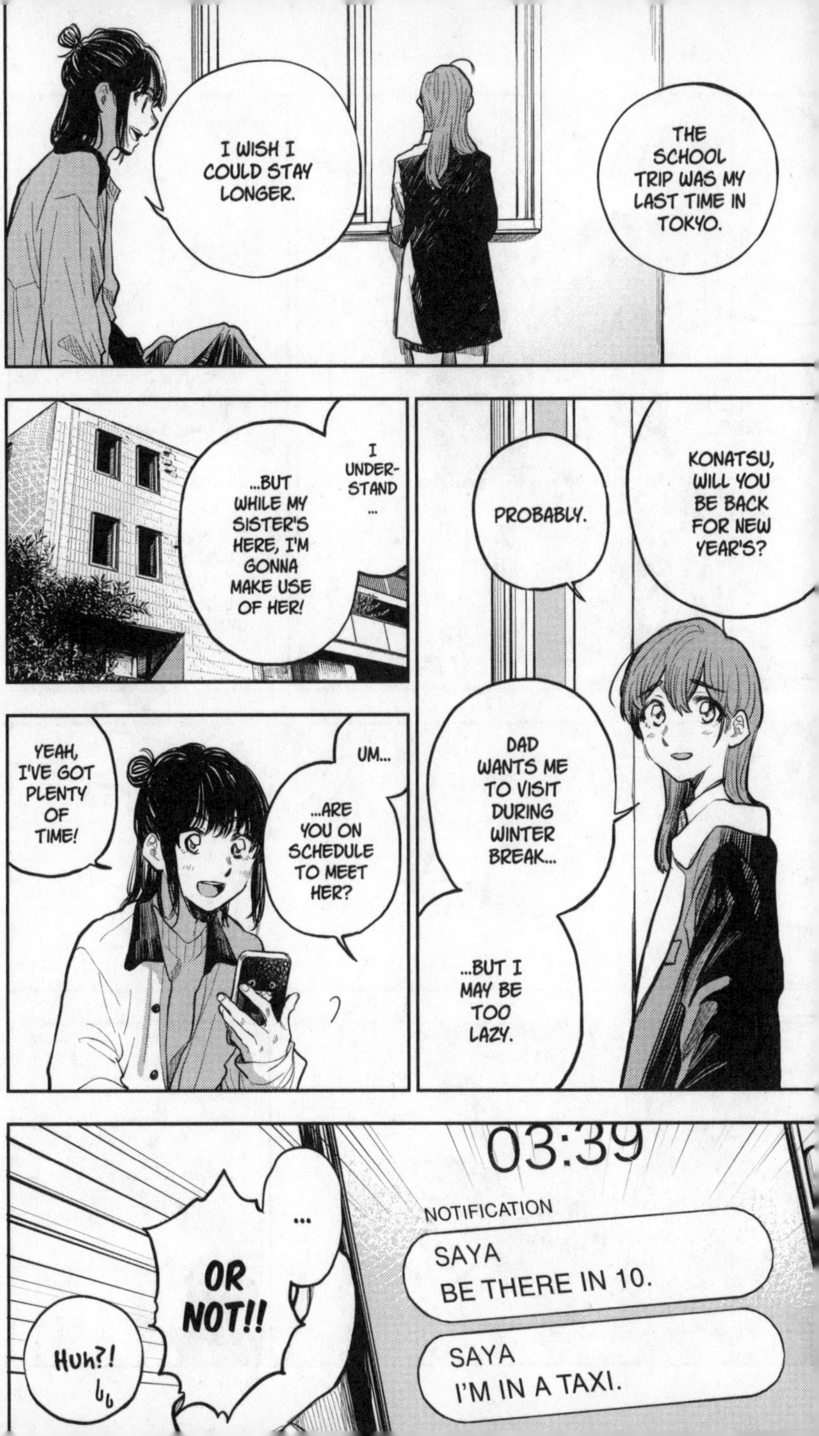
THE SCHOOL TRIP WAS MY LAST TIME IN TOKYO.
I WISH I COULD STAY LONGER.
KONATSU, WILL YOU BE BACK FOR NEW YEAR'S?
PROBABLY.
DAD WANTS ME TO VISIT DURING WINTER BREAK...
...BUT I MAY BE TOO LAZY.
I UNDER-STAND...
...BUT WHILE MY SISTER'S HERE, I'M GONNA MAKE USE OF HER!
UM...
...ARE YOU ON SCHEDULE TO MEET HER?
YEAH, I'VE GOT PLENTY OF TIME!
03:39
NOTIFICATION
SAYA
BE THERE IN 10.
SAYA
I'M IN A TAXI.
...
OR NOT!!
Huh?!

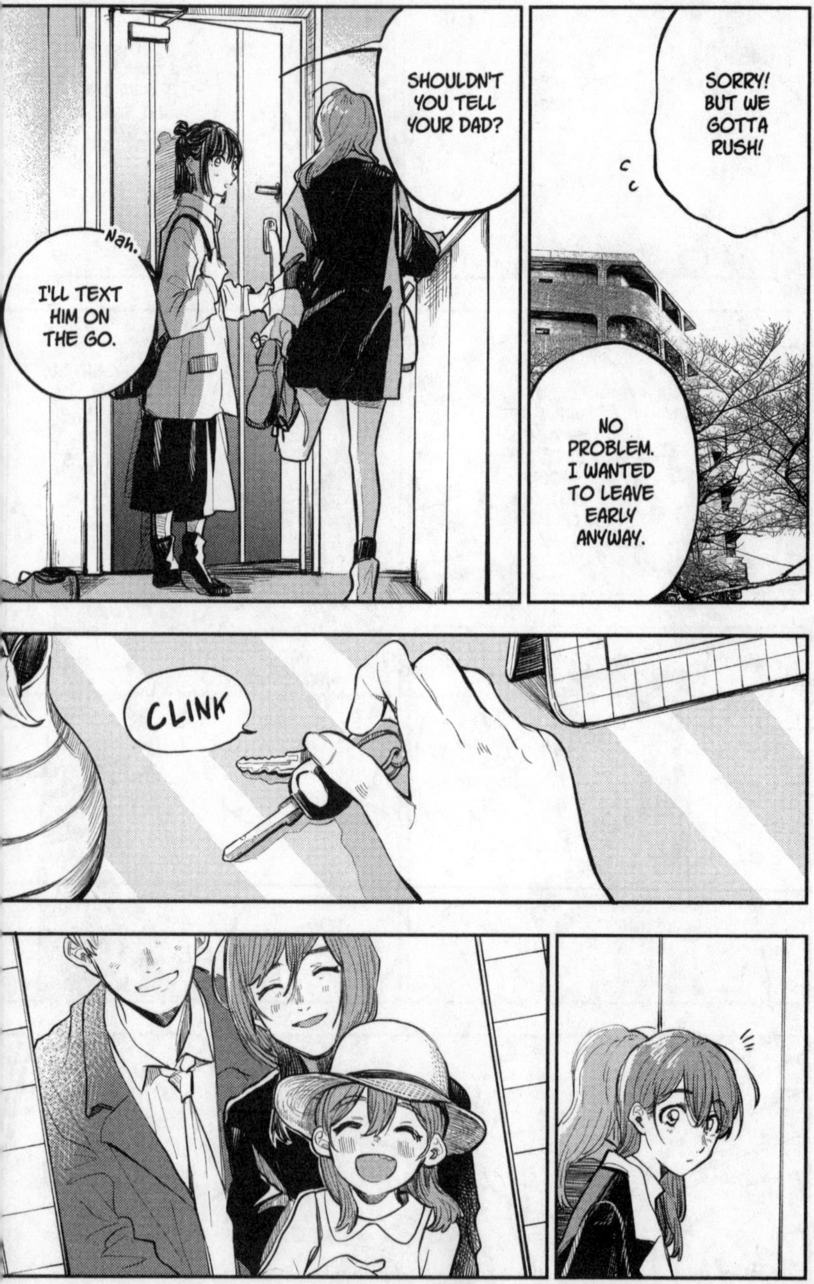
SORRY! BUT WE GOTTA RUSH!
NO PROBLEM. I WANTED TO LEAVE EARLY ANYWAY.
SHOULDN'T YOU TELL YOUR DAD?
Nah.
I'LL TEXT HIM ON THE GO.
CLINK

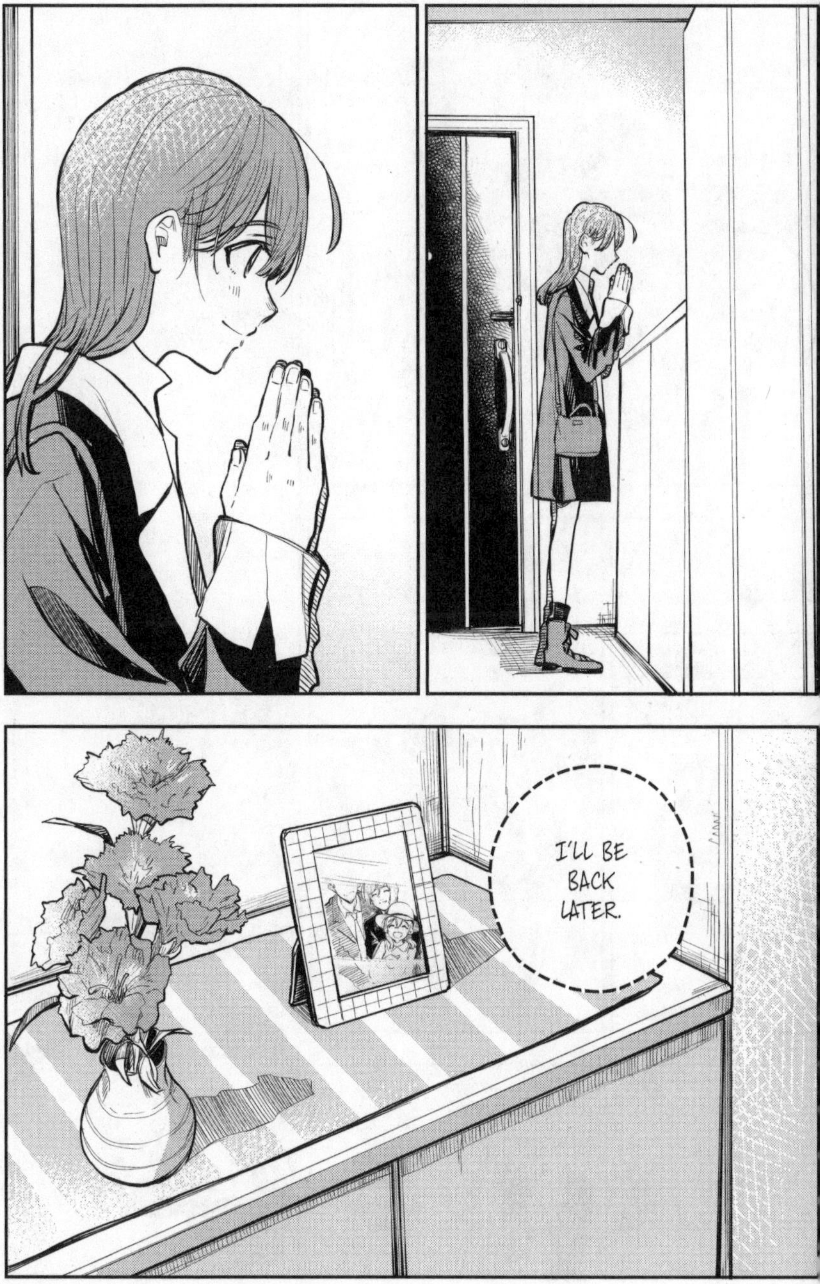
I'LL BE BACK LATER.

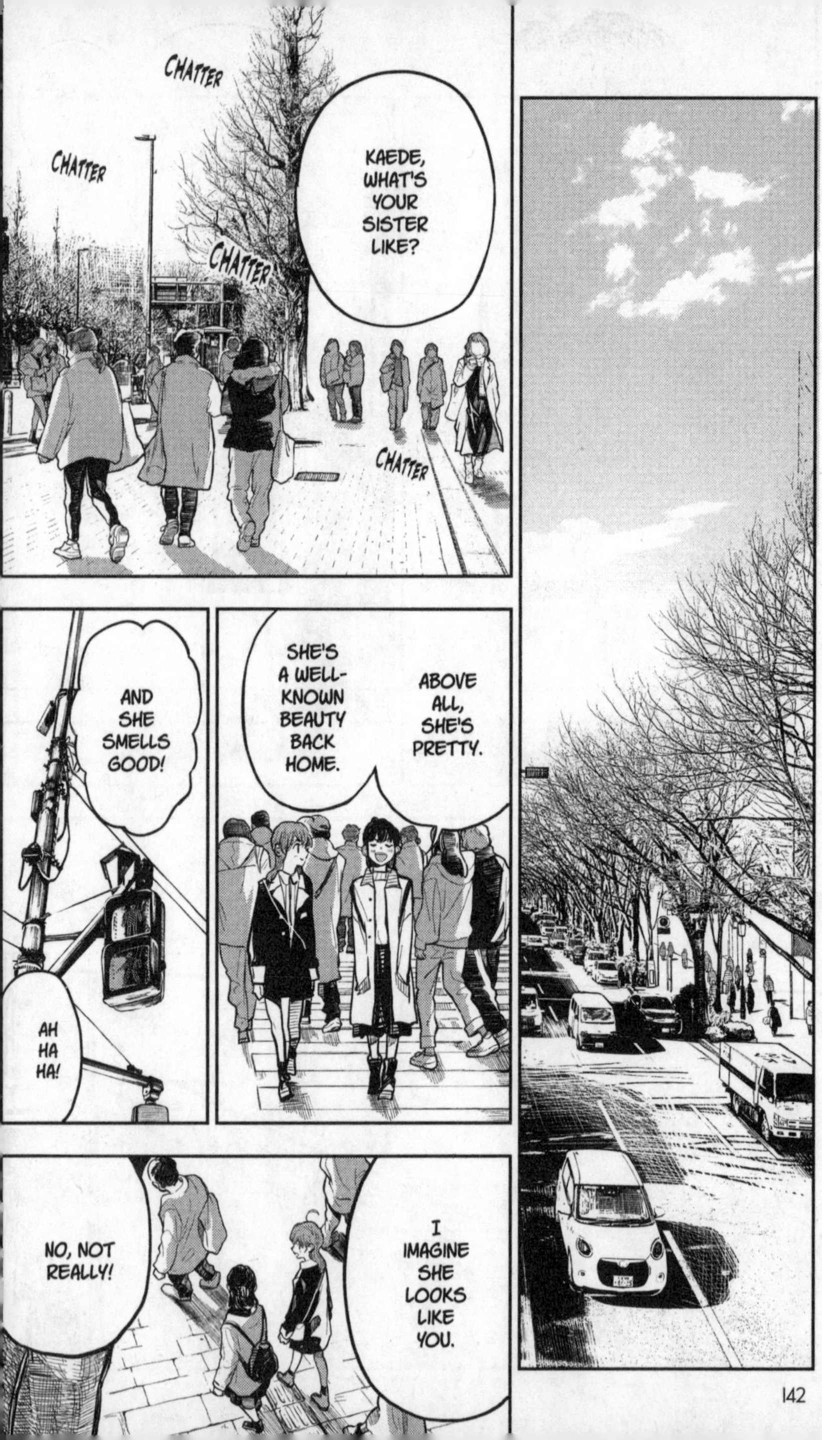
KAEDE, WHAT'S YOUR SISTER LIKE?
CHATTER
CHATTER
CHATTER
CHATTER
SHE'S A WELL-KNOWN BEAUTY BACK HOME.
ABOVE ALL, SHE'S PRETTY.
AND SHE SMELLS GOOD!
AH HA HA!
I IMAGINE SHE LOOKS LIKE YOU.
NO, NOT REALLY!

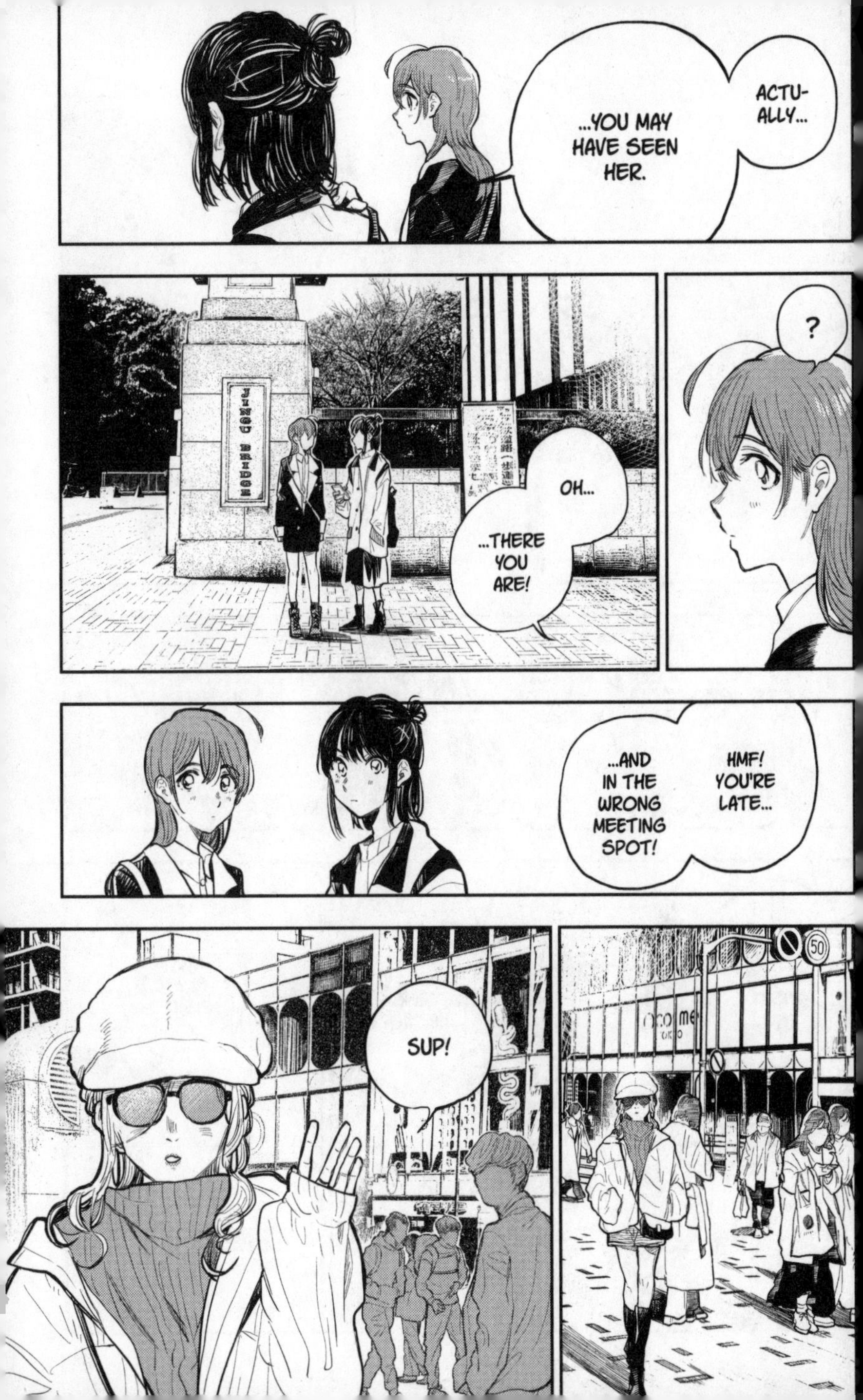
ACTU-ALLY...
...YOU MAY HAVE SEEN HER.
?
JINGU BRIDGE
OH...
...THERE YOU ARE!
HMF! YOU'RE LATE...
...AND IN THE WRONG MEETING SPOT!
50
SUP!

...?
UM, KAEDE?
THAT IS YOU, RIGHT?
OR... NOT?
DID I GET SOME-THING WRONG?
NO, THIS IS THE RIGHT TIME...

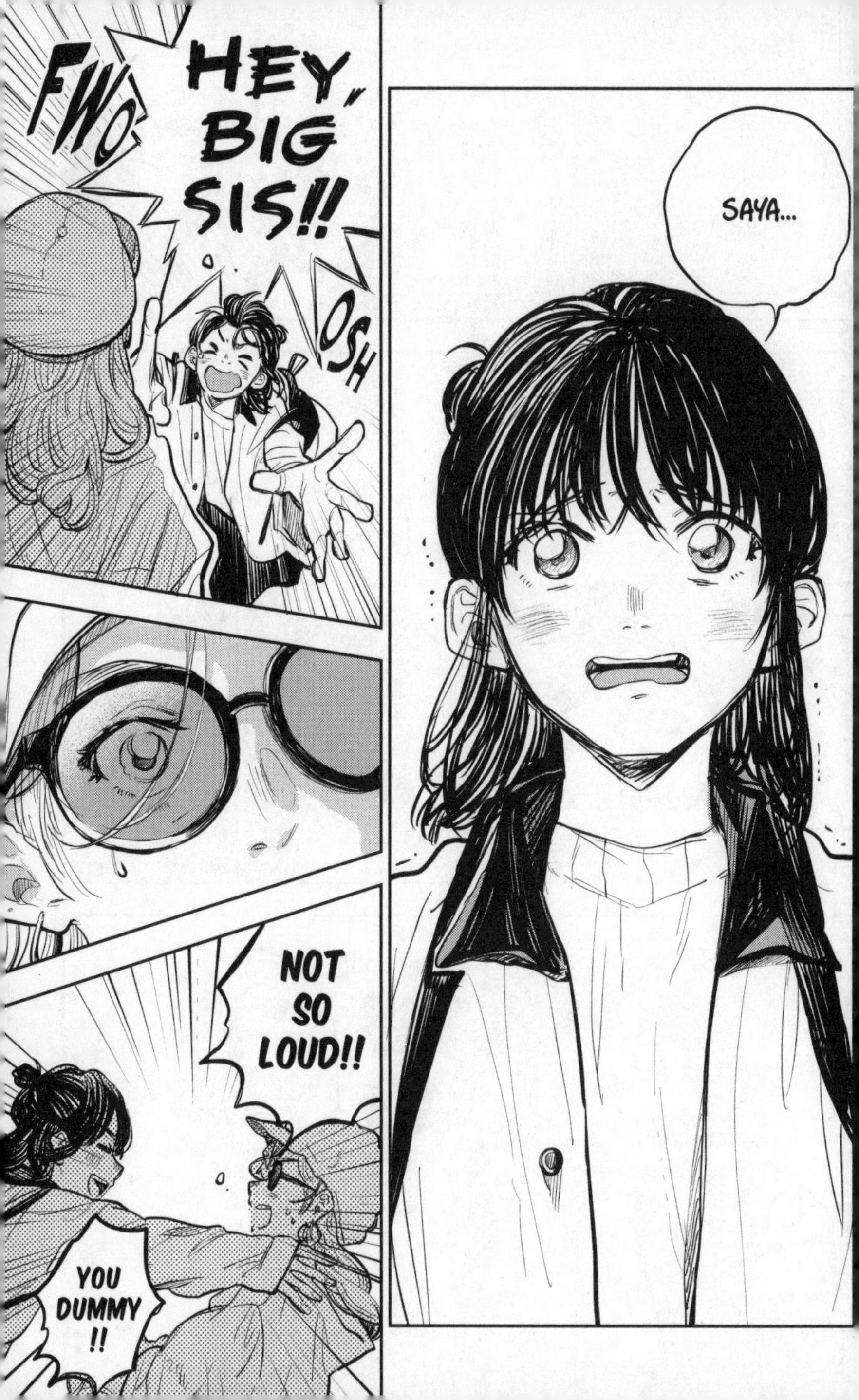
SAYA...
FWOOSH
HEY, BIG SIS!!
NOT SO LOUD!!
YOU DUMMY!!

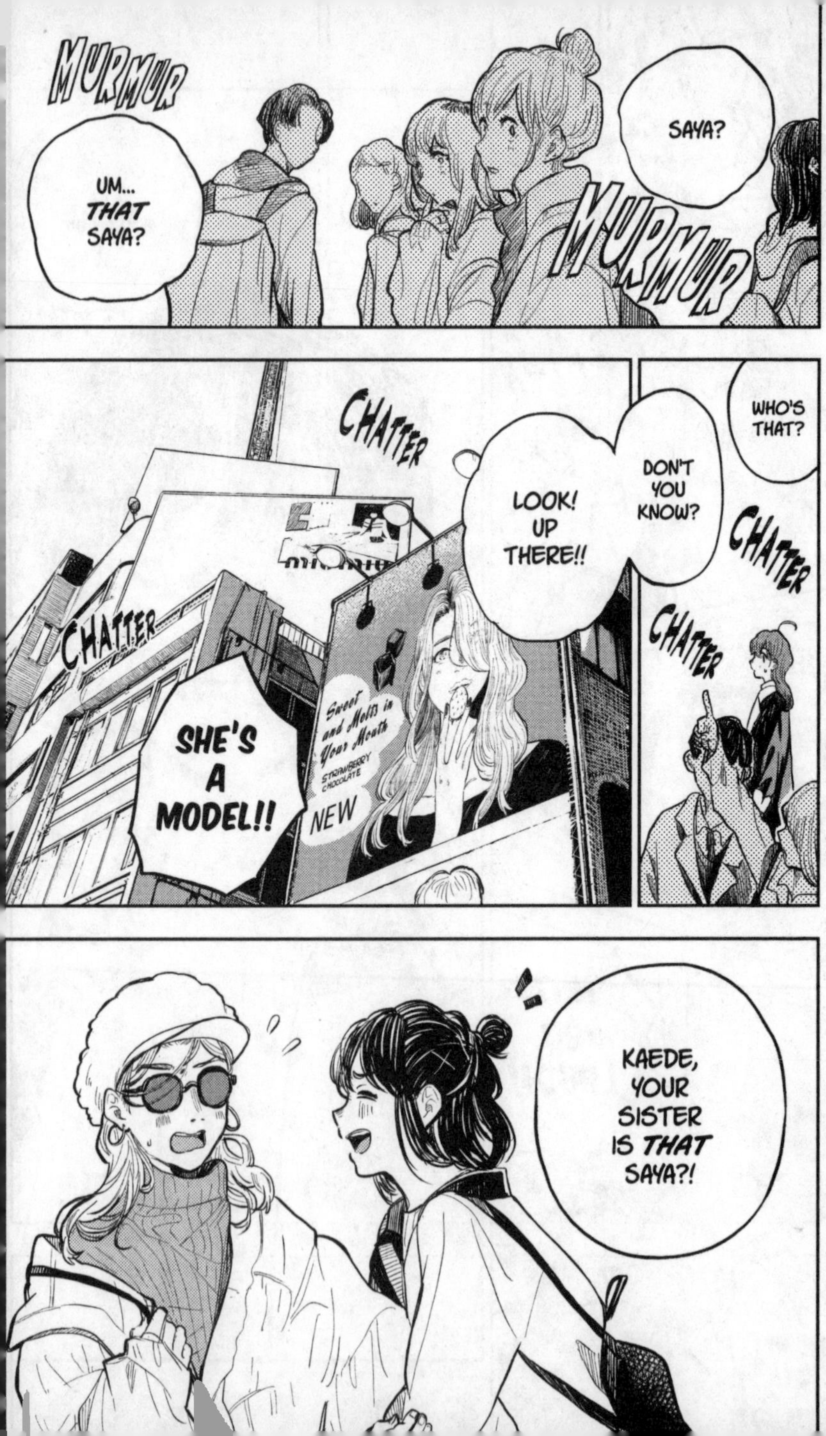
SAYA?
MURMUR
MURMUR
UM... THAT SAYA?
WHO'S THAT?
DON'T YOU KNOW?
CHATTER
CHATTER
LOOK! UP THERE!!
CHATTER
CHATTER
SHE'S A MODEL!!
Sweet and Melts in Your Mouth
STRAWBERRY CHOCOLATE
NEW
KAEDE, YOUR SISTER IS THAT SAYA?!

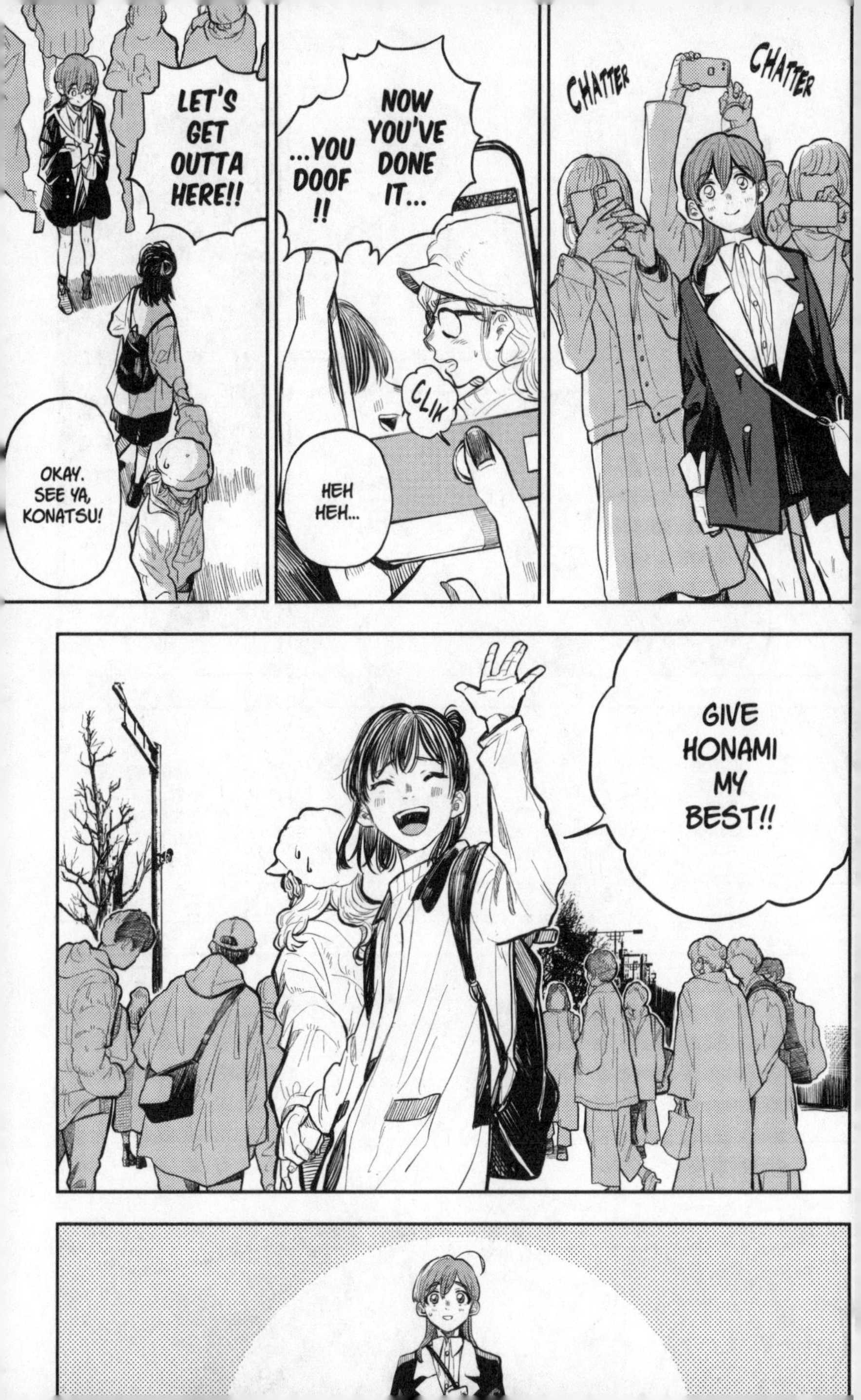
CHATTER
CHATTER
NOW YOU'VE DONE IT...
...YOU DOOF!!
CLIK
HEH HEH...
LET'S GET OUTTA HERE!!
OKAY. SEE YA, KONATSU!
GIVE HONAMI MY BEST!!

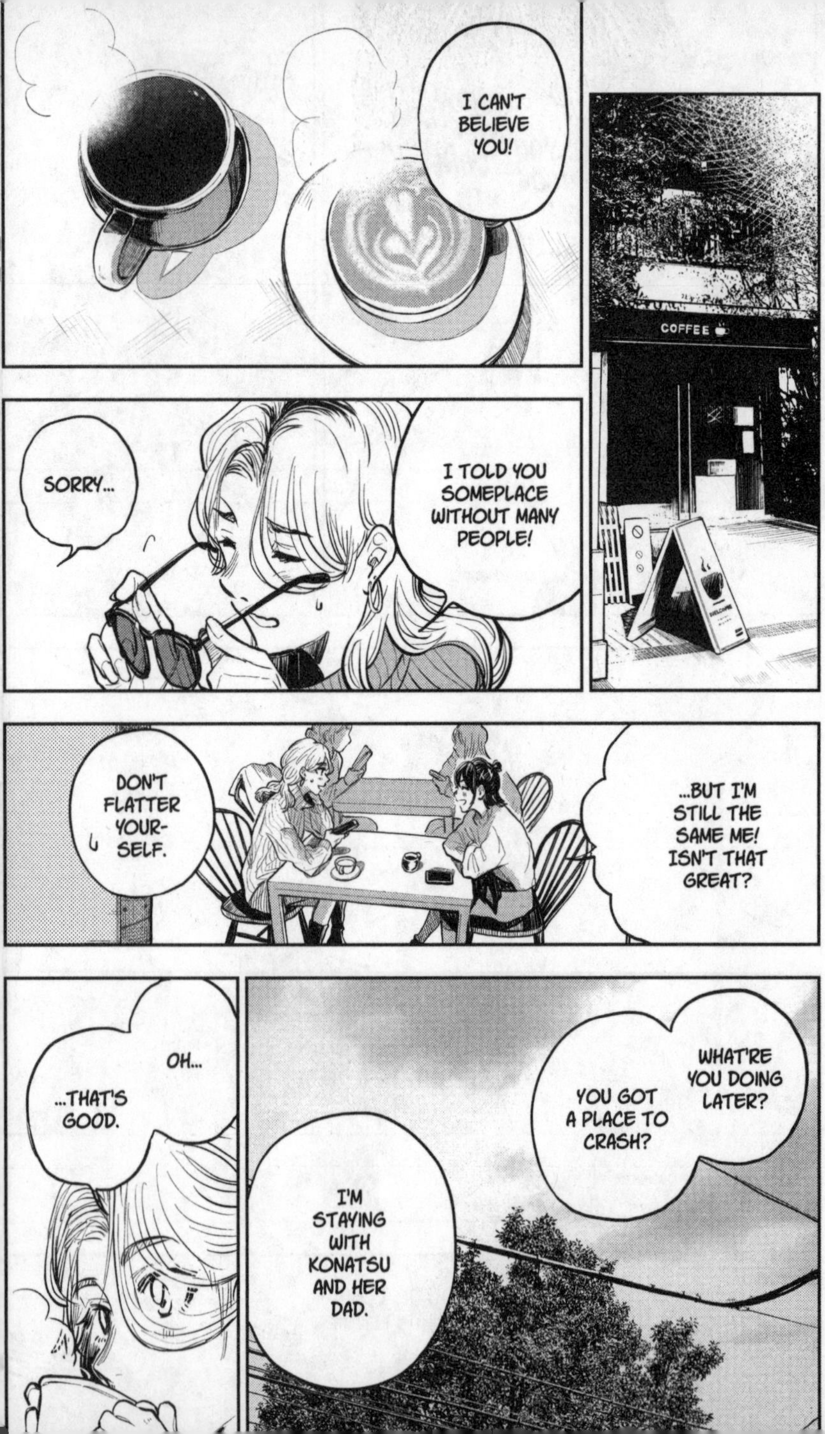
COFFEE
I CAN'T BELIEVE YOU!
I TOLD YOU SOMEPLACE WITHOUT MANY PEOPLE!
SORRY...
...BUT I'M STILL THE SAME ME! ISN'T THAT GREAT?
DON'T FLATTER YOUR-SELF.
WHAT'RE YOU DOING LATER?
YOU GOT A PLACE TO CRASH?
I'M STAYING WITH KONATSU AND HER DAD.
OH...
...THAT'S GOOD.

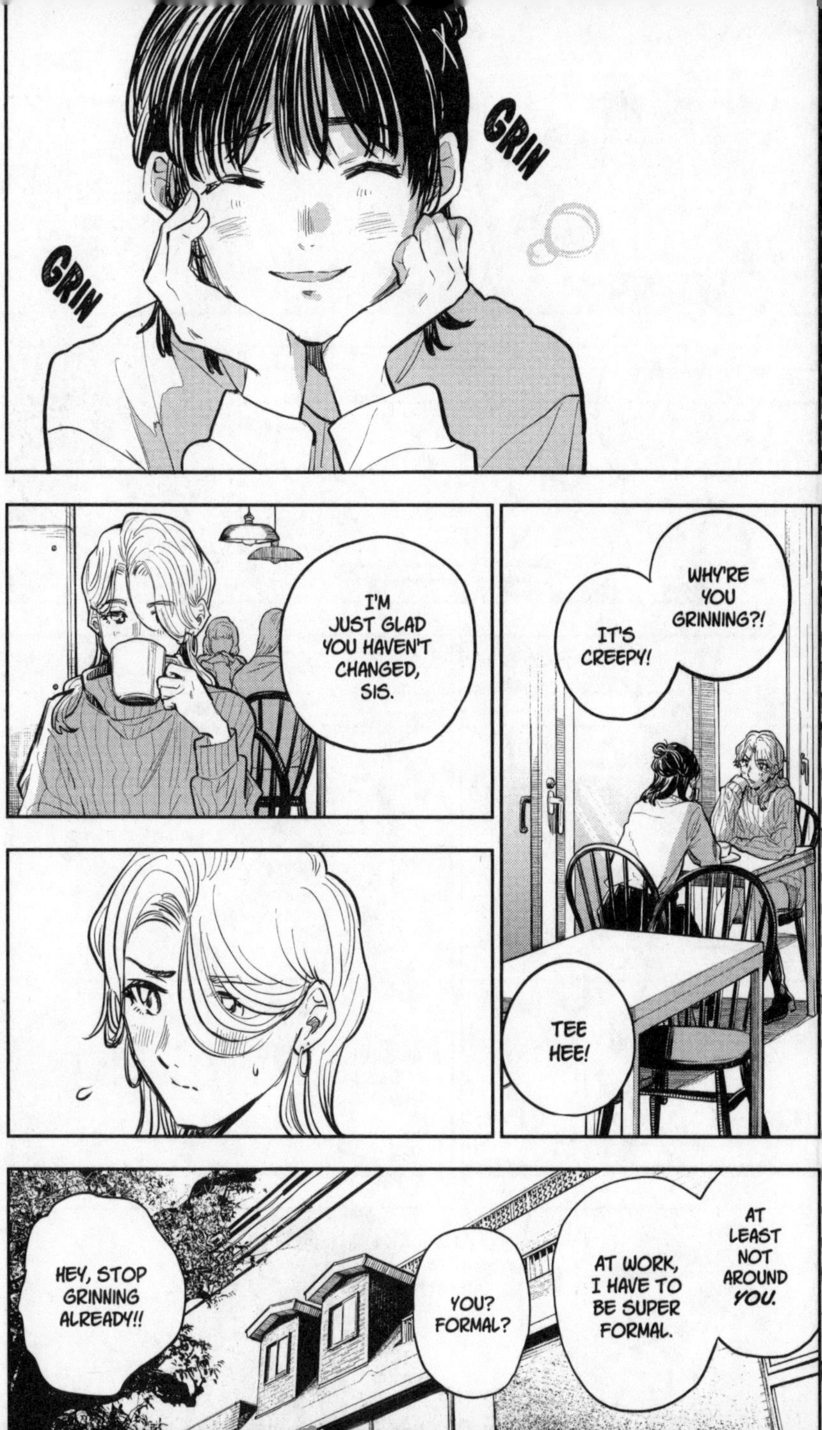
GRIN
GRIN
WHY'RE YOU GRINNING?!
IT'S CREEPY!
TEE HEE!
I'M JUST GLAD YOU HAVEN'T CHANGED, SIS.
AT LEAST NOT AROUND *YOU.*
AT WORK, I HAVE TO BE SUPER FORMAL.
YOU? FORMAL?
HEY, STOP GRINNING ALREADY!!

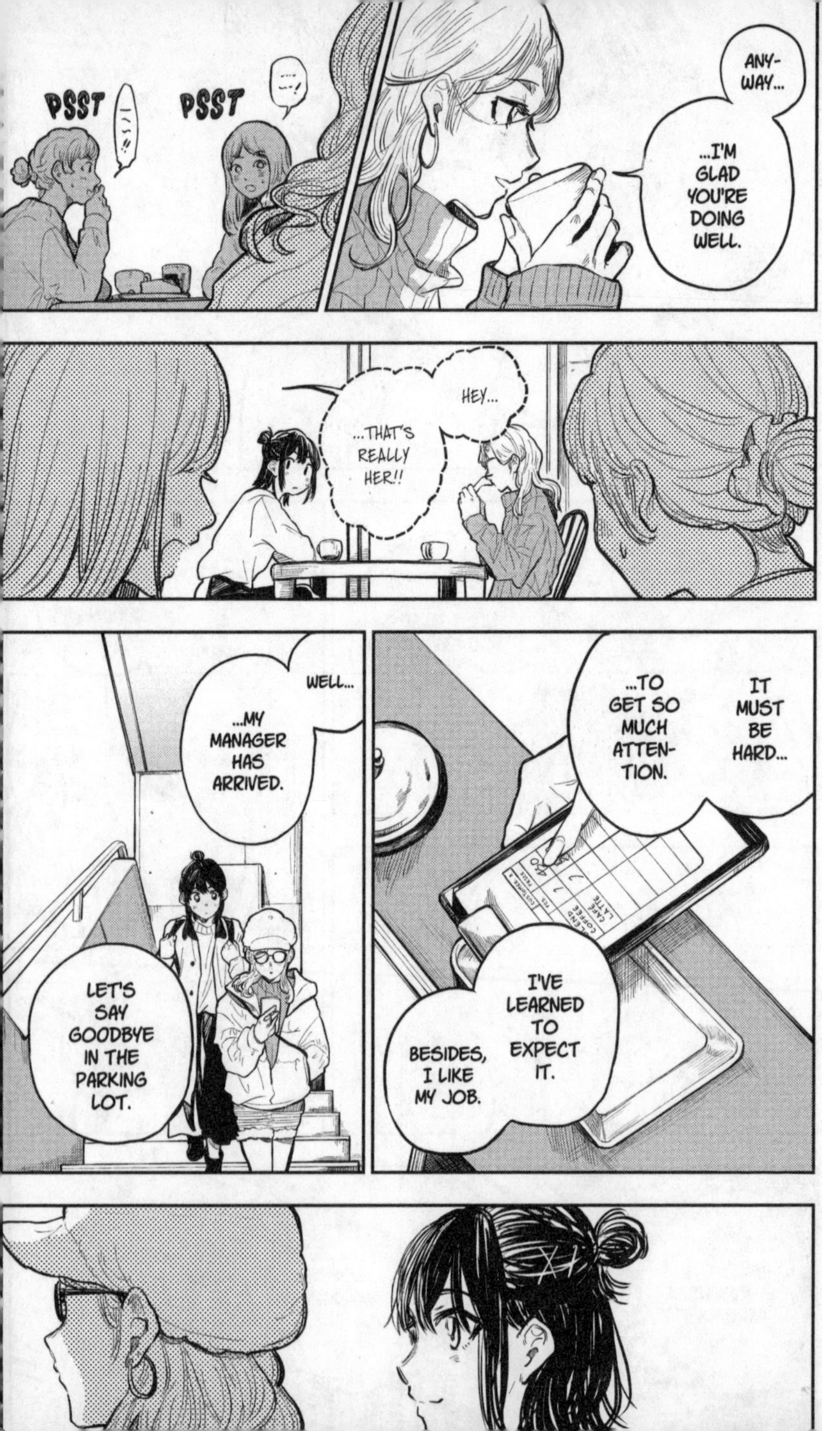
ANY-WAY...
...I'M GLAD YOU'RE DOING WELL.
PSST
PSST
HEY...
...THAT'S REALLY HER!!
IT MUST BE HARD...
...TO GET SO MUCH ATTEN-TION.
I'VE LEARNED TO EXPECT IT.
BESIDES, I LIKE MY JOB.
WELL...
...MY MANAGER HAS ARRIVED.
LET'S SAY GOODBYE IN THE PARKING LOT.

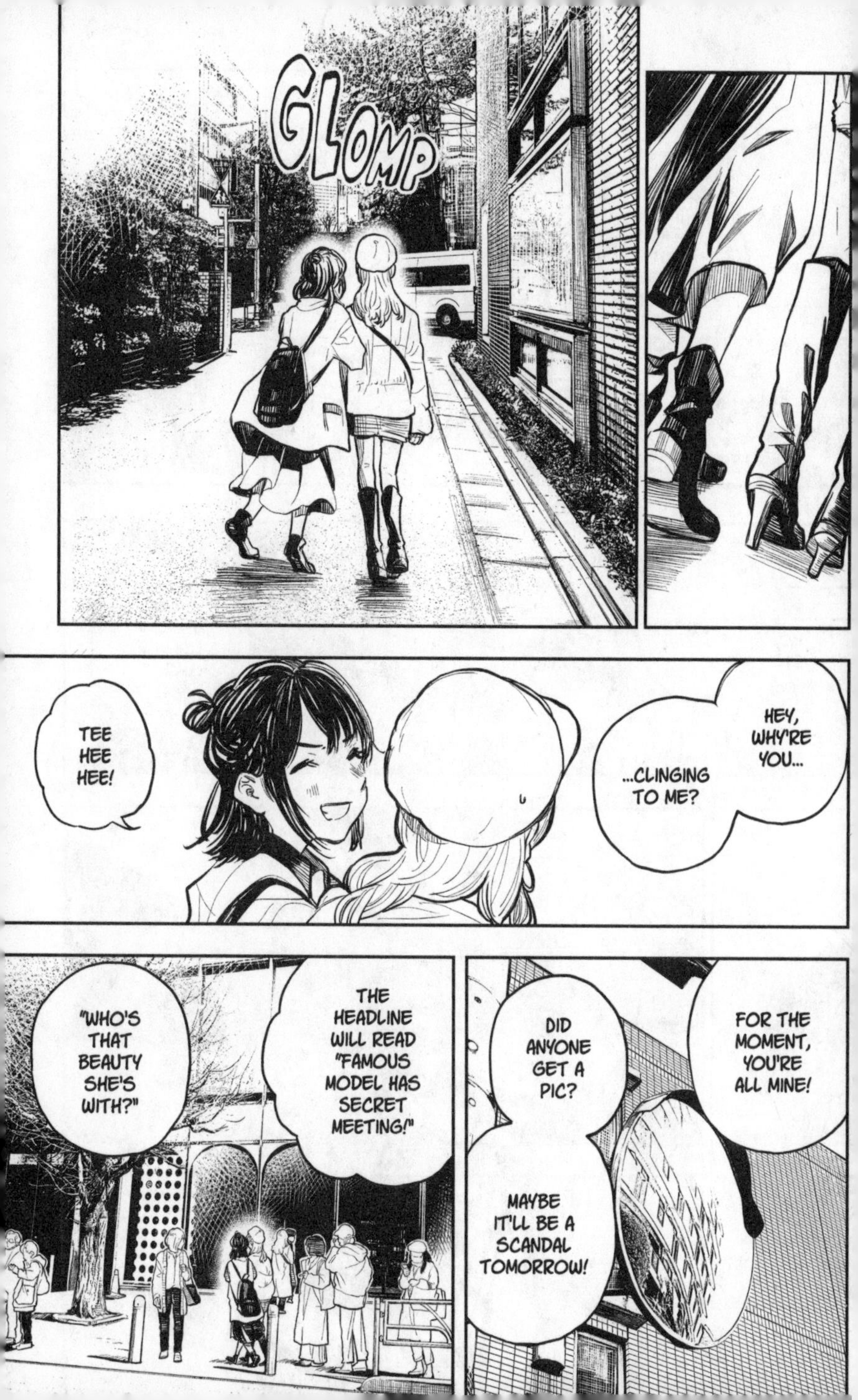
GLOMP
HEY, WHY'RE YOU...
...CLINGING TO ME?
TEE HEE HEE!
FOR THE MOMENT, YOU'RE ALL MINE!
DID ANYONE GET A PIC?
MAYBE IT'LL BE A SCANDAL TOMORROW!
THE HEADLINE WILL READ "FAMOUS MODEL HAS SECRET MEETING!"
"WHO'S THAT BEAUTY SHE'S WITH?"

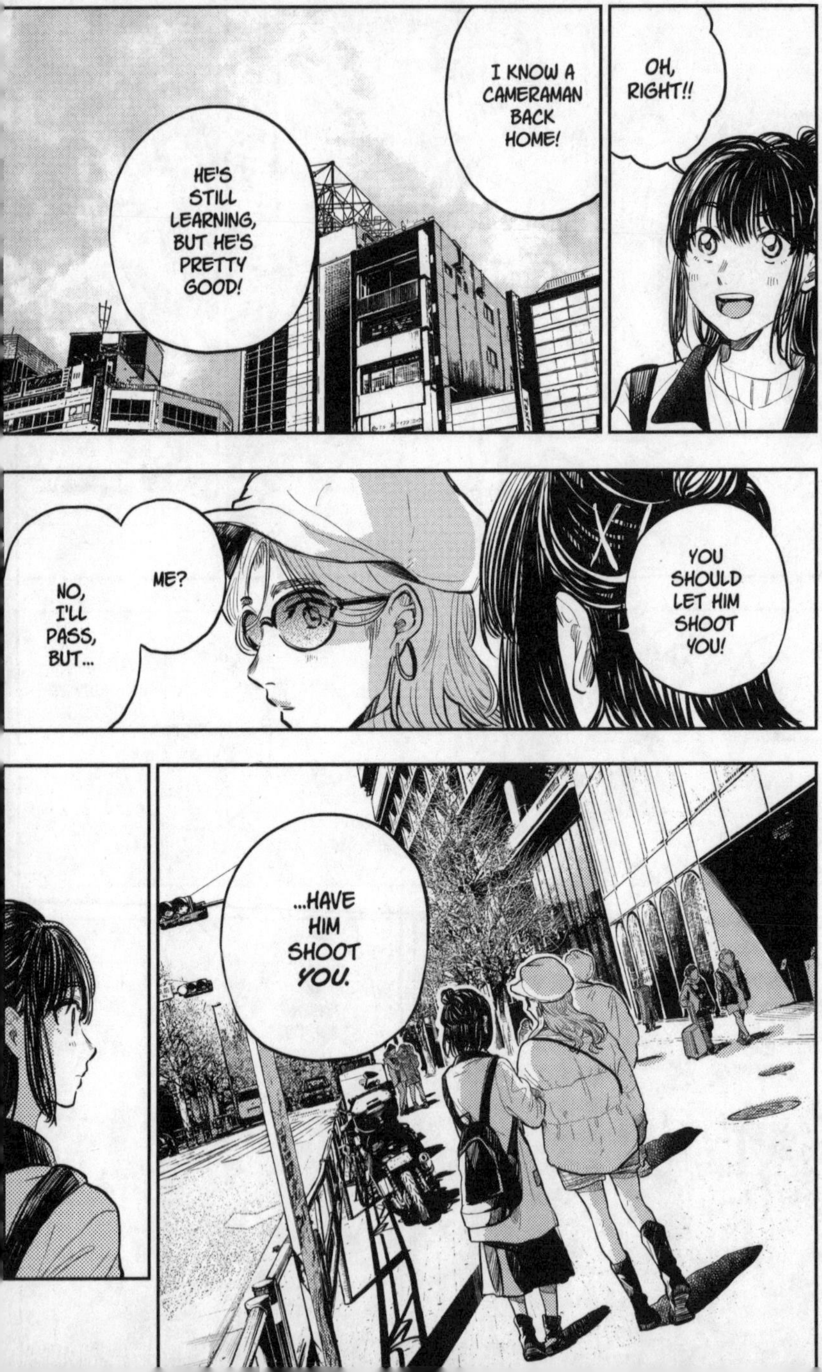
OH, RIGHT!!
I KNOW A CAMERAMAN BACK HOME!
HE'S STILL LEARNING, BUT HE'S PRETTY GOOD!
YOU SHOULD LET HIM SHOOT YOU!
ME?
NO, I'LL PASS, BUT...
...HAVE HIM SHOOT *YOU*.

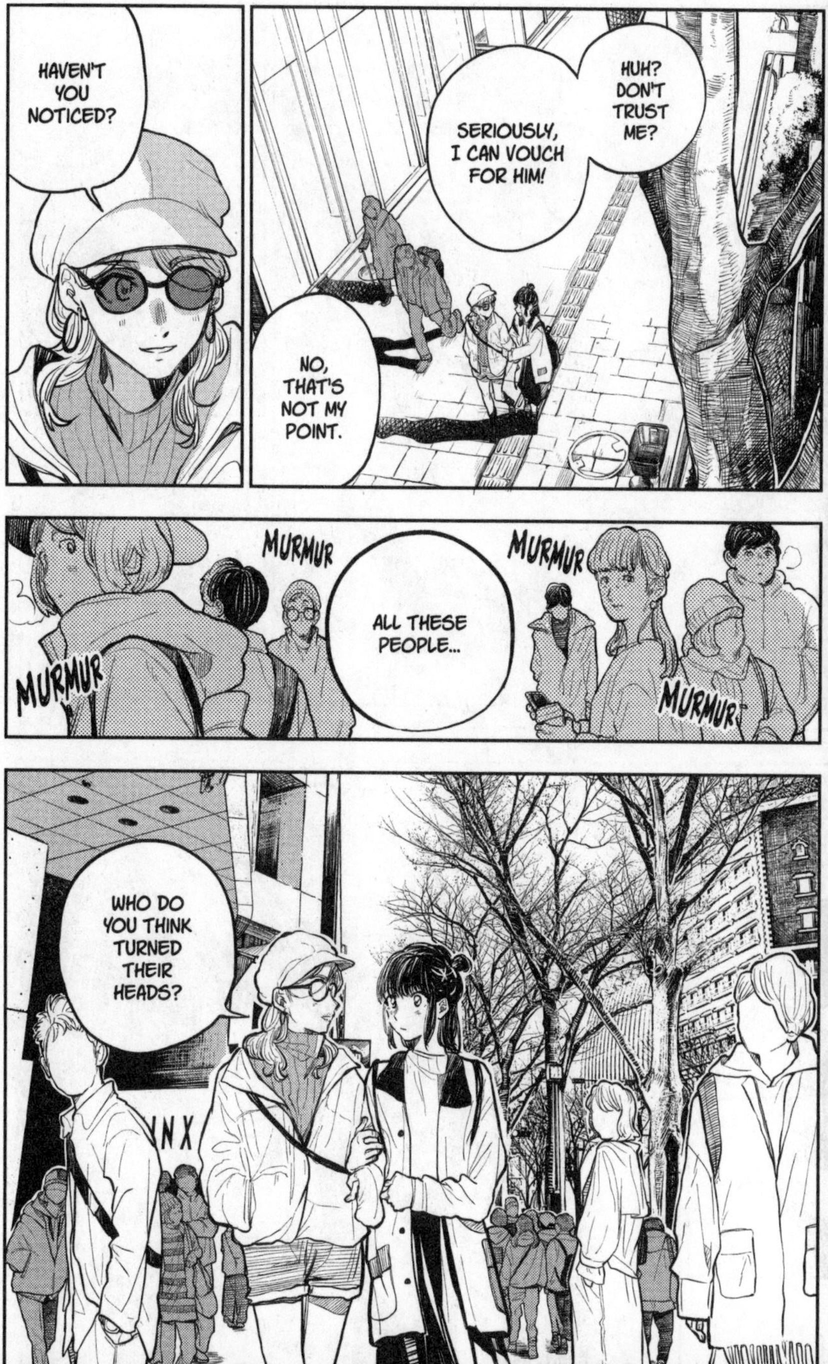
HUH? DON'T TRUST ME?
SERIOUSLY, I CAN VOUCH FOR HIM!
NO, THAT'S NOT MY POINT.
HAVEN'T YOU NOTICED?
MURMUR
MURMUR
MURMUR
ALL THESE PEOPLE...
MURMUR
WHO DO YOU THINK TURNED THEIR HEADS?

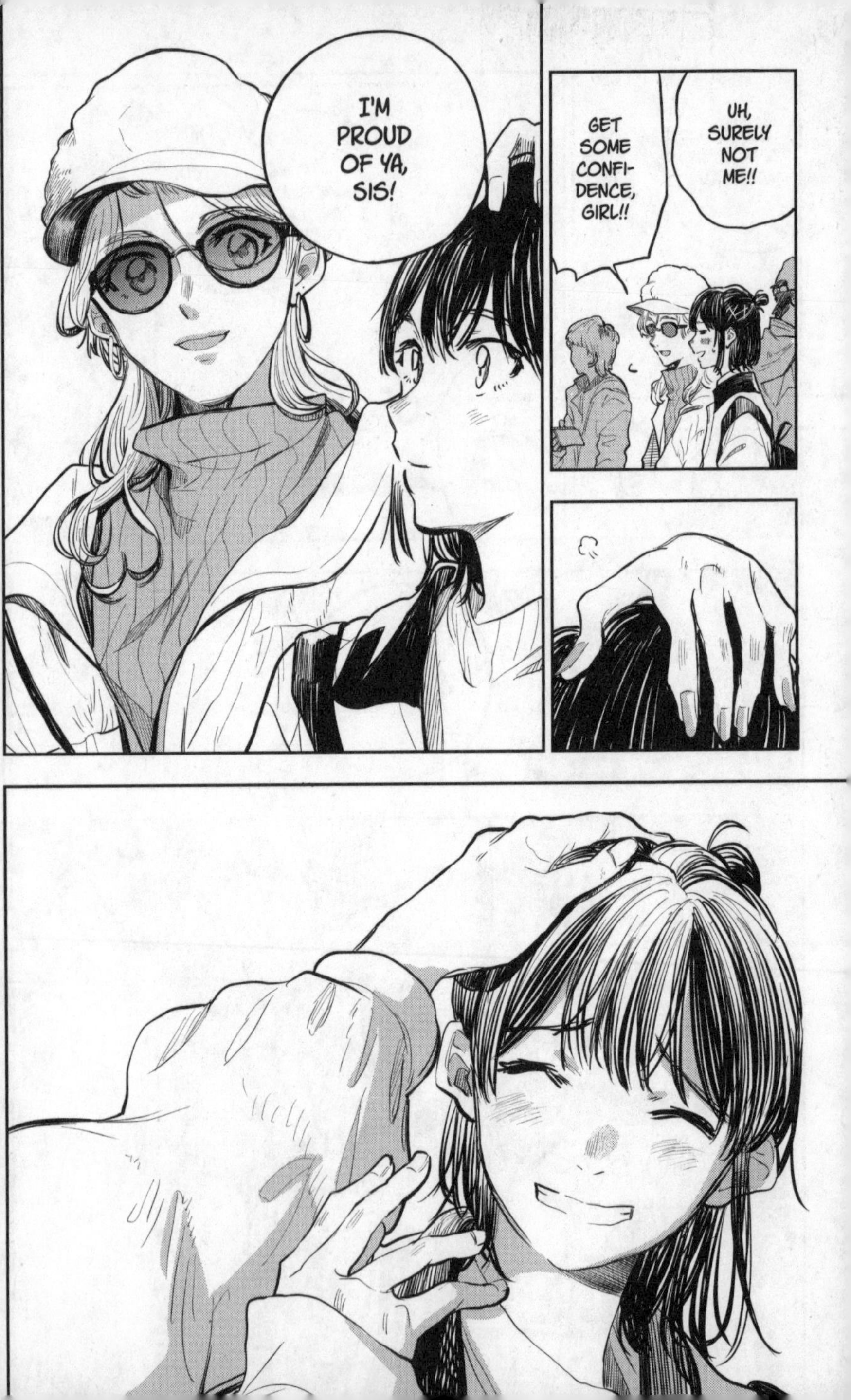
UH, SURELY NOT ME!!
GET SOME CONFI-DENCE, GIRL!!
I'M PROUD OF YA, SIS!

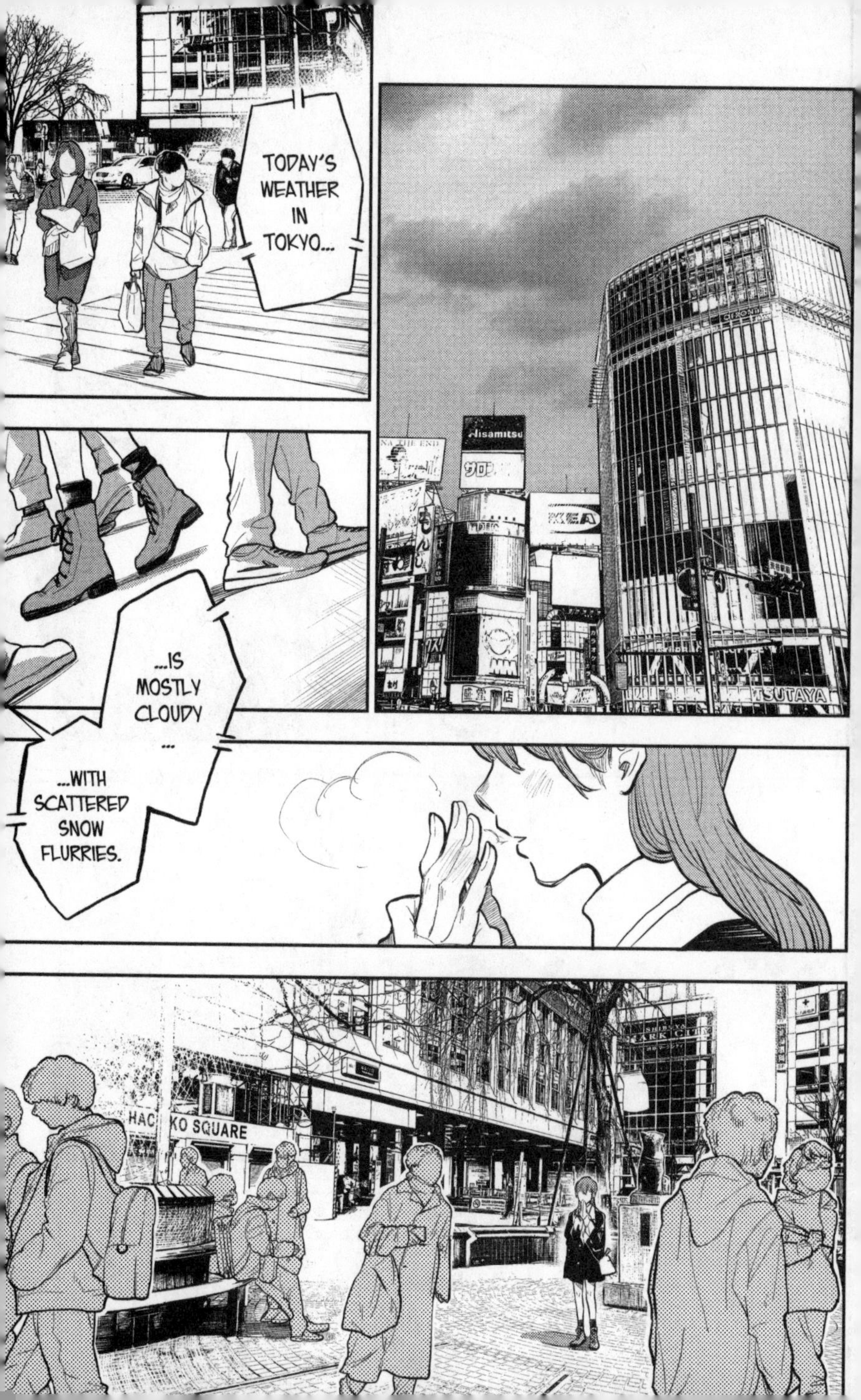
Hisamitsu
TSUTAYA
TODAY'S WEATHER IN TOKYO...
...IS MOSTLY CLOUDY ...
...WITH SCATTERED SNOW FLURRIES.

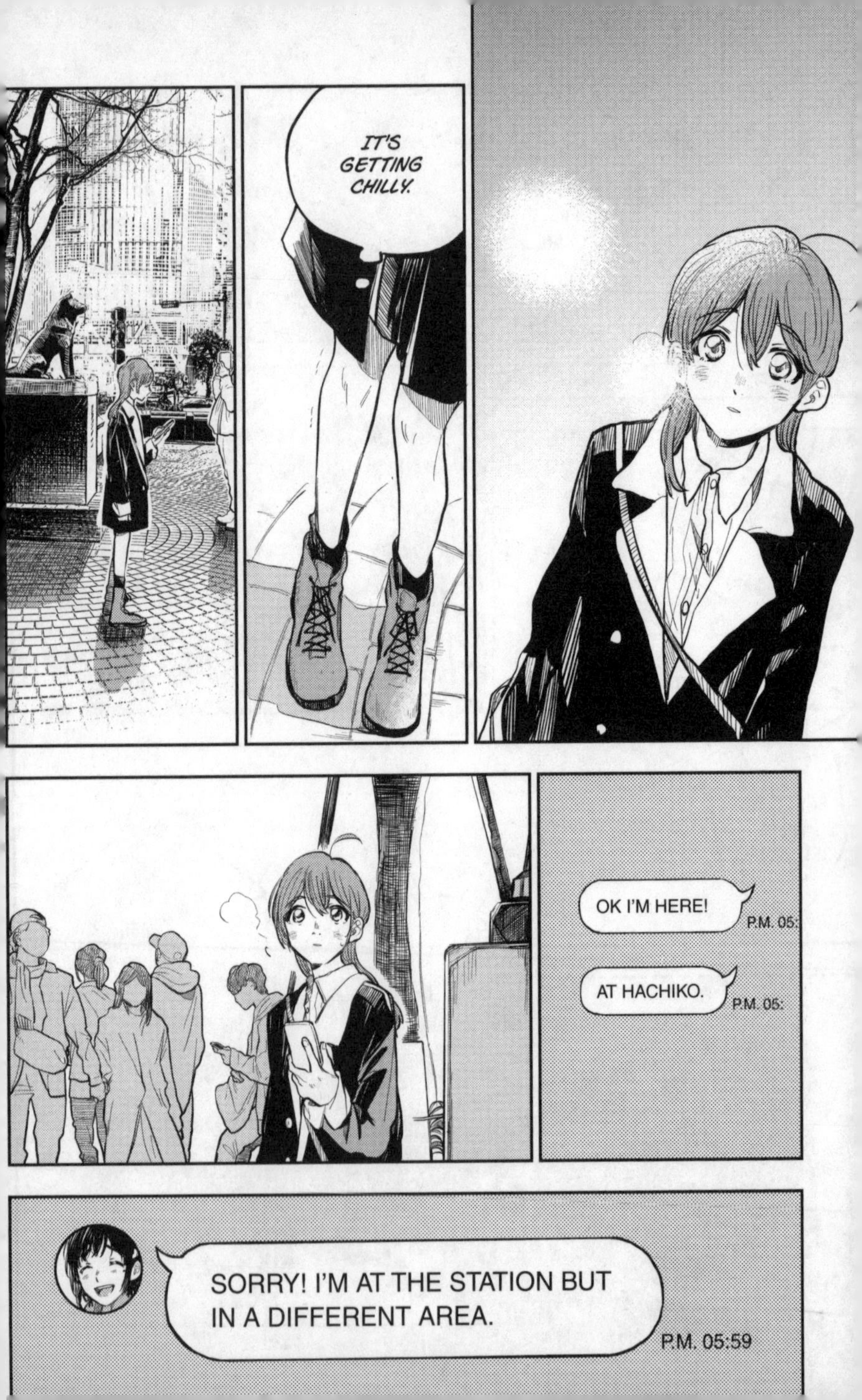
IT'S GETTING CHILLY.
OK I'M HERE!
P.M. 05:
AT HACHIKO.
P.M. 05:
SORRY! I'M AT THE STATION BUT IN A DIFFERENT AREA.
P.M. 05:59

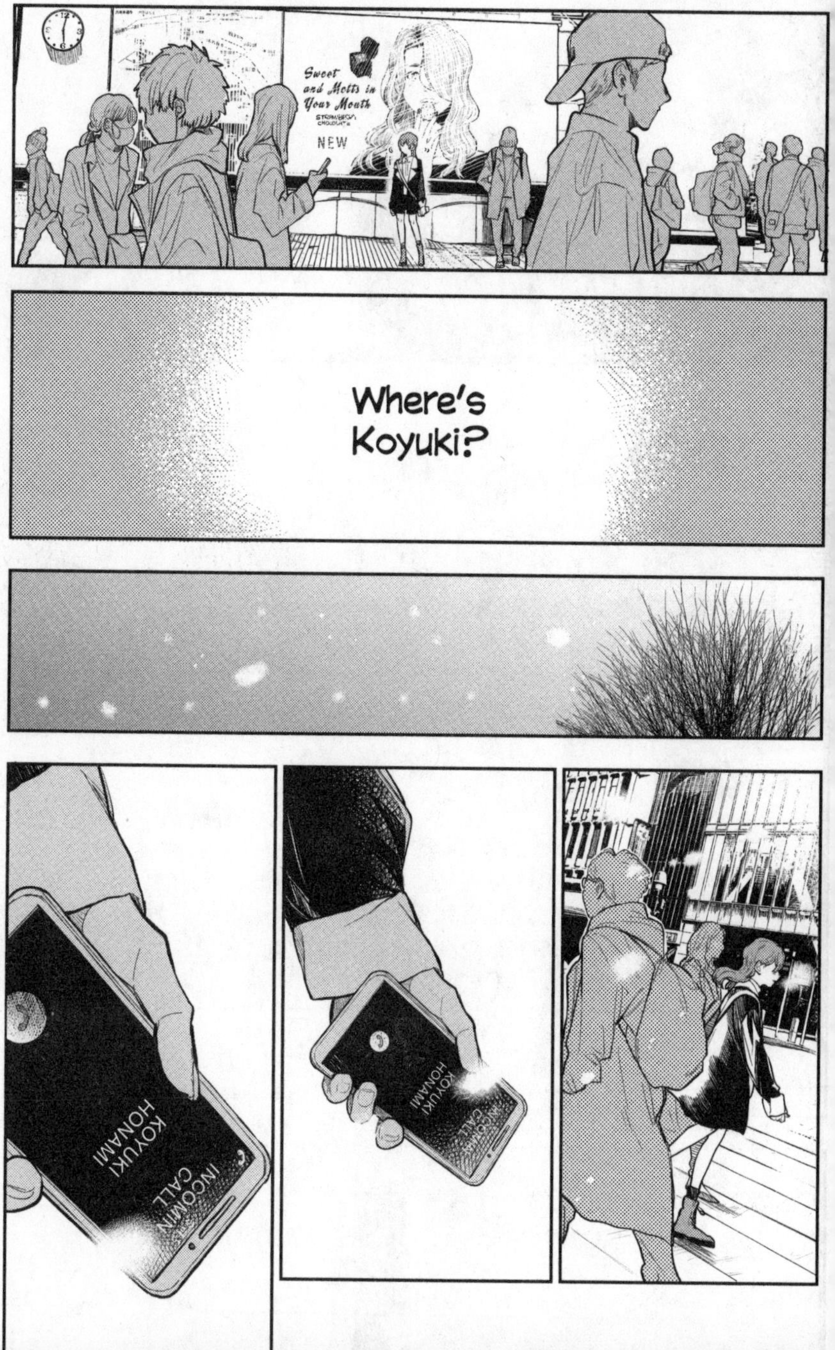
Sweet and Melts in Your Mouth
STRAWBERRY CHOCOLATE
NEW
Where's Koyuki?
KOYUKI HONAMI
INCOMIN CALL
KOYUKI HONAMI

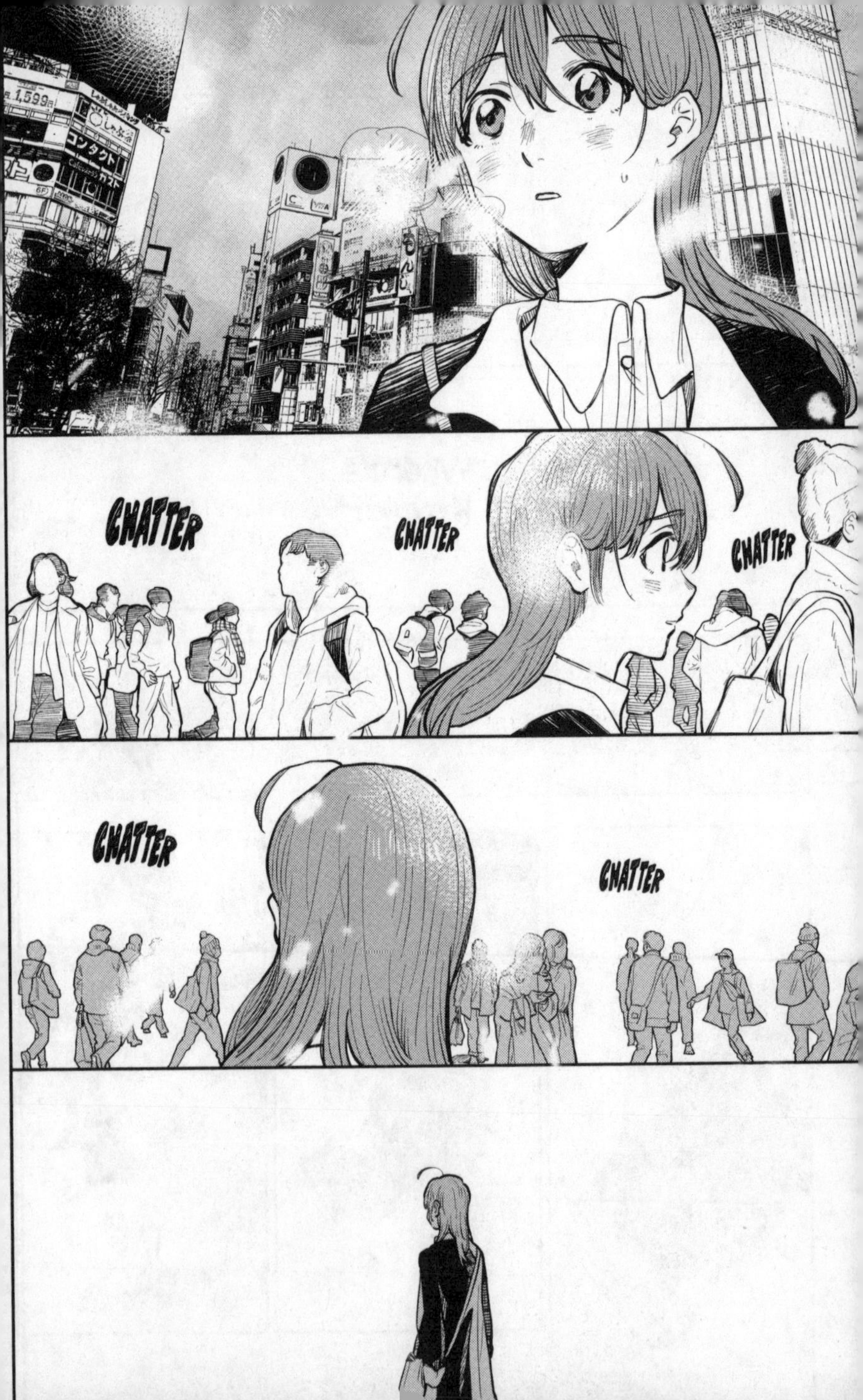
CHATTER
CHATTER
CHATTER
CHATTER
CHATTER

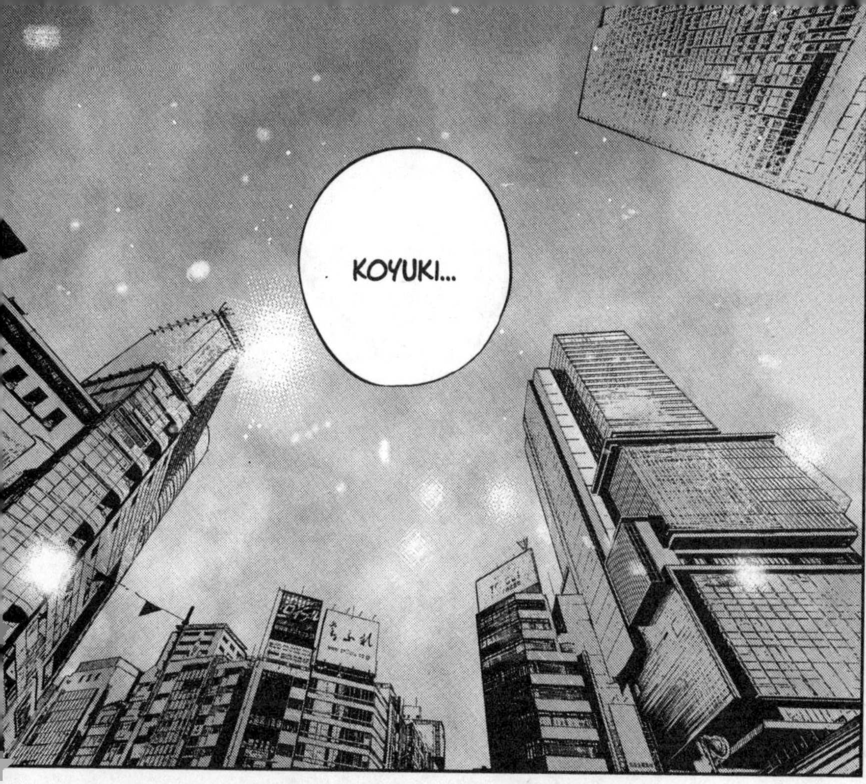
KOYUKI...
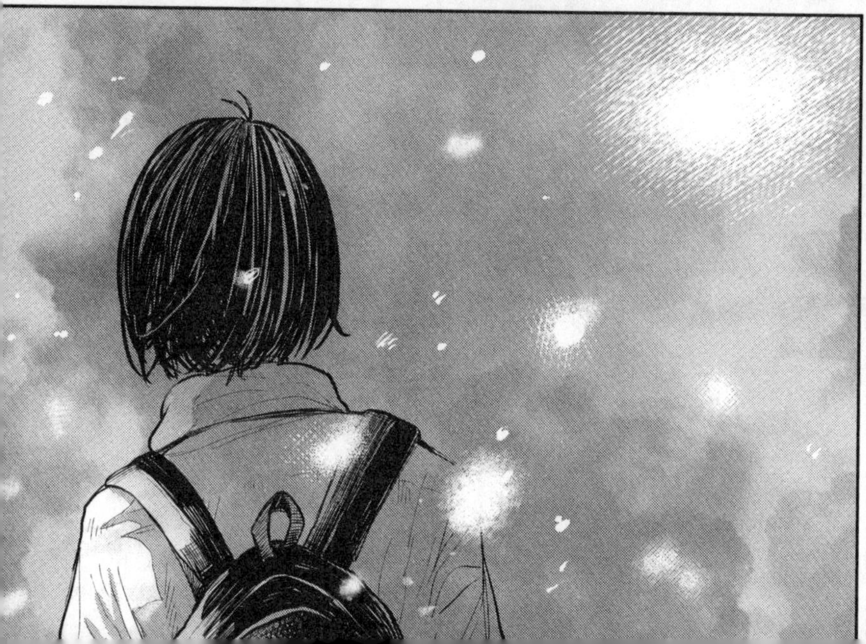

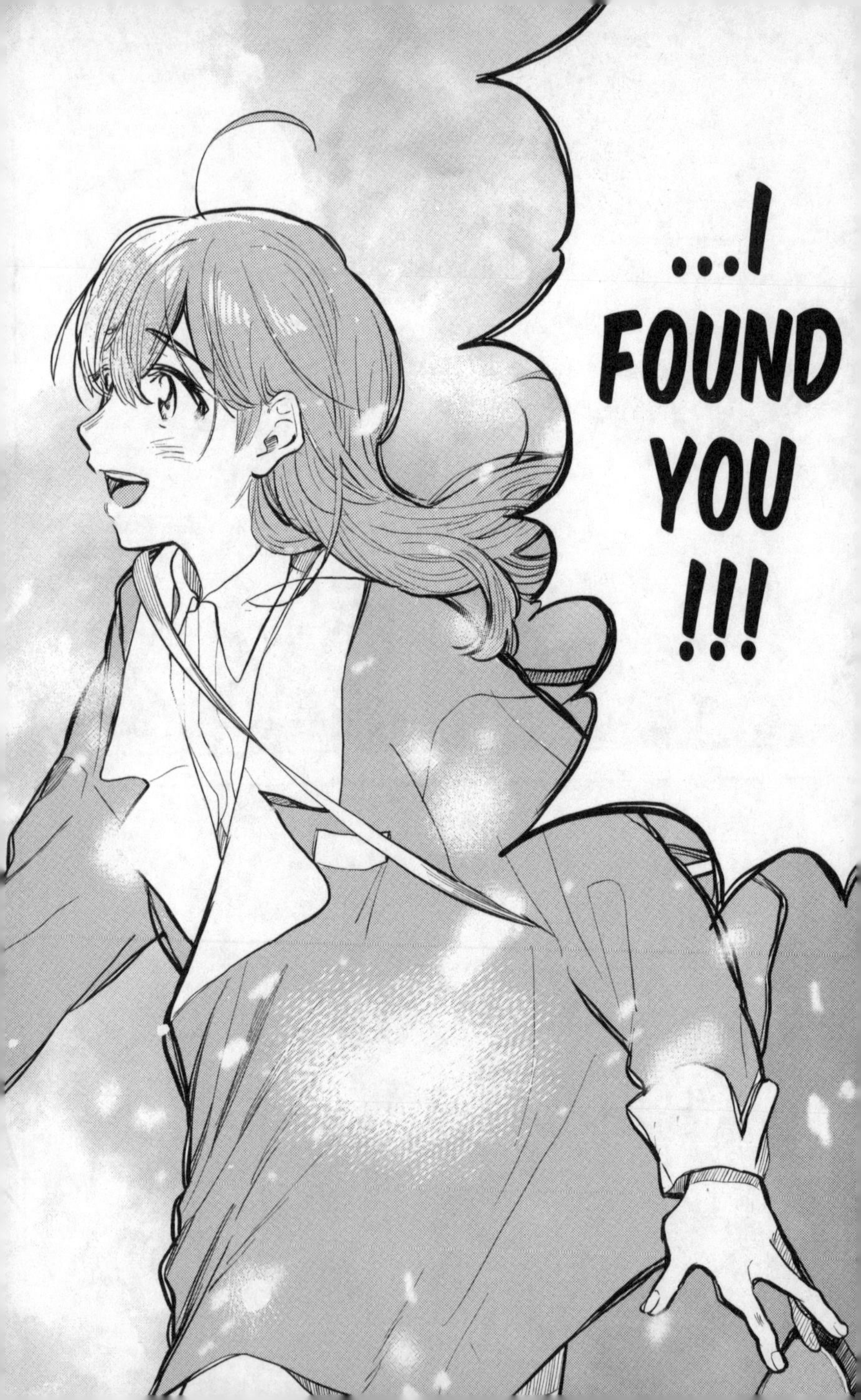
...I FOUND YOU !!!

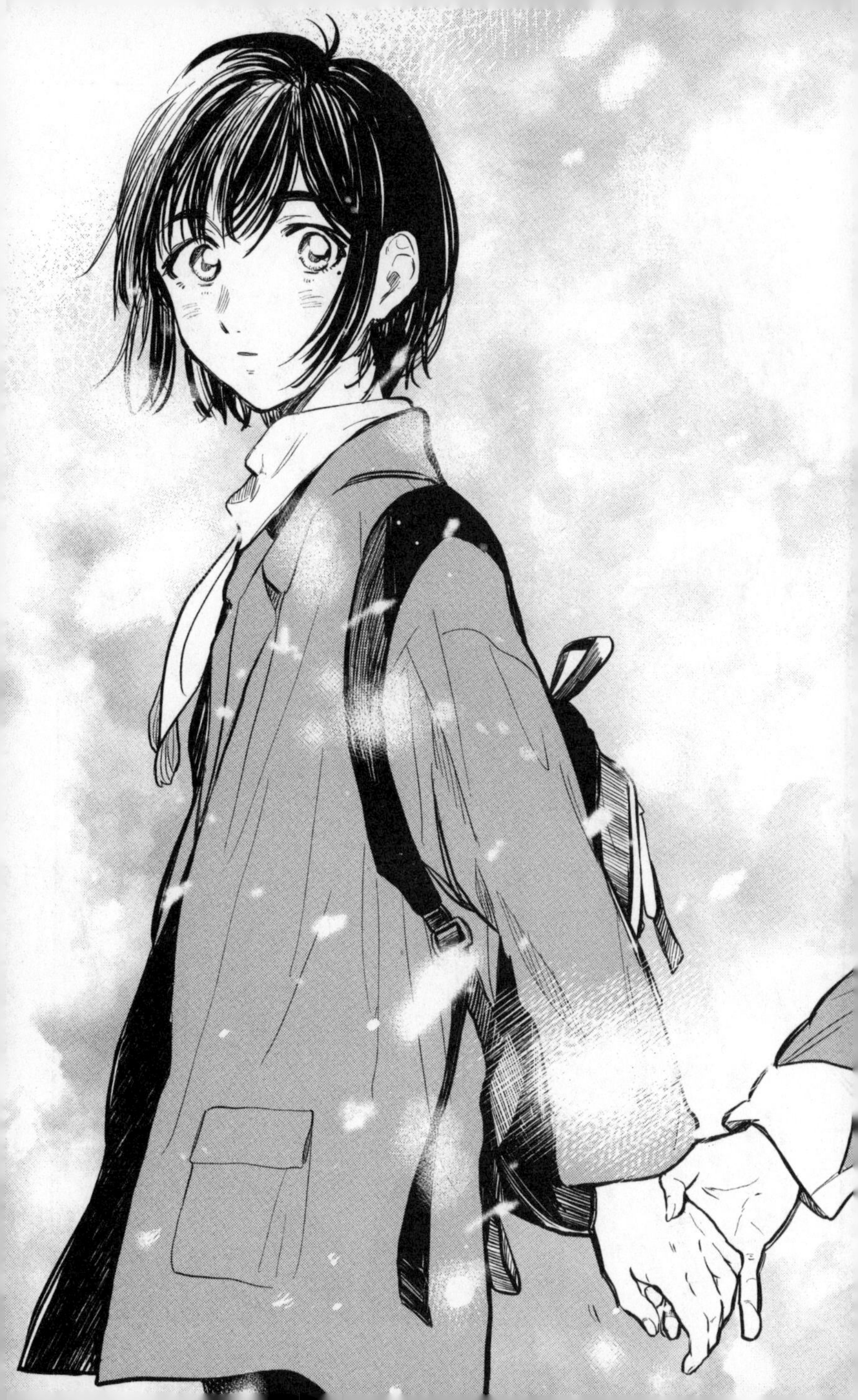

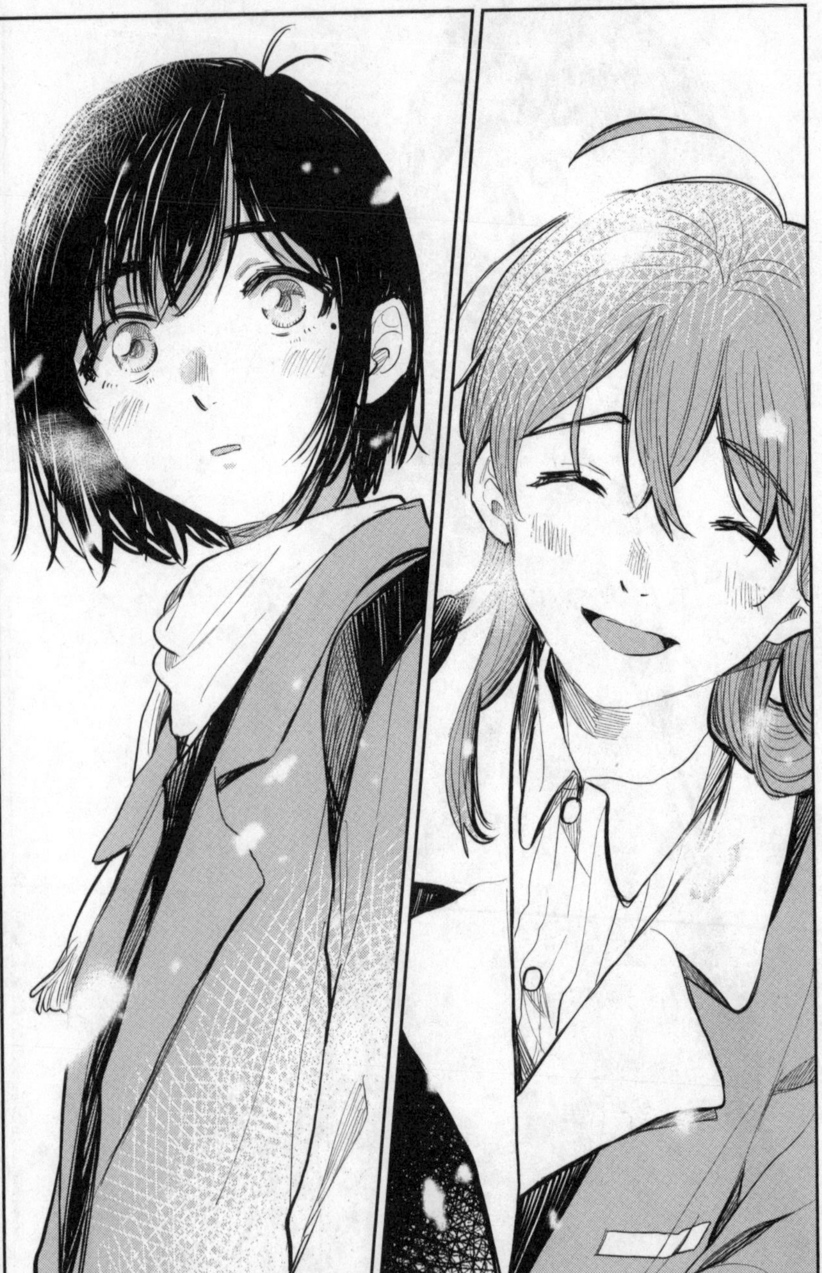

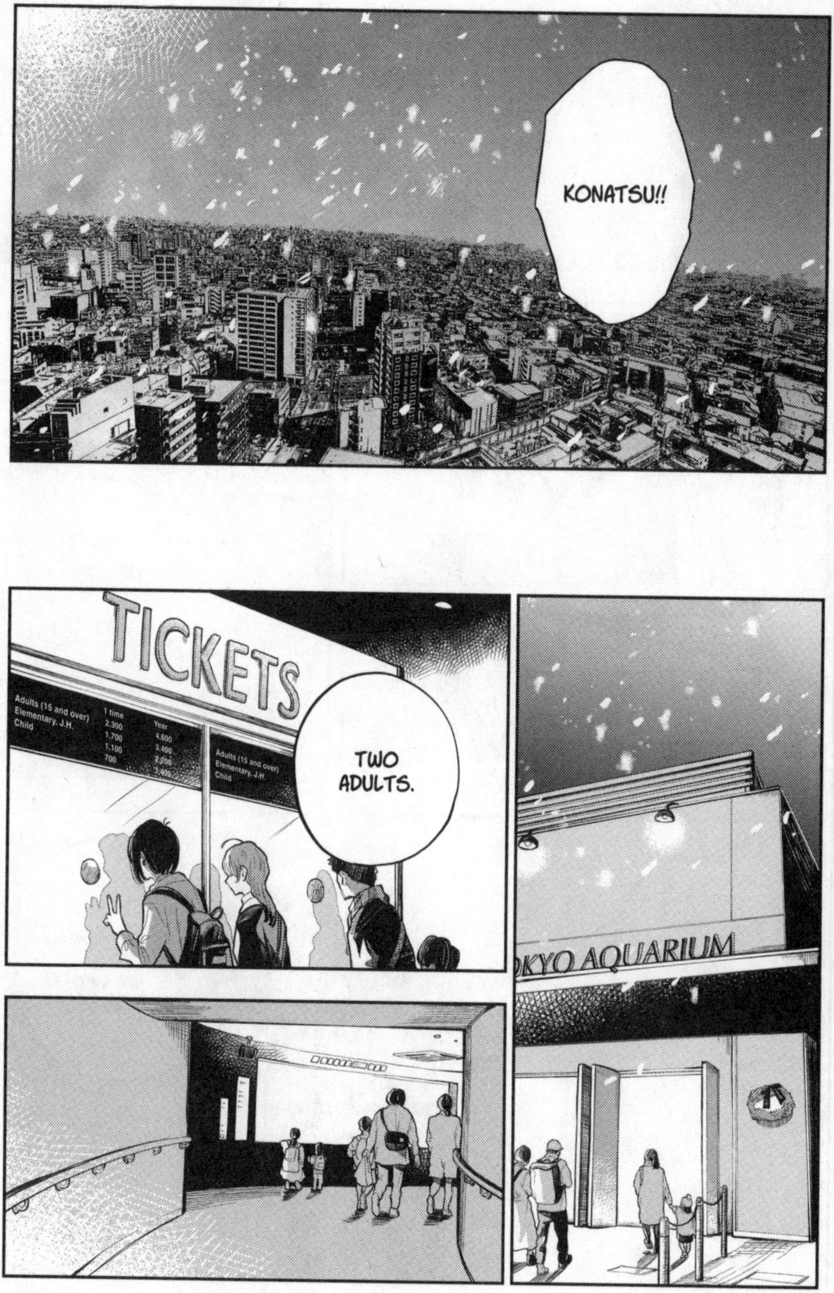
KONATSU!!
OKYO AQUARIUM
TICKETS
Adults (15 and over)
Elementary, J.H.
Child
1 time
2,300
1,700
1,100
700
Year
4,600
3,400
2,200
1,400
Adults (15 and over)
Elementary, J.H.
Child
TWO ADULTS.

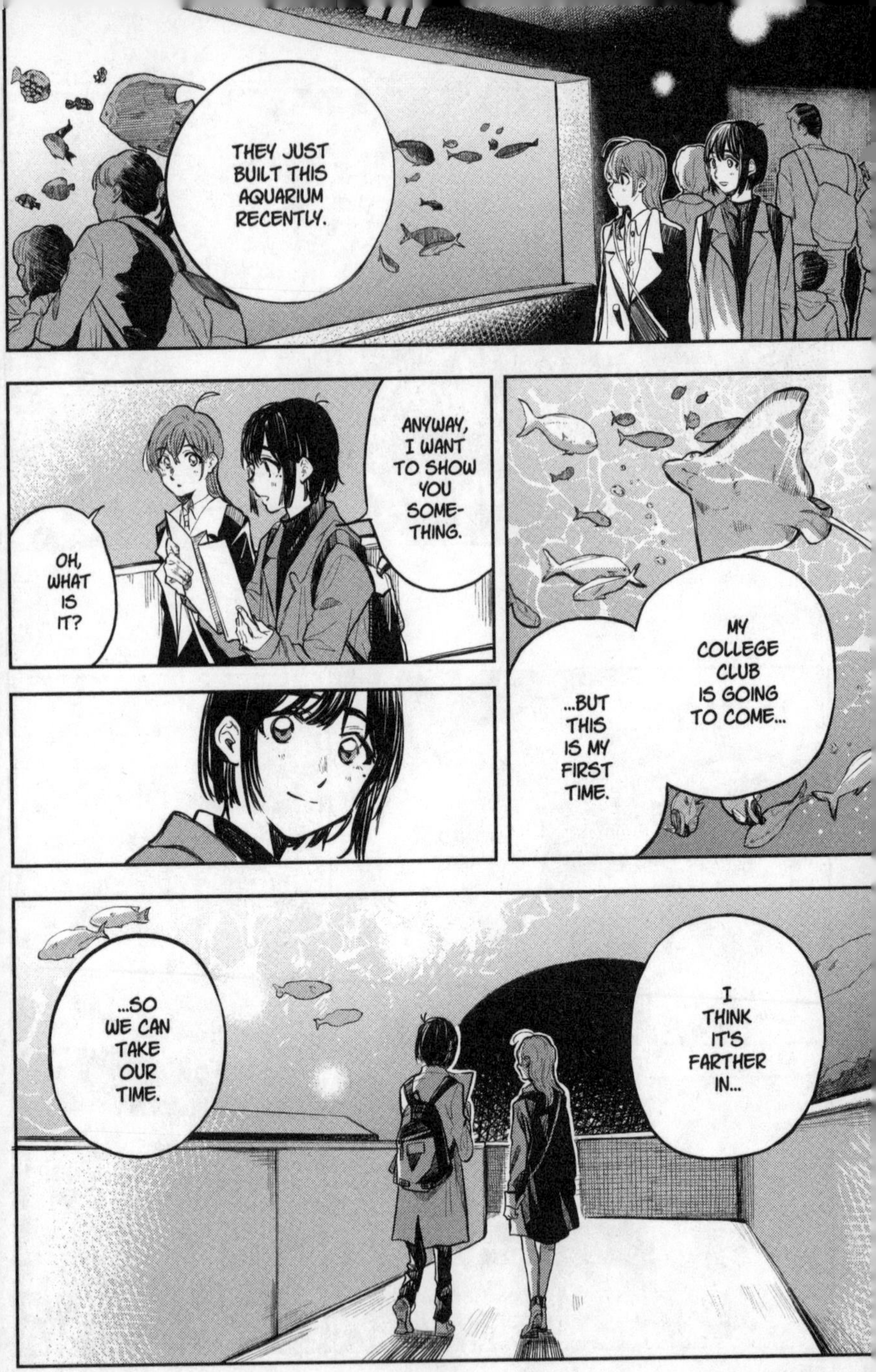
THEY JUST BUILT THIS AQUARIUM RECENTLY.
MY COLLEGE CLUB IS GOING TO COME...
...BUT THIS IS MY FIRST TIME.
ANYWAY, I WANT TO SHOW YOU SOMETHING.
OH, WHAT IS IT?
I THINK IT'S FARTHER IN...
...SO WE CAN TAKE OUR TIME.

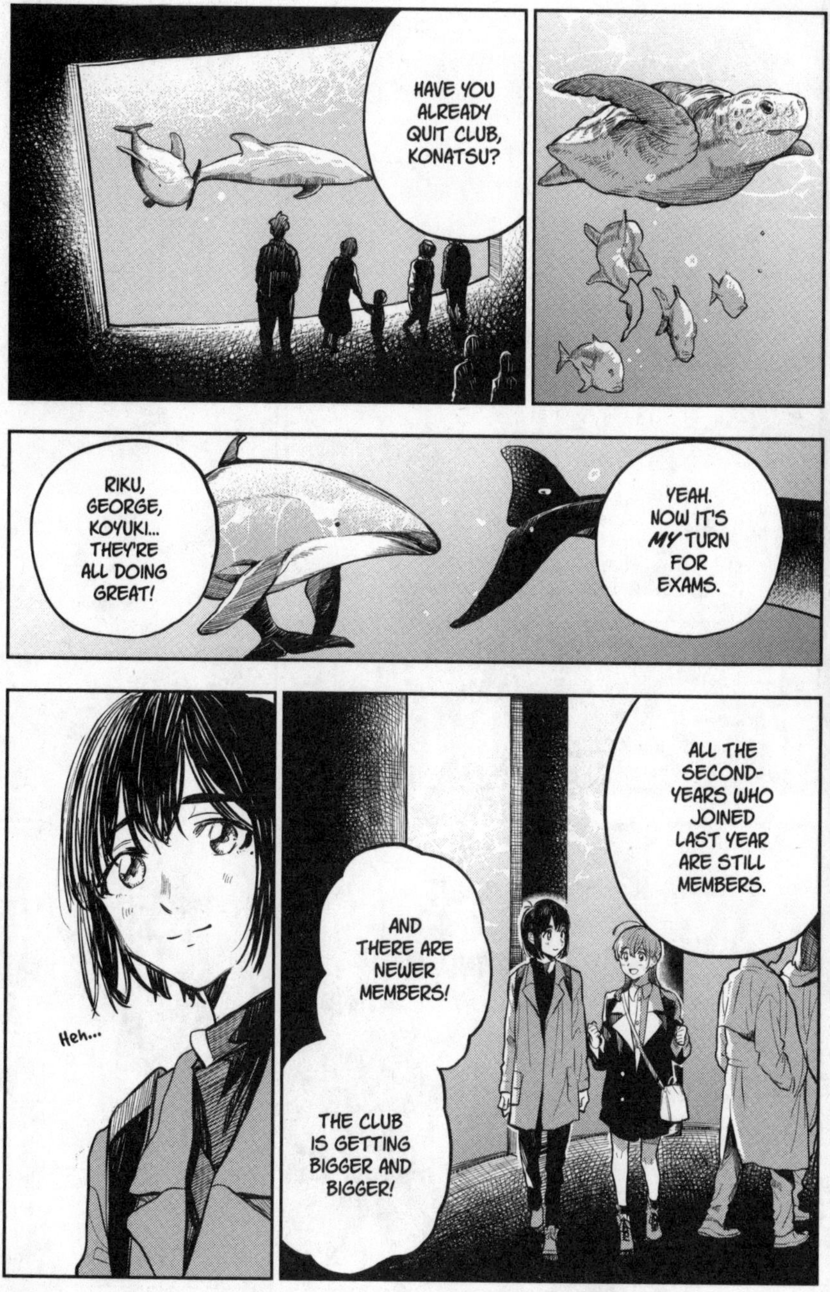
HAVE YOU ALREADY QUIT CLUB, KONATSU?
YEAH. NOW IT'S *MY* TURN FOR EXAMS.
RIKU, GEORGE, KOYUKI... THEY'RE ALL DOING GREAT!
ALL THE SECOND-YEARS WHO JOINED LAST YEAR ARE STILL MEMBERS.
AND THERE ARE NEWER MEMBERS!
THE CLUB IS GETTING BIGGER AND BIGGER!
Heh...

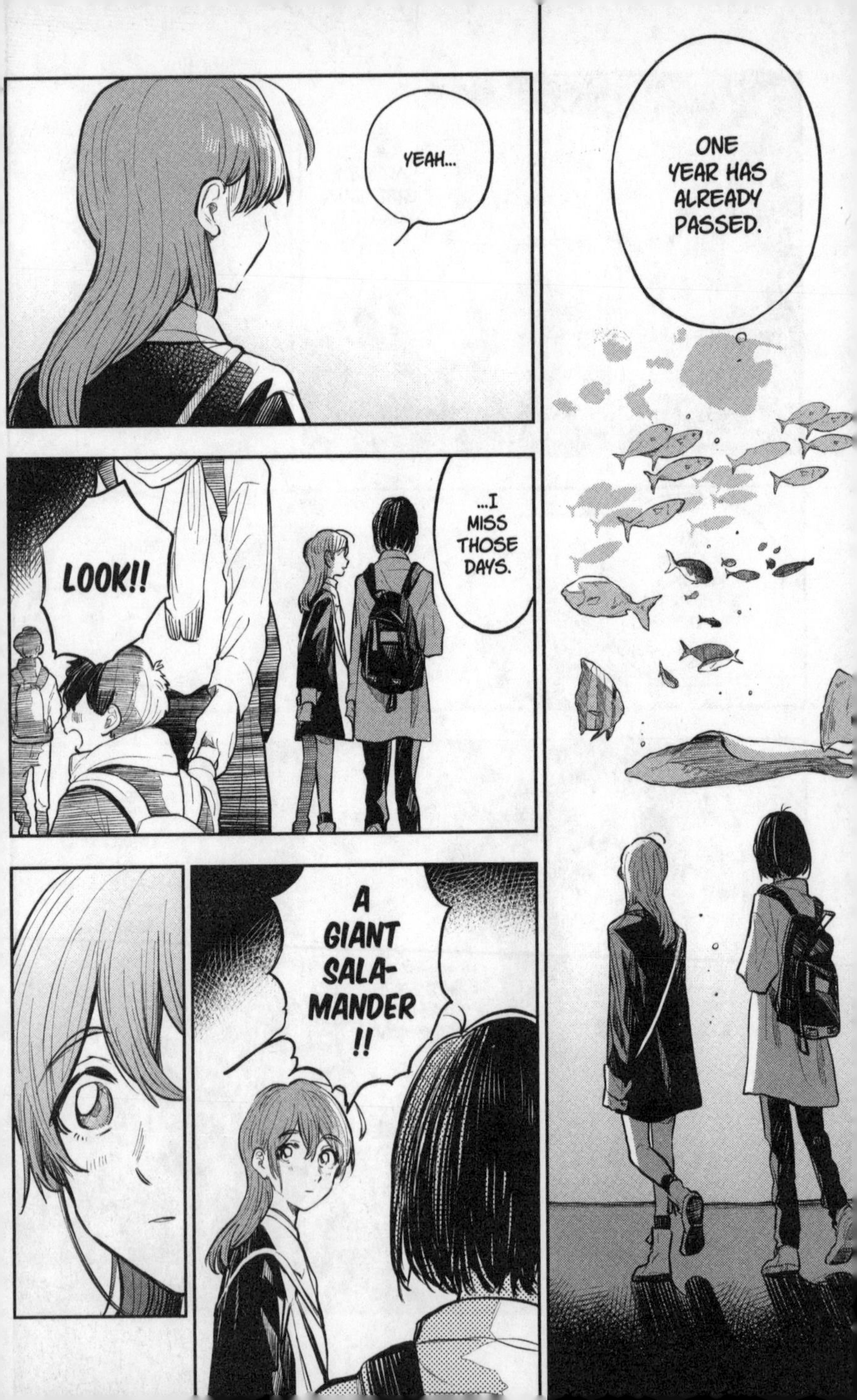
ONE YEAR HAS ALREADY PASSED.
YEAH...
...I MISS THOSE DAYS.
LOOK!!
A GIANT SALAMANDER!!

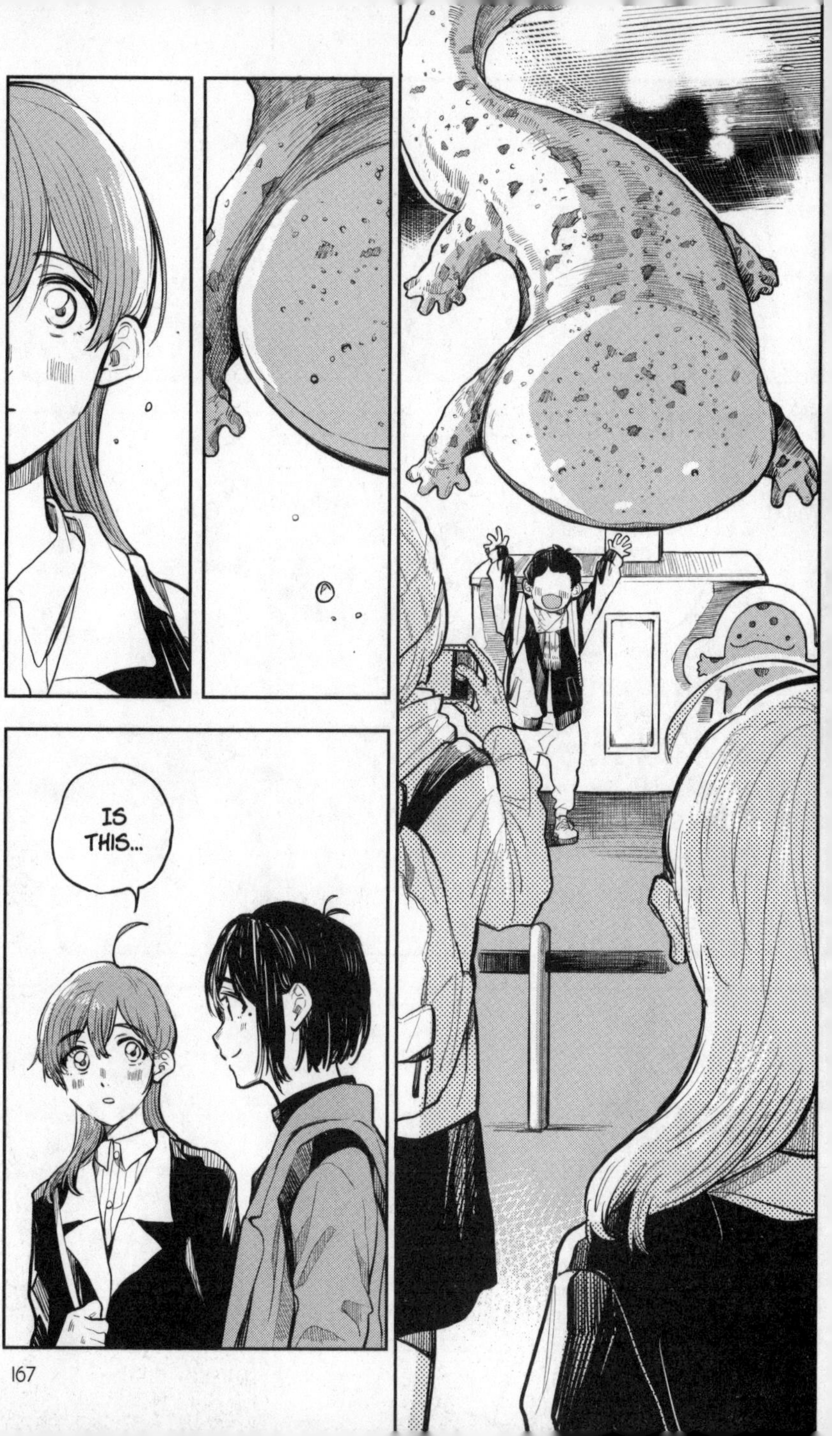
IS THIS...

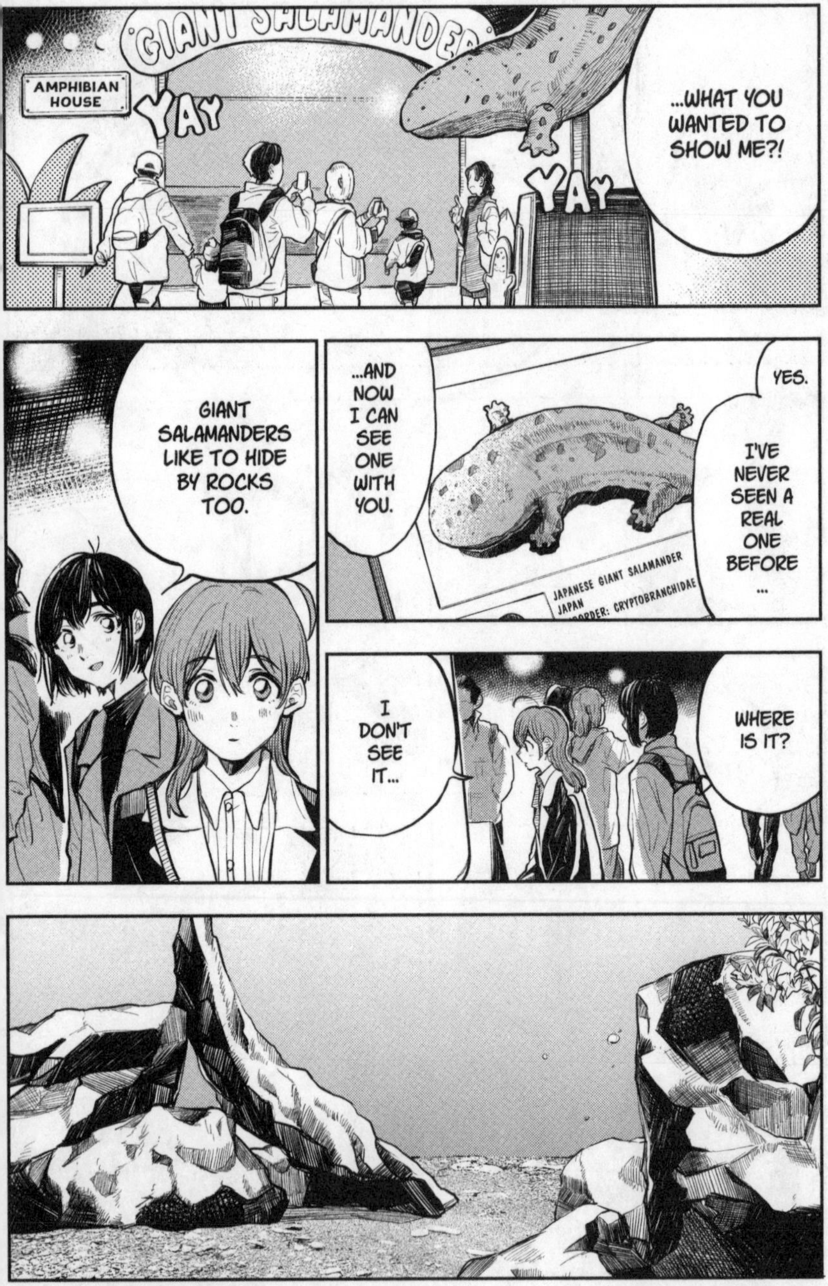
GIANT SALAMANDER
AMPHIBIAN HOUSE
YAY
YAY
...WHAT YOU WANTED TO SHOW ME?!
YES.
I'VE NEVER SEEN A REAL ONE BEFORE...
JAPANESE GIANT SALAMANDER
JAPAN
CRYPTOBRANCHIDAE
...AND NOW I CAN SEE ONE WITH YOU.
WHERE IS IT?
I DON'T SEE IT...
GIANT SALAMANDERS LIKE TO HIDE BY ROCKS TOO.

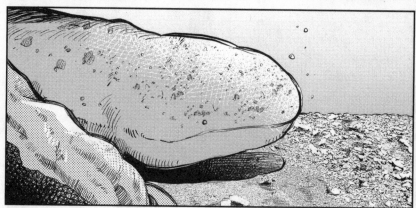

LOOK, KOYUKI!

THERE IT IS!

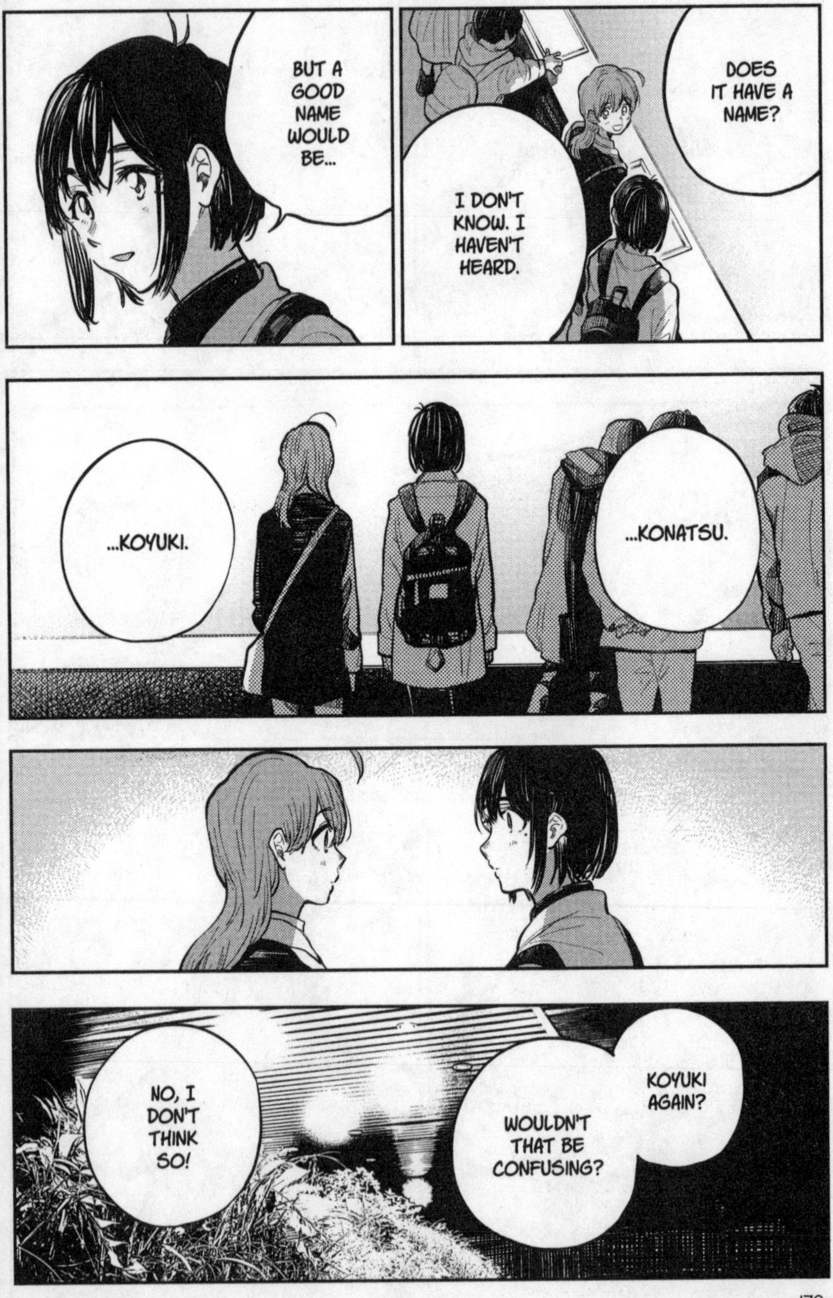
DOES IT HAVE A NAME?
I DON'T KNOW. I HAVEN'T HEARD.
BUT A GOOD NAME WOULD BE...
...KONATSU.
...KOYUKI.
KOYUKI AGAIN?
WOULDN'T THAT BE CONFUSING?
NO, I DON'T THINK SO!

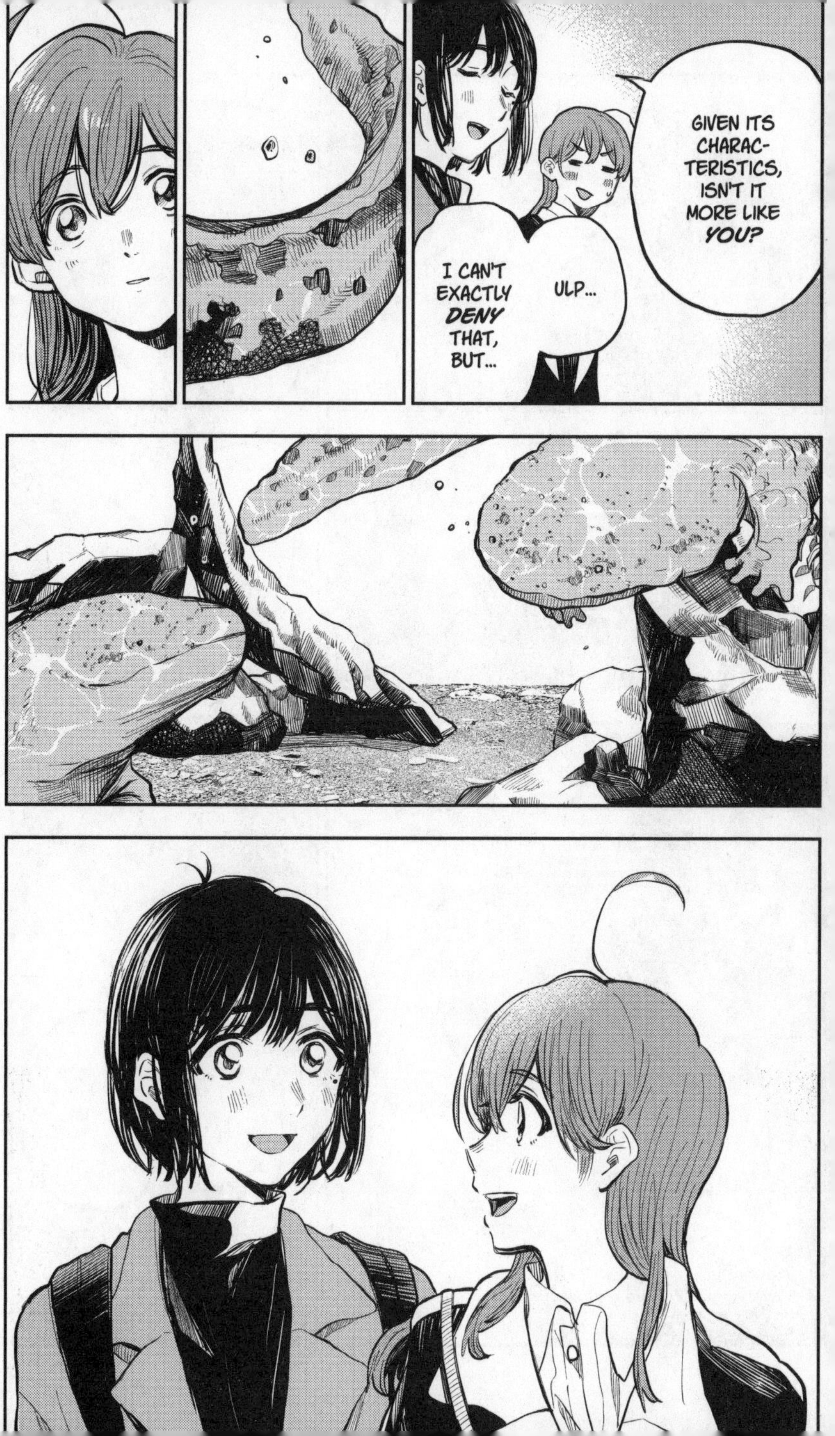
GIVEN ITS CHARAC-TERISTICS, ISN'T IT MORE LIKE *YOU?*
ULP...
I CAN'T EXACTLY *DENY* THAT, BUT...

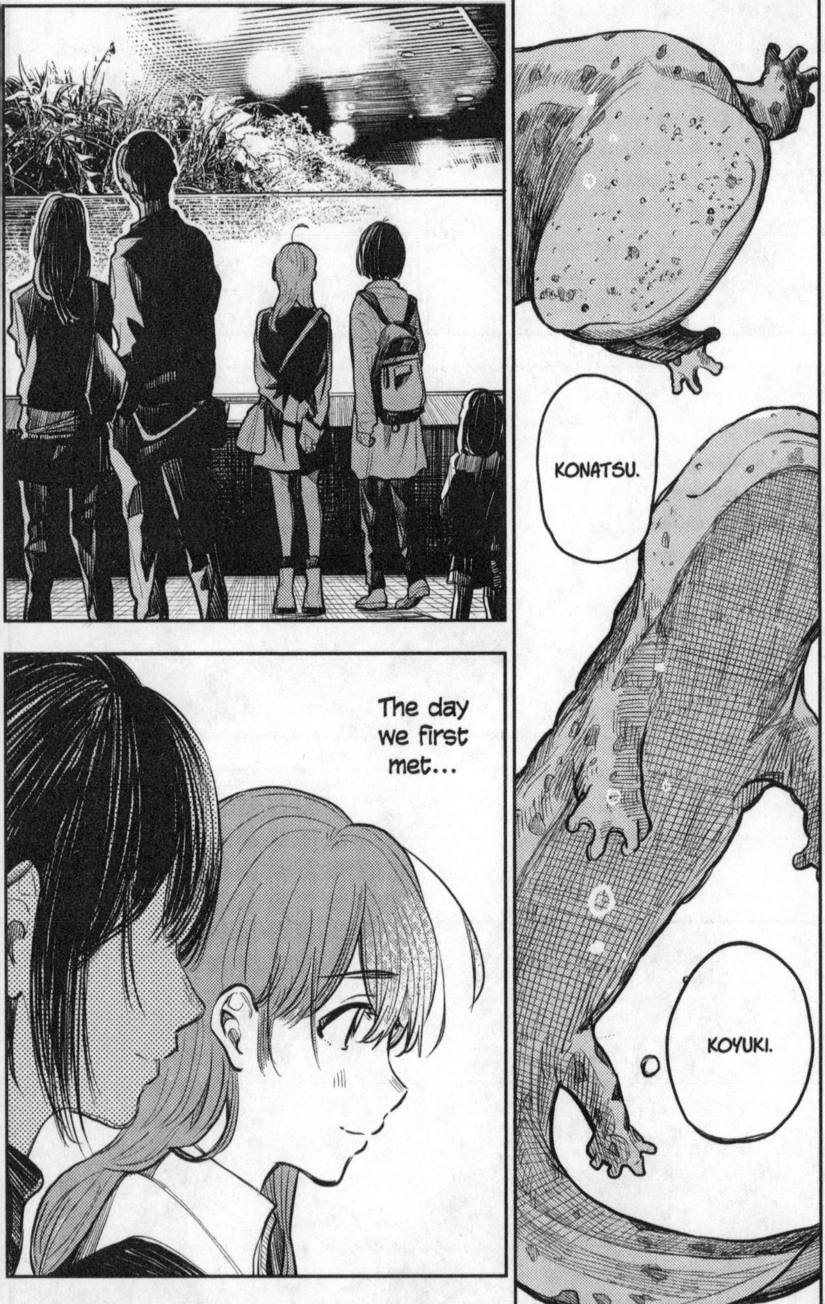
KONATSU.
KOYUKI.
The day we first met...

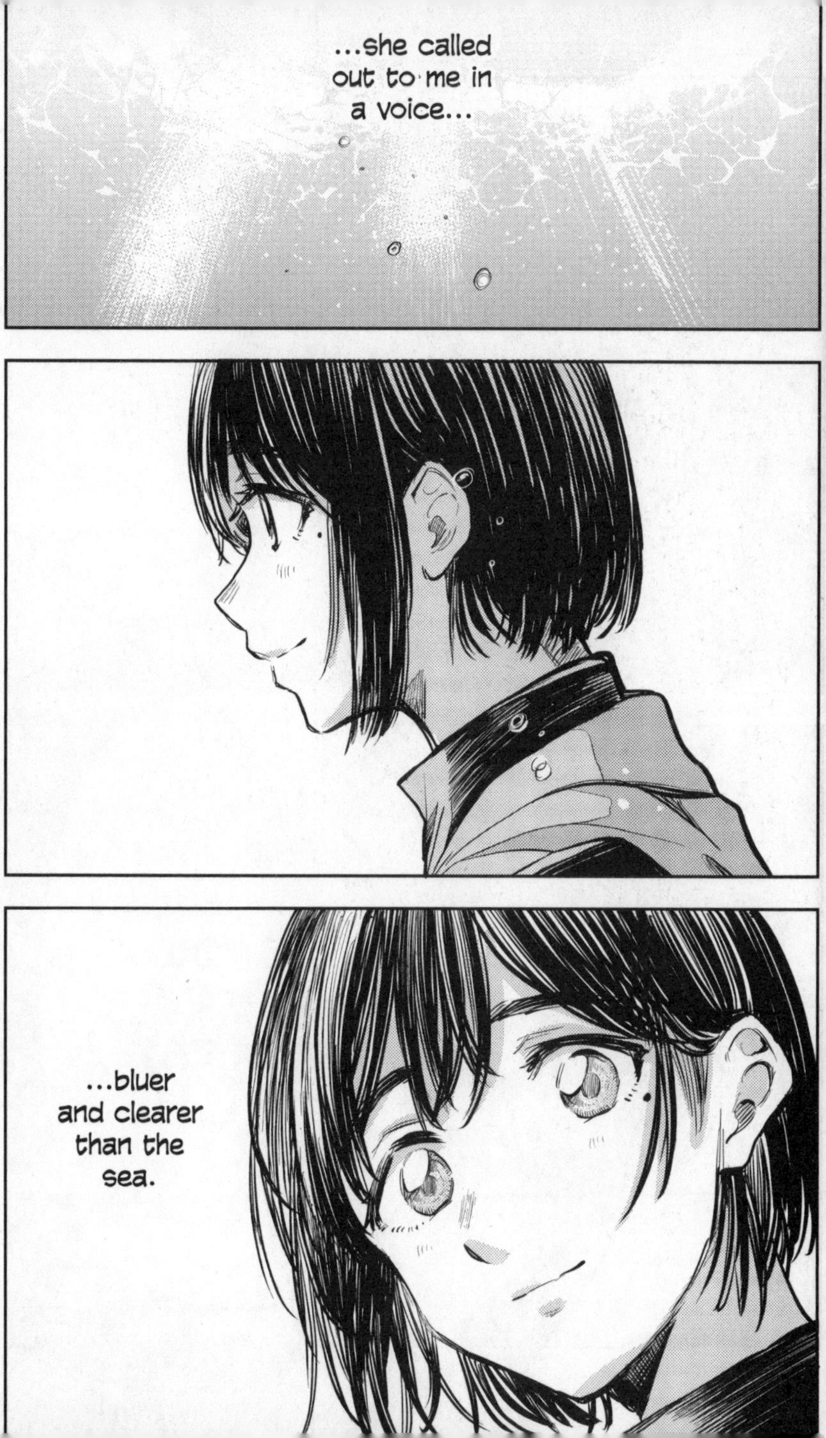
...she called out to me in a voice...
...bluer and clearer than the sea.

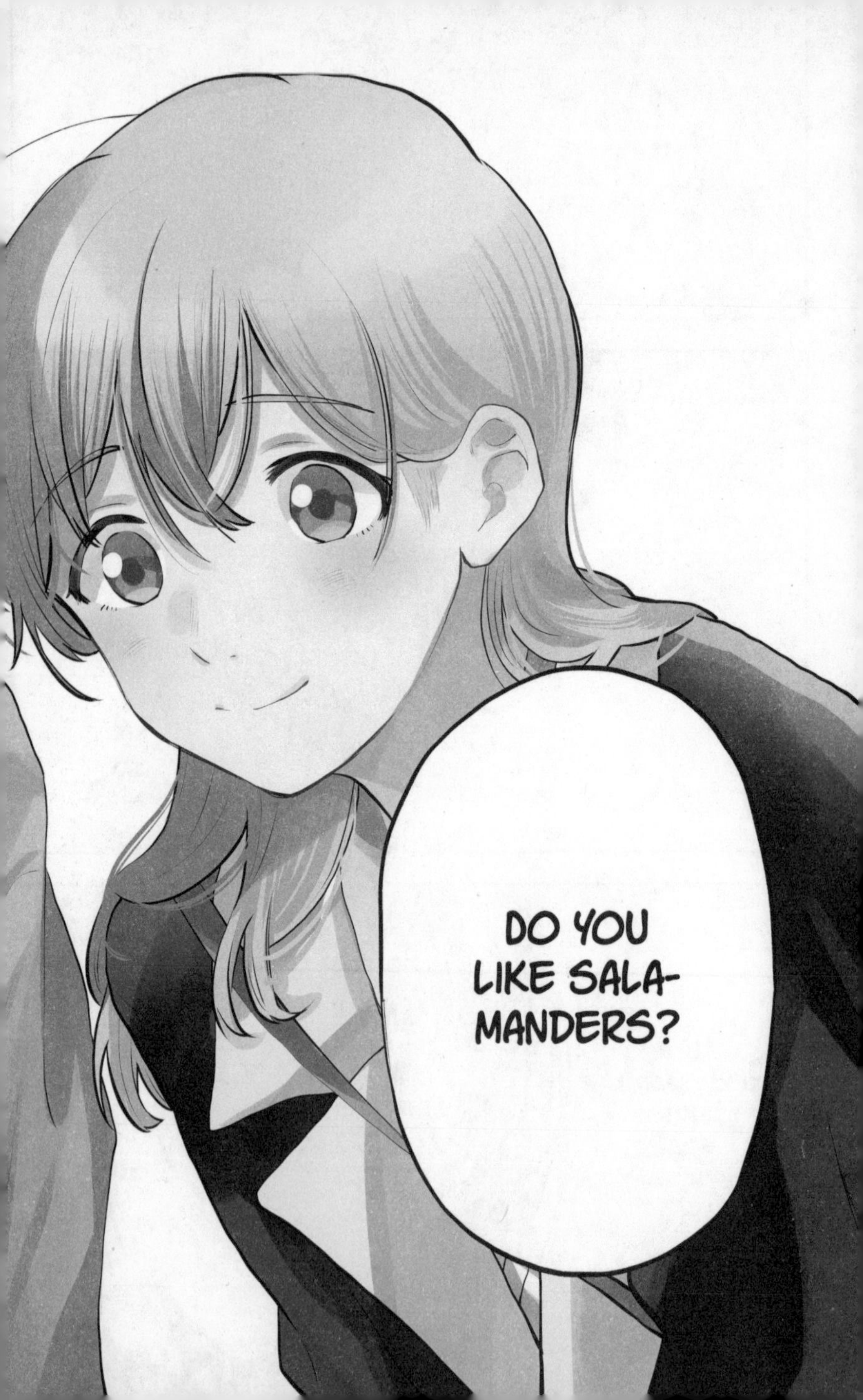
DO YOU LIKE SALA-MANDERS?

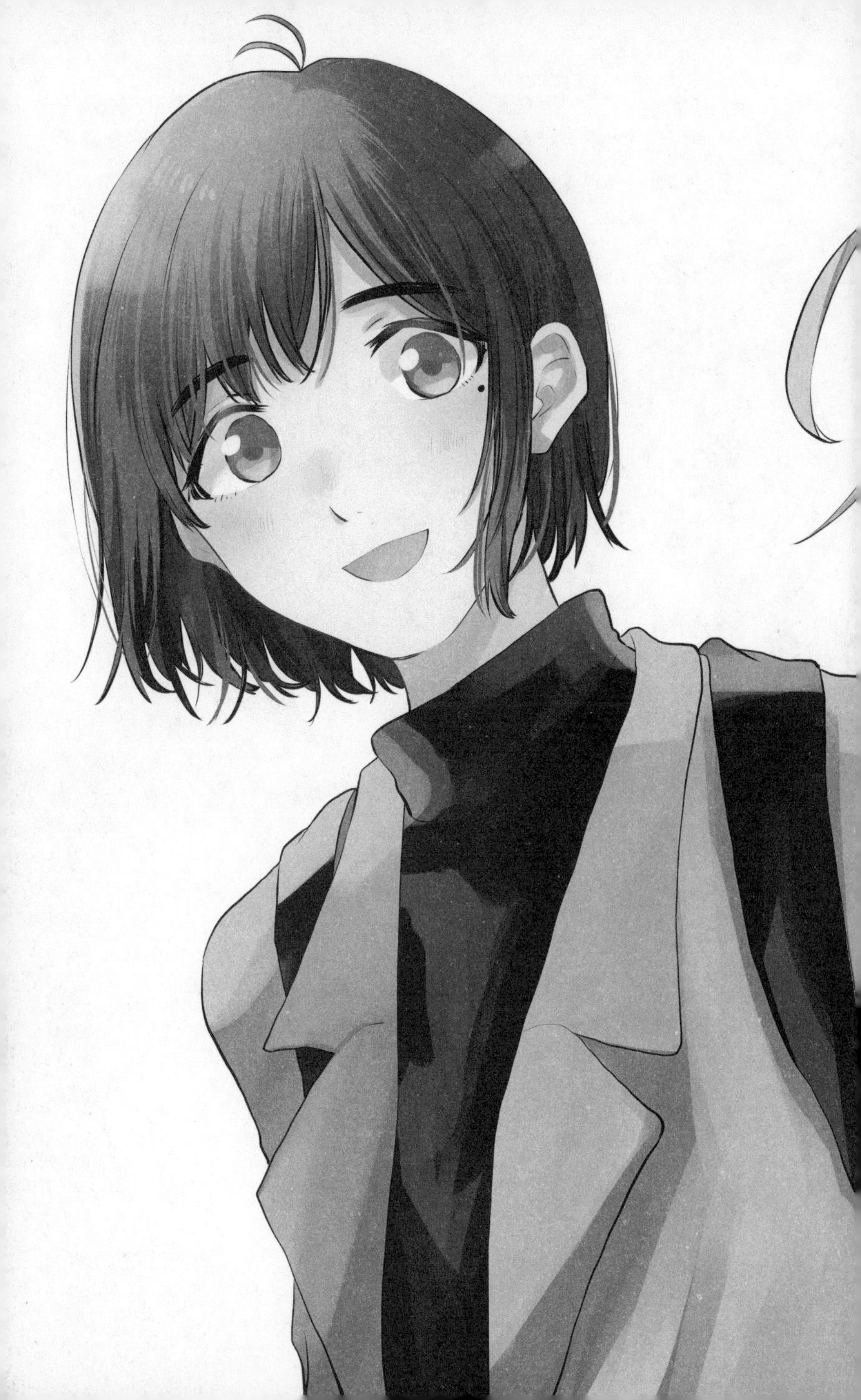

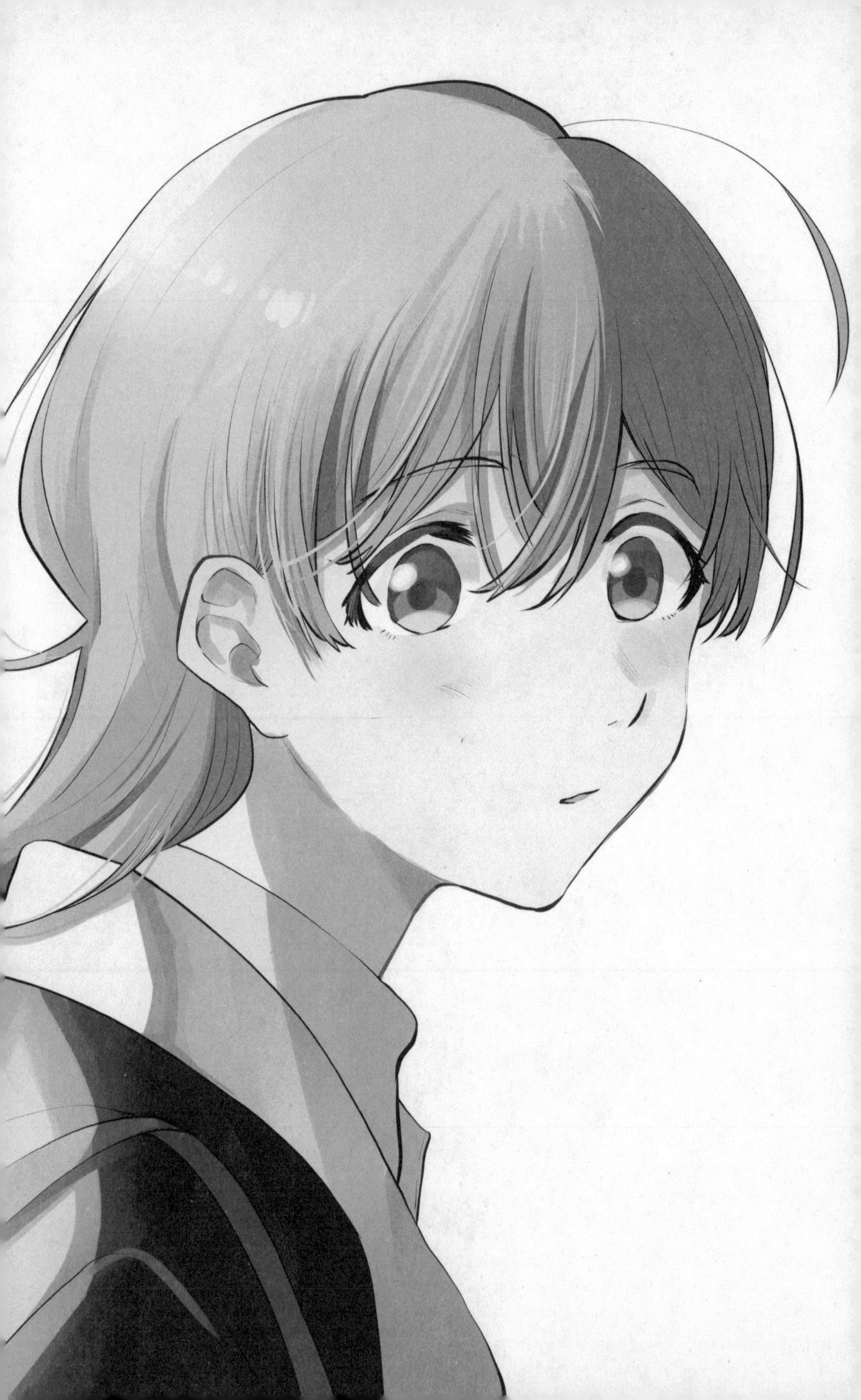

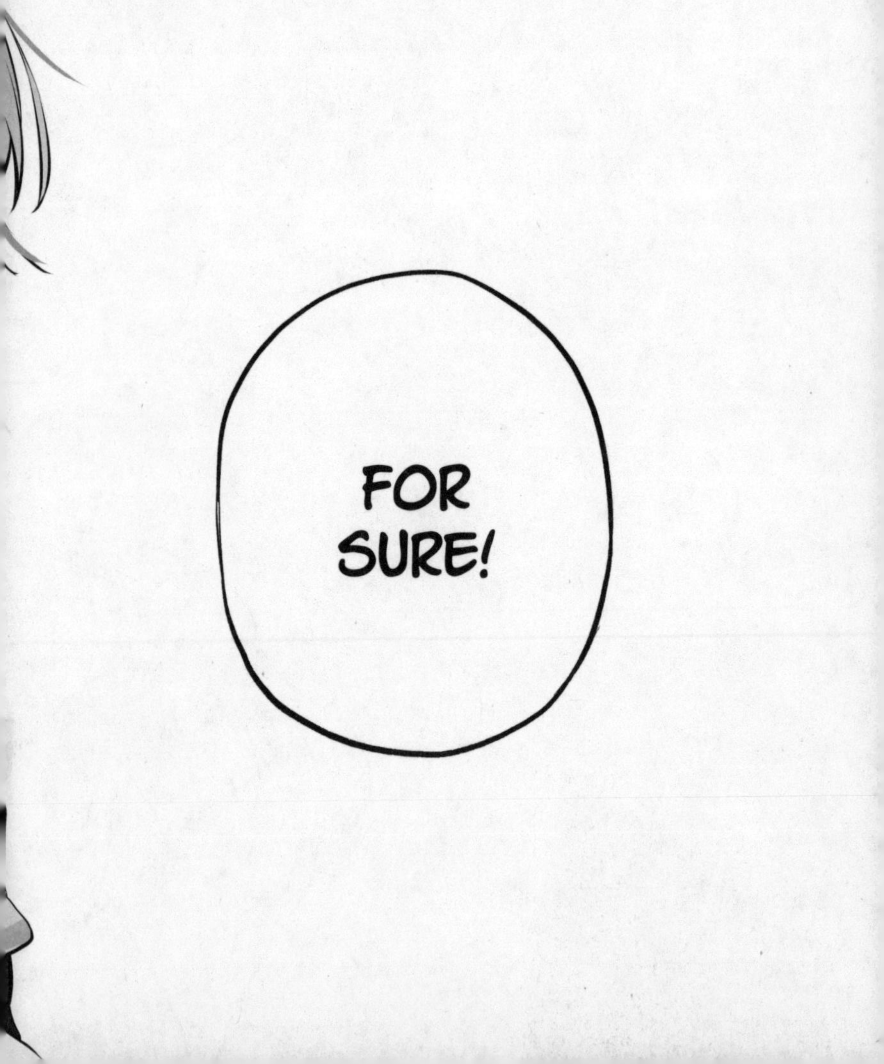
FOR SURE!

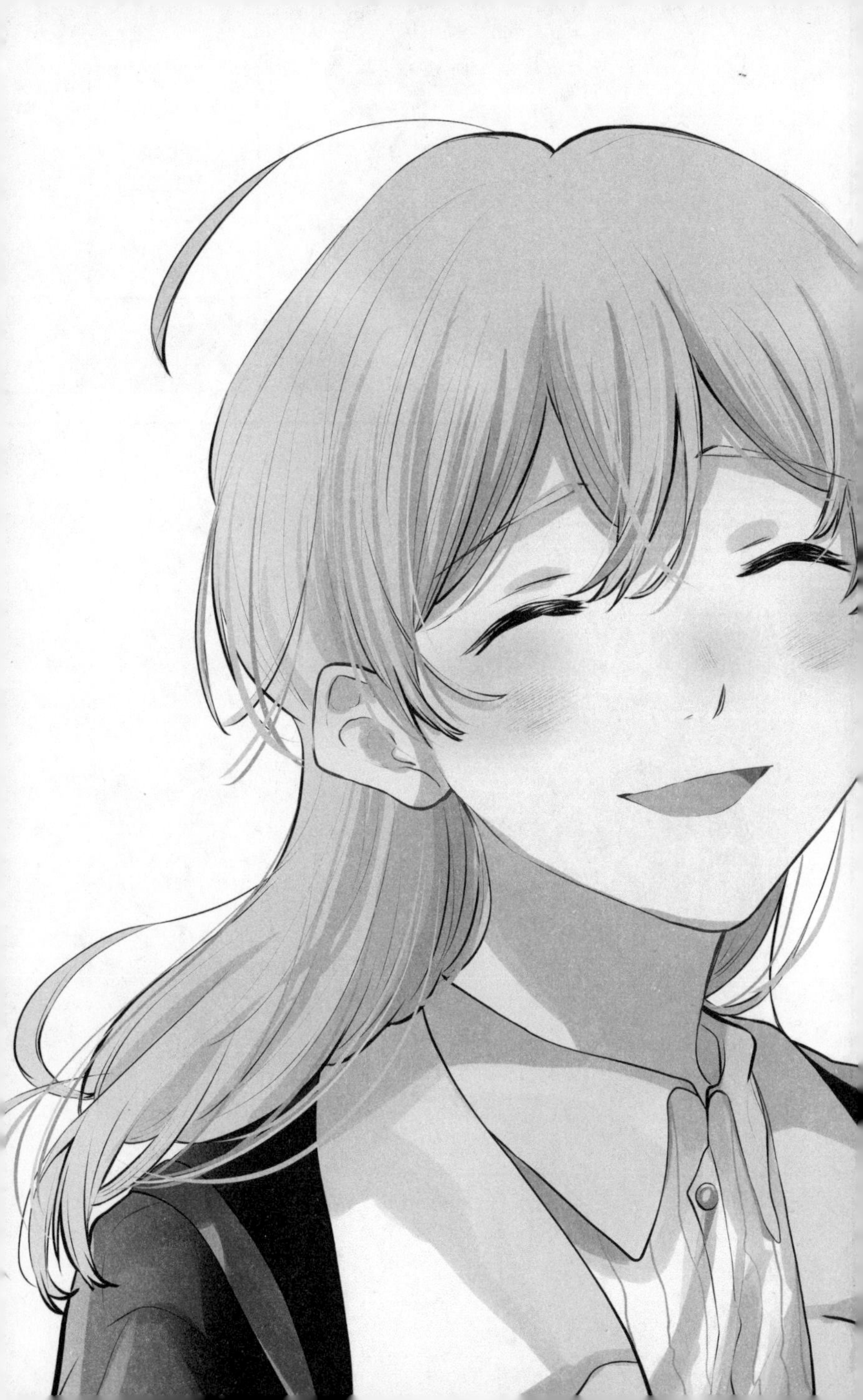

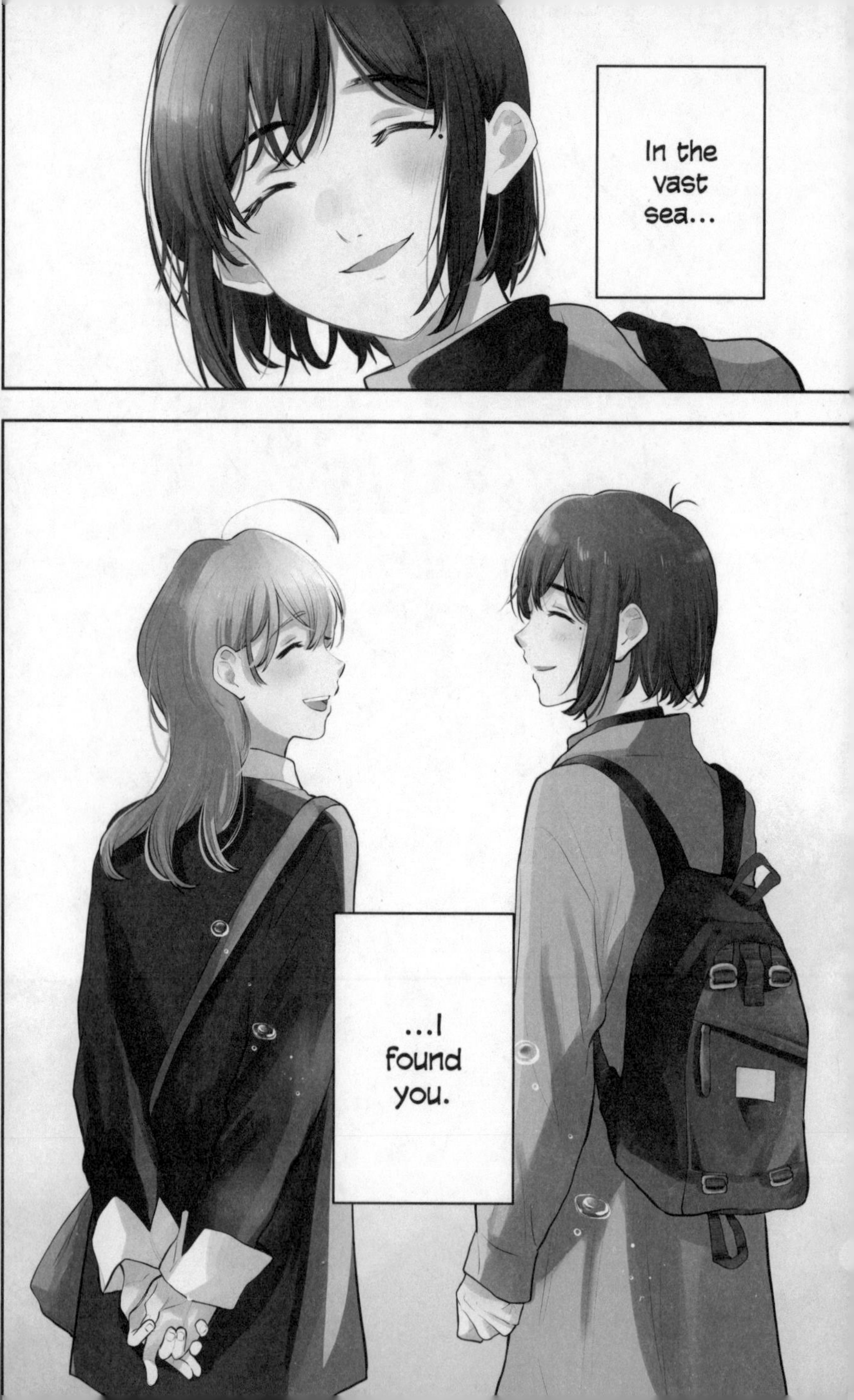
In the vast sea...
...I found you.

Fin.

A Tropical Fish Yearns for Snow

Makoto Hagino

Research Cooperation:

Ehime Prefectural Nagahama High School Aquarium Club

Designer:

BALCOLONY

Special Thanks:

Everyone who supported me this whole time

Everyone involved with this series

R.I.P.

hinata

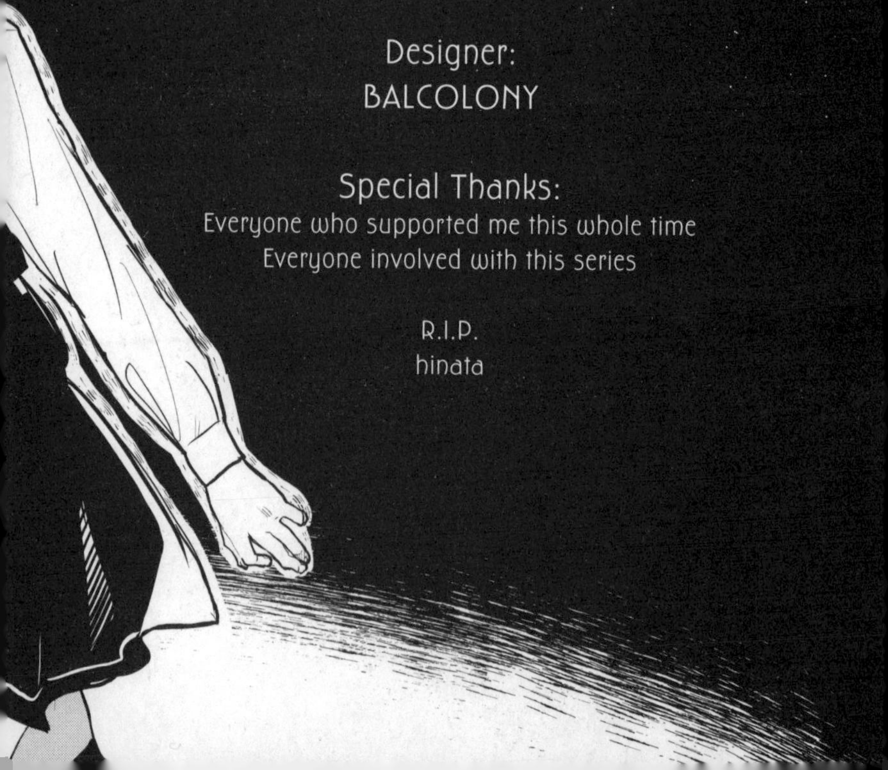

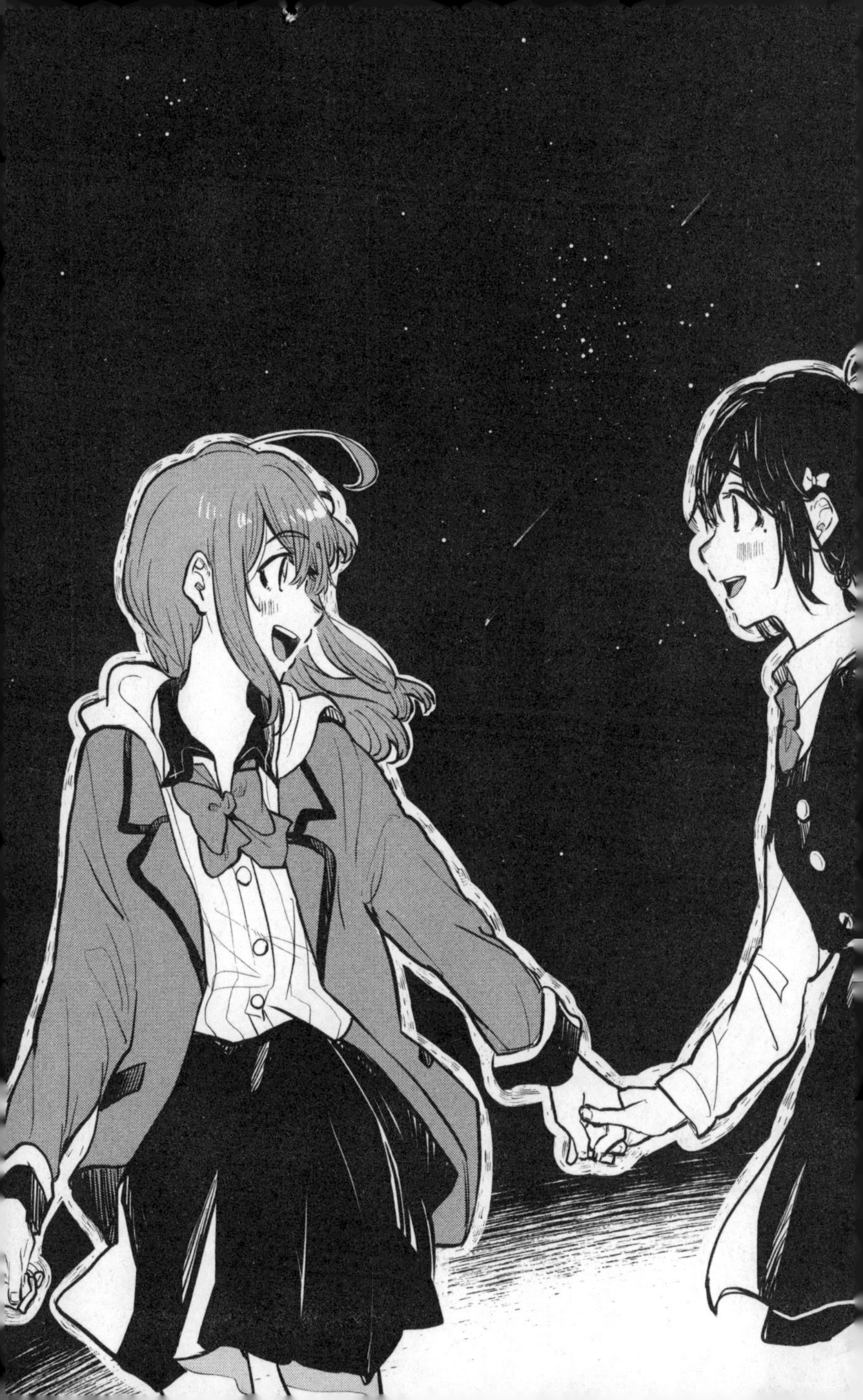

A TROPICAL FISH YEARNS FOR SNOW
Vol. 9
VIZ Media Edition

STORY AND ART BY
MAKOTO HAGINO

English Translation & Adaptation/John Werry
Touch-Up Art & Lettering/Eve Grandt
Design/Yukiko Whitley
Editor/Pancha Diaz

NETTAIGYO WA YUKI NI KOGARERU Vol. 9
©Makoto Hagino 2021
First published in Japan in 2021 by KADOKAWA CORPORATION, Tokyo.
English translation rights arranged with KADOKAWA CORPORATION, Tokyo.

Printed in Canada

Published by VIZ Media, LLC
P.O. Box 77010
San Francisco, CA 94107

10 9 8 7 6 5 4 3 2 1
First printing, July 2022

PARENTAL ADVISORY
A TROPICAL FISH YEARNS FOR SNOW is rated T
for Teen and is recommended for ages 13 and up.

viz.com

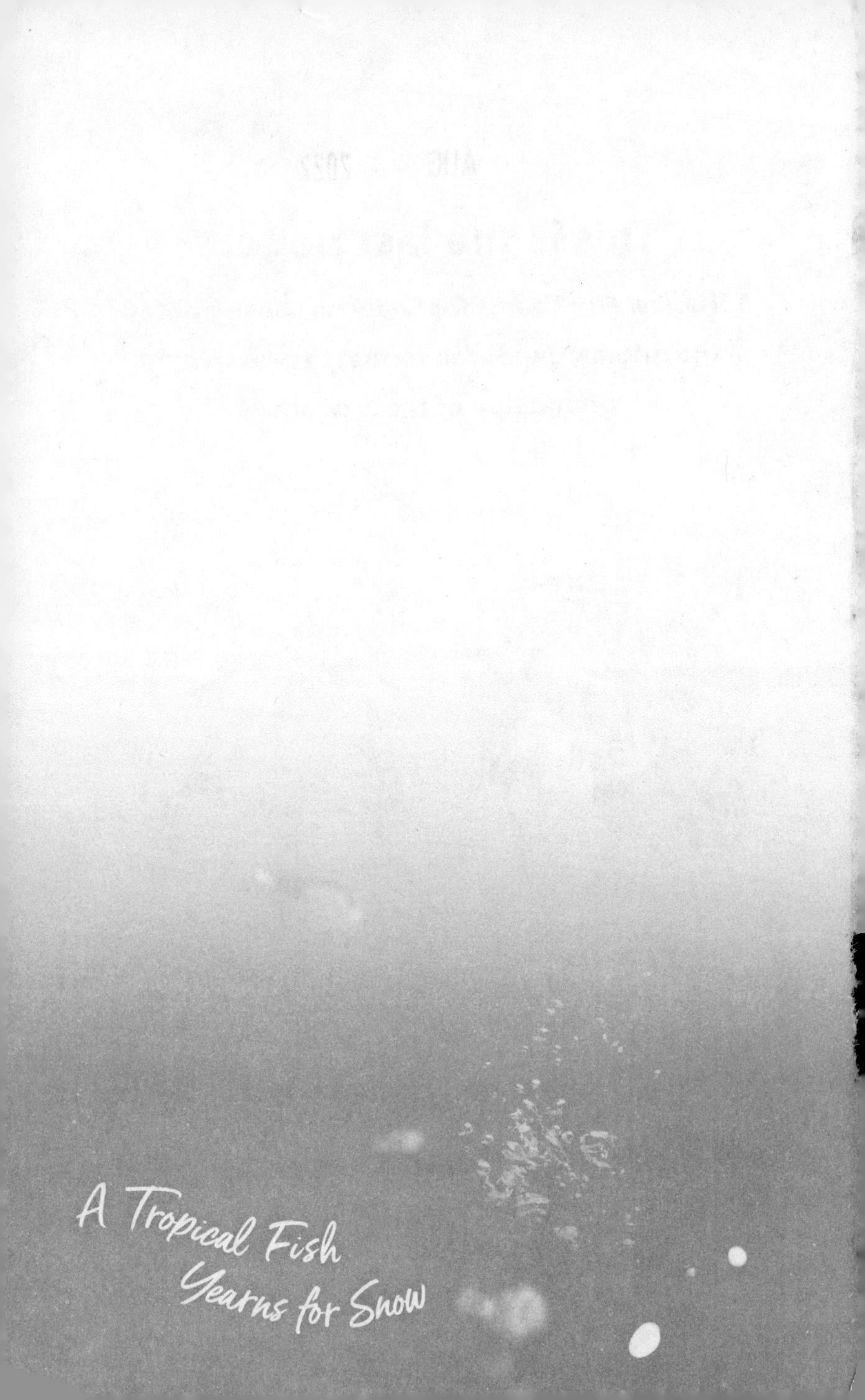
A Tropical Fish
Yearns for Snow

This is the last page.

A Tropical Fish Yearns for Snow **has been printed in the original Japanese format to preserve the orientation of the artwork.**

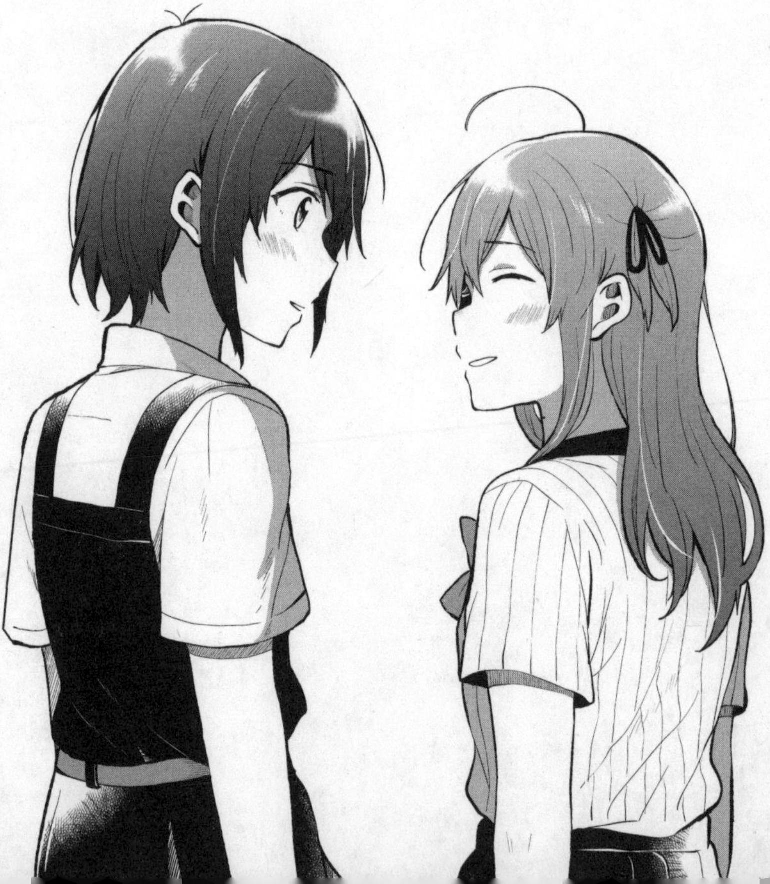